The Slave in Legal and Political Philosophy

This book explores how the figure of the slave has been used to construct ideas of freedom in Western political and legal philosophy.

The figure of the slave has supported philosophical and legal defences of colonialism, coloniality and the supremacy of the white subject. Yet for Giorgio Agamben, the slave stands (almost counterintuitively) as an exemplar of a potential form of future positive political existence. Developing this line of thought, the book reads key thinkers Agamben engages with in his thought and writings – including Aristotle, Saint Paul and G W F Hegel – and draws on decolonial theory to argue that the lives of people who were enslaved and unfree, and their actions and gestures, can point towards a paradigmatic form of political belonging. By reading Agamben in a decolonial direction, we can imagine alternative forms of agency, recognition and subjectivity, which can challenge the necropolitical world of racial capitalism in which we live.

This study will appeal to scholars, researchers and graduate students with an interest in the thought of Giorgio Agamben, radical politics, legal and political philosophy and decolonial theory.

Tom Frost is a Senior Lecturer at Kent Law School, UK.

The Slave in Legal and Political Philosophy

Agamben and His Interlocutors

Tom Frost

Routledge
Taylor & Francis Group
a GlassHouse Book

First published 2025
by Routledge
4 Park Square, Milton Park, Abingdon, Oxon OX14 4RN

and by Routledge
605 Third Avenue, New York, NY 10158

Routledge is an imprint of the Taylor & Francis Group, an informa business

A GlassHouse book

British Library Cataloguing-in-Publication Data
A catalogue record for this book is available from the British Library

Library of Congress Cataloging-in-Publication Data
Names: Frost, Tom (Lecturer in Law), author.
Title: The Slave in Legal and Political Philosophy:
Agamben and his Interlocutors / Tom Frost.
Description: 1. | New York: Routledge, 2025. |
Includes bibliographical references and index.
Identifiers: LCCN 2024045409 (print) |
LCCN 2024045410 (ebook) | ISBN 9781032301273 (hardback) |
ISBN 9781032301280 (paperback) | ISBN 9781003303534 (ebook)
Subjects: LCSH: Agamben, Giorgio, 1942-. | Slavery–Law and legislation. |
Enslaved persons–Legal status, laws, etc. | Law–Philosophy. |
Political science–Philosophy. | Slavery–Political aspects.
Classification: LCC K3267.G56 2025 (print) | LCC K3267 (ebook) |
DDC 342.08/7–dc23/eng/20241009
LC record available at https://lccn.loc.gov/2024045409
LC ebook record available at https://lccn.loc.gov/2024045410

ISBN: 9781032301273 (hbk)
ISBN: 9781032301280 (pbk)
ISBN: 9781003303534 (ebk)

DOI: 10.4324/9781003303534

Typeset in Sabon
by Deanta Global Publishing Services, Chennai, India

Contents

Preface

This monograph draws upon research which I have previously published in academic journals, including:
Frost, T (2014) 'Thinking relationality in Agamben and Levinas', *Griffith Law Review*, 23, 210–31.

This study is also a direct development of my first monograph:
Frost, T (2021) *Law, Relationality and the Ethical Life: Agamben and Levinas*, Abingdon: Routledge.

All journals and publishers have given their permission for these articles to have their arguments developed in this book. I would like to thank all the anonymous reviewers for these publications for their criticisms, suggestions and comments. This feedback has proven invaluable for these publications as well as this book's arguments.

I am indebted to J M Bernstein's lectures on Hegel's *The Phenomenology of Spirit*, which helped my arguments in relation to the master-slave dialectic (https://bernsteintapes.com).

In this study, I started to apply a concept that I first developed during my doctorate, namely that of hyper-hermeneutics. This is designed to be a form of living through which small actions can challenge and deactivate oppressive biopolitical systems of control. I believe that it provides a way of showing how forms of living in the present, following Agamben's ideas, can form the basis of a new politics.

This study aims to place Agamben's thought in the service of those of us living in this necropolitical world of racial capitalism, as well as those impacted by it on a daily basis.

I should note here a point about 'race' and 'racialisation'. 'Race' is an ideological category, controlling how we think, speak and act. Race is not neutral. It enables a prior exercise of power, and racialisation produces racial subjects. Agamben reads all identities as differential constructs. Everyone is racialised. White people are racialised as 'White', a point that should not be missed or minimised. For this reason, I have capitalised the terms 'Black', 'Blackness', 'White' and 'Whiteness' when I have used them throughout the book. I have not changed the capitalisation of these terms where I have quoted other authors. To refer to 'white/ness' in the lower case whilst only captalising 'Black/ness' affirms the hegemony of White/ness and treats it as the societal norm, from which all other identities diverge.[1]

Like Agamben, I remain an optimist. That there does not appear to be a easy solution to the troubles of the world does not mean a way forward is impossible. To paraphrase James Baldwin, to be alive is to be optimistic. Human life is not an academic matter (despite being covered in many academic books and publications).

For the reader, I hope that there will be some kernels of use found within the following pages. Any mistakes or errors in the text are mine and mine alone.

1 Wolfe, P (2002) *Race and racialisation: Some thoughts*, Postcolonial Studies: Culture, Politics, Economy, 5, 51-62.

Table of Cases

Why the enslaved?

To begin with, a division

This is a book about the enslaved person, and their position in Western European legal and political philosophy. The enslaved person places us face-to-face with fundamental political questions. What does it mean to belong to a society? Where is the boundary between those with political agency and those with none? Does a slave have any autonomy? What is the most accurate definition of enslavement? What does it mean to own another human being? What is the difference between slavery as a lived condition and slavery as a metaphor, and how has that metaphor been deployed?

More importantly, how does this debate relate to the lived realities of the enslaved? Enslaved people have been living their lives, and resisting their treatment and status, for longer than philosophers have been writing about the figure of the slave. New possibilities were being created through these lived experiences. My primary point of reference for this book is the Italian philosopher Giorgio Agamben. For Agamben, the slave is an exemplar of a form of future positive political existence, but a form that has not been considered by Western law, philosophy or politics. Such a claim may be curious, to say the least. How is it possible to base *political* life, or any form of political existence, on a figure such as the slave? I make a key distinction in this book between the 'enslaved' and the 'slave'. The term 'slave' abstracts the individuals being talked about, illustrating the natural or normative production of a negation as a natural consequence of a person being so classified. To speak of the 'enslaved' focuses on the life and lived experiences of those persons classified as slaves.[1]

Slavery is mentioned throughout Agamben's philosophy. Previously I faulted Agamben for abstracting the historical cruelty of slavery to use it as a concept in a philosophical endeavour.[2] Whilst Agamben's own treatment

1 Adébísí (2023) 83.
2 Frost (2021) 159.

DOI: 10.4324/9781003303534-1

of slavery is not without flaws, on reflection I was too quick to dismiss his thought on this matter. Agamben uses the figure of the slave to point towards a form of living which can undo or deactivate forms of political violence that both dog the present and have allowed for enslavement. Agamben's work on slavery, and his linking of slavery to his proposed coming politics, has not been the subject of a sustained academic study. Agamben's slave becomes a paradigm for the good life.[3] This book follows Ype de Boer's hypothesis that Agamben's thought can be aligned with decolonial attempts to develop a form of consciousness that is emancipated from 'colonial logics', specifically in the critique of the figure of the master.[4] For de Boer, if we only recognise in enslaved people a dehumanised figure, life is valued from the master's perspective. This in turn makes a category error of keeping systems of exclusion and institutional violence in place.[5]

Slavery resists attempts to reduce it to a set of binary oppositions. As Malcolm Bull points out, the slave is a personality without personhood.[6] Slavery operates as a division. It is a division of the *polis*, a division of how we conceive of freedom, and a division of how we conceive of justice.[7] Perhaps that is no surprise. As Alain Badiou has remarked, "from the outset everything is in some sense divided".[8]

Justin Clemens sees the slave as a paradox, at the same time both foundational and aporetic for philosophy. For Clemens, philosophy cannot make up its mind as to whether the slave is rational or irrational, a disagreement that can be traced to Plato and Aristotle.[9] In Plato's *Meno*, Meno asks Socrates if he can prove the claim that "all learning is recollection", which is connected to the idea of an immortal soul. Socrates responds by calling over a slave boy with no mathematical training. Socrates then helps the boy to work out how to double the area of a square.[10] Socrates uses this example to show Meno that this knowledge was recollected by the slave's immortal soul and not taught to him.[11] But Plato remained ambiguous on slavery. Clemens asks: "did Plato think or refuse to think slavery? Did Plato affirm or deny the very idea of slavery? Was Plato himself on the side of the slave or the master?"[12]

3 de Boer (2023) 227–8.
4 de Boer (2023) 228.
5 de Boer (2023) 228.
6 Bull (1998) 124.
7 Clemens (2018) 135.
8 Badiou (2017) 35.
9 Clemens (2018) 135.
10 Plato (2005) 82a–85c.
11 Plato (2005) 85c.
12 Clemens (2018) 136.

Aristotle tried to accommodate the contradictions of slavery within his work. Two claims are passed down to subsequent writings on slavery.[13] First, Aristotle assumed enslaved peoples had a dual identity. Slaves (douloi) are human beings who are not properly human. The slave sits at the axis of human and animal. A slave is an animate instrument, whose exclusion from politics provides the foundation for the economy and understanding freedom, whose body can be deployed without questioning.[14] Second, following Bull, Aristotle assumed that the master's humanity took the place of the slave's. Aristotle made a comparison between what he called legal slavery and what he called natural slavery. A natural slave is a being who is by their very nature, suitable for enslavement. A legal slave is a being who, by chance, is classified as a slave by the laws of the nation or state in which they live. For Aristotle, the only 'true' slaves are natural slaves who are legally enslaved. Any natural citizens who happen to have been enslaved must be freed, and those natural slaves who are by chance free must be enslaved.[15] Bull's view is that Aristotle bequeaths to Western thought the idea that there exists inhuman beings who can be enslaved, and freemen and citizens who can never be enslaved.[16]

There are two points following this. The first is the importance of tracing the *figure* of the slave in Western philosophical thought. What role does this *figure* play in our philosophical understandings of knowledge, freedom and belonging? The second is the concrete fact that enslaved people have been carving out their own understandings of freedom, quite separate from philosophical debates. My approach to these two points is a variation of what Lewis Gordon calls 'disciplinary decadence'. For Gordon this is a discipline so rooted in colonial practices that it considers itself complete, self-created and immortal.[17] Such decadence exposes a gap in our methodologies in respect of populations objectified when the discipline was formed. Historically marginalised populations, non-normative people, cannot be fitted into the strictures of the discipline; they become problems, rather than people who face problems.[18] Gordon speaks of colonial practices. I wish to extend the analogy to the ways in which enslaved people, throughout Western political and philosophical thought, are treated as a non-normative remainder which cannot be accounted for, and yet is required by the structure of the system.

13 Bull (1998) 124.
14 Clemens (2018) 136.
15 Bull (1998) 101–2.
16 Bull (1998) 102.
17 Gordon (2015) 4–5; Gordon (2014) 86.
18 Gordon (2014) 81–92.

The divided nature of life

Laura Brace explains that the politics of slavery has centred on the issue of how slavery should be defined, and whether and how slavery should be seen as an absolute condition or a fixed status.[19] Seymour Drescher wrote that the most frequently used part of the status is a recognised right by some to possess, buy, sell, discipline, transport, liberate or dispose of the bodies and behaviour of others.[20] The idea of slavery carries a "mythic potency".[21]

Chasing an all-encompassing and elusive definition is not my focus, in part because it poses problems. Here I find Kostas Vlassopoulos's writing helpful. Vlassopoulos argues that 'essentialist' approaches make it difficult to account for diversity and difference. Slavery is often seen from the masters' point of view, the group which controlled the institution. In this sense, enslaved people become passive objects of exploitation, able to acquiesce to their enslaved status or to revolt and try to become free. Vlassopoulos notes that they are not seen as historical agents who shaped slavery's configuration historically.[22]

Slave agency and the wider relationships that shaped slavery are often missing from definitions of slavery.[23] Orlando Patterson saw enslaved people as natally alienated and socially dead.[24] Extrapolating from Patterson, our ideas of freedom can be seen as a paradoxical concept. Freedom and the highest good is to not be under the constraint of another. It requires people to be deprived of it to gain meaning. For Patterson, slavery is the required counterpoint to freedom. Freedom is always doubled. The claiming of rights requires the exclusion of others from those rights, which Patterson ties to the social death of enslaved individuals.

For Brace, the distinction between freedom and unfreedom is an ongoing social struggle, with slavery constituting colonialism and political thought, as well as the meanings of class, gender and race. Brace also notes that slavery is "part of the answer to the questions about which identities are visible, whose identity matters and who counts as a human and as a person".[25] The slave is deracinated and only exists through the master. This is why Patterson described slavery as a "relation of domination".[26]

The slave is a divided figure, and the notion of a 'division' is central to Agamben's philosophy. Agamben contends that our notion of 'life' is divided

19 Brace (2018) 1.
20 Drescher (2009) 5.
21 Blackburn (1988) 269.
22 Vlassopoulos (2021) 2.
23 Vlassopoulos (2021) 5.
24 Patterson (1982) 13.
25 Brace (2018) 8.
26 Patterson (1982) 335.

in Western political thought. It is a political concept, not a biological one.[27] Agamben investigates the divisions and caesurae which separate man from 'non-man'.[28] What this means is that "everything happens as if, in our culture, life were *what cannot be defined, yet, precisely for this reason, must be ceaselessly articulated and divided*".[29]

This division works on several levels. First, life is divided into two, what Agamben terms *bios* and *zoè*. He traces this division to Aristotle, claiming that the 'Greeks' used two terms to refer to life.[30] *Bios* is the (political) form of life proper to an individual or group, and *zoè* is the basic fact of living common to all living beings. Crucially, for Agamben's thought, each term is determinable only in its relation to the other.[31] Natural life is not accessible. It is only experienced through its being taken up in a political system.[32] This is what Agamben calls an 'inclusive exclusion'. Agamben explains that:

> This division separates the living being from itself and from its immediate relationship with its environment.[33]

This division operates on several levels – vegetal and relational, organic and animal, animal and human. The divisions pass as a 'mobile border' within living man. They operate as an 'apparatus' that decides who (or what) is human and who is not human.[34] An apparatus, or *dispositif*, is:

> [L]iterally anything that has in some way the capacity to capture, orient, determine, intercept, model, control, or secure the gestures, behaviours, opinions, or discourses of living beings.[35]

This includes prisons, schools, juridical measures (and to this I can include the legal exploitation of enslaved people), but also writing, literature, philosophy and even language itself, the "most ancient of apparatuses".[36] Agamben's thought is based on a massive (in his own words) division. On the one hand, living beings, and on the other, *dispositifs* in which living beings are incessantly captured:

27 Agamben (1998) 161.
28 Agamben (2004) 16.
29 Agamben (2004) 13.
30 Agamben (1998) 1.
31 Agamben (2016) xix.
32 Kotsko (2020) 83.
33 Agamben (2009b) 16.
34 Agamben (2004) 15.
35 Agamben (2009b) 17.
36 Agamben (2009b) 17.

> To recapitulate, we have then two great classes: living beings (or substances) and dispositives, and between these two, as a third class, subjects. I call a subject that which results from the relation and, so to speak, from the relentless fight between living beings and dispositives.[37]

The product of this constant separation and division of life is inevitably a remainder.[38] This remainder is 'bare life', which is cast out from the *polis*, and a figure lacking rights or recognition.[39]

The separation of man from 'non-man' also operates as an "anthropological machine". This machine *creates* the human with and against the animal.[40] The machine has two sides:

> If, in the machine of the moderns, the outside is produced through the exclusion of an inside and the inhuman produced by animalizing the human, here [the machine of earlier times] the inside is obtained through the inclusion of an outside, and the non-man is produced by the humanization of an animal: the man-ape, the *enfant sauvage* or *Homo ferus*, but also and above all the slave, the barbarian, and the foreigner, as figures of an animal in human form.[41]

The human-animal divide sets up the very possibility of politics. Man retains a privileged position in the dichotomy of man-animal.[42] Humanity is premised upon the exclusion of animality and is defined as not-animality. The category of human is empty as it is continually shifting.[43] As Salzani describes, this makes the human not something with precise, historical and immutable content, but a contingent form that is always held in relation to other living beings and to itself.[44] The dividing line between the animal and the human passes through man internally.[45] The 'missing link' between animals and men has always been filled by figures who are considered subhuman animals, like slaves.[46]

What does this mean? This 'empty space' establishes the 'human'. This is done by opposing *bios* to *zoè*, man to animal, human to inhuman. This

37 Agamben (2009b) 19. The spelling of 'dispositive' is from the English translation of the work.
38 Agamben (2016) xix–xx.
39 Agamben (1998) 1, 181.
40 Oliver (2007) 1.
41 Agamben (2004) 37.
42 Agamben (2004) 79.
43 Agamben (2004) 91.
44 Salzani (2022) 40.
45 Agamben (2004) 16.
46 Oliver (2007) 8.

anthropological, or human-creating machine, functions through an exclusion (which is also always already a capturing) and an inclusion (which is also always already an exclusion). This always leads to one part being subjected and dominated by the other. The human being is dislocated and displaced. The human being obtains a bare life, whose separation and exclusion from itself grounds political existence.[47]

Without bare life, and without that bare figure of existence, political life cannot exist, and the human being cannot be produced. Our political existence *requires* this remainder. This division allows the life we label as 'human being' to gain a capacity to live a political life.[48] Bare life encompasses political existence while simultaneously being anathema to the very system it maintains. The anthropological machine means that man must recognise himself as a non-man in order to become human.[49] Moreover, Salzani notes that for Agamben, man is Man with a capital "M", a gender-neutral category which negates the existence of women and other genders.[50] He goes on to say (referencing the work of Kelly Oliver) that the binaries of man/animal and man/woman are inseparable in the history of Western thought. Femininity is linked to animality, a not-quite-human category, contrasted to the human 'Man'. The violence that women have been subjected to is similar to the violence perpetrated against non-human animals.[51] For Emma Jones, it is more accurate to speak of an 'andrological machine' rather than an anthropological machine. Stopping the anthropological machine is not possible without stopping the andrological machine. The division made between man and animal is complicit with the division made between man and woman. Agamben does not contemplate this connection.[52] I attempt to grapple with this legacy.

Bare life is left at the mercy of sovereign and governmental action and decisions. It is exemplified by politically liminal figures that lack the rights and legal protections we take for granted, like the camp inmate. It is to these figures that Agamben draws attention, writing that "it is only in the burning house that the fundamental architectural problem becomes visible for the first time".[53] It may appear that the 'slave' would stand as a paradigmatic figure of bare life, not least because in *The Open* the slave is described as a figure of an animal in human form.[54] But the opposite is the case. The key is to render the anthropological machine inoperative, and the slave (or the enslaved person, as I interpret this) is able to render the machine inoperative

47 Agamben (2004) 38; Agamben (2016) 199, 203.
48 Agamben (2016) 203.
49 Agamben (2004) 26–7.
50 Salzani (2022) xii.
51 Salzani (2022) 2–3; Oliver (2009) 230–1.
52 Jones (2007) 36.
53 Agamben (1999c) 115; Kotsko (2020) 50.
54 Agamben (2004) 37.

and points to a life that is not divided or controlled.[55] This is a life that consists of the potential *not to* adhere to the species' limited set of possibilities.[56] Human potential constitutes human freedom. To be free is to be capable of one's own impotentiality, to be free for good and evil.[57]

Agamben and the slave

Agamben's starting point is Aristotle. Reading Aristotle, Agamben contends that the slave is a human being but is also an 'animate instrument'. The master uses the slave's body. In using the body of the slave the master uses his own body. For Agamben, the slave is intimately connected to the very definition of the human being. This is what Agamben calls the 'use of bodies', where a zone of indifference emerges between one's own body and that of another. Slavery, Agamben argues, retains a memory of this original operation.[58] This leads to a claim that I explore through this book: that the perversion of the proper human relation occurs when the reciprocal relation of use is appropriated and reified juridically through constituting slavery as a social institution.[59] What does this mean? I explore the idea of a 'properly human relation' through the actions and lives of enslaved people themselves, and how legal and political philosophy (including Agamben's work) has been unable to capture those lived experiences in their conceptualisation of the figure of the slave.

Slaves have a precarious juridico-political position. They are included in the *polis* through their exclusion. Their lives are the material presupposition for the good life of others.[60] de Boer mentions that if we view these bare lives as something that is never to occur again, we repeat the scission of the living being and will repeat the constant re-creation of bare life.[61] Any true ethics and politics must consider the lives formerly excluded from considerations of the good life.[62] Judith Butler has made a similar argument. For Butler, those who find themselves in positions of radical exposure to violence are not reduced to mere being, nor deprived of all forms of agency.[63] The term 'bare life' does not describe the modes of agency and action undertaken by those forms of life. To be cast out of the *polis* is still to be saturated in power

55 Agamben (2004) 92.
56 Agamben (1999a) 182; Salzani (2022) 14.
57 Agamben (1999a) 182–183.
58 Agamben (2016) 14.
59 Agamben (2016) 14.
60 de Boer (2023) 230.
61 de Boer (2023) 233.
62 de Boer (2023) 233.
63 Butler (2015) 79.

relations, which should be a point of departure for thinking forms of political being.[64]

Agamben does not aim to provide a historically accurate analysis of all forms of slavery but uses the enslaved to bring something into view, a form of human existence that may otherwise elude historians.[65] In a similar vein, decolonial thought involves discovering and developing potentialities that were not factually actualised.[66] The invention of slavery as a juridical institution allowed the capturing of living beings and deployed the use of the body as a means of production.[67] Slavery is also an ancient category of technology. For Agamben, slavery's abolition in modernity freed up the possibility of technology, of the living instrument.[68] Yet the use of the slave's body is not assimilable to the labour of us moderns. Clemens explains that a slave is the master's animate organ. The slave's exclusion from politics creates the economy. The slave's body is available to be deployed without question. The slave produces without really producing.[69] Slavery therefore allows us to understand and counter the forms of technological repression that we experience in modernity and postmodernity.

Agamben's hypothesis is that the slave is a human being without work who makes possible the work of the human being, which is to live a human life, a political life.[70] The slave represents the capture of a figure of human action within the law, which remains for us to recognise.[71] The slave's community is vital yet treated as sub-human. The slave's servitude is seen as both natural and able to be refigured as seen fit.[72]

This book does three main things. First, I read key thinkers that Agamben engages with in his thought and writings to show how the figure of the slave (in contrast to the enslaved person) has been used to construct ideas of freedom in political and legal philosophy. This use of the slave shows that it is not just a crucial figure for Agamben. Aristotle, St Paul and Hegel all engage with the figure of the slave and slavery as part of their political philosophies. I then seek to develop and explore the connections between these philosophies that Agamben does not make in his works and use examples of the agency of the enslaved to show how the figure of the slave can never account for the agency and resistance of the enslaved. This serves as a background to and justification of my argument that the *figure of the slave*, and not the *enslaved*

64 Butler (2015) 80.
65 de Boer (2023) 233; Agamben (2009a) 31.
66 de Boer (2023) 234.
67 Agamben (2016) 11, 78–9.
68 Agamben (2016) 78–9.
69 Clemens (2018) 139.
70 Agamben (2016) 22–3.
71 Agamben (2016) 23.
72 Clemens (2018) 140.

person, is a necessary figure for Western political theory. Recognition at the centre of politics, law, and rights requires the existence of a non-human in the slave who cannot be recognised.

This leads to my claim that the figure of the slave has helped construct and orient philosophical and legal defences of colonialism, coloniality and the supremacy of the White subject. In my discussion of Western European thought, I cannot separate out the history of philosophy from the history of colonialism. As de Boer states, Western modernity has condemned slavery. However, Western thought's ideas of what constitutes the 'good life' remain based on Aristotelian thought. Specifically, they are based on Aristotle's definition of the master as a male human being, who is legitimised by the *polis* to "lay claim to his possessions and develop his proper humanity".[73] de Boer mentions that our presupposed ideal in overcoming the problem of slavery is to create a civilisation composed fully of masters. But de Boer continues that maintaining the high standard of living in Western societies has been possible only through the reliance on slave-like labour in the Global South.[74] Aristotle's view of natural law provided the template for race becoming an epistemology of domination, an ordering principle and the moral authority of a political order.[75] Aristotle inferiorised women,[76] non-Greeks and all labourers, including slaves,[77] articulating an uncompromising racial construct.[78] Cedric Robinson claimed that from the twelfth century onwards, one European ruling order after another, and clerical and secular propagandists, reiterated this racial calculus.[79] Peter Garnsay traced Aristotle's influence into the first 400 years of Christianity;[80] Moses Finley traced Aristotle's influence into the modern age.[81]

This genealogy has led meaningful political life to be centred on a specifically White, male and European subject. In a sense, the figure of the slave becomes a means to an end and a crucial concept of the colonial enterprise. Colonialism is a political and economic relation. In this relation, the sovereignty of a people rests on the power of another people or nation. Coloniality, in contrast, references long-standing patterns of power that emerged because of colonialism. Coloniality defines culture, labour and knowledge production, but this definition takes place beyond the decisions of colonial administrations and is something much more deep-rooted and

73 de Boer (2023) 237.
74 de Boer (2023) 237.
75 Robinson (2021) li.
76 Aristotle (1984b) 1260a12.
77 Aristotle (1984a) 1095b20.
78 Robinson (2021) li.
79 Robinson (2021) li.
80 Garnsay (1996).
81 Finley (1998).

pervasive.[82] Coloniality controls the economy, authority and even gender and sexuality.[83] This has been termed the colonial matrix of power, or CMP. The CMP has existed from 1500 to the present day, representing the era of the Westernisation of the planet.[84] Today, Whiteness is a legal and global power structure that institutionalises the asymmetries of power that exist across the globe.[85] Today, borders exist everywhere, based on the racial, sexual and epistemological divisions imposed by coloniality.[86] We live in a world where Whiteness is an orientation, or our starting point.[87] This is a consequence of the divisible and stratified nature of life, and of how political life has been described in an exclusionary manner.

Principles like freedom and formal equality encouraged slave-owning and slave-trading, and after abolition, fuelled a paternalistic colonialism by Europeans. It is against this dominant reading that this book stands. Such a caricature can efface the close connection between slavery, race and gender, as well as ignoring how colonial slavery was intertwined with the development of modern capitalism. Gender cannot be separated from colonialism. European colonialism exploited the planet for the benefit of man, and the gender system racialised women as inferior to fit the processes of Eurocentric global capitalism.[88] The capitalist system itself is today racial, highlighting coercion and productivity in capital investment and forms of exchange.[89]

Second, this book explores how and why the slave is a transformative figure for Agamben. I develop Agamben's use of the figure of the slave to engage with the lived realities of slavery.[90] I supplement Agamben's writings with examples of the historical agency of enslaved people and unfree individuals, as well as the different legal structures that have governed slavery and the various legal rights that the enslaved and unfree had. Agamben's thought focuses on ancient slavery, not modern slavery. He does not engage with the various forms of contemporary slavery that exist in the CMP. Ancient slavery was enmeshed in the economy in a similar way to the Atlantic slave trade. The body of the slave is also the site of physical, sexual and psychological abuse and domination. These are the areas of Agamben's philosophy that I develop.

Third, I view the enslaved person as an exemplar or figure of future politics, based around the figure of 'form-of-life'. The book seeks to focus on the

82 Maldonado-Torres (2007) 243.
83 Quijano (2000a) 342–86.
84 Mignolo (2021) ix–x.
85 Darien-Smith (2015) 649–50.
86 Mignolo and Walsh (2018) 112.
87 Ahmed (2007) 150–1.
88 Lugones (2008) 1–17.
89 Robinson (2021) 26.
90 Agamben (1998) 12.

position of those sites labelled the 'darker side' of modernity by coloniality.[91] Today's world is necropolitical, populated by 'outsiders', populations deemed surplus and expendable to capitalist production.[92] But we still see survivors, those who have stood in the path of death, yet remain alive.[93] Form-of-life is the name given by Agamben to a form of existence that does not depend on the presuppositional relation between *bios* and *zoè*, or the anthropological machine and the dialectic between man and non-man. Similarly, as de Boer explains, decolonial thought attempts to focus on alternative ways of forming community, for example, by the communities of fugitive slaves or Maroons.[94] Form-of-life is a life of potential, involving the use of the body in a way which makes it impossible to divide the living being and create bare life.

In this vein, I reinterpret form-of-life to sketch a hopeful future politics and agency. Today, this requires disobedience to the ontologies built in an imaginary of Western epistemology.[95] Decoloniality dismantles power relations that reproduce racial, gender and geopolitical hierarchies in the CMP.[96] In short, I read Agamben in light of decolonisation's aims to disrupt and change the order of the world.[97] Agamben is in no way a decolonial or postcolonial thinker. Agamben's thought is Eurocentric, and he has stated that only "European man" can approach "his truth" through a confrontation with the past. Africa is not even mentioned, along with Central and South America. Europe, in contrast, offers a culture that remains vital ever after the end of history, meaning its history can help attain a "new life".[98] But Europe cannot be understood without considering European colonialism. The legacies of decolonial politics cannot be found in Greece and Rome.[99]

The structures Agamben critiques create an *ethos* that perceives existence instrumentally as a means toward unachievable ends.[100] de Boer notes that Agamben's thought is similar to decolonial critiques of the modern as producing 'neoliberal subjectivity', and to rid ourselves of this colonial logic, we need to critique institutions, historical injustices and this form of subjectivity.[101] The world needs transforming, and the transformative potential is to be found in the oppressed and neglected; expressions of humanity are to be

91 Mignolo and Walsh (2018) 111.
92 Phipps (2020) 123.
93 Mbembé (2019) 36.
94 de Boer (2023) 236.
95 Mignolo (2021) 489–90.
96 Maldonado-Torres (2011).
97 Fanon (2005) 36.
98 Savà (2012).
99 Mignolo (2021) 489.
100 de Boer (2023) 237.
101 de Boer (2023) 237.

found in inhumane circumstances.[102] The enslaved person provides us with the possibility of an alternative vision of an ethical existence. This sets the stage for a fruitful encounter between Agamben and decolonial theory.[103]

In one sense, this book gives a very 'unfaithful' reading to Agamben. My aim is to show how form-of-life can be fruitfully read with decolonial theory to think of a hopeful form of future politics, given the continued colonial control of the world.[104] Here I follow the spirit of Agamben's own words:

> The genuinely philosophical element contained in a work – be it artistic, scientific, or theoretical work – is its capacity to be developed, something that has remained – or has willingly been left – unspoken and that needs to be found and seized.[105]

This means that, at some point, it is no longer possible to distinguish what is our work and what belongs to the author in question. For Agamben, it is a joyous moment when every claim to originality fades away.[106]

The enslaved person should not be seen as the antithesis of freedom, grounding our Eurocentric ideas of freedom and agency by being their opposite. The historical reality of the lives of people who were enslaved and unfree can provide an alternative construction of the ideas of agency, recognition and subjectivity, ideas which are central to legal and political philosophy. It can also show how race in the early modern world created and reproduced material distinctions between groups of humanity.[107] This is not to reify the lives of the enslaved, nor to engage in a type of orientalist analysis, nor indeed to focus on the deaths and abuse of the enslaved as a foundation for a different form of politics and freedom.

I draw influence from Saidiya Hartman, who viewed the autobiographical example as a way of "engaging and countering the violence of abstraction".[108] These are insurgent lives lived in rebellion, waywardness, refusal, love and mutual aid.[109] Alexander Weheliye sees in these stories "the lines of flight, freedom dreams, practices of liberation, possibilities of other worlds" of people coded as property and as totally powerless.[110] I seek to explore how to substantively respond to these "miniscule movements" and "glimmers of hope" (in Weheliye's words), without effacing the annihilation of the people

102 de Boer (2023) 239–40.
103 de Boer (2023) 241.
104 Hall (2017) 24.
105 Agamben (2019) 14–15.
106 Agamben (2019b) 15.
107 Quijano (2000b) 534.
108 Hartman (2008) 7.
109 Hartman (2019) xiv.
110 Weheliye (2014); Brace (2018) 4.

who made them.[111] The institution of slavery involved a constant conflict with those who were enslaved. When enough alternative worlds are built by enslaved people, then the mastery itself may cease to maintain its imperial status.[112]

The enslaved were historical agents, seeking to change their slave relationship. Given the nature of slavery throughout Western history and the fact that enslaved people had little to no power, they were often unsuccessful. But slave agency did exist.[113] If we focus on acts of resistance through the lens of linearity, we could view them as a series of defeats. But they are an accumulated and accumulating commitment to act in the hope of an unpredictable future.[114] In what we call modernity and the CMP, the era of European colonialism, the colonial ordering and understanding of the world has always been challenged and resisted.[115]

A Note on Method

The lives and actions of the enslaved and unfree point towards a form of acting and living that I term *hyper-hermeneutics*, which can render inoperative systems or institutions of control. Enslavement, in all its forms, is the *paradigmatic* example of such a system. It is this hyper-hermeneutic politics that I argue underpins Agamben's form-of-life, which provides a way out of the cul de sacs of the present. Agamben's concept of the 'paradigm' is crucial here. Paradigms are historical phenomena that "constitute and make intelligible a broader historical-problematic context".[116] The paradigm is neither inside nor outside the set of phenomena that it identifies. It is the real particular case that is set apart from what it is meant to exemplify.[117] A term, once taken as a paradigm, is 'deactivated' from its normal use.[118]

Agamben reads these paradigms as constructing a 'paradigmatic circle',[119] which allows form-of-life to deactivate apparatuses of control.[120] These paradigms are gestural.[121] Such gestures reveal the possibility of a new way of being to be brought about.[122] The paradigmatic gestures of the enslaved separate themselves from oppressive and dominating legal and political structures,

111 Weheliye (2014) 12.
112 Gordon and Gordon (2006) ix.
113 Vlassopoulos (2021) 8.
114 Verges (2021) 5.
115 Nanni (2017) 19.
116 Agamben (2009a) 9.
117 de la Durantaye (2009) 218–19.
118 Agamben (2009a) 18.
119 Agamben (2009a) 27–8.
120 Agamben (1999b) 174.
121 Agamben (2009a) 27.
122 Agamben (2016) 214–19.

revealing new ways of belonging. There is a history of these acts which can be excavated from the historical record – there has always been resistance to enslavement which aligns very closely with Agamben's conception of freedom. Gestures of resistance may be subtle, or they may be revolutionary. It is these actions that I consider here.

The slave is an embodied individual within modern capitalism and capitalism's connections to racism and coloniality. Importantly, the enslaved, whilst being treated as a mere instrument of production in fact (through acts of culture, music and the body) acted against the very institution which enslaved them. These are examples (in Agamben's register) of living one's life as a form. Resistance and insurgence have the potential in the agency of the *how*.[123] The possibility of becoming human requires the affirmation of a different humanity. It demands one's own foundation in the creation of forms of life that could be characterised as fully human. A fully human form of life results from a struggle for life. This helps emerge from sterile and arid regions of existence, what Frantz Fanon called the zone of nonbeing.[124] I then connect slavery to technology and contemporary neoliberalism. European states have not self-decolonised, and there remains a kinship between colonial predation and contemporary neoliberal appropriation. Neo-colonialism and neoliberal capitalism remain resilient, but the enslaved can point to a future away from a divided subject to a common humanity.

The book's argument

This study comprises eight chapters. In the first two chapters, I outline Agamben's philosophy and his writings on form-of-life. I also explore why the acts of enslaved peoples can provide the basis for rethinking this form-of-life.

Chapter One considers form-of-life, outlining the features of this way of living. Agamben states that form-of-life exists in unedifying places and does not yet exist in its fullness. Despite this, elements of form-of-life are hidden in the present, in potentially contemptible areas. I argue that slavery is one such contemptible area. Agamben sees the human being whose *ergon* is the use of the body as being the slave. I explain Agamben's position – that the slave represents the capture within the law of a figure of human acting that remains for us to recognise. The use of the body and absence of 'work' of the slave (used in a sense distinct from slavery as an institution) evoke the paradigm of a human activity reducible neither to labour, production nor praxis. Slavery retains a memory of the original operation of what is properly human.

Chapter Two outlines the philosophical method and arguments that I use to underpin the book's arguments and conclusions. It considers the

123 Mignolo and Walsh (2018) 48.
124 Fanon (1970) 2.

Eurocentric limitations to Agamben's writings in pursuing a project that focuses on enslaved people. Agamben's focus on the primacy of Europe has the potential to undermine the force of his argument. But Agamben's work provides a fruitful basis for being read with decolonial thought. This enables us to view the actions and lives of enslaved people as carving out forms of life that do not depend on a divisible idea of freedom.

Agamben's conception of 'destituent potential' rejects the idea that political action consists in instrumentally realising a specific doctrine, plan or philosophy. Destitution tears down, dismantles and cancels prevailing political representations, apparatuses and institutions without proposing others to replace them. It is an ethical task demanding that those who inhabit the destitute terrain learn to move within it and deactivate the anthropological machine. It is lived through the paradigm. The paradigm is akin to an example, a historical phenomenon that makes intelligible a broader historical and problematic context. Once a term becomes a paradigm it is deactivated from its normal use. I propose a philosophical approach called 'hyper-hermeneutics', which is a form of hermeneutics. I use hermeneutics to understand the potential within human lives (whether they are counted as lives worth living or not) to effect changes within modes of power and control that shape the modern world. Hyper-hermeneutics is a paradigm; it is a form of acting through which small acts and gestures of living one's life as a form can be a form of revolutionary action that can challenge and deactivate oppressive political systems. These paradigmatic gestures are not revolutionary. They are slight shifts in modes of living that allow forms of life to become forms-of-life.

Finally, using slavery in England as an example, I show how hyper-hermeneutic acts of resistance by the enslaved helped end the slave trade. I consider the English case of *Somerset v Stewart*. Famously mislabelled as the case which freed all slaves in England, the reality is more complex. Lord Mansfield delivered a compromise judgment, and slavery continued to exist until the 1830s in England. Slavery was ended in part because enslaved people acted as though *Somerset* freed them.

Chapter Three, Chapter Four and Chapter Five consider key interlocutors for Agamben who all have attempted to theorise the figure of the slave – Aristotle, St Paul and Hegel. These chapters demonstrate how the lives and agency of enslaved peoples are not adequately accounted for by these theorisations. They provide this study with a theoretical architecture and a framework to consider my decolonial reading and application of Agamben, a necessary reading given the colonial ordering of the present.

Chapter Three considers Aristotle's theory of slavery. It contrasts the position of the slave in Aristotle and slavery in the Greek city states. Aristotle's view of humanity as bifurcated into beings who can and cannot be enslaved is found throughout Western European thought. This chapter connects Aristotle's writings to coloniality, showing how Aristotle provided the philosophical defence for the Atlantic slave trade and early modern chattel slavery, and how his work provided the basis for race becoming an epistemology of domination. This provides context for a discussion of how Agamben has interpreted Aristotle with respect to the idea of 'use'. The use of the body of the enslaved person opens the possibility of a different form of being human, the potential of which has been captured in the history of slavery. Yet the status of the slave is much more indeterminate than Aristotle gives credit for, and the role of passive and active resistance by slaves is more endemic than Aristotle intimates. It is in that resistance that we may see the germ of what Agamben terms the use of bodies. The focus on Aristotle provides a philosophical foundation for Agamben and shows how and why enslaved people construct alternative forms of freedom.

Chapter Four considers slavery in St Paul, who I view as an intermediary between Aristotle and Hegel. Paul is the bridge to the ancient world but also to the importance of communal action, which played a key part in the actions and lives of enslaved people in early modernity and modernity. Both St Paul and Aristotle write of the *doulos*, or slave, and Agamben refers to both without theorising the connection between the two. This chapter concludes that Aristotle's theory of slavery is incompatible with slavery in the Pauline Epistles. The slave as an 'animate instrument' (in Aristotle) cannot be reconciled with Paul's messianic completion of the law as exemplified in the slave (*doulos*). I explore the historical realities of slavery in Paul's world to explore the roles of agency and resistance which are not reflected in the Epistles. What we see in Roman slavery are enslaved people, through small and seemingly insignificant actions, trying to carve out their own modes of freedom.

For Agamben, the slave in Paul is invested with the messianic vocation. This allows him to treat the slave as a rational being and to set aside the institution itself. Paul's messianism is based on the 'as not', the revocation of every vocation, and the deactivation of every apparatus. This 'as not' is connected to the use of the body and Paul's radical equality. Connecting the work of Agamben to Furio Jesi, I explain how this deactivation affects machines of control, be they mythological or anthropological. I use this to consider the nature of time and the difference between *chronos* and *kairos*. *Chronos* represents the idea of time running in a straight line with direction and purpose, a homogeneous continuum. Agamben, following Paul, states that we must reconceive time as *kairos*. *Kairos* is fulfilled time, the time of the now.

I connect this to strands of decolonial thought, which develops alternative ways of relating to time and community. Time has a crucial communal dimension, created through communal events, and experienced through hyper-hermeneutics gestures to become real for people. In the final part of the chapter, using the figure of Spartacus, I apply Jesi's and Agamben's writings on time and messianism. I argue that the *example* of the 'slave' operates as a figure of emancipation for future political struggles, connecting back to *kairos* and the way the past can be grasped to inform present political action. The time of the now cannot be separated from what has gone before, and the coming politics involves an excavation of the past.

Chapter Five focuses on the Hegelian master-slave dialectic setting the stage for the remaining three chapters' consideration of slavery, colonialism, capitalism and neoliberalism. A decolonial line of argument naturally flows from a discussion of Hegel. It is through Hegel's master-slave dialectic that the figure of the slave gains a crucial destiny in the philosophical anthropology of the West, in shaping subsequent understandings of political belonging and freedom. The dialectic is the model for the mutual recognition of all by all. I draw connections between Aristotle's 'use of the body', and Paul's messianic conception of time as *kairos* that can deactivate apparatuses of control, rendering them inoperative. Agamben then connects Hegel's use of *Aufhebung* or *aufheben* to Paul's use of *katargēsis* or inoperativity. In this sense, Hegel's thought is read messianically by Agamben.

Hegel's account cannot be separated from early modern colonial slavery. Race is the historical limitation to the master-slave dialectic in Hegel, as it was heavily influenced by the successful rebellion in Haiti. The history of Haiti shows the importance of traditions for political action. Life's divisibility is the constant in our conceptions of freedom; the resistance of the enslaved is a commonality. Form-of-life reaches back to past examples to help shape action in the present. But Hegel moved away from the radicality of his writings on slavery, towards a racist and derogatory view of Africa and Africans, which reflected the view of the slave-owning classes of the time. The chapter ends with Alexander Kojève's interpretation of Hegel's dialectic. Kojève's figure of the 'workless slave' is read as form-of-life, its inoperativity is an originary feature of the human condition.

The final chapters consider how the connections Agamben makes between slavery, the use of bodies and the coming politics can deactivate the apparatuses of biopolitical control that incessantly create bare life. The enslaved person holds the potential for future politics today. Form-of-life, given a decolonial reading, can present a form of political agency that can challenge the coloniality of the present day. The examples of bare life in modernity focused upon by Agamben occur in the shadow of the CMP. The camp occurs in the same modern world as the slave ship. The biopolitical body is structured by colonial and racial logic.

Chapter Six engages with elements of decolonial theory to show the centrality of race, coloniality and enslavement to the modern world and modern epistemologies (including Agamben's thought). The position of the slave in the legal and political thought of Europe was both *materially* and *symbolically* significant. I show how racialism merged with capitalism. Central to modern racial capitalism and coloniality is the Atlantic slave trade, and the transformation of human life into an object of economic transaction. I discuss the way the concept of 'domination' relates to the figure of the slave to structure Western conceptions of freedom, both in terms of the body and in terms of what is permitted speech. I use Afropessimism to show how (analogously to Agamben) what is 'Human' is based on a divided Life, constructed on a (Black) Death.

A decolonial critique of the CMP interrogates the coloniality that has shaped the modern world. In this way, form-of-life can be removed from a reading that restricts it to a liberal Western juridical subject. There remains a surplus which escapes all attempts at capture within a social or legal status. The key is a focus on destitution and abolishing current categories and conditions of oppression. To support this, I draw on the work of Alexander Weheliye. For Weheliye, potential libidinal currents slumber in all acts of political domination, of which slavery is one. I consider such libidinal currents in the example of women's bodies that not only resisted enslavement and domination but carved out modes of survival and community in the face of such political and bodily oppression.

Chapter Seven shows how small acts and gestures of enslaved people have been able to point towards new forms of political belonging not based on the divided subject. Living in the 'now' means living for yourself but also with others, deactivating apparatuses through actions that become examples that impact future gestures. The enslaved person is an embodied individual within capitalism. In the context of the plantation, the humanity of the slave appears as the figure of a shadow and the slave condition results from domination and expulsion from humanity altogether. We need to search for what Agamben terms a 'remnant', a people embodying resistance to the existing political hegemony through their gestures, their way of being.

I explore the ways in which enslaved people in Caribbean societies transformed the colonial order by maintaining an alternative perspective towards time, work and self. There is a history of enslaved people being treated as mere instruments of production, yet drawing upon any object, instrument, language or gesture and turning it into a stylised performance. This chapter also returns to the aftermath of the Haitian Revolution. The struggle in Haiti was between the workers and the oligarchs who ran the country. The lives of the workers are examples of a radically different political imaginary. These types of acts have led to new forms of culture, political organisation, and the legal recognition of alternative forms of subjectivity. One such form is found in the figure of the 'zombii', a form of life that points towards a life in contact with one another, beyond the control of necropolitical capitalism. Forms of resistance against dominant and totalising power do exist, and they point the way towards conceptions of belonging that are just, just as they are.

The final chapter, Chapter Eight, draws together the arguments of the book. I explain my thesis that the figure of the slave continually appears and reappears as legal and political philosophy defines personhood and agency. Even today when slavery is abolished in international law and legally anathema, the figure of the slave remains ever-present. The formal emancipation of enslaved people has given way to a different form of unfreedom in the capitalist world. I discuss the way the figure of the slave constructs Marxist and anarchist critiques of wage slavery. I consider how living in the Anthropocene and in the CMP have led to a world populated by hyper-exploited outsiders who are necessary for the functioning of the economy. I broaden the discussion to neoliberalism, and how debt helps reinforce an 'unfreedom' at the heart of the economy. I also consider the position of debt and how space is 'raced', contending that a non-Statist anarchism can be problematic in repeating the logic of coloniality. I then consider Agamben's claim that a slave is an ancient category of technology. Drawing on Martin Heidegger's thought, I make the argument that today's dependence on technology is akin to the ancient world's dependence on chattel slavery. I discuss this with reference to Donna Haraway's work on the 'cyborg' and Maurizio Lazzarato's 'machinic enslavement', contending that modernity's approach to technology repeats the Aristotelian idea that some beings are naturally slaves. Ultimately, Agamben's politics is optimistic, but his anarchistic tendencies remain borne of Eurocentrism and coloniality. I end the chapter, and the book, by returning to my decolonial 'correction' of Agamben's thought. The form-of-life of the enslaved person points toward a form of politics able to deactivate the apparatuses of control that exist around the world and were born of the CMP.

Reference List

Adébísí, F (2023) *Decolonisation and Legal Knowledge: Reflections on Power and Possibility*, Bristol: Bristol University Press.

Agamben, G (1998) *Homo Sacer: Sovereign Power and Bare Life*, Heller-Roazen, D (trans.), Stanford: Stanford University Press.

Agamben, G (1999a) 'On Potentiality' in *Potentialities: Collected Essays in Philosophy*, Heller-Roazen, D (trans.), Stanford: Stanford University Press, 177–84.

Agamben, G (1999b) 'The Messiah and the Sovereign: The Problem of Law in Walter Benjamin' in *Potentialities: Collected Essays in Philosophy*, Heller-Roazen, D (trans.), Stanford: Stanford University Press, 160–74.

Agamben, G (1999c) *The Man Without Content*, Albert, G (trans.), Stanford: Stanford University Press.

Agamben, G (2004) *The Open: Man and Animal*, Attell, K (trans.), Stanford: Stanford University Press.

Agamben, G (2009a) *The Signature of All Things: On Method*, D'Isanto, L and Attell, K (trans.), New York: Zone Books.

Agamben, G (2009b) *What is an Apparatus? and Other Essays*, Kishik, D and Pedatella, S (trans.), Stanford: Stanford University Press.

Agamben, G (2016) *The Use of Bodies*, Kotsko, A (trans.), Stanford: Stanford University Press.

Agamben, G (2019) *Creation and Anarchy: The Work of Art and the Religion of Capitalism*, Kotsko, A (trans.), Stanford: Stanford University Press.

Ahmed, S (2007) 'A Phenomenology of Whiteness', *Feminist Theory*, 8, 149–68.
Aristotle (1984a) 'Nicomachean Ethics' in *The Complete Works of Aristotle, Volume Two*, Barnes, J (ed.), Princeton: Princeton University Press.
Aristotle (1984b) 'Politics' in *The Complete Works of Aristotle, Volume Two*, Barnes, J (ed.), Princeton: Princeton University Press.
Badiou, A (2017) 'Hegel's Master and Slave', *Crisis and Critique*, 4, 34–47.
Blackburn, R (1988) 'Defining Slavery – Its Special Features and Social Role' in Archer, L (ed.), *Slavery and Other Forms of Unfree Labour*, London: Routledge, 262–80.
Brace, L (2018) *The Politics of Slavery*, Edinburgh: Edinburgh University Press.
Bull, M (1998) 'Slavery and the Multiple Self', *New Left Review*, 231, 94–131.
Butler, J (2015) *Notes Toward a Performative Theory of Assembly*, Cambridge: Harvard University Press.
Clemens, J (2018) 'As Fire Burns: Philosophy, Slavery, Technology', *Crisis & Critique*, 6, 130–45.
Darien-Smith, E (2015) 'Postcolonial Law' in Wright, J (ed.), *International Encyclopedia of the Social & Behavioural Sciences*, 2nd edn, Amsterdam: Elsevier, 647–51.
de Boer, Y (2023) 'The Figure of the Slave as an Ethical Paradigm in the Work of Agamben', *Netherlands Journal of Legal Philosophy*, 52, 227–41.
de la Durantaye, L (2009) *Giorgio Agamben: A Critical Introduction*, Stanford: Stanford University Press.
Drescher, S (2009) *Abolition: A History of Slavery and Antislavery*, Cambridge: Cambridge University Press.
Fanon, F (1970) *Black Skin, White Masks*, Markmann, C (trans.), London: Paladin.
Fanon, F (2005) *The Wretched of the Earth*, Farrington, C (trans.), New York: Grove Press.
Finley, M (1998) *Ancient Slavery and Modern Ideology*, Princeton: Markus Wiener Publishers.
Frost, T (2021) *Law, Relationality and the Ethical Life: Agamben and Levinas*, Abingdon: Routledge.
Garnsay, P (1996) *Ideas of Slavery from Aristotle to Augustine*, New York: Cambridge University Press.
Gordon, L (2014) 'Disciplinary Decadence and Decolonisation of Knowledge', *Africa Development*, 39, 81–92.
Gordon, L (2015) *Disciplinary Decadence: Living Thought in Trying Times*, Abingdon: Routledge.
Gordon, L and Gordon, J (2006) 'Introduction: Not Only the Master's Tools' in Gordon, L and Gordon, J (eds.), *Not Only the Master's Tools: African-American Studies in Theory and Practice*, Boulder: Paradigm.
Hall, S (2017) *Familiar Stranger*, Durham: Duke University Press.
Hartman, S (2008) 'Venus in Two Acts', *Small Axe*, 12, 1–14.
Hartman, S (2019) *Wayward Lives, Beautiful Experiments*, New York: W W Norton.
Jones, E (2007) 'In the Presence of the Living Cockroach: The Moment of Aliveness and the Gendered Body in Agamben and Lispector', *PhaenEx*, 2, 24–41.
Kotsko, A (2020) *Agamben's Philosophical Trajectory*, Edinburgh: Edinburgh University Press.

Lugones, M (2008) 'The Coloniality of Gender', *Worlds & Knowledges Otherwise*, 2, 1–17.

Maldonado-Torres, N (2007) 'On the Coloniality of Bring: Contributions to the Development of a Concept', *Cultural Studies*, 21, 240–70.

Maldonado-Torres, N (2011) 'Thinking Through the Decolonial Turn: Post-continental Interventions in Theory, Philosophy, and Critique – An Introduction', *Transmodernity: Journal of Peripheral Production of the Luso-Hispanic World*, 1. http://dx.doi.org/10.5070/T412011805.

Mbembé, A (2019) *Necropolitics*, Durham: Duke University Press.

Mignolo, W (2021) *The Politics of Decolonial Investigations*, Durham: Duke University Press.

Mignolo, W and Walsh, C (2018) *On Decoloniality: Concepts, Analytics, Praxis*, Durham: Duke University Press.

Nanni, G (2017) *The Colonisation of Time: Ritual, Routine and Resistance in the British Empire*, Manchester: Manchester University Press.

Oliver, K (2007) 'Stopping the Anthropological Machine: Agamben with Heidegger and Merleau-Ponty', *PhænEx: Journal of Existential and Phenomenological Theory and Culture*, 2, 1–23.

Oliver, K (2009) *Animal Lessons: How They Teach Us to Be Human*, New York: Columbia University Press.

Patterson, O (1982) *Slavery and Social Death: A Comparative Study*, Cambridge: Harvard University Press.

Phipps, A (2020) *Me, Not You: The Trouble with Mainstream Feminism*, Manchester: Manchester University Press.

Plato (2005) 'Meno' in *The Collected Dialogues, Including the Letters*, Hamilton, E and Cairns, H (eds.), Princeton: Princeton University Press.

Quijano, A (2000a) 'Coloniality of Power and Social Classification', *Journal of World Systems*, 6, 342–86.

Quijano, A (2000b) 'Coloniality of Power, Eurocentrism, and Latin America', *Nepantia: Views from the South*, 1, 533–80.

Robinson, C (2021) *Black Marxism: The Making of the Black Radical Tradition*, London: Penguin Books.

Salzani, C (2022) *Agamben and the Animal*, Newcastle upon Tyne: Cambridge Scholars Publishing.

Savà, P (2012) '"God Didn't Die, He Was Transformed into Money" – An Interview with Giorgio Agamben' (16 August 2012) https://libcom.org/article/god-didnt-die-he-was-transformed-money-interview-giorgio-agamben-peppe-sava.

Verges, F (2021) *A Decolonial Feminism*, Bohrer, A (trans.), London: Pluto Press.

Vlassopoulos, K (2021) *Historicising Ancient Slavery*, Edinburgh: Edinburgh University Press.

Weheliye, A (2014) *Habeas Viscus: Racializing Assemblages, Biopolitics, and Black Feminist Theories of the Human*, Durham: Duke University Press.

Chapter 1

Slavery and the coming politics

Introduction

My starting point for this study is 'form-of-life'. Much attention has been paid to Agamben's writings on bare life, or *homo sacer*, but there has been little focus on how Agamben uses the figure of the slave to support a positive politics. This chapter begins by exploring the immanent, non-relational 'form-of-life' which Agamben posits as being able to 'deactivate' the forms of biopolitical control which ceaselessly produce bare life. Form-of-life involves the use of the body in a way which makes it impossible to divide the living being and produce the remainder of bare life. The first part of this chapter sketches out the contours of form-of-life and explains why it is so crucial to Agamben's overall philosophical project.

The next part of the chapter considers Agamben's writings on the slave (and he writes on the slave, rather than the enslaved person) and slavery. Form-of-life does exist today, but in unedifying places. One of these places is in the body of the slave. The use of the body and absence of 'work' of the figure of the slave (used in a sense distinct from slavery as an institution) evokes the paradigm of a human activity that cannot be reduced to labour, production or praxis. The slave stands at the threshold that separates and joins *zoè* and *bios*.[1] But the slave and slavery are concepts fraught with conceptual difficulties and cannot be presented in terms of binary oppositions.

Slavery (Agamben's examples are drawn primarily from ancient Greece and the Roman Empire) retains a memory of the original anthropogenetic operation of what is properly human. Slavery is to ancient humanity what technology is to modern humanity – both watch over the threshold that allows access to the 'truly human condition'.[2] For Agamben, this operation is perverted when slavery is appropriated juridically as a 'social institution'.[3]

1 Agamben (2016) 78.
2 Agamben (2016) 78.
3 Agamben (2016) 14.

DOI: 10.4324/9781003303534-2

It is a curious phrasing, not least because slavery has always operated as a social institution.

What is a life lived as its form?

What is form-of-life? What does it mean to live one's life as a form? To explore these questions, we must explain how Agamben's philosophy focuses on the lived existence of singular lives, standing in opposition to operations of power which lead to life being constantly articulated and divided. Agamben rejects any attempt to find the locus of radical transformation in the State or the law.[4] Agamben's is not a 'traditional' political project.[5] He does not seek to be identified with key terms of the Western political tradition, such as:

> [S]overeignty, right, nation, people, democracy and general will [which] refer to a reality that no longer has anything to do with what these concepts used to designate – and those who continue to use these concepts uncritically literally do not know what they are talking about.[6]

Fred Moten has criticised the (in his words) American reception of Agamben that does not recognise the severity of his critique of movements of power and knowledge that separate life from its forms.[7] Agamben's form-of-life is a quickening, forgetive force.[8] For Lorenzo Chiesa, this means that we must *live* and at the same time to *think* of politics "set free from every figure of relation" (and representation).[9]

This non-relational togetherness requires the 'use of bodies'. Another body is possible for the human being, where use becomes common use and it is not possible to divide that body into a bare life. This means that a form of life can express itself as a hyphenated 'form-of-life', where life immanently lives its own mode of being in a non-relational 'contact'.[10] Agamben explains:

> In this way, philosophy is presented as an attempt to construct a life at once "superpolitical and apolitical" (*hypsipolis apolis*): separated in the ban from the city, it nevertheless becomes intimate and inseparable from itself, in a non-relation that has the form of an "exile of one alone to one alone." "Alone with one alone" ("alone by oneself") can only mean: to be together beyond every relation. Form-of-life is this ban that no longer

4 Prozorov (2010) 1056.
5 Agamben (1998) 46–7; Prozorov (2014) 183; Prozorov (2017) 172–3.
6 Agamben (2000) 110.
7 Moten (2018) 262.
8 Moten (2018) 144.
9 Chiesa (2018) [2].
10 Chiesa (2018) [5].

> has the form of a bond or an exclusion-inclusion of bare life but that of an intimacy without relation.[11]

The community of forms-of-life simply exists with no essence.[12] The 'coming community' is a community of singularities who share nothing more than their singularity.[13] Form-of-life:

> [H]as no identity, it is not determinate with respect to a concept, but neither is it simply indeterminate; rather it is determined only through its relation to an *idea*, that is, to the totality of its possibilities. Through this relation ... singularity borders all possibility and thus receives its *omnimoda determinatio* not from its participation in a determinate concept of some actual property ... but *only by means of this bordering* ... the relation to an empty and indeterminate totality ... Whatever adds to singularity only an emptiness ... Whatever is singularity plus an empty space, a singularity that is *finite* ... Whatever is the event of an outside.[14]

Form-of-life is encountered in unexpected figures: the 'glorious body' that is nothing but the earthly body divested of its functions and open to a new use,[15] objects of profanation and play,[16] and Franciscan monasticism.[17] All these figures are exposed in the bare facticity of their existence or 'being-thus'.[18] These forms of life are "elusive elements" which, while appearing to docilely submit to control and domination, actually escape the grasp of it.[19] Agamben questions whether such docility can "even threaten the governmental machine". However, hope for the future lies with this docility.[20] We must think a figure that is "the beginning and, at the same time, the vanishing point of every politics".[21]

Form-of-life is "a being that is its own bare existence, [a] life that, being its own form, remains inseparable from it".[22] For Aristotle, *zoè* and *bios* are not opposed to each other. *Zoè* is the fact of being alive; *bios* is the 'mode of life' enacted by a living being.[23] Form-of-life is the 'becoming' of something

11 Agamben (2016) 236.
12 Agamben (2007b) 1–3, 17–21; Agamben (2000) 94–5.
13 Agamben (2007b) 9.
14 Agamben (2007b) 67.
15 Agamben (2010a) 91–103.
16 Agamben (2007a) 73–91.
17 Agamben (2013) 122.
18 Prozorov (2017) 180.
19 Prozorov (2010) 1054.
20 Agamben (2009) 23.
21 Agamben (2009) 31; Agamben (2011) 65.
22 Agamben (1998) 188.
23 Backman (2017) 16.

other out of what we are, representing what remains after the biopolitical machinery of the West has been rendered inoperative.[24] Agamben's use of 'machine' has implications. Michael Lewis explains that a 'machine' is opposed to dialectical thought. The machine is dead and automatic, whereas dialectical thought is 'living' on the side of life. When a machine repeats an action, it does not produce a memory that it can learn from and conduct a new or improved action, a difference.[25] For Agamben, history is unfurled through a machine that leads to a collapse into indifference, exhaustion and emptiness, and gives rise to all manner of sinister events. The only choice left for us is to put the machines that have governed Western history permanently out of action.[26]

Form-of-life is a being of *potential.* Man is essentially inoperative. No work or vocation can define man, and it is not possible to assign a nature or essence to man.[27] Inoperativity cannot be thought of as "a praxis or potentiality of a special kind, which maintains a constitutive relation to its own inoperativity".[28] Inoperativity means that the individual has nothing to do.[29] There is no purpose to be fulfilled. It is:

> [A] matter of ... an inoperativity internal to the operation itself, a *sui generis* praxis that, in the work, first and foremost, exposes and contemplates potentiality, a potentiality that does not precede the work, but accompanies it, makes it live, and opens it to possibilities. The life that contemplates its own potentiality to act and not to act becomes inoperative in all its operations, lives only in its livableness.[30]

Inoperativity must be achieved by a process of 'deactivation' in which all human and divine works are *rendered* inoperative.[31] Deactivation is a "properly human and political praxis".[32] Lewis explains that the new possibilities of human life found through this deactivation will reveal what the machine has tried to progressively obliterate.[33] To completely neutralise a power it must be deposed and made inoperative.[34]

24 Fusco (2023) 6.
25 Lewis (2022) 70.
26 Lewis (2022) 71.
27 Agamben (2017) 52; Prozorov (2009) 530.
28 Agamben (2017) 53.
29 Agamben (2017) 51; Aristotle (1984b) 1097b 22–30.
30 Agamben (2017) 54.
31 Lewis (2022) 96.
32 Agamben (2011) xiii.
33 Lewis (2022) 97.
34 Agamben (2014) 71.

Agamben's construction of potentiality rests on his reading of Aristotle's *Metaphysics*, and Aristotle's ambiguous term '*dunamis*'.[35] Kevin Attell has argued that *dunamis* has two senses that are relevant for Agamben's interpretation – possibility and capacity. Possibility refers to a pure logical possibility. Capacity infers an individual could realise a potentiality if not prevented by external conditions.[36] Aristotle's hierarchy of life is structured by the dialectic of potential and act. Aristotle states that a thing is capable of which it is said to have the potentiality.[37] It is possible for me to exercise a capacity or potentiality if I am not prevented from doing so. Yet these external conditions do not determine whether these capacities exist. Agamben's reading argues that potentialities persist even when they are not in act.[38]

Dunamis's counterpart is *adunamia*. This is "potentiality not to" or "impotentiality". Without *adunamia*, *dunamis* or potentiality would immediately lead to actuality.[39] In being actualised, impotentiality is exhausted and preserved in actualisation. This means that potentiality does not have to be sacrificed. An existence *as* potentiality is not the potential to do something but also the potential to *not-do*, the potential not to pass into actuality.[40]

Agamben's thought affirms existing possibilities and is an injunction to seize them and a warning about the dangers of not doing so.[41] It is difficult to easily translate this writing on potentiality into a clear and practical political project. This can be shown through Agamben's statement that the negation of potentiality is 'evil':

> [The] only ethical experience ... is the experience of being (one's own) potentiality, of being (one's own) possibility ... The only evil consists instead in the decision to remain in a deficit of existence, to appropriate the power to not-be as a substance and a foundation beyond existence or to regard potentiality itself ... as a fault that must always be repressed.[42]

Ethical experience is the experience of potential. Unethical existence is a choice to stay in a deficit of existence, rejecting one's own potential. Agamben has recognised the paradox at the heart of his philosophy. It is almost counter-intuitive to formulate as a demand or duty the freedom from any essence, identity or vocation:

35 Seshadri (2014) 473.
36 Attell (2009) 39–40.
37 Aristotle (1984a) 1047a 24–6.
38 Attell (2009) 40.
39 Attell (2009) 41.
40 Agamben (1999a) 180.
41 Agamben (2007b) 64.
42 Agamben (2007b) 44; Prozorov (2014) 184–5.

> [T]here is in effect something that humans *are and have to be*, but this ... is the simple fact of one's own existence as possibility or potentiality. But precisely because of this things get complicated.[43]

The singular being retains a potential to live life as a 'mode', or a 'how'.[44] Form-of-life is a being *with the capacity for living ethically*. Agamben claims that form-of-life is continually generated by its manner of being.[45] To live life as a form means one *must* actively act to bring about this condition. The ethical subject must constitute itself.[46] The community to come will also be grasped and lived through its mode of being.[47] Every body is affected by its form-of-life as by a *clinamen*. For Jean-Luc Nancy, this represents the inclination from one toward the other.[48] Community is exposure of singularities to other singularities.[49] This coming politics can be found in 'use'.[50] Use is internal to potential, preventing potential from being consumed in the act. Use drives potential to make itself a potential of potential, to be capable of its own potential (and own impotential).[51] Every use is first of all the use of the self: "to enter into a relation of use with something, I must be affected by it, constitute myself as one who makes use of it".[52] It is with the figure of the slave that Agamben develops his use of use.

The figure of the slave

The slave is a far more important figure in Agamben's thought than has been credited to date. Form-of-life "does not yet exist in its fullness" and is found in places that "necessarily appear unedifying".[53] We must apply Walter Benjamin's principle according to which the elements of the end point for the way of living in question are hidden in the present, in insignificant and contemptible areas.[54] One of these places is in the body of the slave. In discussing Agamben here I use 'slave' in the figurative sense, as Agamben's references are not to the lived experiences of enslaved people. Agamben claims that the absence of 'work' for the slave, and the use of the body point toward

43 Agamben (2007b) 43.
44 Agamben (2016) 157, 164; Agamben (2018b) 30.
45 Agamben (2016) 224.
46 Agamben (2016) 231.
47 Agamben (2016) 228.
48 Nancy (1991) 3–4.
49 Nancy (1991) 60.
50 Agamben (2016) 81.
51 Agamben (2016) 93.
52 Agamben (2016) 30.
53 Agamben (2016) 227.
54 Agamben (2016) 227.

a paradigm of a human activity that cannot be reduce to labour, production or praxis.[55]

The categories of the slave and slavery are concepts which are fraught with conceptual difficulties. Whilst slavery is an extreme form of the relation of domination, it cannot be neatly presented in terms of binary oppositions.[56] There is no clear distinction between slavery and non-slavery. What we can say is that Agamben is not interested in the *institution* of slavery, but the *figure* of the slave. I wish to change this focus in this study onto the enslaved person, as the label 'slave' distances the actual human being from the production of a category of negation.[57]

Agamben's main engagement with slavery occurs in *The Use of Bodies*, when he discusses ancient slavery and Aristotle's work in particular.[58] But references to slaves and slavery were already present in earlier publications.[59] Bikundo notes that Agamben references slavery and related terms in at least 13 of his works.[60] These references include the master-slave dialectic in Hegel;[61] a slave's role in the funeral ceremony of a dead Roman Emperor;[62] how slaves figure in property disputes in ancient Rome;[63] and the Emancipation Proclamation.[64]

In earlier works Agamben seemed to avoid making connections to slavery where it appeared obvious to do so. Edwin Bikundo explains that in *Homo Sacer*, Agamben overlooked Roman law, which had a primary distinction between slaves and free men,[65] in favour of the figure of *homo sacer*, the sacred man standing as a paradigm for bare life.[66] Slave and other forms of personhood in Roman law were not "metaphysical" but "purely technical and functional" categories, meaning that slaves could be treated as both persons and things, which seems to accord with Agamben's thoughts on bare life.[67] Agamben considered Aristotle's *Politics* without mentioning Aristotle's defence of slavery.[68] Bikundo also explains that Thomas Hobbes is used by Agamben to argue that bare life is the basis on which politics in the nation

55 Agamben (2016) 20.
56 Wallon (1879) 409.
57 Adébísí (2023) 84.
58 Agamben (2016) 23.
59 Bikundo (2022) 5.
60 Bikundo (2022) 7; Fiskesjö (2012) 166.
61 Agamben (2006) 46-47; Agamben (2002) 108–9.
62 Agamben (1998) 95.
63 Agamben (2010b) 60.
64 Agamben (2005) 21.
65 Buckland (2010) 1.
66 Bikundo (2022) 5; Bignall and Svirsky (2012) 1.
67 Mussawir and Parsley (2017) 48; DeLombard (2019) 497, quoting Gaius's *Institutes*.
68 Agamben (1998) 2.

state is built upon.[69] Bikundo notes that Agamben misses a connection made by Susan Buck-Morss, which is that slavery is a consequence of Hobbes's state of nature and the war of all against all.[70]

This is not to suggest that Agamben has missed an obvious definition or commonly held view of enslavement. There have been repeated efforts to define what is meant by slavery. An important example is Orlando Patterson, who saw slavery as 'social death', the slave's exclusion from the social order and their subjugation.[71] Without the master the slave does not exist independently.[72] For Patterson, our social construction of freedom was made possible by the relation of slavery.[73] Western thought views freedom in terms of an absence of restrictions.[74] If Patterson is correct, then slavery had to exist before people could conceive of the idea of freedom as a meaningful and useful value, and an ideal to be striven for.[75] Without slavery there would be no free men. Slavery is the boundary and limit of freedom. Only with slavery did one person have the freedom to do absolutely as he or she pleased with another.[76] Patterson explains:

> Before slavery people simply could not have conceived of the thing we call freedom. Men and women in premodern, nonslaveholding societies did not, could not, value the removal of restraint as an ideal. Individuals yearned only for the security of being positively anchored in a network of power and authority. Happiness was membership; being was belonging; leadership was the ultimate demonstration of these two qualities. It is an abuse of language to refer to membership and belonging as a kind of freedom; freedom is not a faculty or a power to do something.[77]

Slavery is a relation of human parasitism.[78] The dominator, in dominating another, also makes themselves dependent on the one that has been dominated.[79] 'Man' became a performative idea, which created inequalities and hierarchies used to exclude and oppress the other. Likewise, the classification of 'human' was attributed to dominant people by themselves. This also enabled

69 Bikundo (2022) 6; Agamben (1998) 125.
70 Bikundo (2022) 6; Agamben (1998) 26–7; Buck-Morss (2009) 21.
71 Patterson (1982) 79, 86.
72 Patterson (1982) 1.
73 Patterson (1991).
74 Cranston (1953) 19.
75 Patterson (2008) 117.
76 Patterson (2008) 117.
77 Patterson (1982) 340.
78 Patterson (1982) 335.
79 Patterson (1982) 336. There is an clear evocation here of the Hegelian dialectic, which is developed in later chapters.

them to define others.[80] For Patterson this leads to an enigma: "are we to esteem slavery for what it has wrought, or must we challenge our conception of freedom and the value we place upon it?".[81] I explore the latter option.

To place slavery and freedom in opposition is not to accept the two exist in a neat binary. For example, during the early Middle Ages there was no *legal* distinction between slaves and serfs.[82] Kostas Vlassopoulos notes that many historians project an 'ideal type' of slaves working under their master's direct control, and an 'ideal type' of serfs who would live and work on their own and give up part of their produce to the manor lord.[83] The reality was different. People who were legally slaves lived in conditions of stereotypical serfdom because of the interplay between the needs of the masters, the wishes of the slaves and the negotiations that ensued.[84]

Today, slavery persists and new forms have been created.[85] Jessica Whyte notes that what Walter Benjamin said of fascism in the twentieth century is true of slavery and forced labour in the twenty-first century:

> The current amazement that the things we are experiencing are 'still' possible in the twentieth century is *not* philosophical. This amazement is not the beginning of knowledge – unless it is the knowledge that the view of history which gives rise to it is untenable.[86]

As Kevin Bales has described, slavery is the dark side of global capitalism.[87] People get rich using slaves, and then dispose of them when they have exhausted their usefulness. Forms of unfree labour continue to exist, in a "specifically capitalist form".[88] Whyte also references Ian Baucom, writing about the history of Atlantic slavery, who suggests that "what has been begun does not end but endures", as the time of modernity "accumulates" on the foundation of the Atlantic slave trade.[89] How are we to reconcile the existence of slavery with its formal abolition?[90]

80 Mpofu and Steyn (2021) 1.
81 Patterson (1982) 342.
82 Vlassopoulos (2021) 43.
83 Vlassopoulos (2021) 58.
84 Vlassopoulos (2021) 46.
85 Whyte (2010).
86 Benjamin (2003) 392; Whyte (2010).
87 Bales (2004) 4.
88 Federici, Caffentzis and Alidou (2000).
89 Baucom (2005) 333.
90 Paz-Fuchs (2016) 758.

The slave in Agamben

Beginnings

Agamben's treatment of the slave does not rely on a binary definition. The slave (and again this is used as a figure, rather than an enslaved person) is a threshold. A free person implies a slave as a condition of its possibility.[91] Theories of recognition are dependent on the figure of the slave. The attribute 'human' can be both given and taken away. The threat of withdrawing or denying this attribute ends up defining life within a climate of fear. This in turn makes the very status of human both fragile and uncertain.[92] The slave has oriented legal, political and philosophical thought:

> The slave is, on the one hand a human animal (or an animal human) and, on the other hand and to the same extent, a living instrument (or an instrument-human). That is to say, the slave constitutes in the history of anthropogenesis a double threshold, in which animal life crosses over to the human just as the living (the human) crosses over into the inorganic (into the instrument) and vice versa.[93]

The slave has a mixed character which blurs our categories of humanity. Kelly Oliver states that early forms of the anthropological machine operated by humanising animals. This meant that some 'people', like slaves, were considered animals in human form.[94] Saidiya Hartman explains that the captive was both an object of property and a person, and whilst this is a striking contradiction of chattel slavery, we have not yet considered the constitution of this human life.[95] Oliver explains that humanity needs the exclusion of animality (in the figure of the slave). The slave-animal operates as the mysterious beating heart both concealed and revealed at the centre of humanity.[96] This is a life separated and excluded from itself – the slave.[97] In such a reading, the precise definitions of a slave, a serf, an indentured labourer or a worker forced by their circumstances to sign a disadvantageous employment contract matter less than the necessary existence of bare life which helps us define freedom.

It is necessary here to explore Agamben's reading of Aristotle in a little detail. Adam Kotsko sees Agamben's focus as unexpected.[98] Agamben sees

91 Agamben (2016) 20.
92 Soyinka (2004).
93 Agamben (2016) 78–9; Bikundo (2022) 18.
94 Oliver (2007) 1.
95 Hartman (1997) 5.
96 Oliver (2007) 7.
97 Agamben (2004) 38.
98 Kotsko (2020) 159.

the proper response to Aristotle's defence of slavery not as one of outrage at the philosopher illegitimately depriving the slave of characteristics of humanity. Instead, Agamben sees those characteristics as burdens rather than benefits.[99] Aristotle's writings on slavery point towards a different experience of humanity that our existing definitions of humanity have denigrated.[100] Gian-Giacomo Fusco explains that the figure of the slave is presented as a being of pure potentiality. This figure's status proves that humans retain an ability to create "a multitude of vocations in the form of the potential".[101]

Agamben presents Aristotle's view of slaves as follows. Slaves follow their nature which reflects the order of things, making it possible for them to act in agreement toward a common goal.[102] Agamben reads Aristotle as explaining that the city is composed of families or households. The family is composed of slaves and free people.[103] Furthermore, there are three types of relations defining the family: the despotic relation between the master and slaves; the matrimonial relation between the husband and wife; and the parental relation between the father and children.[104] The master-slave relation is the most important, evidenced by Aristotle saying that the latter two relations lacked a proper name. It is not a political, but an economic-domestic relationship.[105]

In the *Politics*, the phrase "the use of the body" defines the nature of the slave.[106] In contrast, "the work of the human being is the being-at-work of the soul according to the *logos*".[107] The use of the body of the slave is purposeless: "by putting in use his own body, the slave is, for that very reason, used by the master, and in using the body of the slave, the master is, in reality, using his own body".[108] The body of the slave is situated in a zone of indifference between one's own body and the body of another.[109] This means that, for Aristotle, there are some human beings whose *ergon* (their proper function) is not properly human or is different from that of other human beings.[110] To put it another way, "to command and be commanded are not only necessary parts of things but also expedient".[111] The foundation of slavery in Aristotle is 'physical', consisting in a difference with respect to

99 Kotsko (2020) 159; Agamben (2016) 8.
100 Kotsko (2020) 160–1.
101 Fusco (2023) 46.
102 Agamben (2011) 81–2.
103 Aristotle (1984c) 1253b 3–5.
104 Aristotle (1984c) 1253b 7–11.
105 Agamben (2016) 4.
106 Agamben (2016) 3; Aristotle (1984c) 1254b 17–20.
107 Aristotle (1984b) 1098a 7.
108 Agamben (2016) 14.
109 Agamben (2016) 22.
110 Agamben (2016) 5.
111 Aristotle (1984c) 1254a 21–2.

the body of the free person.[112] Through this, Aristotle justifies the command of some men over others. Equality between inferior and superior is hurtful, and it is natural for the soul to control the body and the intellect the passions. The same is true for human beings.[113]

Agamben references Yan Thomas in making a claim that the classical world only thought of human activity from their results, and did not consider the process of labour needed to produce those results. Thomas analysed Roman law, and argued that there labour is acknowledged juridically in contracts for the *locatio operarum* of an enslaved person by the person who had the usufruct of the slave.[114] The slave's labour was isolated by separating the use, or *usus* (which refers to the personal use of the body of the enslaved), from the *fructus*, which could be disposed of in the open market.[115] These distinctions between title, use and usufruct are essential ingredients in the legal doctrines of Roman civil law and the Anglo-American common law:

> Usufruct was the right to enjoy the property of another and to take his fruits, but not to destroy it, or fundamentally alter its character ... Usufruct being incorporeal could not be possessed, but the notion of quasi-possession was applied to it.[116]

Usufruct involves the use and taking of the benefits of a piece of property belonging to another, but it does not involve the destruction or the change in the character of the thing. It also lasts only so long as the character remains unchanged. *Usus* is a similar right to the use of the thing only.[117] *Usus* was defined as a "fraction of usufruct" or "*usufruct* without the *fructus*".[118] Vlassopoulos explains that Ulpian imagined Roman slaves as agricultural tenants who were separate from Roman slaves who were farm hands and counted as farm equipment.[119] Vlassopoulos argues that Thomas illustrates another distinction created by Roman jurists which distinguished between the ownership of slaves and the usufruct deriving from the ownership of slaves. Usufruct was further divisible between the use of slaves by the master's (or other beneficiary's) direct authority, and the financial gain from a slave being leased to a third party.[120] For Agamben, the use of the slave, even

112 Agamben (2016) 8; Aristotle (1984c) 1254b28ff, 1255a 1–2, 1255b 4.
113 Aristotle (1984c) 1254b 5–16.
114 Agamben (2016) 15.
115 Agamben (2016) 15–16; Thomas (1998) 222.
116 Buckland (2007) 269–270.
117 Jolowicz (2009) 282.
118 Buckland (2007) 273; Goldie (1985) 692.
119 Vlassopoulos (2021) 58.
120 Vlassopoulos (2021) 59.

when the owner has ceded it to others, always remains inseparable from the use of his body.[121]

The original anthropogenetic relation

There is more to Agamben's focus on the slave and the use of the body. 'Use' has a singular nature – in entering into a relationship of use with a thing, I am affected by this relationship, and I constitute myself as someone who makes use of the relationship.[122] This means that the self is nothing other than use-of-oneself.[123] Slavery retains a memory of the "original anthropogenetic operation" of what is properly human. This is because the relationship between a human being and nature is not immediate, but it is mediated by the human being's relationship with other human beings. In Agamben's words:

> I can constitute myself as ethical subject of my relationship with nature solely because this relationship is mediated by the relationship with other human beings.[124]

In slavery, the relationship of the master with nature is mediated through the relationship of the slave with nature.[125] By putting in use his own body, the slave is used by the master. In using the body of the slave, the master is using his own body.[126] Mediating one's own relation with nature through the relation with another human being is, for Agamben, from the very beginning what is properly human.[127] Using one another is not *in itself* perverted or immoral but part of the human condition.[128]

The relation's perversion begins when the reciprocal relation of use is made juridical through constituting slavery as a social institution.[129] For Agamben, if I try to appropriate mediation for myself by means of the other, then the relation of use becomes a relationship of exploitation.[130] This is a curious claim, especially as there is no historical evidence of this pure sphere of use that existed prior to the practice of ancient slavery.[131] There needs to

121 Agamben (2016) 16.
122 Agamben (2016) 30.
123 Agamben (2016) 54.
124 Agamben (2016) 15.
125 Fusco (2023) 51.
126 van der Heiden (2020) 314.
127 Agamben (2016) 14.
128 de Boer (2023) 236.
129 Agamben (2016) 14.
130 Agamben (2016) 15.
131 Frost (2021) 161.

be a category shift from considering an abstracted figure of the slave and the institution of enslavement, to the lives, acts and gestures of enslaved people.

The master-slave relation is described as the capture in the juridical order of a use of bodies as an originary pre-juridical relation. It is through the inclusion of this relation that the juridical order founds itself. The juridical order defines the master-slave relation in terms of property. The original form of property is the way the use of bodies is captured by the law.[132] Gert-Jan van der Heiden notes that this use can lead to an abuse. This happens when juridification leads to some people identifying solely as masters and others identifying solely as slaves.[133] On this reading, the *invention* of slavery as a "juridical institution" captured and divided living beings and transformed bodies into 'productive' systems. The fact that the juridical institution of slavery 'captures' living beings indicates that slavery (as a juridical institution) is an apparatus or *dispositif*. We are also told that this *invention* "temporarily blocked the development of the technological instrument".[134]

There is a symmetry between the figure of the slave and the machine – technology.[135] The machine, like the slave, intends to liberate human beings from necessity. For the ancient Greeks the liberation promised by the slave was political life. For us moderns, technology promises the possibility of mastering the forces of nature:

> [T]he symmetry between the slave and the machine ... concerns the ultimate achievement of anthropogenesis, the becoming fully human of the living human being. ... In this sense, slavery is to ancient humanity what technology is to modern humanity: both as bare life, watch over the threshold that allows access to the truly human condition (and both have shown themselves to be inadequate to the task, the modern way revealing itself in the end to be no less dehumanizing than the ancient).[136]

The technological hold over modernity holds back the finding of what is truly human. Only when slavery was abolished did the possibility of technology, "the living instrument", emerge.[137]

The mentioning of slavery's 'abolition' implies a distinction between the ancient slave trade, the early modern slave trade driven by European empires, and what is called modern slavery. Technology has meant that the relationship between human beings and nature is not mediated by another

132 Agamben (2016) 36.
133 van der Heiden (2020) 314; Agamben (2016) 14.
134 Agamben (2016) 79.
135 Agamben (2016) 77.
136 Agamben (2016) 78.
137 Agamben (2016) 79.

human (the slave), but by an apparatus. In our dependence on technology, we have estranged ourselves from the animal and organic and drawn close to the machine and the inorganic to the point of almost identifying with them, as a human-machine.[138] This, for Agamben, has produced a new and unheard-of form of slavery.[139] Humanity has lost its immediate relation to its own animality. The fundamental question posed by Agamben's analysis is how exactly can such a relation of domination operate as the gatekeeper to form-of-life?

Ype de Boer helpfully explains that Agamben's target is the way Western politics has been modelled on the figure of the master, with our ideal civilisation being one which is composed only of masters.[140] de Boer goes on to say that the very idea of mastering existence for Agamben perverts what it means to be a human being. Mastery means enslaving it in relation to a certain goal.[141] For Agamben, to live together means to mutually use each other's bodies.[142] The use of the body reflects the human being's fundamental inoperativity, which opens it up to all kinds of activity.[143] van der Heiden explains this means that sometimes we are the user in this use and sometimes the one who is being used. This mutual use means the poles of master and slave are not fixed but rather continuously changing.[144] In the phrase "the use of the body", the body is what is *used* and what is *using*. Understanding "the use of the body" means thinking this other possible body of the human being.[145]

What does this mean? In *Beyond the Periphery of the Skin*, Silvia Federici argues that one of capitalism's main projects has been the transformation of the body into 'work machines'.[146] This leads to the exploitation of living labour, with multiple histories existing of how the body was articulated using racial, sexual and generational hierarchies and oppression. The history of the body cannot be told without telling the history of those who were enslaved, colonised or turned into unpaid wage workers.[147] The body is our most powerful means of self-expression, and the evidence of histories of rebellion as well as oppression.[148] As such the body is a ground for resistance, the power to act, to transform itself,[149] to be affected and to affect, to be moved and

138 Agamben (2016) 79.
139 Agamben (2016) 79.
140 de Boer (2023) 237.
141 de Boer (2023) 237.
142 Agamben (2016) 14–15.
143 de Boer (2023) 238.
144 van der Heiden (2020) 314.
145 Agamben (2016) 9.
146 Federici (2020) 10.
147 Federici (2020) 11.
148 Federici (2020) 53.
149 Federici (2020) 119.

to move, in an indestructible capacity exhausted only by death.[150] Enslaved people have been resisting and transforming themselves through use, and it is these examples I wish to consider.

Use and praxis

Modernity understands the human being's productive activity as praxis, a "manifestation of a will that produces a concrete effect".[151] Modernity has understood all of the human being's 'doing' as praxis. On this reading, praxis starts from work, the production of material life.[152] All activity then becomes associated with the biological processes underpinning work.[153] Modern thought has remained wedded to an interpretation of praxis as will and vital impulse. It has not been able to conceive of the human being's 'doing' differently.[154] But this has meant, for Agamben, that we have not recognised that "it could be, and in other eras has been, conceived differently".[155]

In relation to the use of the body of the slave, Agamben states that 'use' can stand as "a new figure of human praxis",[156] one which is not reduced to work and biological processes. This new practice is evocative of Agamben's reference to *poiēsis*, in that it refers back to a new form of life, or existence, for the human. Agamben explains that "in using the body of the slave, the master is in reality using his own body".[157] Backman states that the 'work' of Aristotle's slave consists in making use of their bodies as animate instruments and being used to uphold the master's 'way of life' (*bios*) by liberating it from the necessities of survival.[158] An instrument of the master's *bios*, the slave's activity is neither an end in itself nor a process towards an end.[159] Aristotle's slave only 'represents' but never is.[160] Susan Brophy concludes that this means it can both portray bare life and operate as a point from which we can contemplate what it means "to use the body absent compulsive praxis".[161]

Use does not exhaust being and praxis in each other.[162] Use is distinct from will, and is connected to the Aristotelian concept of habit, or *hexis*. 'Habitual use' is "a potential that is never separate from act, which never needs to be

150 Federici (2020) 124,
151 Agamben (1999b) 68; Lagaay and Rauch (2020) 93–6.
152 Agamben (1999b) 70.
153 Rae (2018) 989.
154 Agamben (1999b) 71.
155 Agamben (1999b) 68.
156 Brophy (2021) 196; Agamben (2016) 30.
157 Brophy (2021) 196; Agamben (2016) 14.
158 Backman (2017) 22; Aristotle (1984c) 1.4.1253b32-33, 1254a7-8, 1.5.1254b24-6.
159 Backman (2017) 22; Agamben (2016) 18–21.
160 Agamben (2016) 23.
161 Brophy (2021) 196.
162 Brophy (2021) 196; Agamben (2016) 65.

put to work".[163] Habit is an *ethos*, a means of constituting oneself as a subject by habitually making use of oneself and the world in a certain way – a form-of-life.[164] This life lives only its liveability.[165] The use of life is the good life and an antidote to a politics of mastery that excludes those who do not fit its arbitrary description.[166]

This is why the enslaved person is important. An expression of humanity is found in an inhumane place. It stands as an attempt to deactivate the primacy of the master, which is complicit in keeping violent and oppressive systems in place. The world needs transforming, and this fact brings Agamben's aims into contact with the aims of decolonial thought.[167] This transformation can be found in the *ethos* of individuals and communities who have been oppressed or neglected, but who are seeking to make use of their lives and the world in a certain way, in the face of systems and structures of control and violence. We need to search for forms of living that are never prescribed but preserve their character as a real possibility.[168] Form-of-life does not need to 'master' its relations to the world, its surroundings and others. de Boer notes that there is a difference between the individual shifting to live their life as a form and as a habit, and the communal exercise and implementation of the same.[169] In the actions and lives of enslaved people throughout history we find many examples of the same.

Conclusion

Agamben has referred to slaves and slavery in a number of works over many years. It was in *The Use of Bodies* that it became clear that the slave is a far more important figure to Agamben's thought than had previously been credited, and closely connected to form-of-life. It is in the figure of form-of-life that Agamben sees the potential to deactivate apparatuses of control and division which endlessly produce and reproduce bare life. Agamben focuses on the figure of the slave in Aristotle. This slave, far from being a paradigmatic figure of bare life, cast out from rights and legal protections, and excluded from society, contains the kernel of a life that is lived through use, a pure means. What is this use? Using one's life counters the machines of domination that have structured Western politics since the days of the ancient Greek city states by refusing to accept a life based on mastery, or a political order based on divisible ideas of freedom.

163 Backman (2017) 22; Agamben (2016) 58.
164 Backman (2017) 23; Agamben (2016) 62.
165 Agamben (2016) 5.
166 de Boer (2023) 240.
167 de Boer (2023) 240.
168 Agamben (2016) 207–8.
169 de Boer (2023) 241.

As we will explore in the next chapter, the transformative potential of form-of-life is a *destituent potential*, and one which has been lived by enslaved people. This renders inoperative the anthropological machine, showing that life can be lived in a different, purposeless way. Destitution aims to make inoperativity a concrete political option. What needs to be done now is to explore how the use of the body of enslaved people enables us to live our lives as a form. What does a destituent potential look like, and how do we bring it about as individuals and communally? In the next chapter I introduce the concept of 'hyper-hermeneutics' as a practice to show how form-of-life can exist even in unedifying places. I also explore how the enslaved person's acts and lives can help us trace this form of political belonging as an alternative form of political belonging and life.

Reference List

Adébísí, F (2023) *Decolonisation and Legal Knowledge: Reflections on Power and Possibility*, Bristol: Bristol University Press.

Agamben, G (1998) *Homo Sacer: Sovereign Power and Bare Life,* Heller-Roazen, D (trans.), Stanford: Stanford University Press.

Agamben, G (1999a) 'On Potentiality' in *Potentialities: Collected Essays in Philosophy*, Heller-Roazen, D (trans.), Stanford: Stanford University Press, 177-84.

Agamben, G (1999b) *The Man Without Content*, Albert, G (trans.), Stanford: Stanford University Press.

Agamben, G (2000) *Means Without End: Notes on Politics*, Binetti, V and Casarino, C (trans.), Minneapolis: University of Minnesota Press.

Agamben, G (2002) *Remnants of Auschwitz: The Witness and the Archive*, Heller-Roazen D (trans.), New York: Zone Books.

Agamben, G (2004) *The Open: Man and Animal*, Attell, K (trans.), Stanford: Stanford University Press.

Agamben, G (2005) *State of Exception*, Attell, K (trans.), Chicago: University of Chicago Press.

Agamben, G (2006) *Language and Death: The Place of Negativity*, Pinkus, K and Hardt, M (trans.), Minneapolis: University of Minnesota Press.

Agamben, G (2007a) *Profanations*, Fort, J (trans.), Princeton: Princeton University Press.

Agamben, G (2007b) *The Coming Community*, Hardt, M (trans.), Minneapolis: University of Minnesota Press.

Agamben, G (2009) *What Is an Apparatus? and Other Essays*, Kishik, D and Pedatella, S (trans.), Stanford: Stanford University Press.

Agamben, G (2010a) *Nudities*, Kishik, D and Pedatella, S (trans.), Stanford: Stanford University Press.

Agamben, G (2010b) *The Sacrament of Language: An Archaeology of the Oath*, Kotsko, A (trans.), Stanford, Stanford University Press.

Agamben, G (2011) *The Kingdom and the Glory: For a Theological Genealogy of Economy and Government*, Chiesa, L and Mandarini, M (trans.), Stanford: Stanford University Press.

Agamben, G (2013) *The Highest Poverty: Monastic Rules and Form-of-Life*, Kotsko, A (trans.), Stanford: Stanford University Press.

Agamben, G (2014) 'What Is a Destituent Power?', *Environment and Planning D: Society and Space*, 32, 65–74.

Agamben, G (2016) *The Use of Bodies*, Kotsko, A (trans.), Stanford: Stanford University Press.

Agamben, G (2017) *The Fire and the Tale*, Chiesa, L (trans.), Stanford: Stanford University Press.

Agamben, G (2018a) *Karman: A Brief Treatise on Action, Guilt and Gesture*, Kotsko, A (trans.), Stanford: Stanford University Press.

Agamben, G (2018b) *What Is Philosophy?*, Chiesa, L (trans.), Stanford: Stanford University Press.

Aristotle (1984a) 'Metaphysics' in *The Complete Works of Aristotle, Volume Two*, Barnes, J (ed.), Princeton: Princeton University Press.

Aristotle (1984b) 'Nicomachean Ethics' in *The Complete Works of Aristotle, Volume Two*, Barnes, J (ed.), Princeton: Princeton University Press.

Aristotle (1984c) 'Politics' in *The Complete Works of Aristotle, Volume Two*, Barnes, J (ed.), Princeton: Princeton University Press.

Attell, K (2009) 'Potentiality, Actuality, Constituent Power', *Diacritics*, 39, 35–53.

Backman, J (2017) 'Aristotle' in Kotsko, A and Salzani, C (eds.), *Agamben's Philosophical Lineage*, Edinburgh: Edinburgh University Press, 15–26.

Bales, K (2004) *Disposable People: New Slavery in the Global Economy*, Berkley and Los Angeles: University of California Press.

Baucom, I (2005) *Spectres of the Atlantic: Finance Capital, Slavery, and the Philosophy of the Atlantic*, Durham and London: Duke University Press.

Benjamin, W (2003) 'On the Concept of History' in *Walter Benjamin, Selected Writings, Volume 4: 1938–1940*, Jennings, M (ed.), Cambridge: Harvard University Press, 389–400.

Bignall, S and Svirsky, M (2012) 'Introduction: Agamben and Colonialism' in Bignall, S and Svirsky, M (eds.), *Agamben and Colonialism*, Edinburgh: Edinburgh University Press, 1–14.

Bikundo, E (2022) 'Follow Your Leader – I Prefer Not to: Slavery, Giorgio Agamben and Herman Melville', *Law, Culture and the Humanities*, 18, 4–19.

Brophy, S (2021) 'A Politics Like No Other: Agamben, Fanon, and the Colonial Fracture' in Norris, M and Dickinson, C (eds.), *Agamben and the Existentialists*, Edinburgh: Edinburgh University Press, 191–211.

Buckland, W (2007) *A Text-Book of Roman Law from Augustus to Justinian*, 3rd edn, Cambridge: Cambridge University Press.

Buckland, W (2010) *The Roman Law of Slavery: The Condition of the Slave in Private Law from Augustus to Justinian*, New York: Cambridge University Press.

Buck-Morss, S (2009) *Hegel, Haiti and Universal History*, Pittsburgh: University of Pittsburgh Press.

Chiesa, L (2018) 'Superpolitically Apolitical: On Agamben's Use of Bodies', *Journal of Italian Philosophy*, 1, 22–26.

Cranston, M (1953) *Freedom*, New York: Basic Books.

de Boer, Y (2023) 'The Figure of the Slave as an Ethical Paradigm in the Work of Agamben', *Netherlands Journal of Legal Philosophy*, 52, 227–41.

DeLombard, J (2019) 'Dehumanizing Slave Personhood', *American Literature*, 91, 491–521.
Federici, S (2020) *Beyond the Periphery of the Skin: Rethinking, Remaking, and Reclaiming the Body in Contemporary Capitalism*, Oakland: PM Press.
Federici, S, Caffentzis, G and Alidou, O (2000) *A Thousand Flowers: Social Struggles Against Structural Adjustment in African Universities*, Africa World Press: Asmara.
Fiskesjö, M (2012) 'Outlaws, Barbarians, Slaves: Critical Reflections on Agamben's Homo Sacer', *HAU: Journal of Ethnographic Theory*, 21, 161–80.
Frost, T (2021) *Law, Relationality and the Ethical Life: Agamben and Levinas*, Abingdon: Routledge.
Fusco, G-G (2023) *Form of Life: Agamben and the Destitution of Rules*, Edinburgh: Edinburgh University Press.
Goldie, L F E (1985) 'Title and Use (And Usufruct) – An Ancient Distinction too Oft Forgot', *American Journal of International Law*, 79, 689–714.
Hartman, S (1997) *Scenes of Subjection: Terror, Slavery, and Self-Making in Nineteenth-Century America*, Oxford: Oxford University Press.
Jolowicz, H F (2009) *Historical Introduction to the Study of Roman Law*, 3rd edn, Cambridge: Cambridge University Press.
Kotsko, A (2020) *Agamben's Philosophical Trajectory*, Edinburgh: Edinburgh University Press.
Lagaay, A and Rauch, M F (2020) 'Scenes of Indifference. The Addressee of the Adventure', *Etica & Politica / Ethics & Politics*, 22, 87–108.
Lewis, M (2022) 'The Machine in Esposito and Agamben', *Journal of Italian Philosophy*, 5, 69–106.
Moten, F (2018) *The Universal Machine*, Durham: Duke University Press.
Mpofu, W and Steyn, M (2021) 'The Trouble with the Human' in Steyn, M and Mpofu, W (eds.), *Decolonising the Human: Reflections from Africa on Difference and Oppression*, Johannesburg: Wits University Press, 1–24.
Mussawir, E and Parsley, C (2017) 'The Law of Persons Today: At the Margins of Jurisprudence', *Law and Humanities*, 11, 44–83.
Nancy, J-L (1991) *The Inoperative Community*, Connon, P (trans.), Minneapolis: University of Minnesota Press.
Oliver, K (2007) 'Stopping the Anthropological Machine: Agamben with Heidegger and Merleau-Ponty', *PhænEx: Journal of Existential and Phenomenological Theory and Culture*, 2, 1–23.
Patterson, O (1982) *Slavery and Social Death: A Comparative Study*, Cambridge: Harvard University Press.
Patterson, O (1991) *Freedom, vol 1: Freedom in the Making of Western Culture*, New York: Basic Books.
Patterson, O (2008) 'Freedom, Slavery, and the Modern Construction of Rights' in Joas, H and Wiegandt, K (eds.), *The Cultural Values of Europe*, Liverpool: Liverpool University Press, 115–51.
Paz-Fuchs, A (2016) 'Badges of Modern Slavery', *Modern Law Review*, 79, 757–85.
Prozorov, S (2009) 'Giorgio Agamben and the End of History: Inoperative Praxis and the Interruption of the Dialectic', *European Journal of Social Theory*, 12, 523–42.
Prozorov, S (2010) 'Why Giorgio Agamben Is an Optimist', *Philosophy and Social Criticism*, 36, 1053–73.

Prozorov, S (2014) *Agamben and Politics: A Critical Introduction*, Edinburgh: Edinburgh University Press.
Prozorov, S (2017) 'Agamben, Badiou and Affirmative Biopolitics' in *Agamben and Radical Politics*, McLoughlin, D (ed.), Cambridge: Cambridge University Press, 165–88.
Rae, G (2018) 'Agency and Will in Agamben's Coming Politics', *Philosophy & Social Criticism*, 44, 978–96.
Seshadri, K (2014) 'Agamben, the Thought of *Sterēsis*: An Introduction to Two Essays', *Critical Inquiry*, 40, 470–9.
Soyinka, W (2004) *Climate of Fear*, London: Profile Books.
Thomas, Y (1998) 'L''usage' et les 'fruits' de l'esclave', *Enquête*, 7, 203–30.
van der Heiden, G-J (2020) 'On Use and Care: A Debate between Agamben and Heidegger', *International Journal of Philosophy and Theology*, 81, 310–27.
Vlassopoulos, K (2021) *Historicising Ancient Slavery*, Edinburgh: Edinburgh University Press.
Wallon, H (1879) *Histoire de l'escavage dans l'antiquité*, Paris: Hachette.
Whyte, J (2010) ''A New Use of the Self': Giorgio Agamben on the Coming Community', *Theory & Event*, 13.

Chapter 2

The potential of resistance

Introduction

This chapter considers how Agamben's work can develop an alternative form of political agency. Agamben's 'philosophical archaeology' is his method underpinning his writings on the use of the body and form-of-life. I consider the limitations to Agamben's writings in pursuing a project that focuses on enslaved people, rather than the figure of the slave. Notwithstanding these limitations, Agamben's work provides a fruitful basis for being read with decolonial thought, enabling us to view the actions and lives of enslaved people not just as resistance, but as carving out forms of life that do not depend on a divisible idea of freedom. These forms are found in unedifying places,[1] but my point, paraphrasing Cedric Robinson, is not to exhaust this subject, only to suggest that it is there.[2]

First, I explore how Agamben's thought and philosophical focus is decidedly Eurocentric. This has implications for his writings on slavery. He speaks of us living in a "global civil war",[3] and a "bloody mystification of a new planetary order".[4] What is missing is the biopolitical experimentation of slavery, exemplified in the Atlantic slave trade, which is inextricably tied up with European colonialism and the shape of our world. Agamben is a fierce critic of the modern world, but his focus on the primacy of Europe has the potential to undermine the force of his argument. Just as importantly as his diagnosis, Agamben's work seeks to find a way out of the impasse we face today.

Second, I explore the concept of 'destituent potential', which rejects the idea that political action consists in instrumentally realising a specific doctrine, plan or philosophy. Destitution dismantles prevailing political representations and institutions without proposing others to replace them. It is an

1 Agamben (2007a) 87.
2 Robinson (2021) lii.
3 Agamben (2005a) 2.
4 Agamben (1998) 14.

DOI: 10.4324/9781003303534-3

ethical task demanding that those who inhabit the destitute terrain learn to move within it and deactivate the anthropological machine.

Third, I show how this deactivation is enacted through a method I developed based on Agamben's thought, termed 'hyper-hermeneutics'. This is a form of hermeneutics, which is about interpretation and the conditions for understanding. I use hermeneutics to understand the potential within human lives (whether they are counted as lives worth living or not) to effect changes within modes of power and control that shape the world. The preposition 'hyper' is of crucial importance, as Agamben deploys the same term to describe an enslaved person whose life is lived as a form. I situate this in relation to Agamben's wider philosophical method which he terms 'philosophical archaeology'.

This destituent form of living deactivates apparatuses of control and is lived through the paradigm – specifically paradigmatic gestures and actions. I situate Agamben's paradigm within the wider theoretical literature on the term. I explore what it means to view the enslaved person as a paradigm, and how the 'figure of the slave' is transmitted through the Western philosophical tradition as a signature. Importantly, these paradigmatic actions in Agamben's thought do not have to be revolutionary. They are slight shifts in modes of living that allow forms of life to become forms-of-life. The bounds of human possibility are only limited by human knowledge and human experience, and neither are finite.[5]

Finally, I show how resistance by enslaved people to the institution of slavery and the slave trade helped end it in England. This is an example of how the enslaved person, rather than the figure of the slave, can bring about alternative modes of living through their actions. My main focus is the 1772 case of *Somerset v Stewart*, famously (mis)read as freeing all slaves resident in England. Lord Mansfield's ruling was in fact a compromise, stating that a master could not forcibly remove a slave from England. Slavery was in part ended through the contributions of enslaved people living in England. They acted as though *Somerset* had freed them, living their life as a form, deactivating the apparatus of the slave law. It is these hyper-hermeneutic actions and gestures that this book explores by drawing on historical and legal studies, showing that enslaved people themselves were carving out their own understandings of freedom.

Agamben, slavery and Europe

The socially dead slave appears as the ideal human tool, perfectly flexible, unattached and deracinated.[6] The same description can be applied to bare

5 Adébísí (2023) 13.
6 Patterson (1982) 337.

life in Agamben's work, a hollowed-out and ahistorical subject that can be applied in trans-historical situations. *Zoè* and *bios* constitute each other whilst including and excluding each other at the same time.[7] It is through a sovereign decision that life gains meaning, and bare life is created. As Susan Dianne Brophy explains, we derive value from the experience of a relation. But in the non-relational creation of bare life there is no such condition, and as a result, we cannot judge the value of anything, including life.[8] The idea of a 'people' presupposes the existence of a class of bodies that are *wretched*, oppressed and defeated.[9] For Agamben, it is more honest and useful:

> [T]o investigate carefully the juridical procedures and deployments of power by which human beings could be so completely deprived of their rights and prerogatives that no acts committed against them could appear ... as a crime.[10]

Elvira Basevich notes that for Agamben, race is not natural or to be safeguarded.[11] The question of what is assumed to be 'natural' is dependent on a sovereign judgment. The danger of sovereign power creating bare life is concentrated on certain groups based on their race and historical exclusion by the state. These are apparatuses of control. Basevich notes that if one thinks of this from the point of view of race, racial categories are neither natural nor are racial and ethnic differences inherently problematic. Race becomes problematic within a power structure that affirms Whiteness and oppresses groups that fall outside of that artificial norm.[12] Fusco, referencing Agamben, notes that there is nothing natural in the existing forms of human life.[13] Racism is a global hierarchy of superiority and inferiority produced by the institutions of the capitalist and colonial world system.[14] It acts as a *dispositif*, transforming living beings into subjects. Achille Mbembé calls this the "Becoming Black of the World",[15] where Blackness is a product of the racism that reduced living beings "to matters of appearance, skin and colour".[16] The term 'Black' was developed through the histories of colonialism and enslavement to refer to the name "of the slave, man-of-metal, man-merchandise, man-money".[17]

7 Agamben (1998) 153.
8 Brophy (2021) 194.
9 Agamben (1998) 177.
10 Agamben (1998) 171.
11 Basevich (2012) 75; Agamben (1998) 148.
12 Basevich (2012) 75.
13 Fusco (2023) 23; Agamben (2016) 208.
14 Grosfoguel (2016) 10.
15 Mbembé (2017) 6.
16 Mbembé (2017) 2.
17 Mbembé (2017) 47.

Agamben's bare life neglects the history and legacy of racialisation, colonialism and slavery.[18] To consider the effects of the apparatus of racialisation would have forced Agamben's analyses to extend much further beyond the European continent. Agamben does (correctly) note that the judgment of the physical body is "immediately political" such that race "is not a biological given" but a contingent historical construction.[19] He also writes that race is not evinced by "measurable characteristics".[20] But there is no clear acknowledgment of how non-European peoples are viewed as disposable lives in modernity, due to colonialism's reordering of human interactions and relations.[21] This neglect could be explained as Agamben's discourse is almost unashamedly Eurocentric. We read that in seeking to comprehend the present, human beings find themselves compelled to interrogate the past.[22] Yet there is a crucial qualifier – this interrogation is done by "we Europeans":

> Europeans – unlike, for example, Asians and Americans, for whom history and the past have a completely different significance – can gain access to their truth only by means of a confrontation with the past, only by settling accounts with their history.[23]

Europe's past is colonialism and racialisation. Africa is dismissed through an omission – it is included in Agamben's thought as part of an amorphous 'Third World':

> [T]oday's democratico-capitalist project of eliminating the poor classes through development not only reproduces within itself the people that is excluded but also transforms the entire population of the Third World into bare life.[24]

The 'Third World' is an undifferentiated, passive mass. We have an example of what Edward Said termed 'Orientalism', where European culture benefits from an approach which sets it against the 'Orient' through dominating, restructuring and having authority over it.[25] Not mentioned is that the development of the 'Third World' is also a consequence of Western invasion and colonisation and racial capitalism.[26] Agamben continues:

18 Weheliye (2014) 32–6; Jackson (2013) 670.
19 Agamben (1998) 148.
20 Agamben (1998) 147.
21 Adébísí (2023) 21.
22 Agamben (2019) 1.
23 Agamben (2019) 1.
24 Agamben (1998) 180.
25 Said (1978) 2–3.
26 Brophy (2021) 202.

> Only a politics that will have learned to take the fundamental biopolitical fracture of the West into account will be able to stop this oscillation and to put an end to the civil war that divides the peoples and the cities of the earth.[27]

We could here make a connection between the fundamental biopolitical fracture and the dehumanising process that created this global civil war and bare life in the 'Third World'. Agamben provides no direct consideration of how (following Maldonado-Torres) forms of slavish and colonial power relations are reproduced and sustained even after slavery and juridical colonialism have been abolished.[28] Agamben also does not consider how the oppressed assimilate oppressor consciousness, leading them to become accessories of their own oppression, which is seen as natural.[29]

What is missing in Agamben is an interrogation of this colonial logic.[30] Frantz Fanon said Europe is "literally the creation of the Third World", as it was built on plundering the world's wealth.[31] Instead, we see a defence of Europe. Agamben's (non-)treatment of Africa represents a trend which is all too common by European authors. As Chinua Achebe noted, although Africa's landmass is closer than any other to the mainland of Europe, Africa occupies in the European psychological disposition the farthest point of otherness, and Europe's very antithesis.[32] British writing about Africa changed in content once the slave trade reached its highest level in the eighteenth century. Writing became pejorative, slavery was defended as desirable, changing Africans for the better through contact with their European masters.[33] Joseph Conrad's *Heart of Darkness* is an example of fanciful writing about Africans presented as serious literature.[34] Conrad describes a journey up the River Congo in the 1890s as though it were the very first encounter between conscious European humanity and an unconscious, primeval hegemony that had apparently seen nobody since the world was created.[35] Conrad described his travels as follows:

27 Agamben (1998) 180.
28 Maldonado-Torres (2007) 240–70.
29 Freire (1993).
30 Brophy (2021) 202–3.
31 Fanon (2005) 58.
32 Achebe (2009) 17.
33 Hammond and Jablow (1992) 22–3.
34 Achebe (2009) 21–2.
35 Achebe (2009) 22.

> We were wanderers on a prehistoric earth, on the earth that wore the aspect of an unknown planet. We could have fancied ourselves the first of men taking possession of an accursed inheritance.[36]

Conrad admits that *Heart of Darkness* "pushed a little (and only very little) beyond the actual facts of the case" to bring home the truth of Africa to the reader.[37] Conrad's novella shows how telling stories of Africa and its people have been the "self-appointed responsibility of white people", done to "suit a white purpose".[38]

We also have no mention or reference to the 'boomerang effect', mentioned by (but not originating with) Hannah Arendt and Michel Foucault, key reference points in Agamben's work. Arendt argued that the Nazi racism underpinning the Holocaust had been tested in African colonial possessions,[39] and Foucault saw the methods of colonial control brought back to the West in the form of internal colonialism.[40] W E B Du Bois saw an analogy between colonialism and fascism,[41] and Aimé Césaire and Fanon contended that Europe had been racist long before the Holocaust, and what made the Final Solution singular was its application to other Whites.[42] Césaire went further, arguing that this form of colonisation ultimately works to decivilise the coloniser.[43]

Instead, following Alexander Kojève, Agamben claims that the "American Way of Life" was conceived of as a post-historical animality.[44] The Japanese were living in a post-historical society but had not ceased to be 'human'.[45] In Japan, there was a snobbery, exemplified in the tea ceremony, a life structured by formalised values that are empty of all human content in the historical sense.[46] The post-historical figure of the human, which survived the historical drama, introduces a fringe of ultrahistory.[47] In this fringe, man presumes that other human beings must survive to function as their support. Life is not possible without the subjection of other lives.[48] Agamben states that for Kojève, the subject we term 'man' is not something concrete. 'Man' exists by way of a mass of dialectical tensions which are riven by caesurae. These caesurae separate what Agamben terms "anthropophorous"

36 Conrad (1972) 37.
37 Conrad (1972) 4.
38 Achebe (2011) 61.
39 Arendt (1966) 206.
40 Foucault (2003) 103.
41 Du Bois (1965) 23.
42 Stovall (2022) 219.
43 Césaire (1973) 35.
44 Kojève (1969) 159.
45 Agamben (2004) 10.
46 Kojève (1969) 161–2; Agamben (2004) 11.
47 Agamben (2004) 11–12.
48 Agamben (2004) 12.

animality, an animal that bears and 'gives birth' to the human and the human that emerges from that animality. Man exists in a tension. Man is historical only in the sense of transcending and transforming the underlying animality that supports him. What is more, man is historical only to the degree that he is capable of mastering and destroying this animality.[49]

The body of the anthropophorous animal is unresolved in post-history. The contradictions of contemporary philosophy today are connected to this dialectical tension of man, a figure drawn and divided between the human and the animal.[50] Whilst America and Japan conceive of man, without any historical content, we read that:

> Europe could offer the alternative of a culture that remains human and vital even after the end of history, because it is capable of confronting itself with its own history in its totality and of drawing from this confrontation a new life.[51]

However, it is precisely here that we need to pause. A confrontation with Europe's history must involve a reckoning with the slave trade, colonialism, racial capitalism and the deployment of race as a means of ordering societies.

Agamben has recognised that the slave stands at the threshold of the separation of *zoè* and *bios*, and even asks rhetorically:

> Aristotle developed his idea of the human being starting from the paradigm of the free man, even if this latter implies the slave as his condition of possibility. One can imagine that he could have developed an entirely other anthropology if he had taken account of the slave.[52]

Agamben can be criticised on the basis that slavery appears to be his concern only insofar as its violence is revealed to rely on a prior form of intimacy, use.[53] But 'slave' is a category that has changing meanings.[54] The slave is not called, but trained to be an object, or not to be.[55] Today the 'slave' illustrates the production of negation as a natural consequence of being racialised Black.[56] As Folúké Adébísí explains, the effect of being racialised Black in

49 Agamben (2004) 12, 19; Kojève (1979) 554.
50 Agamben (2004) 12.
51 Agamben (2019) 1–2.
52 Agamben (2016) 20.
53 Sorentino (2019) 652.
54 Wilderson (2010) 15.
55 Farley (2004) 228.
56 Adébísí (2023) 83.

a world ordered by colonial logics is to permanently exist in the category 'slave' and its changing meanings.[57]

Agamben's inquiries do not focus on racial slavery. Instead, Agamben states that "ancient philosophers not only did not problematize slavery but seemed to accept it as obvious and natural".[58] We need to reflect on what it would mean to consider that "ontology and politics correspond perfectly" through the enslaved person and especially the enslaved person of the Atlantic slave trade, given that the modern world and modern capitalism exist in the shadow of this trade in human beings.[59]

To do this we can turn to a figure Agamben has written about in *Remnants of Auschwitz*, Primo Levi, and specifically Paul Gilroy's analysis of Levi's works. In discussing the concentration camps of the Holocaust, Levi explains that slave labour was a key purpose in the camps, alongside killing political opponents and exterminating inferior races.[60] What Gilroy gleans from Levi is that the nature of the journey to the camps of the Holocaust had an equivalent in the literature and racial slavery of the Atlantic slave trade.[61]

Slavery is one of the first instances of biopolitical experimentation.[62] The Jewish and the Black traditions are the two most powerful traditions that have taken to their deepest philosophical consequences our understanding of bondage, captivity, exile, death – and therefore, freedom.[63] The Black philosophical critique of modernity has been deeply influenced by the historical experience of captivity, bondage, colonial subjugation and racism. Bondage always rests, at least partly, on the power to arrogate another human being's labour without his or her consent.[64]

That is why in many Black narratives of freedom, liberty is imagined first as the recovery of the capacity to take care of oneself once again – a capacity which is defined as "the right to self-determination".[65] Even more important in the calculus of freedom is self-ownership.[66] We must challenge the operation of racism, understood as the state-sanctioned or extra-legal production and exploitation of group-differentiated vulnerability to premature death.[67] Taking this into account, Agamben's work needs to be able to explain how the suspension or deactivation of the biopolitical order can be brought about,

57 Adébísí (2023) 84.
58 Agamben (2016) 7.
59 Agamben (2016) 129.
60 Gilroy (1993) 215, citing Levi (1988) 100.
61 Gilroy (1993) 220.
62 Mbembé (2003) 21.
63 Mbembé (2005) 294.
64 Mbembé, (2005) 296.
65 Mbembé (2005) 296–7.
66 Mbembé (2005) 297.
67 Gilmore (2007) 28.

and what role form-of-life plays in this. If the anthropological machine is rendered inoperative, this presumes that it still continues to exist in some deactivated form.[68] What are the specific limits to the coming politics?

The basis for the coming politics can be found in Agamben's writings on destitution. We must challenge Agamben's claim to see Europe as the future. If this is the case, then form-of-life can only ever be a narrowly conceived liberal juridical Western subject.[69] Even if we were to accept that Agamben's work should only apply to the Global North, this is problematic, considering the way racial capitalism operates in those countries, and how colonialism and coloniality shaped and formed both Europe and North America.[70] We are better to follow the example of Fanon here, who wrote in 1961: "Today we are present at the stasis of Europe".[71]

On destituent potentiality

Destituent potentiality requires a willingness to radically put into questions the ways we think of the grounds and strategies of politics.[72] Strategy here means that every thought, however abstract it may be, is marked by historical and temporal signs and is engaged in a strategy and agency.[73] Philosophy always has a political potential, and we must take into account the time and place of ideas, their genealogies and the potential for development that they possess.[74] This is not a variation of a revolutionary struggle we are familiar with.[75] Form-of-life is a life of destituent potential. Destitution frees ourselves from the concept of 'realisation' which dominates Western thought and politics. 'Realisation' is the way in which political action seeks to *realise* (in facts or deeds), a doctrine, philosophy, ideal or plan, translating into reality something that is clearly intended not to be real or not yet real.[76]

Agamben seeks to distance himself from realisation. For example, Agamben considers the position the verb *aufheben* plays in Hegel's dialectic, which has a double meaning of both to abolish or stop and to conserve.[77] Hegel's error was to maintain a paradigm of realisation in his thought, specifically the realisation of the law. For Hegel, to realise also means to abolish, "the realization remains, but insofar as the abolished is conserved and the

68 Brophy (2021) 203.
69 Brophy (2021) 205.
70 Olusoga (2016).
71 Fanon (2005) 314.
72 Agamben (2023) 9.
73 Agamben (2006).
74 de la Durantaye (2012) 232.
75 Agamben (2023) 9.
76 Agamben (2023) 10.
77 Agamben (2023) 11.

conserved abolished, this becomes an infinite process" of realisation.[78] The metaphysics of realisation separates the possible from the real and of potentiality from the act. It is a machine, which like the anthropological machine separates its two sides yet articulates them together.[79] This is why revolutions run aground – there is no opening in which the possible is translated into reality and politics is finally realised. This opening does not exist because the possible is already real and absolutely unrealisable.[80] This entails changing our strategies completely.[81]

Instead of seeking to realise a particular vision of the world and making it in that image, destitution invokes a desire to tear down and cancel prevailing political representations and institutions without proposing others to replace them.[82] Attacking institutions enables them to consolidate and reinvigorate their power.[83] 'Destitution' means that to resist something it must be countered using 'as-not':

> The 'as not' is a destitution without refusal. To live in the form of the as-not means to deactivate every juridical and social property, without establishing a new identity.[84]

Political subjectivity in the modern sense of a conscious agent with a vision of a future society to be realised is refused.[85] Destituent potential is not negative but points to the liberation of something already present.[86] As Gian-Giacomo Fusco explains, inoperativity is the form of the coming politics, and destitution is its operative logic. An inoperative politics remodels human action in a non-purposeful sense, liberating the potential immanent to all forms of life.[87] This is an ethical gesture which renders inoperative the forces shaping human lives, and this constitutes an immanent form of inhabiting the world.[88]

For Agamben, all identities are a differential construct. Some regard these differences as essential. Others regard them as arbitrary constructs. The person who regards differences as arbitrary constructs focuses on living their life as a form.[89] A striving *to other* oneself or others makes no sense. Everybody

78 Agamben (2023) 12.
79 Agamben (2023) 15.
80 Agamben (2023) 16.
81 Agamben (2023) 17.
82 Tarì (2021) 13; Invisible Committee (2017) 80.
83 Bolt Rasmussen (2023) 26.
84 Agamben (2014) 71.
85 Bolt Rasmussen (2023) 26.
86 Fusco (2023) 6; Aarons (2020) 51; Invisible Committee (2017) 76.
87 Fusco (2023) 58.
88 Fusco (2023) 66.
89 Agamben (2016) 231.

should take care of themselves to become a true self, which is a form of destituent politics:

> The constitution of a form-of-life coincides ... completely with the destitution of the social and biological conditions into which it finds itself thrown. The form-of-life is, in this sense, the revocation of all factical vocations, which deposes and puts in tension from within the same gesture by which it is maintained and dwells in them.[90]

Agamben writes that destituent potential "welcomes non-Being, and this welcoming of non-Being *is potentiality*, fundamental passivity".[91] Because the fundamental passivity of potentiality arises from the act of *welcoming* non-Being, it is dependent on a form of action.[92] Focusing on a *passive* interpretation of Agamben implies that there is nothing we can do to bring about a coming politics.[93] Living one's life as a form involves a decision in favour of potentiality *as such*, actualising the potentiality *for* potentiality, setting aside the potentiality not to be.[94]

Fusco notes that such an inoperative politics is difficult for a Western mind to conceive, as we are attuned to a law backed up with violence and separate from the institutions of the state.[95] Fusco turns to the work of Pierre Clastres to explore Indigenous peoples in South America, who he saw as living without a state, and outside the Western conception of power as coercion, with an essential alterity and multiplicity,[96] and focused on a non-coercive power.[97] Such societies show that a world beyond capitalism, and a society outside the nation state, is possible.[98] Fusco concludes that the destitution of law, the idea of a form of non-coercive regulation, must be thought only beyond and against our civilisation.[99]

But perhaps not that far at all. The zone of non-Being (or nonbeing) also appears in Fanon as an extraordinarily sterile and arid region.[100] Fanon credits European colonialism with the creation of damned peoples who are physically marked through their deviation from a predetermined standard.[101] Kojo

90 Agamben (2014) 74.
91 Agamben (1999a) 182.
92 Rae (2018) 979.
93 Rae (2018) 980.
94 Prozorov (2010) 1068.
95 Fusco (2023) 110.
96 Clastres (1989) 189.
97 Clastres (1989) 47.
98 de Castro (2010) 15.
99 Fusco (2023) 115.
100 Fanon (1970) 2.
101 Koram (2022) 101.

Koram sees the subjectivity of the colonised in a condition of damnation as a theological connection.[102] Thus the zone of non-Being is a real hell, a place that encapsulates the lived experience of the racialised or colonised other.[103] But this is a hell where an authentic upheaval can be born.[104] To draw an analogy, both Fanon and Agamben accept that we need to transform our ideas of what constitutes the 'human' which will be placed at the heart of our future political struggles. Fanon determines that the future struggle is decolonial, whereas Agamben couches it in terms of destituent potential.[105] We need to read the two traditions together and think of a destituent decoloniality.

On hyper-hermeneutics

I use Agamben's writings on the slave to show how enslaved people's lives and actions can found new forms of legal and political acting and agency, in a world which has been shaped by colonial forms of domination and structured by coloniality. My claims centre around a form of acting I have termed 'hyper-hermeneutics'. This is analogous to the way Agamben deploys the preposition 'hyper' in his discussion of slavery. Saint Paul in Philemon uses the phrase *hyper doulon*, 'more than a slave', to refer to the recently baptised Onesimus.[106] Agamben claims this formulation epitomises a messianic deactivation of the law. But Agamben modifies the term, speaking of an "extraordinary hapax, *hyper doulos*, 'super slave, slave to the second power'".[107] This involves Agamben bringing together two unrelated Pauline texts, the reiteration of *hōs mē* in 1 Corinthians 7 and Paul's advocacy for Onesimus in Philemon.[108] Without naming Onesimus, Agamben appropriates the phrase *hyper doulon*, and the attribution of a messianic vocation to "the" (singular, unnamed, presumptively male) slave is consistent with Agamben's positioning of the slave as a liminal figure at the threshold of a form-of-life, the contemplative way of living he deems truly human.[109]

Agamben first transliterates the phrase *hyper doulon*.[110] He later alters the phrase, without comment, to *hyper doulos*.[111] The noun *doulon* is in the accusative case. When governing the accusative case, *hyper* means 'over' or 'beyond'. *Hyper* would not be used with the nominative case. In changing the

102 Koram (2022) 110.
103 Koram (2022) 109; Fanon (2005) 140.
104 Fanon (1970) 10.
105 Fanon (1970) 112.
106 Philemon 16.
107 Agamben (2005b) 28–9.
108 Glancy (2020) 18.
109 Glancy (2020) 18–19.
110 Agamben (2005b) 13.
111 Agamben (2005b) 29.

accusative *doulon* to the nominative *doulos*, Agamben construes the *hyper* as an adjective, meaning 'super'.[112] This is inconsistent with Greek usage, but the Greek preposition *hyper* is generally translated with the Latin preposition *super*.

Jennifer Glancy sees the super slave as *Übermensch*. This is purely Agamben's construction. Form-of-life is a messianic figure whose indifference to the law is sufficient to disarm the law.[113] Glancy sees this disarming or suspension of the law as magical, but it is this view I challenge. Agamben seeks and claims to find an archaic nucleus of slavery in mutual use, a zone of indifference between one body and another. What are the power relations within such relations? How is the usefulness or uselessness of another person determined? Agamben's assertion of a messianic vocation for the slave who lives "as not" requires indifference to the violence and other forms of coercion that counter the potentiality inherent in the refusal to be used.[114]

To address these concerns, form-of-life itself should be read as 'hyper-hermeneutic'. Form-of-life retains a hermeneutic structure but is constructed through singular paradigmatic examples. Agamben's 'paradigm' is a real particular case set apart from what it is meant to exemplify.[115] Agamben reads paradigms as constructing a 'paradigmatic circle',[116] allowing form-of-life to exist outside the hermeneutic circle.[117] By stepping outside this hermeneutic circle, form-of-life can deactivate apparatuses of control.[118] These paradigms are gestural.[119] These gestures are coterminous with a contemplative life.[120] Before exploring this, we need to consider the method underpinning Agamben's thought, 'philosophical archaeology'.

Philosophical archaeology

'Philosophical archaeology' has three elements: the paradigm; the signature; and the *archē*.[121] Agamben defines his archaeology as follows:

> [W]e may call "archaeology" that practice which in any historical investigation has to do not with origins but with the moment of a phenomenon's arising and must therefore engage anew the sources and tradition.

112 Glancy (2020) 19.
113 Glancy (2020) 19.
114 Glancy (2020) 19.
115 de la Durantaye (2009) 218–19.
116 Agamben (2009a) 27–8.
117 Heidegger (1962) 182–195.
118 Agamben (1999b) 174.
119 Agamben (2009a) 27.
120 Agamben (2016) 214–19.
121 Watkin (2013) 4.

> It cannot confront tradition without deconstructing the paradigms, techniques, and practices through which tradition regulates the forms of transmission, conditions access to sources, and in the final analysis determines the very status of the knowing subject.[122]

Instead of looking for origins, philosophical archaeology searches for the point of emergence of the phenomenon, its *archē*.[123] The *archē* is not a past in a linear historical sense, nor a lived experience. It is a moment of arising that takes place in the future, but it is also a form of the past in the future. It is "the past that will have been when the archaeologist's gesture ... has cleared away the ghosts of the unconscious and the tight-knit fabric of tradition which blocks access to history".[124] Access to this moment is only obtained by "returning back to the point where it was covered over and neutralised by tradition".[125]

The paradigm, an actual historical phenomenon, is used by Agamben to illustrate the broader historical-problematic context produced by the machines that divide and separate life.[126] Paradigms are also able to point the way toward the coming politics, as Agamben uses the slave as representing a paradigm for form-of-life. In using paradigms in both ways, Agamben aims to focus on phenomena that have eluded the historian's view.[127] The paradigm is drawn from history, but it is like an example in that it constitutes and represents its own singularity.[128] It also defines the intelligibility of the group of which it is a part and that it also constitutes.[129] Agamben explains his method did not reduce the historical aspect of the paradigm, but he tries to contextualise them in his work. Paradigms are a historical method of working through understanding the world in which we live.[130]

There is one paradigm Agamben identifies that informs my overall argument and the later chapters consideration of decolonial thought – colonialism. Agamben considers the paradigm of colonialism as a way to understand life in our cities and societies today.[131] Colonialism begins with the metropolis, a colonial term. The metropolis is a Mother City, and the term refers to the relationship between cities and colonies. The Greek *polis* as a model of the political city is excluded from the relation between metropolis and colony.

122 Agamben (2009a) 89.
123 Agamben (2009a) 81.
124 Agamben (2009a) 107.
125 Agamben (2009a) 105.
126 Raulff and Agamben (2004) 610.
127 Agamben (2009a) 31.
128 Agamben (2009a) 9.
129 Agamben (2009a) 17.
130 Agamben (2001) 19.
131 de la Durantaye (2012) 233.

The current idea of the metropolis as an urban, continuous and homogeneous fabric needs reconsidering.[132] This historical phenomenon emerged in Western culture's early colony formation, which means ancient Greece.[133] Metropolis was used by Greek colonists to refer to the nurturing point of departure and return.[134]

What defines the relationship between the state and colonies is the original meaning of 'metropolis', which was a "maximum dislocation" and a "political and spatial dishomogeneity".[135] Agamben notes this dislocation and dishomogeneity *within* every metropolis and every *polis*, and this is characteristic of all of today's cities and states and the way they supervise and punish their body politic.[136] The city is a *dispositif*, or apparatus, which captures and takes hold of living beings.[137] This *dispositif* was replaced by the *dispositif* of the metropolis when power became the government of the living and of things in the early modern period.[138] There is no *dispositif* without the process of subjectivation resulting from the relation between living beings and apparatuses. Subject means to become attached to an individuality, but it also means subjugation to an external power. Every time an identity is assumed or assigned, the living being is also subjugated, which can also involve 'de-subjectification'.[139] 'De-subjects' will be figures of bare life.[140] More than this, the metropolis is a new paradigm, separate from the *polis*. The form of the *polis* has shifted to a new spatialisation that de-politicises.[141] Colonialism is a process of the control and subjection, disciplining and punishment of subjects (those subjected to colonial power).[142] The metropolis involves a huge process of creating subjectivity. For Agamben, our task is to reach a point of ungovernability, where the system is brought to a standstill and the coming politics begins.[143]

Finally, signatures. A signature "makes a sign intelligible" by determining its existence through its usage.[144] The signature describes the mode of distribution of paradigms through time and across discourses.[145] For William Watkin, signatures have a historical moment of arising (*archē*) when they

132 Agamben (2006).
133 de la Durantaye (2012) 232–3.
134 de la Durantaye (2012) 233.
135 Agamben (2006).
136 de la Durantaye (2012) 233–4.
137 Agamben (2009b) 17.
138 Agamben (2006).
139 Agamben (2009b) 19; Agamben (2006).
140 Agamben (2016) xix–xx.
141 Agamben (2006).
142 de la Durantaye (2012) 237.
143 Agamben (2006).
144 Agamben (2009a) 42.
145 Watkin (2013) 4.

become active in sanctioning 'knowledge systems', controlling how we think, speak and act. The signature is actualised through different discourses but is kept consistent by each discourse by its sharing in common a series of terms – these terms are 'paradigms'.[146] Watkin goes on – signatures are in a mode of opposition to the very paradigms they sanction and legitimate. Signatures exist if they make a consistent set of paradigms over time sufficient to be named, for example 'life'. Until these paradigms are corralled under the signatory term 'life', the signature does not exist. The signature 'life' occurs *after* its paradigm – the paradigms are paradigms because they exist due to the signature in operation.[147] For our purposes we can say that 'slavery' also operates as a signature, sanctioning not just how we think about freedom but also how the signature of 'slavery' has produced paradigms of unfreedom throughout the history of Western European political thought. Just as political life requires a bare life to hold itself against, our conceptions of freedom require paradigms of unfreedom to find their meaning.

Paradigms as examples

In Plato the paradigm has its place in dialectics. Agamben claims his paradigmatic method is expressed in Book 6 of the *Republic* through Plato's dialectic.[148] For Plato, dialectics treats hypotheses as hypotheses – underpinnings or springboards that enable us to access an *archē* that is unhypothetical, the first principle of everything.[149] Dialectic seeks knowledge of the Forms by thinking about or viewing the Forms directly. A parallel could be drawn here to the idea of form-of-life existing as such. Such a claim also places Agamben's paradigmatic method as part of a long philosophical heritage and is not his only reference back to Plato and the idea of grasping 'the thing itself'.[150] Hypotheses are never presupposed. In a similar vein, the knowability of the paradigm is never presupposed.

The paradigm takes a single singularity and raises it to the status of example.[151] Agamben turns to Aristotle's *Prior Analytics* for the epistemology of the example. There, Aristotle states that:

> It is clear that the paradigm does not function as a part with respect to the whole, nor as a whole with respect to the part, but as a part with respect

146 Watkin (2013) xv.
147 Watkin (2013) xv; Frost (2021) 57–61.
148 Agamben (2009a) 25; Plato (2005) 509d–511e.
149 Plato (2005) 511b2–c1; Benson (2015) 237–270.
150 Agamben (1999c); Agamben (2023) 13–14.
151 Watkin (2013) 16–17; Agamben (2009a) 25–6.

> to the part, if both are under the same but one is better known than the other.[152]

Agamben claims Aristotle's treatment of the paradigm does not move beyond his observations in *Prior Analytics*.[153] But Michèle Lowrie and Susanne Lüdemann note that Aristotle's *paradeigma* is actually an umbrella term. In the *Rhetoric* Aristotle states that the example is a form of rhetorical induction, with an enthymeme (an argument where one premise is not explicitly stated) being a form of rhetorical deduction.[154] Agamben follows *Prior Analytics*, privileging the radical singularity of the example being a part with respect to a part, and not as a form of induction, but as an analogy.[155]

In the *Rhetoric*, each paradigm is only a particular. The relationship between paradigm and paradigm is one of resemblance, a kind of induction. As a result a principle can never be fully gained via paradigmatic induction. At best it is hinted at or claimed. A genus does not precede the examples *qua* paradigms but is a product or effect of the relation of similitude between them, arriving from the analogous force shared between the paradigmatic instances.[156]

Agamben's focus on singularity rather than induction is a desire to be discharged from the general altogether.[157] Fusco explains that by moving from singularity to singularity the paradigm makes every singular case into an exemplar of a general rule that can never be stated a priori.[158] A paradigm is the real particular case set apart from what it is meant to exemplify.[159] We must understand Agamben's interpretation of exemplarity as a deliberate philosophical choice, but one which reflects a long tradition. Following Foucault, Agamben's paradigm is both an *exemplar* and a model, and an *exemplum* which allows statements and discursive practices to be gathered into a new intelligible ensemble and in a new problematic context.[160] A paradigm:

> [I]mplies the total abandonment of the particular-general couple as the model of logical inference. The rule … is not a generality pre-existing singular cases and applicable to them, nor is it something resulting from the

152 Agamben (2009a) 19, quoting Aristotle (1984a) 69a13–15.
153 Agamben (2009a) 19.
154 Lowrie and Lüdemann (2015) 2; Aristotle (1984b) 1326a37–1356b5.
155 Agamben (2009a) 19, 31.
156 Fleming (2015) 198.
157 Lowrie and Lüdemann (2015) 2.
158 Fusco (2023) 17; Agamben (2009a) 22.
159 de la Durantaye (2009) 218–19.
160 Agamben (2009a) 18.

> exhaustive enumeration of specific cases. Instead, it is the exhibition alone of the paradigmatic cases that constitute a rule.[161]

The emphasis on a paradigm as a model finds a precursor in the Roman and Christian traditions. In Rome, exemplarity was treated as a practice starting from a set of values embodied in known figures that offer models to be imitated or avoided, fulfilling the functions of a role model.[162] Exempla often served as popular narratives recounting the great feats of glory undertaken in Rome's name.[163] The Roman example does things through stories which share some of the moral force of narratives such as parables or fables.[164] A longer narrative was used to set up expectations in a homogeneous society where everyone is presumed to know the standard stories.[165] This tradition influenced Agamben. He traces the origins of form-of-life to Cicero, Seneca and Quintilian, where the syntagma *forma vitae* has the meaning of 'example, model', and *forma* is equivalent to exemplar and exemplum.[166]

In the medieval period, the exemplum was deployed by ecclesiastical writers in two meanings. Firstly, as an 'example' in a general sense, frequently termed *similitudo*. Secondly, as an illustrative story.[167] In contrast to classical literature's exemplum which refers to the role model of a historical or legendary person, in medieval literature, an exemplum is a short narrative with the potential to provide a moral lesson, either implicitly or explicitly.[168] Between the fourth and twelfth centuries, the early Christian exemplum presented perfect ethical behaviour according to the precepts of Christianity and illustrated man's sole means of relationship with the divine order.[169] At the beginning of the thirteenth century, the exemplum underwent a profound change. Frederic Tubach traces this to the appearance of the Franciscan Order which led to increased social awareness of the Church. Exempla became socially oriented. The exemplum becomes a mirror of life, a personalised expression and a literary tradition.[170]

Classical and medieval exempla are related. Citing an example of a person implies that person undertook an action, and a narrative comes into being as a person is said to have performed such an action. In Christian literature, the two concepts meet in Christ. Christ is the ideal personal exemplum, and

161 Agamben (2009a) 21.
162 Langlands (2015) 69; Speed (1995) 312.
163 Tubach (1962) 409.
164 Lowrie and Lüdemann (2015) 9.
165 Roller (2004) 2, 10.
166 Agamben (2013) 94.
167 Tubach (1962) 408.
168 Speed (1995) 312.
169 Tubach (1962) 409–10.
170 Tubach (1962) 412, 417.

Christ's actions, or the actions of his followers, or antagonists, are the primary subject of Christian exempla.[171]

Agamben notes the importance of the Franciscans, who made the *forma vitae*, form-of-life, a term of monastic literature.[172] St Francis of Assisi and the Franciscan Order tried to integrate monastic rules developed by the Church into a form-of-life itself, so that rule and life would become indistinguishable. Francis wanted the monks to live according to the "form of the Holy Gospel", not the laws of the Roman Church.[173] The form of the Holy Gospel was to live the very life of Christ.[174] Christ's life is a form-of-life, a way of life that is an example in the sense that the life adheres to a form or model from which it cannot be separated.[175] Francis's own life was a summary and example for his followers.[176] The monk orders his form-of-life through his own way of being and interpreting the form of the Holy Gospel, and also through reference to the examples provided by other monks. Form-of-life dwells together, and its way of being is structured by reference to others.[177]

In this way a paradigm, the example, form-of-life, becomes the basis for the coming politics. It is a life that is not possible to be separated into something like bare life. It is also a model. Form-of-life is not an atomised individual existence. The 'reference to others' is crucial here. Agamben's paradigm locates itself at the crossing of diachrony and synchrony. This makes our present as intelligible as the past of the object.[178] If we treat the enslaved person as a form-of-life, then the actions and behaviours of forms-of-life in the past can provide a model, or a structure of behaviour, for the present. As Agamben states, a chronological archive can be "cleaved open to produce a paradigm" to make the whole archive legible.[179] This cleavage, I contend, is hyper-hermeneutic, and develops Agamben's reading of the paradigm.

The paradigmatic circle and paradigmatic gestures

Agamben's thought remains within the hermeneutic tradition.[180] Agamben notes, with respect to reading the works of Foucault, that:

171 Speed (1995) 312.
172 Agamben (2013) 96.
173 Agamben (2013) 97.
174 Agamben (2013) 111.
175 Agamben (2013) 95.
176 Agamben (2013) 101–2.
177 Frost (2014) 219.
178 Agamben (2009a) 32.
179 Agamben (2009a) 32.
180 Agamben (2009b) 13.

> Whenever we interpret and develop the text of an author in this way, there comes a moment when we are aware of our inability to proceed any further without contravening the most elementary rules of hermeneutics.[181]

Hyper-hermeneutics conveys Agamben's response to perceived *aporias* within Martin Heidegger's hermeneutic circle. Agamben proposes a *paradigmatic circle*, which deactivates the hermeneutic circle.[182] My term 'hyper' in hyper-hermeneutics connotes Agamben's attempt to escape the hermeneutic circle, which he does through non-hermeneutic means, namely the paradigm. For Agamben, the hermeneutic circle acquires its true meaning from within this paradigmatic method.

Our starting point is Heidegger's construction of *Dasein*, and how *Dasein* lives in the world temporally. Simplifying matters for the purpose of my argument here, I will here consider *Dasein* as referring to the living being in the world, and the insights here can apply to form-of-life. Understanding is a fundamental character of *Dasein*,[183] guiding *Dasein* to comprehend what its possibilities are.[184] Understanding happens through projection, what Heidegger terms being thrown before its own possibilities of living.[185] Understanding is connected to interpretation, which Heidegger states is *Dasein*'s own possibility of developing itself.[186] Interpretation allows *Dasein* to work out the possibilities projected through understanding and being thrown. To understand is to give the structure of something 'as' something to a phenomenon. The 'as' relates to the purpose of the thing in question, making an assertion that characterises it.[187] The interpretation that leads to a thematic assertion about something *as* something is itself grounded in fore-having, fore-sight and fore-conception. These are known as the 'fore-structures' of interpretation, grounded on things *Dasein* has in advance, sees in advance and grasps in advance respectively.[188]

Dasein's own possibilities must be understood as being structured by the world into which *Dasein* was thrown. The hermeneutic circle is the structure of *Dasein*'s understanding of the world that *Dasein* has in advance of any interpretation, the expression of the fore-structure of *Dasein* itself. But the circle must be approached in the 'right way'. The circle hides a possibility of the most primordial kind of knowing. Heidegger warns against resting any interpretation on popular conceptions without first questioning those

181 Agamben (2009b) 13.
182 Agamben (2009a) 27.
183 Heidegger (1962) 182.
184 Heidegger (1962) 184.
185 Heidegger (1962) 185.
186 Heidegger (1962) 188.
187 Heidegger (1962) 189.
188 Heidegger (1962) 190–1.

conceptions themselves.[189] It is vital to focus upon and understand the fore-structures that make up the world into which *Dasein* is thrown.[190]

It is this claim that we need to understand the world's fore-structures that forms the basis for Agamben's critique. Agamben acknowledges *Being and Time* as an attempt to reconcile the difficulties of hermeneutics.[191] But Agamben challenges the idea that *Dasein* can come to the circle in the right way, and that these fore-structures can be worked out.[192] Agamben sees the pre-understanding of these fore-structures as elusive. On this reading, the hermeneutic circle appears defined by an ineffable foundation that can never be grasped. Agamben sees that any interpretative response to the hermeneutic circle is futile:

> This can only mean – and the circle then seems to become even more "vicious" – that the inquirer must be able to recognise in phenomena the signature of a pre-understanding that depends on their own existential structure.[193]

Pre-understanding depends on the existential structure of the phenomena in question, meaning that any pre-understanding of those fore-structures is impossible. The interpreter can never come to the circle in the right way as the interpreter will not have the pre-understanding of the world required to do so. This is why Agamben moves from hermeneutics to paradigms. Agamben maintains that the 'things themselves' (which I read here to refer to form-of-life) cannot be reached through the hermeneutic circle, or even through a pre-understanding.

In contrast, the paradigmatic circle allows for the phenomenon's intelligibility to be understood through the paradigm itself.[194] A singular paradigm allows for an understanding of a constellation of phenomena which the paradigm stands as an example:

> The paradigmatic gesture moves not from the particular to the whole and from the whole to the particular but from the singular to the singular. The phenomenon, exposed in the medium of its knowability, shows the whole of which it is the paradigm. With regard to phenomena, this is not a presupposition (a "hypothesis"): as a "non-presupposed principle", it stands neither in the past nor in the present but in their exemplary constellation.[195]

189 Heidegger (1962) 195.
190 Heidegger (1962) 195.
191 Agamben (2009a) 27.
192 Agamben (2009a) 27.
193 Agamben (2009a) 27.
194 Agamben (2009a) 27.
195 Agamben (2009a) 27–8.

This paradigmatic method makes Agamben's approach 'hyper-hermeneutic'. The paradigm does not need a fore but makes those phenomena intelligible through its own operation. The paradigm, the singular gesture, can break the circle of oppression tied through hermeneutics to current forms of political belonging. Form-of-life cannot be based on the hermeneutic circle. Form-of-life must be understood paradigmatically.

Agamben uses a number of different paradigms to represent form-of-life. They include the nude body,[196] an adult pornographic actress who remains expressionless in her films[197] and the protesters in Tiananmen Square.[198] All these figures stand as paradigmatic examples for singular life. Each shows the whole of which it is the paradigm. Such a hyper-hermeneutic method points to a singular nature of form-of-life existing apart from the hermeneutics of the world we live in. It points to a life being lived as an example, without needing to be beholden to the structures of understanding and interpretation of this world shaped by coloniality.

If the paradigm is a singular example, then a single act must be able to form the basis for effecting destituent potential. The all-important moment for form-of-life becomes the singular paradigmatic gesture. This paradigmatic gesture renders inoperative existing forms of political belonging, including the self-referential nature of the hermeneutic circle. What would such a paradigmatic gesture look like? Destituent acts cannot be prescribed and would not need to be decisive or revolutionary. These paradigmatic acts are truly political. Singular beings are in-common, joined through their own experience of the limit of their finitude. A gesture does not produce, but it opens the proper sphere of that which is human.[199] Agamben puts at the core of his philosophical journey the singular events that exceed the limits of subjectivities and promise the coming of another world out of the gestures in this one.[200] Gesture is an activity which, in the manner in which it is carried out, at the same time stops itself, exposes itself and holds itself at a distance.[201] By rendering works inoperative, gesture opens them to a new, possible use.[202]

How can these gestures be connected to freeing what Agamben terms "archaic nucleus" imprisoned within the juridical institution of slavery?[203] How can we understand the way the *legal* understanding of the master-slave relationship that Agamben alleges has lost access to the use of bodies?[204]

196 Agamben (2010) 91–103.
197 Agamben (2007a) 90–1.
198 Agamben (2007b) 85–7.
199 Agamben (2000) 57.
200 Agamben (2018a) 80.
201 DeCaroli (2020) 271.
202 Agamben (2018a) 84–5.
203 Agamben (2016) 78.
204 Agamben (2016) 36–7.

Agamben's focus appears to be a modest form of action. Agamben states that:

> [T]he strongest objection against the principle of sovereignty is contained in Melville's Bartleby, the scrivener who, with his "I would prefer not to", resists every possibility of deciding between potentiality and the potentiality not to.[205]

Edwin Bikundo explains that Agamben is implying that a violent rebellion by an enslaved person is deploying violence within the system's parameters. The oppressive legal system's survival is guaranteed by the very terms of the violent exchange. Preferring not to participate is instead the genuine position of rejecting or refusing the system as such.[206]

But let us pause here and consider the terms of this refusal. Following Aníbal Quijano, Eurocentric colonialism and imperialism has caused direct political, social and cultural domination over the conquered of all continents.[207] This colonial paradigm of power produced specific social discriminations later codified as 'racial', 'ethnic' or 'anthropological'. Today, the majority of the exploited, dominated and discriminated peoples in the world are precisely members of the 'races', 'ethnicities' or 'nations' into which the colonised populations were categorised by European colonialism. European (Western) culture continues to dominate.[208] This is what Quijano calls 'European modernity/rationality': a dominated cultural complex presented as a universal paradigm of knowledge for humanity.[209] How does one challenge a totality?

Precisely through a refusal. Those enslaved persons who 'prefer not to' appear to point to the nucleus of a form-of-life (and freedom) that deactivates the institution of slavery which has captured and divided life. This is at the same time intriguing and elusive. Slave rebellions have been documented throughout the recorded history of slave ownership. They retained important symbolism and meaning even if they were not successful. Cedric Robinson saw the first waves of "African New World revolts" as a total rejection of the experience of enslavement and racism.[210]

Agamben's thought implies we should not be searching for violent activities by default, but gestures of resistance that may be slight, but can in fact be revolutionary. As Fanon noted, when a life is declared to be a sub-human

205 Agamben (1998) 48.
206 Bikundo (2022) 12.
207 Quijano (2007) 168.
208 Quijano (2007) 169.
209 Quijano (2007) 176.
210 Robinson (2021) xiv.

or a non-human, they exist in a zone of contested humanity or negation.[211] All resistance is an accumulated and accumulating commitment to act for the hope of the future.[212] Refusal is central. This is a refusal to live by the colonial matrix of power. This is a form of 're-existence', which references ways to exist (and not just to resist) as subjects. Re-existence seeks to build projects of society and life in the face of adverse conditions and to ultimately seek to occupy a social and cultural place of dignity, re-existing with others in radically distinct terms.[213]

It is these gestures that are a theme of this book, and which are explored in its arguments. The aim here, following Saidiya Hartman, is to narrate counter-histories of slavery, which is also inseparable from writing a history of the present, an incomplete project of freedom.[214] Hartman notes that there is a scarcity of African narratives of captivity and enslavement. This is true. But more broadly there is a scarcity of slave narratives about slavery.[215] Narratives which are perceived as inauthentic or unoriginal have been criticised.[216] But silence is created by privileging some forms of writing and certain voices and viewpoints over others. This does not mean that nothing is being said or done. Silence can also be a strategy to protect your identity from pathologisation.[217]

How does one tell impossible stories?[218] We must make visible the production of disposable lives to describe the "resistance of the object".[219] It is an impossible writing which attempts to say that which resists being said, but which depends upon the limits of the archive.[220] I want to consider what destituent gestures of enslaved people could be, using English law in the eighteenth century as an example. Resistance by enslaved people to the institution of slavery and the slave trade in England helped bring it to an end.

Slavery and resistance in England

The background to Somerset v Stewart

Enslaved people were socially and legally anomalous in Great Britain as there were no statutes sanctioning the institution.[221] The Crown's legal position

211 Fanon (1970) 82.
212 Verges (2021) 5.
213 Achinte (2012) 30.
214 Hartman (2008) 4.
215 Hartman (2008) 3.
216 Olney (1984) 46–73.
217 Holsey (2008) 235.
218 Hartman (2008) 10.
219 Hartman (2008) 11–12; Moten (2003) 14.
220 Hartman (2008) 12.
221 Drescher (1989) 87.

from 1677 onwards was that 'Blacks' were goods under the Navigation Acts.[222] Chattel slavery was supported by the common law. Actions in tort to protect property rights in slaves succeeded in many cases.[223] This position was buttressed in 1729 by Attorney General Philip Yorke and Solicitor General Charles Talbot, a decision given after dinner in Lincoln's Inn, without the status of a court judgment.[224] Ships were key juridical forms that were vital to the expansion of British imperial power.[225] The Navigation Acts created a monopoly over seaborne trade with the Americas, and the British Parliament designated African captives as chattel property.[226] Without the slave ships, plantations in British colonies could not have produced sugar, cotton or other commodities and supplied them to Europe.[227]

As British admiralty law granted ships a legal personality, the laws of slavery and the laws of the sea denied African captives their humanity.[228] Hartman characterises the slave ship as a womb or abyss, the belly of the world.[229] The feminisation of ships was an integral aspect of British maritime customs. Ships also had husbands – agents on land responsible for repairs and general upkeep – and sisters, ships that were built in the same year and by the same company.[230] Françoise Verges has explored the interplay between gender and slavery in the Atlantic. For Verges, slave owners viewed Black women as sexual objects. As enslaved people, they did not fully belong to humanity. Gender is a historical and cultural category, which differs from the metropolis to the colony, between colonies, and even within the same colony. For racialised women, affirming what it means *to be a woman* has been a battleground.[231]

'Unfree' slaves were transported on the 'free sea'. This was thought to necessitate legal regimes of racial coercion and death aboard moving ships.[232] The slave ship was a *dispositif* that controlled human beings, a combination of war machine, mobile prison and factory.[233] It produced the subject of the slave, which became a commodity for the global labour market.[234] Without the terrors of shipboard administration, slave ships might not have survived

222 Davies (1957) 331–2.
223 *Butts v Penny* (1677) 2 Lev 201, 3 Keb 785; *Gelly v Cleve* (1694) 1 Ld Raym 147.
224 Wiecek (1974) 93–4.
225 Mawani (2022) 21.
226 Mawani (2022) 23–4; Mtubani (1981) 73.
227 Mawani (2022) 23.
228 Mawani (2018) 86; NourbeSe Philip (2008) 196.
229 Hartman (2008) 166.
230 Mawani (2022) 30.
231 Verges (2021) 31.
232 Mawani (2018) 87.
233 Rediker (2007) 299.
234 Rediker (2007) 338; Youngquist (2011) 4.

their passage across the Atlantic.[235] Even with the terror, resistance was common, and this had financial implications.

In 1720, the British Government sanctioned the foundation of two joint-stock insurance companies – the London Assurance and the Royal Exchange Assurance.[236] The English thought of the slave as a commodity or thing, and not as a captive or a subject.[237] Enslaved Africans entered English law as an exceptional commodity, with no claim to freedom and no legal personality.[238] Ship owners were unable to file insurance claims for the first five per cent of their losses.[239]

In *Gregson v Gilbert*, the owners of the slave ship *Zong* brought a legal case against their insurers, who failed to pay out for the murder of slaves on a voyage to Jamaica. Ottobah Cugoano, an active abolitionist, wrote of the *Zong* as a "melancholy instance" of "the vast carnage and murders committed by the British instigators of slavery".[240] Insurance contracts did not cover the mortality or 'natural deaths' of the enslaved people on the crossing of the Atlantic. But ship owners could be compensated for 'accidental death' and for murdering anyone suspected of insurrection.[241] The implication here is clear. The agency of enslaved people is recognised, whilst at the same time denied. The crew of the *Zong* had thrown 132 slaves into the sea, on the basis that they did not have enough fresh water aboard to ensure the enslaved people did not die of thirst. Despite this claim of necessity, evidence showed that the ship's water supplies were sufficient. Legal argument was predicated on the fact that "It has been decided, whether wisely or unwisely is not now the question, that a portion of our fellow-creatures may become the subject of property".[242]

The 'Free Air' of England

England had a contradictory and longstanding popular tradition that an enslaved person's coming to England by itself resulted in their emancipation. From 1540 to 1771 most courts and legal authorities agreed that the common law did not recognise chattel slavery in England, and enslaved people who came to England were not fully emancipated, being subject to a form of "slavish servitude" that constituted "near slavery".[243]

235 Walvin (2019) 43.
236 Rupprecht (2008) 273.
237 Shilliam (2012) 594.
238 Bush (1993) 443.
239 Walvin (2013) 120.
240 Cugoano (1999) 111.
241 Oldham (2007) 308–10; Armstrong (2004) 170.
242 *Gregson v Gilbert* (1783) 3 Doug 232, 233.
243 van Cleve (2006) 604, 611.

Earlier court judgments had reached similar conclusions. In 1701 Lord Chief Justice Holt declared that "as soon as a negro comes into England, he becomes free, one may be a villein in England but not a slave".[244] There were an estimated 10,000 to 15,000 Black people in England in 1770. Drescher notes that Black servants in England had the same capital value as was annually invested in the British Atlantic slave trade.[245]

The case of *Somerset v Stewart* threatened a definitive answer on the question of slavery's legality in England. Lord Mansfield, the Lord Chief Justice, realised this. He deliberated for six months. When he issued his judgment, it was a deliberate compromise. This led to foreseeable controversy and misinterpretation on important points,[246] which Lord Mansfield thought was a necessary price to pay for political peace on slavery in England.[247] In this case Lord Mansfield declared:

> The state of slavery is of such a nature, that it is incapable of being introduced on any reasons, moral or political; but only positive law, which preserves its force long after the reasons, occasion, and time itself from whence it was created, is erased from memory: it's so odious, that nothing can be suffered to support it, but positive law.[248]

Somerset did not bring immediate freedom to all slaves in England. Lord Mansfield did not intend his ruling to emancipate enslaved people.[249] He intended for enslaved people to continue in 'near slavery'.[250] Lord Mansfield ruled that an enslaved person's master could not forcibly send the slave out of the realm.[251] Any use of force against any person in England must be permissible under English law. This effectively barred chattel slavery.[252]

Lord Mansfield tried to stress that his decision was narrow, but he could not prevent its misinterpretation. This showed the nature of the legal world where "things are not what they seem, a world of deceptive appearances and unforeseen consequences".[253] Drescher shows how the judgment took on an existence of its own. West Indian slave owners viewed the *Somerset* judgment as freeing all slaves in England. Drescher quotes 'Veritas', a West Indian writing in the *St James's Chronicle* newspaper in 1788, who claimed that

244 *Smith v Brown and Cooper* (1701) 2 Salk 666.
245 Drescher (2009) 98–9.
246 van Cleve (2006) 634.
247 van Cleve (2006) 638.
248 *Somerset v Stewart* (1772) 98 ER 499, 510 (KB) (Lord Mansfield).
249 Oldham (1988).
250 Davis (1999) 498.
251 Wiecek (1974) 108.
252 van Cleve (2006) 636; Davis (1999) 498.
253 Wiecek (1974) 87.

hundreds of enslaved people had come to England since the legal decision, knew they were on free ground and acted as if they had freedom.[254]

Edward Long, slave owner and staunch defender of the institution, worried that the consequence of *Somerset* was the abolition of slavery and the need for White Britons to do the work of enslaved Africans in the Caribbean.[255] *Somerset* had set the stage for miscegenation,[256] equal political status[257] and the death of English liberty.[258] The lack of legal punishment for running away from their masters meant that enslaved people "soon grow acquainted with a knot of blacks who, having eloped from their respective owners at different times, repose themselves here in ease and indolence".[259]

A belief spread that Lord Mansfield had ruled slavery was inconsistent with the British constitution, and people acted on this assumption.[260] In Britain and British America, enslaved people, opponents of slavery, judges and lawyers saw *Somerset* as abolishing slavery in Britain. This precedent was, in turn, applied to the British American colonies, leading to many enslaved people testing the legality of slavery in American colonial courts.[261]

Slavery was in part ended in England through the escape of enslaved people, with institutional elements such as the understanding of *Somerset*, English libertarianism and the rule of law (a not unproblematic concept in itself) providing a conducive climate to Black resistance. The British air became too pure for slavery mainly because of the brave acts of resistance by members of Britain's Black community. Douglas Lorimer, in reviewing the legal and political status of slaves in England both before and after *Somerset*, explains that:

> If slavery is looked at as a social rather than a legal institution, it is clear that the ending of slavery in England came about not from the decisions of the courts, but from the actions of the slaves. ... The slaves simply refused to be slaves, and fled from masters who insisted on treating them like chattels, and not like free domestic servants. [262]

Thinking that slavery was illegal and knowing that *Somerset* prohibited that deportation to British colonies where slavery was still permitted, enslaved people themselves resisted their owners' authority and quitted their

254 Drescher (2009) 103.
255 Long (1772) 20.
256 Long (1772) 49.
257 Long (1772) 50.
258 Long (1772) 60.
259 Long (1772) 47.
260 Wiecek (1974) 146.
261 Gerzina (1995) 131–2.
262 Lorimer (1984) 135.

households.[263] The abolition of slavery, both in a legal and social context, cannot be told without the actions of the slaves themselves. As long as everyone believed that enslaved people were now free, it served as de facto freedom. Gretchen Gerzina describes how in just three weeks Lord Mansfield's judgment passed into the apocryphal, with enslaved people all over England and even in America leaving their masters and striking out on their own.[264] Dana Rabin notes that in 1820, Prince Hoare credited the decision with securing the lives of Africans who "ceased to be hunted in our streets as a beast of prey ... [and now] slept in security and feared no dangers".[265]

I present these actions as paradigms of form-of-life. Regardless of the status of slavery in English law at the end of the eighteenth century, enslaved people were living their lives as if they were free. This is a tenuous freedom to be sure. Such actions did not mean that the enslaved people suddenly had legal protections or had a secure position in the social order. However, Agamben makes clear that form-of-life can only be found in unedifying places,[266] while appearing to docilely submit to control yet escaping the grasp of it.[267] These forms-of-life exercise lines of flight, freedom, dreams and possibilities of other worlds that represent a form of action and living which cannot be divided and captured by the anthropological machine that creates bare life.[268] Through this book I explore these lines of flight. By focusing on these lines, I argue, we can see enslaved people living their lives as a form.

Conclusion

I have set out to provide a detailed methodological background of Agamben's thought. This aims to underpin my arguments about the agency of enslaved people, and to support my argument that Agamben's thought can provide the basis for developing an alternative form of political agency. But this requires critiquing Agamben's Eurocentrism. We need to leave behind this European perspective. I have explored Agamben's philosophical archaeology and the important position of the paradigm within his thought and method. The paradigm is a historical phenomenon which serves two key purposes. First, paradigms illustrate the broader historical context produced by apparatuses that seek to control the living being and produce subjects and de-subjects. I explored how colonialism is a key but under-theorised paradigm that I will explore and develop in later chapters. Second, the positive paradigm. Form-of-life is a paradigmatic figure, and the enslaved person is

263 Fryer (2018) 207.
264 Gerzina (1995) 132.
265 Rabin (2011) 23–4; Hoare (1820) 93.
266 Agamben (2016) 227.
267 Agamben (2009b) 23.
268 Weheliye (2014) 2.

such a figure. The paradigm is akin to an example. I also explored the long tradition of the example, showing how the paradigm is both an *exemplar* and a model, as well as an *exemplum* that allows statements and practices to be gathered into a new problematic context. This is the paradigm (or example) of form-of-life.

Form-of-life is an example and a model. The actions and lives of enslaved people should not be viewed as resistance to a dominant politics, but as examples (in every sense) of a life lived as a form. This is how the notion of destituent potential should be understood. Destitution is not proposing a new or better system but involves dismantling and cancelling political institutions and modes of thought. Destitution is an ethical task. I argue that destituent forms of life can be enacted through a method I have termed 'hyper-hermeneutics'. This is a form of hermeneutics, and it is through hermeneutics that we can understand the potential within living beings to change modes of power. But the prefix 'hyper' is vitally important. The same term is used by Agamben in referring to a slave who has lived their life as a form.

Hyper-hermeneutics refers to the way lives, through paradigmatic (or exemplary) gestures, can affect slight shifts in modes of living that allow a form of life to become a form-of-life. The paradigmatic method can make a phenomenon (like form-of-life) intelligible through an exemplary act or model. This can deactivate machines and *dispositifs* of control without recourse to destructive violence or large-scale revolutions. As form-of-life is both an exemplum and a model (exemplar), dwelling together, its way of being is structured by reference to other forms-of-life and other exempla and models.

Finally, to illustrate, I showed how slavery in England was ended in part through the contributions of the escape of enslaved people living in England, and their gestures of resistance. These individuals acted as though the legal decision in *Somerset* had freed them. They acted as forms-of-life, living lives as forms, deactivating the application of the slave laws that had oppressed them. The next chapter considers the first of Agamben's interlocutors – Aristotle. Aristotle's writings on slavery have proved extremely influential to Western thought, especially in their transmission of the paradigm of colonialism. But even in the time of the Greek city states, and the original metropolis, we see enslaved people living their lives as destituent forms. It is this I wish to place emphasis on.

Reference List

Aarons, K (2020) 'Destitution and Creation: Agamben's Messianic Gesture', *Journal of Italian Philosophy*, 3, 51–89.

Achebe, C (2009) *Africa's Tarnished Name*, London: Penguin Books.

Achebe, C (2011) *The Education of a British-Protected Child*, London: Penguin Books.

Achinte, A A (2012) 'Epistemes "otras" ¿Epistemes Disruptivas?', *KULA. Antropólogos del Atlántico Sur*, 6, 22–34.

Adébísí, F (2023) *Decolonisation and Legal Knowledge: Reflections on Power and Possibility*, Bristol: Bristol University Press.

Agamben, G (1998) *Homo Sacer: Sovereign Power and Bare Life,* Heller-Roazen, D (trans.), Stanford: Stanford University Press.

Agamben, G (1999a) 'On Potentiality' in *Potentialities: Collected Essays in Philosophy*, Heller-Roazen, D (trans.), Stanford: Stanford University Press, 177-84.

Agamben, G (1999b) 'The Messiah and the Sovereign: The Problem of Law in Walter Benjamin' in *Potentialities: Collected Essays in Philosophy*, Heller-Roazen, D (trans.), Stanford: Stanford University Press, 160–74.

Agamben, G (1999c) 'The Thing Itself' in *Potentialities: Collected Essays in Philosophy*, Heller-Roazen, D (trans.), Stanford: Stanford University Press, 27–38.

Agamben, G (2000) *Means Without End: Notes on Politics*, Binetti, V and Casarino, C (trans.), Minneapolis: University of Minnesota Press.

Agamben, G (2001) 'Das unheilige Leben: ein Gespräch mit dem italienischen Philosophen Giorgio Agamben', interview with Hannah Leitgeb and Cornelia Vismann', *Literaturen*, 2, 16–21.

Agamben, G (2004) *The Open: Man and Animal*, Attell, K (trans.), Stanford: Stanford University Press.

Agamben, G (2005a) *State of Exception*, Attell, K (trans.), Chicago: University of Chicago Press.

Agamben, G (2005b) *The Time That Remains: A Commentary on the Letter to the Romans*, Dailey, P (trans.), Stanford: Stanford University Press.

Agamben, G (2006) 'Metropolis', Bove, A (trans.), *Generation Online*, https://www.generation-online.org/p/fpagamben4.htm.

Agamben, G (2007a) *Profanations*, Fort, J (trans.), Princeton: Princeton University Press.

Agamben, G (2007b) *The Coming Community*, Hardt, M (trans.), Minneapolis: University of Minnesota Press.

Agamben, G (2009a) *The Signature of All Things: On Method*, D'Isanto, L and Attell, K (trans.), New York: Zone Books.

Agamben, G (2009b) *What Is an Apparatus? and Other Essays*, Kishik, D and Pedatella, S (trans.), Stanford: Stanford University Press.

Agamben, G (2010) *Nudities*, Kishik, D and Pedatella, S (trans.), Stanford: Stanford University Press.

Agamben, G (2013) *The Highest Poverty: Monastic Rules and Form-of-Life*, Kotsko, A (trans.), Stanford: Stanford University Press.

Agamben, G (2014) 'What Is a Destituent Power?', *Environment and Planning D: Society and Space*, 32, 65–74.

Agamben, G (2016) *The Use of Bodies*, Kotsko, A (trans.), Stanford: Stanford University Press.

Agamben, G (2018a) *Karman: A Brief Treatise on Action, Guilt and Gesture*, Kotsko, A (trans.), Stanford: Stanford University Press.

Agamben, G (2018b) *Pulcinella: Or Entertainment for Kids in Four Scenes*, Attell, K (trans.), East Peoria, Seagull Books.

Agamben, G (2019) *Creation and Anarchy: The Work of Art and the Religion of Capitalism*, Kotsko, A (trans.), Stanford: Stanford University Press.

Agamben, G (2023) 'Destituent Potentiality and the Critique of Realization', *The South Atlantic Quarterly*, 112, 9–17.

Arendt, H (1966) *The Origins of Totalitarianism*, New York: Harcourt.

Aristotle (1984a) 'Prior Analytics' in *The Complete Works of Aristotle, Volume One*, Barnes, J (ed.), Princeton: Princeton University Press.

Aristotle (1984b) 'Rhetoric' in *The Complete Works of Aristotle, Volume Two*, Barnes, J (ed.), Princeton: Princeton University Press.

Armstrong, T (2004) 'Slavery, Insurance, and Sacrifice in the Black Atlantic' in Klein, B and Mackenthun, G (eds.), *Sea Changes: Historicizing the Ocean*, New York: Routledge, 167–85.

Basevich, E (2012) 'Foucauldian Resonances: Agamben on Race, Citizenship, and the Modern State', *Sofia Philosophical Review*, 6, 61–79.

Benson, H (2015) *Clitophon's Challenge: Dialectic in Plato's Meno, Phaedo, and Republic*, Oxford: Oxford University Press.

Bikundo, E (2022) 'Follow Your Leader – I Prefer Not to: Slavery, Giorgio Agamben and Herman Melville', *Law, Culture and the Humanities*, 18, 4–19.

Bolt Rasmussen, M (2023) 'An Affirmation That Is Entirely Other', *The South Atlantic Quarterly*, 122, 19–31.

Brophy, S (2021) 'A Politics Like No Other: Agamben, Fanon, and the Colonial Fracture' in Norris, M and Dickinson, C (eds.), *Agamben and the Existentialists*, Edinburgh: Edinburgh University Press, 191–211.

Bush, J (1993) 'Free to Enslave: The Foundations of Colonial American Slave Law', *Yale Journal of Law & the Humanities*, 5, 417–70.

Césaire, A (1973) *Discourse on Colonialism*, New York: Monthly Review Press.

Clastres, P (1989) *Society Against the State: Essays in Political Anthropology*, Hurley, R and Stein, A (trans.), New York: Zone Books.

Conrad, J (1972) *Heart of Darkness*, New York: Norton.

Cugoano, O (1999) *Thoughts and Sentiments on the Evil of Slavery*, London: Penguin.

Davies, K (1957) *The Royal African Company*, London: Longmans, Green.

Davis, D B (1999) *The Problem of Slavery in the Age of Revolution, 1770–1823*, Oxford: Oxford University Press.

de Castro, E V (2010) 'The Untimely, Again' in Clastres, P, *Archeology of Violence*, Los Angeles: Semiotext(e), 9–51.

de la Durantaye, L (2009) 'The Paradigm of Colonialism' in Bignall, S and Svirsky, M (eds.), *Agamben and Colonialism*, Edinburgh: Edinburgh University Press, 229–38.

DeCaroli, S (2020) 'That Which Is Born Generates Its Own Use. Giorgio Agamben and Karma', *Etica & Politica / Ethics & Politics*, 22, 247–73.

Drescher, S (1989) 'Manumission in a Society without Slave Law: Eighteenth Century England', *Slavery & Abolition*, 10, 85–101.

Drescher, S (2009) *Abolition: A History of Slavery and Antislavery*, Cambridge: Cambridge University Press.

Du Bois, W E B (1965) *The World and Africa: An Inquiry into the Part Which Africa Has Played in World History*, New York: International Publishers.

Fanon, F (1970) *Black Skin, White Masks*, Markmann, C (trans.), London: Paladin.

Fanon, F (2005) *The Wretched of the Earth*, Farrington, C (trans.), New York: Grove Press.
Farley, A P (2004) 'Perfecting Slavery', *Loyola University Chicago Law Journal*, 36, 225–55.
Fleming, P (2015) 'Beside Oneself: Parapraxis as a Paradigm of Everyday Life (Freud)' in Lowrie, M and Lüdemann, S (eds.), *Exemplarity and Singularity: Thinking Through Particulars in Philosophy, Literature, and Law*, London and New York: Routledge, 192–202.
Foucault, M (2003) *Society Must Be Defended, Lectures at the Collège de France, 1975–76*, Macey, D (trans.), London: Penguin Books.
Friere, P (1993) *Pedagogy of the Oppressed*, London: Penguin Books.
Frost, T (2014) 'Thinking Relationality in Agamben and Levinas', *Griffith Law Review*, 23, 210–31.
Frost, T (2021) *Law, Relationality and the Ethical Life: Agamben and Levinas*, Abingdon: Routledge.
Fryer, P (2018) *Staying Power: The History of Black People in Britain*, London: Pluto Press.
Fusco, G-G (2023) *Form of Life: Agamben and the Destitution of Rules*, Edinburgh: Edinburgh University Press.
Gerzina, G (1995) *Black London: Life Before Emancipation*, Hanover: Dartmouth College Library.
Gilmore, R (2007) *Golden Gulag: Prisons, Surplus, Crisis, and Opposition in Globalizing California*, Berkeley: University of California Press.
Gilroy, P (1993) *The Black Atlantic: Modernity and Double Consciousness*, London: Verso.
Glancy, J (2020) 'On Agamben's Slave without Slavery', *Diacritics*, 38, 4–27.
Grosfoguel, R (2016) 'What Is Racism?', *Journal of World—Systems Research*, 22, 9–15.
Hammond, D and Jablow, A (1992) *The Africa That Never Was: Four Centuries of British Writing about Africa*, Prospect Heights: Waveland Press.
Hartman, S (2008) 'Venus in Two Acts', *Small Axe*, 12, 1–14.
Heidegger, M (1962) *Being and Time*, Macquarrie, J and Robinson, E (trans.), New York: Harper Row.
Hoare, P (1820) *Memoirs of Granville Sharp*, London: Henry Colburn.
Holsey, B (2008) *Routes of Remembrance: Refashioning the Slave Trade in Ghana*, Chicago: University of Chicago Press.
Invisible Committee (2017) *Now*, Hurley, R (trans.), Los Angeles: Semiotext(e).
Jackson, Z (2013) 'Animal: New Directions in the Theorisation of Race and Post-Humanism', *Feminist Studies*, 39, 669–85.
Kojève, A (1969) *Introduction to the Reading of Hegel: Lectures on the Phenomenology of Spirit*, Nichols Jr, J (trans.), Ithaca: Cornell University Press.
Kojève, A (1979) *Introduction à la lecture de Hegel*, Paris: Gallimard.
Koram, K (2022) '"Satan Is Black" – Frantz Fanon's Juridico-Theology of Racialisation and Damnation', *Law, Culture and the Humanities*, 18, 94–113.
Langlands, R (2015) 'Roman Exemplarity: Mediating between General and Particular', in Lowrie, M and Lüdemann, S (eds.), *Exemplarity and Singularity:*

Thinking Through Particulars in Philosophy, Literature, and Law, London and New York: Routledge, 68–80.

Levi, P (1988) *The Drowned and Saved*, London: Abacus.

Long, E (1772) *Candid Reflections Upon the Judgement Lately Awarded by the Court of King's Bench ... on What Is Commonly Called the Negroe-Cause, by a Planter ...*, London: T Lowndes.

Lorimer, D (1984) 'Black Slaves and English Liberty: A Re-examination of Racial Slavery', *Immigrants & Minorities: Historical Studies in Ethnicity, Migration and Diaspora*, 3, 121–150.

Lowrie, M and Lüdemann, S (2015) 'Introduction' in Lowrie, M and Lüdemann, S (eds.), *Exemplarity and Singularity: Thinking Through Particulars in Philosophy, Literature, and Law*, London and New York: Routledge, 1–15.

Maldonado-Torres, N (2007) 'On the Coloniality of Bring: Contributions to the Development of a Concept', *Cultural Studies*, 21, 240–70.

Mawani, R (2018) *Across Oceans of Law: The* Komagata Maru *and Jurisdiction in the Time of Empire*, Durham and London: Duke University Press.

Mawani, R (2022) 'The Ship, The Slave, The Legal Person', *Studies in Law, Politics and Society*, 87B, 19–42.

Mbembé, A (2003) 'Necropolitics', *Public Culture*, 15, 11–40.

Mbembé, A (2005) 'Faces of Freedom: Jewish and Black Experiences', *Interventions*, 7, 293–98.

Mbembé, A (2017) *Critique of Black Reason*, Dubois, L (trans.), Durham: Duke University Press.

Moten, F (2003) *In the Break: The Aesthetics of the Black Radical Tradition*, Minneapolis: University of Minnesota Press.

Mtubani V C D (1981) 'African Slaves and English Law', *Pula: Botswana Journal of African Studies*, 3, 71–75.

NourbeSe Philip, M (2008) *Zong!*, Toronto: The Mercury Press.

Oldham, J (1988) 'New Light on Mansfield and Slavery', *Journal of British Studies*, 27, 45–68.

Oldham, J (2007) 'Insurance Litigation Involving the *Zong* and Other British Slave Ships, 1780–1807', *Journal of Legal History*, 28, 299–318.

Olney, J (1984) ''I Was Born': Slave Narratives, Their Status as Autobiography and as Literature', *Callaloo*, 20, 46–73.

Olusoga, D (2016) *Black and British: A Forgotten History*, London: Pan Macmillan.

Patterson, O (1982) *Slavery and Social Death: A Comparative Study*, Cambridge: Harvard University Press.

Plato (2005) 'Republic' in *The Collected Dialogues, Including the Letters*, Hamilton, E and Cairns, H (eds.), Princeton: Princeton University Press.

Prozorov, S (2010) 'Why Giorgio Agamben Is an Optimist', *Philosophy and Social Criticism*, 36, 1053–73.

Prozorov, S (2014) *Agamben and Politics: A Critical Introduction*, Edinburgh: Edinburgh University Press.

Quijano, A (2007) 'Coloniality and Modernity/Rationality', *Cultural Studies*, 21, 168–78.

Rabin, D (2011) ''In a Country of Liberty?': Slavery, Villeinage and the Making of Whiteness in the Somerset Case (1772)', *History Workshop Journal*, 72, 5–29.

Rae, G (2018) 'Agency and Will in Agamben's Coming Politics', *Philosophy & Social Criticism*, 44, 978–96.
Raulff, U and Agamben, G (2004) 'An Interview with Giorgio Agamben', *German Law Journal*, 5, 609–14.
Rediker, M (2007) *The Slave Ship: A Human History*, New York: W W Norton.
Robinson, C (2021) *Black Marxism: The Making of the Black Radical Tradition*, London: Penguin Books.
Roller, M (2004) 'Exemplarity in Roman Culture: The Cases of Horatius Cocles and Cloelia', *Classical Philology*, 99, 1–56.
Rupprecht, A (2008) ''A Limited Sort of Property': History, Memory and the Slave Ship *Zong*', *Slavery & Abolition*, 29, 265–77.
Said, E (1978) *Orientalism*, New York: Random House.
Shilliam, R (2012) 'Forget English Freedom, Remember Atlantic Slavery: Common Law, Commercial Law and the Significance of Slavery for Classical Political Economy', *New Political Economy*, 17, 591–609.
Sorentino, S-M (2019) 'Natural Slavery, Real Abstraction, and the Virtuality of Anti-Blackness', *Theory & Event*, 22, 630–73.
Speed, D (1995) 'The Spiritual Dimension in Medieval Exempla' in Griffith, M and Tulip, J (eds.), *Religion, Literature and the Arts Project: Conference Proceedings of the Australian International Conference 1995*, Sydney: Australian Catholic University, 312–19.
Stovall, T (2022) *White Freedom: The Racial History of an Idea*, Princeton: Princeton University Press.
Tarì, M (2021) *There Is No Unhappy Revolution: The Communism of Destitution*, Richard Braude (trans.), Brooklyn: Common Notions.
Tubach, F (1962) 'Exempla in the Decline', *Traditio*, 18, 407–17.
van Cleve, G (2006) '*Somerset's Case* and Its Antecedents in Imperial Perspective', *Law and History Review*, 24, 601–45.
Verges, F (2021) *A Decolonial Feminism*, Bohrer, A (trans.), London: Pluto Press.
Walvin, J (2013) *Crossings: Africa, the Americas, and the Atlantic Slave Trade*, London: Reaktion Books.
Walvin, J (2019) *The Zong: A Massacre, the Law and the End of Slavery*, New Haven: Yale University Press.
Watkin, W (2013) *Agamben and Indifference: A Critical Overview*, London and New York: Rowman & Littlefield.
Weheliye, A (2014) *Habeas Viscus: Racializing Assemblages, Biopolitics, and Black Feminist Theories of the Human*, Durham: Duke University Press.
Wiecek, W (1974) '*Somerset*: Lord Mansfield and the Legitimacy of Slavery in the Anglo-American World', *The University of Chicago Law Review*, 42, 86–126.
Wilderson III, F (2010) *Red, White & Black: Cinema and the Structure of US Antagonisms*, Durham: Duke University Press.
Youngquist, P (2011) 'The Mothership Connection', *Cultural Critique*, 77, 1–23.

Chapter 3

Aristotle's slave

Introduction

The following three chapters focus on key interlocutors for Agamben's philosophy: Aristotle, St Paul and G W F Hegel. I interrogate how each considered slavery and the enslaved person in their work, and also how they influenced Agamben's thought. They bequeathed certain ideas of political belonging and freedom to Western European legal and political philosophy. Despite this, the records of lives of enslaved people, as incomplete as they are, are not adequately addressed by Aristotle, Paul and Hegel. No enslaved person is without agency. Resistance to slavery is ubiquitous, and enslaved people have been living their lives as a form for as long as Western thought has been using them to define freedom.

This chapter focuses on Aristotle's theory of slavery. I consider how Aristotle, like Agamben, created an anthropological machine which determined which human beings deserved to partake in the political life of the *polis*. This machine serves to highlight features in Aristotle's thought which are crucial to subsequent interpretations of slavery. The enslaved person sits at the threshold between freedom and unfreedom. Aristotle distinguished between legal slavery and natural slavery. Legal slaves are those who, by chance, happen to be legally slaves. Natural slaves (which did not exist but were an invention by Aristotle) are those who are, by nature, fitted for slavery.

This is transmitted to Western thought – there exist inhuman beings who can be enslaved, and free men and citizens who can never be enslaved. I then go on to consider Aristotle's importance for slavery in the contemporary world. I connect Aristotle's writings to coloniality, specifically explaining how he provided the philosophical defence for early modern chattel slavery, and race becoming an epistemology of domination. This provides context for discussing Agamben's interpretation of Aristotle in respect of the idea of 'use'.

I draw a contrast between the position of the enslaved in Aristotle's philosophical works, and the position of the enslaved in the Greek city states. This is explored through Agamben's reading of Aristotle and the conception of

DOI: 10.4324/9781003303534-4

the enslaved person as an 'animate instrument'. The use of the body of the enslaved opens the possibility of a different form of being human. The legal codification of slavery transforms something free – the common and reciprocal use of bodies – into an extreme form of brutal exploitation. However, Agamben's reading of Aristotle omits both several key features of his conception of slavery, and the actual operation of slavery in the Greek city states.

Finally, this chapter considers how no enslaved person can be considered without a voice. Aristotle points to this in admitting the realities of agency and resistance. This chapter draws on historical and legal sources on slavery in the Greek city states, showing the 'clean' distinctions on which Aristotle drew do not reflect the reality. The status of the enslaved is much more indeterminate than Aristotle gives credit for, and the role of passive and active resistance by the enslaved is more endemic than Aristotle intimates. It is in these actions that we may see the germ of what Agamben terms the use of bodies.

Aristotle's slave

Aristotle's political community is modelled on the free man. The *polis* requires a definition of humanity. Political life is only available for those recognised as human beings.[1] Man is a political animal, a "*polis*-creature".[2] Other forms of life (like the enslaved person) are excluded.[3] Aristotle himself embodied such a form of life. He was living in Athens not as a free man, but as a resident alien, an identity positioned between citizen and enslaved.[4] There was enough ambiguity in the status of slavery that actions, beliefs and institutions in ancient Greece (and Rome) were all impacted by the potential that someone involved may be enslaved.[5] Enslaved people were excluded from the *polis* through being depoliticised. Slavery was as natural as other relationships of superior and inferior, such as soul over body and husband over wife.[6] The 're-politicisation' of slavery occurs through the demand for more inclusion. Tim Christiaens notes that philosophy's response has been to construe new human vocations as alternatives to Aristotle's *polis* to include more people into the political community.[7]

Who is recognised as human and has a right to belong in the *polis* is produced by an anthropological machine. Christiaens argues that this machine imposes a division between humans and animals based on an arbitrary

1 Christiaens (2018) 240–1; Aristotle (1984d) 1252b29–1253a5.
2 Millett (2007) 181.
3 Agamben (2016) 20.
4 Dietz (2012) 279.
5 Finley (1998) 133, 166.
6 Campbell (1974) 284.
7 Christiaens (2018) 240.

selection of 'human' qualities. Sustaining one's humanity requires actualising those human qualities, and the suspension of animality.[8] These elements comprise Aristotle's anthropological machine. In addition to this, the machine in Agamben also involves the suspension of both animal and human potentialities in bare life,[9] and a form-of-life lived without imposed vocations which can deactivate the machine.[10]

In terms of the human-animal division, Aristotle sees human beings as exercising rational discourse, deliberating on benefits and harms, justice and injustice.[11] Human beings pursue higher ends, namely the good life, not mere survival. Not everyone can achieve Aristotle's good life, and the institution of slavery is needed to guarantee the possibility of a good life of virtue for free men.[12] Aristotle's theory of slavery describes a world where slave labour is an essential part of the economy.[13] Greek city states placed slave labour surreptitiously into all areas of production, making slavery appear 'natural'.[14] Slavery was of benefit to the master. Enslaved people performed menial work, allowing the master to dwell on higher pursuits.[15] Slavery, to Aristotle, was good for the enslaved as they lacked the necessary intellectual capacity to make decisions and exercise forethought for themselves.[16]

In belonging to another, enslaved people were less than fully human,[17] even though they remained part of the household, like women.[18] These figures served free men who were trying to attain the good life. The *polis* depended on the enslaved and on women. This gendered aspect of Aristotle is not focused on by Agamben in his commentary. Political philosophy, Aristotle implies, *needed* slavery.[19] The use of the 'slave' in Agamben therefore risks repeating the same gendered and exclusive nature of the *polis* and of political life. This relationship involves an element of exploitation, by which the free man can achieve a political life only through the use and direction of another who is not accorded the same privilege. But the difference between human and animal is one of degree. For Aristotle, a good life involves performing one's humanity well.[20] Christiaens explains that the contemplative life, not political life, is the highest fulfilment of humanity, but this is a solitary

8 Christiaens (2018) 241.
9 Agamben (2004) 37–8.
10 Christiaens (2018) 243; Agamben (2016) 203.
11 Christiaens (2018) 245; Aristotle (1984d) 1253a7–16.
12 Brace (2018) 19–20; Agamben (2016) 21; Aristotle (1984a) 1185a26–35.
13 Bull (1998) 124.
14 Thomson (1955) 204.
15 Campbell (1974) 285.
16 Aristotle (1984d) 1255b30.
17 Rosivach (1999) 146.
18 Ehrenberg (1969) 10; Schofield (1999) 110.
19 Sorentino (2019) 644.
20 Christiaens (2018) 246; Aristotle (1984b) 1097b24–30.

affair.[21] Practical understanding (*phronēsis*) underpins Aristotle's political anthropology and his discussion of slavery.[22] Women, children, the enslaved and animals are a part of the *polis* as a reproductive or social community, but they are not a political community.[23]

Christiaens notes that Aristotle does not provide a clear theory of the passage from animal voice to human reason. The good life is acquired through habitual practice. For Aristotle habit, or *hexis*, means a steady disposition to act acquired through repeated behaviour.[24] *Hexis* is a potentiality that people 'have'. Habit must be cultivated through the repeated correct use of rational choice. A *hexis* is also established by consistently making choices. Good choices foster good habits, but bad choices foster bad habits. Free men, as members of the *polis*, were capable of determining the direction of their own lives.[25] Christiaens explains that to cultivate good habit choices based on reason are favoured over behaviour motivated by sensations.[26] Such behaviour has no place in the *polis* and is a form of animality that is included in the human community and requires vigilance against it becoming dominant.[27]

Malcolm Bull identified that Aristotle highlighted two features of slavery central to its subsequent justifications.[28] The first was an assumption that the enslaved person had two identities. One was 'slave' and the other 'human being'. The first identity functioned like a soulless body; the second had a soul, but not the same soul as a free man. The second was that the humanity of the master took the place of the humanity of the enslaved person. The enslaved person became governed by the soul of the master,[29] an animated instrument, their potentialities used by others.[30] These two features are not reconcilable.

Aristotle does not hit upon a stable substance underpinning the idea of the 'slave' – nature is politically amenable.[31] Because of its in-between position on the 'threshold', slavery in Aristotle haunts the Greek *polis*, making the Greek citizen "*a two-faced being, the bearer*" of enslavement to reason and a political being among equals.[32] This haunting is passed down to future conceptions of freedom. It also effaces the realities of slavery in Aristotle's world.

21 Christiaens (2018) 246; Aristotle (1984b) 1177a11–17.
22 Christiaens (2018) 246; Aristotle (1984b) 1141b23–29.
23 Nyquist (2013) 49.
24 Christiaens (2018) 247.
25 Schofield (1999) 103; Walsh (1997) 499.
26 Christiaens (2018) 247–8; Aristotle (1984b) 1095b19–22.
27 Christiaens (2018) 248.
28 Bull (1998) 124.
29 Bull (1998) 125; Monoson (2011) 134.
30 Campbell (1974) 284; Aristotle (1984d) 1254b17–23.
31 Sorentino (2019) 639; Aristotle (1984d) 1254a13.
32 Agamben (1998) 125; Ziarek (2008) 93–4.

Legal slavery and natural slavery are distinct. Bull explains that for Aristotle, legal slavery applies to those who are by chance enslaved by law.[33] Natural slaves are those who are slaves *by nature*, and who are capable of belonging to another.[34] The only 'true' slaves are natural slaves. A citizen who is enslaved ought to be freed; a natural slave who is legally free should be enslaved.[35] Natural slaves have the same traits that distinguish humans from animals – speech and reason. But for natural slaves their reasoning faculty is deficient. The slave cannot conduct deliberation leading to practical wisdom.[36] Laura Brace reads Aristotle's theory of 'natural' slavery as tracing the way freedom, belonging and labour define what it means not to be enslaved.[37] Brace notes that the idea of a natural slave places emphasis on the deficiencies of the enslaved person, and describes what 'slavishness' is, rather than trying to explain what it means to compel someone to become your property.[38]

Bull explores how Aristotle's division is reinforced through his writing on the soul. The soul commands the body despotically. Natural slaves have incomplete souls.[39] The relationship between master and slave depends on the relationship between soul and body. The souls of slaves cannot master their bodies. Therefore, their bodies can be made subject to the souls of those persons capable of such mastery.[40] But for Aristotle, despotic rule was not exploitative. The enslaved person's economic-domestic subordination to bodily necessity serves as the threshold for politics.[41]

For Bull, Aristotle did not answer how his theory of slavery could be correlated with his theory of the soul. He never resolved how the incomplete soul of the enslaved person and the complete soul of the master are related to the singular body of the enslaved. Bull posits that the 'obvious answer' is that the master's soul performs only those functions the enslaved person's soul cannot. But Aristotle ruled out this division of labour, arguing for the unity of the soul.[42] Aristotle's theory of slavery therefore undermines the theory of the soul on which the theory of slavery depends.[43]

33 Bull (1998) 99.
34 Aristotle (1984d) 1254b2.
35 Bull (1998) 100.
36 Monoson (2011) 135.
37 Brace (2018) 19.
38 Brace (2018) 25.
39 Bull (1998) 100.
40 Bull (1998) 110–11; Aristotle (1984d) 1254b15–22.
41 Sorentino (2019) 634; Aristotle (1984d) 1254a12–14.
42 Bull (1998) 103; Aristotle (1984c) 412a16–28, 414a25–27.
43 Bull (1998) 103.

Aristotle, coloniality and the future

There is a habit of using the ancient world as a springboard for a larger political polemic.[44] This certainly occurred in relation to Aristotle's identification of the 'good life'. de Boer identifies that it was Aristotle who started a tradition that defined the master as a male human being, enabled by the *polis* to claim his possessions and develop his humanity.[45] Because of this tradition, Aristotle's theory of slavery, endowed with paternal authority and a 'rational' basis in 'nature', penetrated the thinking of the European Renaissance, medieval scholasticism, and even eighteenth-century rationalism, influencing natural right philosophers.[46] Opponents of slavery also turned to Aristotle's *Politics* when they sought to criticise the institution.[47]

How could Aristotle be identified with 'racial' slavery? Aristotle's view was not representative of the worldview of the ancients. It was not possible to definitively demonstrate those who were justly enslaved because there was no physical hallmark by which to spot the inferior being of enslaved people, and no operable concept of race (in the way we understand it today).[48] In contrast, freedom for individuals in the world of the Atlantic slave trade carried an external sign of their prior enslavement in the way they were racialised, with negative political and social consequences. But ancient freedmen melted into the population within one or two generations.[49]

Mavis Campbell states that most rational and social justifications of unequal privilege are afterthoughts.[50] Aristotle's 'afterthoughts' were composed at a time of unprecedented imperial expansion in and beyond the Hellenic world, including the conquests of Alexander the Great.[51] These factors made enslaved people so plentiful and cheap that almost every Greek citizen could afford to own enslaved people and they were almost entirely foreigners, or barbarians. Because of this, Aristotle accepted that most enslaved people in his own society were natural slaves.[52] Aristotle positions high-spirited and thoughtful Hellenics between two sorts of barbarians, the unsociable and unintelligent Europeans, and the docile and servile Asians.[53] There is an ethnic division in operation in Aristotle, even if it does not fit within modern conceptions of 'race'. Athenian slaves were born outside Greece or had ancestors born outside Greece. They were given names that marked them

44 Finley (1998) 131.
45 de Boer (2023) 237.
46 Campbell (1974) 284.
47 Bull (1998) 124.
48 Campbell (1974) 289; Aristotle (1984d) 1254b27–34.
49 Finley (1998) 165.
50 Campbell (1974) 290.
51 Dietz (2012) 275.
52 Schofield (1999) 133.
53 Sorentino (2019) 637, quoting Aristotle (1984d) 1285a20–22.

as outsiders which became ethnic labels used to mark them as 'slave'.[54] Not speaking Greek was a sign of a barbarian's lack of reason.[55] They were also labelled as both highly masculinised, effeminate, savage and refined, which was used to emphasise the Greek approach of moderation against extremes.[56]

In this respect, Aristotle's thought reflects the paradigm of colonialism. Slavery, operating in the *dispositif* of the Greek city state, produced subjects (free men) and also de-subjects (enslaved persons). This colonialism controlled, subjected and disciplined those bodies subjected to colonial power.[57] Campbell claims that the Greeks were convinced their achievements were due to some superior inherent virtues, leading to a view developing that enslaving 'barbarians' was a privilege and a duty. Greek culture would bring enlightenment to the barbarians. The attempt to systematise the philosophy of the aristocracy of race, or Greek superiority over others, in technical philosophical terms, was made by Aristotle in his *Politics*.[58]

Aristotle became a chief source in defending the Atlantic slave trade.[59] Thinkers parroted the way Aristotle made subjects inferior, but modernity invented entirely new subjects: Africa, the New World and the Orient.[60] Aristotle's work was so authoritative in sixteenth and seventeenth century Spain that any attack on him was seen as a dangerous heresy.[61] The early Spanish Catholic Bishops, when undecided about the status of 'the native Indians' of the New World, did not hesitate to apply the theory of the natural slave to them.[62] Aristotle's defence of slavery was the basis for the Valladolid debate on the ethics of slavery, which took place in 1550–1551.[63] Held between Bartolomé de Las Casas and Juan Ginés de Sepúlveda (and their allies), the debate attempted to codify the status of Indigenous Americans.[64] Were they humans and of equal status with Europeans, or were they the sort of sub-humans classified by Aristotle as natural slaves? Las Casas saw Aristotle as a gentile burning in Hell whose doctrine did not need to be followed.[65] Sepúlveda translated Aristotle into Latin and he saw the Indians as following the Aristotelian model as inferior slaves.[66] He argued that indigenous people were subhuman because they did not dress, eat or behave like

54 Brace (2018) 32; Rosivach (1999) 129.
55 Brace (2018) 32; Hall (1989) 122–3.
56 Hall (1989) 127–8.
57 de la Durantaye (2012) 237.
58 Campbell (1974) 290.
59 Campbell (1974) 283.
60 Robinson (2001) 330.
61 Campbell (1974) 286; Hanke (1959) 16, 30, 129–130.
62 Campbell (1974) 285; Hanke (1959) 1.
63 LaGrandeur (2020) 99.
64 Brunstetter and Zartner (2011) 733–752.
65 Campbell (1974) 86.
66 Hanke (1959) 44–5.

Europeans and, therefore, were natural slaves to their Spanish conquerors.[67] Las Casas opposed these views, but in his opposition, he applied the Aristotelian model to 'prove' indigenous people were rational beings, satisfying Aristotle's requirements for the 'good life'.[68] In referring to Aristotle, Las Casas strengthened the authority of Aristotle. Sepúlveda's views ultimately prevailed.[69]

Moreover, Las Casas and Sepúlveda conducted their debate as if Black slavery did not exist, even though it was well established in the New World.[70] But Europeans had no moral doubts in seeing Black Africans as inferior beings who conformed to Aristotle's natural slave.[71] Campbell explains that Hugo Grotius was influenced by Aristotle's writings on slavery, and he influenced pro-slavery thought in the Americas. Grotius saw slavery, with Aristotle, as harmonious with natural justice.[72] In colonial Virginia, popular sentiment did not demand the subjection of indigenous peoples, unlike Black Africans.[73] Campbell reads Aristotle as having lost some pre-eminence during the last quarter of the seventeenth century and had a mixed reception in the eighteenth century, but regained support in the nineteenth century, and was used to prove the 'natural inferiority' of the Black African.[74] In the 1850s, Aristotle influenced the school of biological science in the American South which sought to prove "Negro inferiority".[75] Aristotle's theory of slavery found itself pinioned to race and underpinned the logics of coloniality.

Connected to the notion of an enslaved person as an animate instrument to be used by the master are concerns about artificial intelligence. But this is in no way a modern phenomenon. The word 'robot' derived from the Czech *robota*, meaning forced labour.[76] It entered universal knowledge following Karel Capek's 1921 play, *R.U.R. (Rossum's Universal Robots)*. But robots and artificial intelligence existed well before they could be realised, and they have always had a close relationship to the figure of the slave. Robots were created to perform the same jobs as enslaved people – dirty, dangerous and monotonous jobs – which would free their owners to pursue more comfortable pursuits, just as Aristotle had explained.[77] The field of cybernetics was

67 de Las Casas (1583) Appendix; LaGrandeur (2020) 100.
68 Hanke (1959) 173.
69 Campbell (1974) 286.
70 Campbell (1974) 287.
71 Robinson (1971) 18–19.
72 Campbell (1974) 294.
73 Campbell (1974) 287; Williams (1994) 8–9.
74 Campbell (1974) 289.
75 Campbell (1974) 297.
76 Shaw (1998) 25.
77 LaGrandeur (2011) 232.

designed to ensure a position of human mastery and control in a chaotic world following World War Two.[78]

Robots function in classical Greek literature as a utopian substitute for slavery or other forms of bound labour; and the failure of Hellenistic automata to realise this utopia illustrates some basic constraints on the power of technology to disturb social institutions in the ancient world.[79] Adrienne Mayor's work has shown how in the Homeric epics we see 'intelligent' machines – a pair of silver and gold watchdogs which guard the palace of Alcinous with their own intelligent minds,[80] and the ships that take Odysseus home to Ithaca could "navigate by thought".[81] Mayor explains that the Homeric Gods do not keep enslaved people but are not expected to do their own work, so they have automatic gates for their citadel.[82] The metalworking god Hephaestus has an automated machine which controls the heat of his furnace. These bellows operate at Hephaestus's command and vary their work depending on his instructions and desires.[83]

Homer's accounts were influential. Plato's Socrates explicitly likens the automata created by Hephaestus in ancient myth to enslaved people: both will run away unless chained up.[84] Plato's slave is aligned with the automaton. Aristotle draws an explicit connection between Homer's automata and real-world enslaved people. Martin Devecka points to a passage of Aristotle's *Politics* that has been remarked upon by many, including Marx, who saw it as representing the limit of ancient thought on industrial applications of technology:

> For if every instrument could accomplish its own work, obeying or anticipating the will of others, like … the tripods of Hephaestus, which, says the poet, "of their own accord entered the assembly of the Gods"; if, in like manner, the shuttle would weave and the plectrum touch the lyre, chief workmen would not want servants, nor masters slaves.[85]

This is Aristotle's coverage of the promise and peril of artificial and intelligent servants.[86] Aristotle can conceive of a system where manual labour (enslaved people) come together with artificial servants to do useful work, both acting as different types of instruments, using the example of a ship:

78 Lenoir (2002) 210.
79 Devecka (2013) 52.
80 Mayor (2018) 143–4; Homer (2003) 7.91–7.94.
81 Mayor (2018) 151; Homer (2003) 8.556.
82 Mayor (2018) 145; Homer (1992) 5.748–5.749; 8.393.
83 Mayor (2018) 151–2; Homer (1992) 18.469; 18.473.
84 Plato (2005a) 97d–98a.
85 Devecka (2013) 54-55; Aristotle (1984d) 1253b38-1254a1.
86 LaGrandeur (2011) 235.

> Now instruments are of various sorts; some are living, others lifeless; in the rudder, the pilot of the ship has a lifeless, in the look-out man, a living instrument; for in the arts the servant is a kind of instrument. Thus, too, a possession is an instrument for maintaining life. And so, in the arrangement of the family, a slave is a living possession, and property a number of such instruments; and the servant is himself an instrument for instruments.[87]

All instruments, animate and inanimate, human and machine, are extensions of the master, and part of his bodily frame.[88] The problem with artificial slaves is the impulse to create servants more powerful than oneself. This can lead the individual to be absorbed or disappear into those systems.[89]

Aristotle takes the master-slave relationship and crafts an imaginary object out of it, a substitute slave, a thing that could replace a slave.[90] Only when robots (to borrow the term) eliminate the need for slave *and* free labour could Greek slavery be ended, but Aristotle's preference appears to be the replacement of human slaves.[91] Enslaved people can rebel and be unpredictable.[92] But those who exploit intelligent chattels embrace a system in which the same beings have the potential to become a threat to the owners' own humanity, power and autonomy. The existence of human automata is interpreted for its effects on 'us' rather than in terms of what the chattels know, feel and experience.[93] These themes and concerns have persisted in the West from antiquity to modernity.[94]

Agamben on Aristotle's slave

Aristotle assumed the exclusion of natural slaves before the question of the good life could be considered.[95] Christiaens explains that if human life is predicated on the capacity to actualise a specific human vocation, there will always be people failing to do so, who will be marked as bare life.[96] This implies that form-of-life does not result from the enactment of a specific vocation but in the withdrawal from any calling.[97] Christiaens notes that

87 Devecka (2013) 60–1; Aristotle (1984d) 1253b28–34.
88 Aristotle (1984d) 1255b11–12.
89 LaGrandeur (2011) 234.
90 Devecka (2013) 62.
91 Devecka (2013) 55; Aristotle (1984d) 1253b15–1254a10.
92 LaGrandeur (2011) 236–7.
93 Shaw (1998) 43.
94 LaGrandeur (2011) 242; Mayor (2018).
95 Christiaens (2018) 255.
96 Christiaens (2018) 262.
97 Christiaens (2018) 252; Agamben (2016) 22.

this withdrawal is not necessarily a violent rendering impotential of a human vocation, but a way of subverting the anthropological machine.[98]

Agamben argues that the enslaved is "a part (of the body) of the master, in the 'organic' and not simply instrumental sense of the term".[99] While masters do not belong to the enslaved people – they are more than 'just' masters – the identity of the enslaved is solely defined by their position as slave.[100] For this reason, by putting in use his own body, the enslaved is used by the master, and in using the body of the enslaved, the master is using his own body.[101] The enslaved is part of the equipment of the household at the disposal of the master. But this is an unproductive instrument. It produces nothing when put to work but the use of the body.[102] The use of the body must be understood in a practical sense, similar to that of a bed or clothing. The dimension of use is independent of an end.[103]

In the use of the body of the enslaved, the traditional categories used to think of human life have been shuffled.[104] Slavery in Greek antiquity is an exemplar of the human condition.[105] Fusco contends that for Agamben this is not a matter of imagining the enslaved happy. He sees Agamben's reading of slavery as not having any overlaps with modern slavery. Instead, such analysis allegorically tries to highlight thought formations that could help us to imagine a politics to come.[106] Similarly for Christiaens, the phenomenon of slavery provides an example from which people today can learn. The goal is not to repeat or imitate enslaved life, but to take it as proof of humankind's potentiality to cultivate a multitude of vocations.[107]

Christiaens reads Agamben as seeing enslaved people as human, but also suspending the rules of anthropogenesis, as they have the potential for leading a good life but are constitutively incapable of enacting it.[108] Slaves are nothing but the bare potential for humanity.[109] The use of the body of the enslaved person in no way exhausts their potential for other identities. On Christiaens' account, for Agamben they are a void of pure potentiality left when all positive characteristics are subtracted.[110] This means that, for Christiaens, Aristotle's writings on slavery shows us that there is a potential

98 Christiaens (2018) 254–5.
99 Agamben (2016) 13.
100 Vlassopoulos (2021) 100.
101 Agamben (2016) 14.
102 Aristotle (1984d) 1254a1–17.
103 Agamben (2016) 9, 12.
104 Fusco (2023) 48–9.
105 Fusco (2023) 49.
106 Fusco (2023) 50.
107 Christiaens (2018) 253.
108 Christiaens (2018) 249–50.
109 Christiaens (2018) 250.
110 Christiaens (2018) 253.

way of life based on detaching oneself from any imposed identities, which has remained obscured in political philosophy's search for the good life.[111]

The enslaved person's decisive meaning should be restored to them. As Fusco notes, in the slave is the possibility of a human being without vocation or purpose. The political and ethical potential of this different form has been neglected or captured by the juridical institution of slavery and its history.[112] The juridification of slavery is a parodic realisation of a 'use of the body'.[113] The perversion of slavery through its being institutionalised has, for Fusco, corrupted an element of human sociality, turning it into an object of domination.[114] The legal codification of slavery produces an extreme form of brutal exploitation. Such exploitation meant denying individuals the property of their own body.[115]

The use of the body preserves the memory of a form of human activity not reducible to labour or what is today understood as 'work'.[116] For Agamben, in ancient Greece there is no general notion of labour comparable to our own. Productive activities are conceived of with respect to the use value of the object produced.[117] Here Agamben follows Yan Thomas, and argues that the only way the body of the enslaved can have a labour activity is by dividing the body into two, "between two zones of law that correspond respectively to what he is as body and what he is as merchandise, as incorporeal good".[118] The activity of the enslaved is by definition deprived of a proper work.[119] Alfred Sohn-Rethel argued the "real abstraction operating in *exchange*" unites "the birth of philosophy in Greek society of slave-labour, and of the birth of modern science in European society based on wage labour".[120] Fusco notes that for Agamben this means we need to reconsider the assimilation of the modern worker as an equivalent to the figure of the slave. If work means to produce value, the enslaved person does not work.[121]

This separates the ancient and modern concepts of slavery. Modernity views the enslaved as a way to procure labour-power at a fair price with the ultimate aim of making profits. The ancients saw the enslaved as a way of removing labour from the properly human life. Labour was incompatible with

111 Christiaens (2018) 254.
112 Fusco (2023) 47.
113 Agamben (2016) 79.
114 Fusco (2023) 52.
115 Fusco (2023) 52.
116 Agamben (2016) 20.
117 Agamben (2016) 19.
118 Thomas (2002) 233.
119 Agamben (2016) 17.
120 Sohn-Rethel (2020) 23.
121 Fusco (2023) 48.

human life, and the enslaved rendered such a life possible.[122] In Western culture, the re-emergence of the figure of the slave in the modern worker appears as a return of the repressed in a pathological form.[123] Fusco concludes:

> Agamben invites us to see … the possibility of a community and a form-of-life without vocations and substantial identities that consequently is potentially shared by all, which accounts for a possible source of coming happy life. Covered up under the legal-institutional stratification and at the same time alien to social and legal codification, such a form of life finds in the use of the body of the slave a paradigmatic expression.[124]

But this reading (and development) of Aristotle is both a selective reading and also glosses over the way in which Aristotle himself does not accurately present the operation of slavery in the Greek city states.

What ancient slavery was

Slavery is a defining feature of the ancient world.[125] Slavery is a form of property, but defining slavery as property does not tell us about the lives of those enslaved people.[126] Kostas Vlassopoulos asserts that ancient slavery viewed enslaved people passively, with no part to play in shaping their lives or condition. This formulation means enslaved people can either acquiesce to their status as a slave or revolt to try and secure their freedom.[127] In Greek and Roman slave systems, a *modus vivendi* involved accommodations to the problems of daily life faced by a great majority of enslaved people.[128] These quotidian adjustments must have produced a world of seething resentments and unresolved stresses that relapsed inwards on the dominated person.[129] Accommodation was achieved by systematic compulsion.[130] Generations of free women and men defined their relationships with slavery and servitude through *mastery*. Mastery, for William Henry Foster, describes often conflicting and ambiguous environments of power accessed by a variety of people in order to control others, themselves, their immediate surroundings, or their

122 Agamben (2016) 20.
123 Agamben (2016) 21.
124 Fusco (2023) 52.
125 Vlassopoulos (2021) 1.
126 Vlassopoulos (2021) 48–50.
127 Vlassopoulos (2021) 2.
128 Shaw (1998) 48.
129 Veyne (1997) 85–6.
130 Shaw (1998) 49.

entire cultures. Beyond individuals, mastery defined how whole slaveholding societies understood themselves.[131]

Ancient slavery involved excluding enslaved people from aspects of society, including freedom and citizenship.[132] Enslaved people were the first persons to see being free as a value to cherish and the most important thing someone could possess.[133] Vlassopoulos explains an influential view that sees the concept of freedom as 'discovered' of freedom by the ancient Greeks, a momentous contribution to world history.[134] Building on this, I follow Orlando Patterson's arguments about the nature of freedom. For Patterson, the ideal of freedom developed during antiquity and through the Middle Ages in direct relation to slavery and other forms of coerced labour.[135] Patterson contends that a distinct body of ideas and beliefs called 'freedom' have existed in Western Europe from the middle of the fifth century BCE.[136] However, freedom *was* known in the ancient Near East – these societies were also based on a distinction between free man and enslaved.[137]

Patterson further explains that freedom has always been a tripartite complex of beliefs relating to power. Freedom is first the release from the power or control of another agent, institution or immaterial force. We are free to the degree that we are not under the power of another agent (negative liberty). Freedom is second to the power to fulfil one's desires with the minimum of constraint. This includes the power to do with another person whatever one pleases, including bringing about their enslavement (Patterson notes that the harm principle was only developed in the nineteenth century). The third notion of freedom is that one is free to the degree that one shares in the public or communal power of one's society – "freedom as participation", often expressed as belonging or citizenship.[138]

Patterson continues that the priority given to one or other notions varied across classes. The Greek ruling class viewed freedom as power and control as the decisive ideal. Ordinary Greeks viewed freedom as power favourably – everyone wished to be a slave master. A large class of freedmen and resident aliens viewed negative freedom most favourably. All sought to experience freedom as power.[139] Patterson notes that the Greeks constructed two other key features of the culture of freedom which persist in modern times. One was a tradition of discourse about freedom's meaning and significance.

131 Foster (2010) 2.
132 Vlassopoulos (2021) 52.
133 Patterson (1991) 9.
134 Vlassopoulos (2021) 120–1.
135 Patterson (2007) 31.
136 Patterson (2007) 32.
137 Vlassopoulos (2021) 122.
138 Patterson (2007) 32.
139 Patterson (2007) 33.

The other was the distinction between inner and outer freedom, along with the contestation about the relative significance of each.[140] The unprecedented existence of large-scale slavery in Greece (and later Rome) was a necessary condition for this invention.[141]

But in Ancient Greece, Patterson argues, freedom began as a woman's value, because women first lived in terror of enslavement, and first came to value its absence.[142] Patterson's reading of Homer leads to his claims that nearly all Homer's references to slavery are to women, and all but one of his references to freedom involved women.[143] Women were not expected to be able to defend themselves, so suffered no irreparable loss of honour in their submission. They could have their status restored as legitimate members of their master's or their own community. Freedom was possible for women, and it could be hoped or yearned for openly. Patterson's conclusion is that because women had less to lose, they had more to hope for. In that hope was born the Western valuation of personal freedom.[144] Stephanie Smallwood has echoed this, contending that New World slavery relied on the nature of freedom existing in Western Europe, a notion in turn built on an understanding of property authored by slavery.[145]

Vlasspoulos explains that 'Greek slavery' is used when referring to slavery in classical Athens, rather than slavery across the Greek-speaking world. Until recently, the servile systems of other Greek communities were considered as forms of serfdom.[146] Vlassopoulos notes that Greek slavery is coterminous with classical Athens because Athens is the best known ancient Greek community, and Athenian slavery is read as representative of all forms of slavery in the Greek world.[147] This is the location from which Aristotle wrote, but every ancient society was a slave society.[148] This means that the 'use of the body' which Agamben (in turn) uses, is a culturally specific claim.

What of Athenian slavery? Enslaved people in Athens were outsiders in a double sense. Moses Finley explored how the Solonic revolution in Athens at the beginning of the sixth century BCE brought an end to debt bondage and the return of Athenians who had been sold into slavery abroad, but not the emancipation of others, non-Athenians, who were enslaved in Athens.[149]

140 Patterson (2007) 33–4.
141 Patterson (2007) 34; Finley (1981) 115.
142 Patterson (1991) 51.
143 Patterson (1991) 51–2.
144 Patterson (1991) 54.
145 Smallwood (2004) 297.
146 Vlassopoulos (2021) 167.
147 Vlassopoulos (2021) 168.
148 Vlassopoulos (2021) 203.
149 Finley (1959) 156.

Barbarian and enslaved were by nature one and the same.[150] The majority of enslaved people in Athens were household slaves, the property of an individual *oikos*. The domestic slaves were the head of a hierarchy of slaves, which had enslaved miners (who were the most expendable) at its base. Paul Cartledge explains that manufacturing was assumed to warp the spirit of the free Greek.[151] It was shameful to be poor and made to perform slavish labour.[152] Brace states that all prosperous Athenians owned some enslaved people and used them for agricultural work.[153] If an enslaved person had a powerful master they could become more influential than many free people.[154] Slaveholding in classical Athens extended beyond the top strata of the population.[155] Both free people and the enslaved adopted a variety of roles in various arenas, roles which were recognised by free people and enslaved alike. For example, enslaved artisans in Athens worked and lived on their own, paying a proportion of their income to their masters.[156] This complicated social structure often meant that masters needed the support of the political community to exercise their power over the enslaved.[157]

Violence and threats of violence against enslaved people was ever present. Force compelled enslaved people to act, and public violence was used to frighten many, not just punish a few. Peter Hunt explains that this violence also defined the roles of enslaved people and citizens within typical Greek worldviews.[158] Individual violence could involve physical beating or the deprivation of food for an insubordinate remark, stealing or delaying the carrying out of an order. Violence was meant to ensure the enslaved person would not repeat the 'error'.[159] Hunt notes that enslaved people did suffer more than others, but violence was routinely used in judicial punishments and in the household.[160]

But it was commodification that became the fullest expression of slavery in the Greek city states. Enslaved people were commodified in a process. Igor Kopytoff explains that the capture or sale of an individual strips them of their previous social identity and makes them a non-person. The process continues with the enslaved person being acquired by a person or group and being re-socialised in the host group. The enslaved person acquires new statuses and

150 Brace (2018) 32.
151 Cartledge (1993) 173.
152 Brace (2018) 30.
153 Brace (2018) 29; Fisher (1993) 41.
154 Vlassopoulos (2021) 119.
155 Lewis (2018) 167–94.
156 Vlassopoulos (2021) 104.
157 Plato (2005b) 578d–579b.
158 Hunt (2016) 136.
159 Hunt (2016) 140.
160 Hunt (2016) 158.

begins new personal relationships, but they remain a potential commodity with an exchange value that can be realised by their re-sale.[161] Despite all of this, enslaved people never lacked a voice.

The blurred threshold of the enslaved person

Nothing is more elusive than the psychology of the enslaved person, especially given the lack of direct evidence from the ancient world. Data is pieced together from fragments in literature, philosophy and surviving legal records.[162] Agency and resistance came in many forms. Hunt notes that the largest differences existed between different types of enslaved people, and not between different time periods. He explains that the forms of agency and resistance practised by enslaved people in the household in fifth-century BCE Athens and in first-century CE Rome households had more in common with each other than with agricultural slaves.[163]

The identification of the enslaved person with the body was central to what it meant to be enslaved in Athens, extending beyond their purchase and their labour.[164] As Clemens claims, the enslaved person enables: a use that is not labour, an economy separate from the political, and a concept of servitude that is both natural and always open to change and reconfiguration.[165] Enslaved people lived multiple identities and also sought to create a world of their own, against the world of slavery and their masters (this is something akin to a destituent gesture, and one which is paralleled in the early modern and modern worlds as well). Vlassopoulos argues that this made enslaved people historical agents who strove to create new vocations for themselves and to redefine their lives and live them for their own benefit. Due to the power imbalance, enslaved people rarely achieved their aims, but the battles they won or did not lose were important.[166] What was true in ancient Greece was also true in the sugar plantations in the Americas: dehumanisation is never completed. Because of this, slavery should not always be (as Patterson would have it) social death.

Legally, free men could own property, a right prohibited to enslaved people.[167] The law also assumed enslaved people were persons, with some honour that deserved to be protected. If an enslaved person was killed by someone other than the master, the master could prosecute the killer.[168] Slaveowners

161 Kopytoff (1986) 65.
162 Cuffel (1966) 323.
163 Hunt (2017) 140.
164 Brace (2018) 30.
165 Clemens (2018) 140.
166 Vlassopoulos (2021) 8.
167 Vlassopoulos (2009) 348.
168 Brace (2018) 30.

had an unrestricted right to manumit enslaved people they owned, and this was exercised frequently. Once freed, enslaved people were subject to a number of conditions, including remaining with their masters for a period of time. This left them in a state of semi-slavery, or semi-freedom.[169] This was noted by Aristotle in writing about freedom, when he noted that the free man does not live under any restraints of another.[170]

No enslaved person was without voice, but they were answerable with their bodies.[171] Their lack of virtue and reason meant they were viewed as not having the moral capacity to tell the truth without compulsion.[172] This compulsion was exacted through judicial torture. An enslaved person's testimony could only be admissible if taken after torture; judicial torture was prohibited for the free man, unless the offence involved religious sacrilege or treason.[173] The Greek word for torture is *basanos*. It then came to mean inquiry by torture. For an enslaved person to have a voice recognised, they had to be tortured so that the noises they made gained political significance. In this sense, torture is not about truth as such, but the truth of the division of the *polis* between slave and free.[174]

In Athenian democracy, enslaved and free exercised the same professions and enslaved people had extensive freedom of movement and initiative, making it impossible to determine status from a profession or living conditions. Enslaved people took advantage of this, but it also made the status of free men precarious. Escaping slavery was one of the defining hopes in the experience of enslaved people.[175] The manumission of the enslaved was not registered, meaning it could be challenged by the former owner or other persons.[176] Athenian democracy meant that rich and poor, landowner and wage labourer, could be citizens. People were protected by association.[177] Pseudo-Xenophon warned that free men often did not dress better than slaves, with their appearance not being superior to enslaved people either.[178]

Enslaved people survived through compromise and accommodation.[179] As Vlassopoulos argues, by working and living together, enslaved people and free men could take advantage of the unclear boundary between free and

169 Brace (2018) 34; Zelnick-Ambramowitz (2005).
170 Aristotle (1984e) 1367a32.
171 Finley (1998) 161.
172 Rosivach (1999) 152.
173 Vlassopoulos (2009) 348.
174 Clemens (2018) 141.
175 Vlassopoulos (2021) 159.
176 Vlassopoulos (2009) 350.
177 Vlassopoulos (2009) 353.
178 Xenophon (2017) 1.10.
179 Finley (1998) 184.

unfree, and enslaved people could even assume citizen identity.[180] Enslaved people were carving out their own world through their families and kinship groups, the skills they had and the professional roles they carried out. This included creating new identities in the course of their life.[181]

Every tactic of resistance to slavery has been recorded. This included being deliberately difficult or feigning ignorance. Hunt notes that enslaved people tried to avoid work by feigning illness or malingering or wandering aimlessly for hours.[182] In support of this claim, Hunt refers to ancient sources. He references Xenophon's claim that motivated enslaved work-gangs do twice as much work a day as disgruntled or unhappy ones.[183] Speaking of Roman slavery, Hunt refers to Columella's complaint that farms deteriorate if worked by 'bad slaves'.[184] Roman agricultural handbooks warn that everything not stored securely would be stolen by enslaved people.[185] Hunt recalls an example of an Athenian enslaved person called Moschion who embezzled from their master, a common occurrence. When Moschion's master died, his heirs grew suspicious. Under torture, Moschion disclosed the location of over 20 years' salary for a skilled worker.[186] There is evidence of sabotage by enslaved people. Enslaved people running away was a recurrent and expensive problem for masters.[187] References to runaway enslaved people are everywhere, dating back to the fifth and fourth century BCE. Papyrus documents from Hellenistic and Roman Egypt show examples of runaways.[188]

In looking at fifth and fourth century BCE classical Greece, slave revolts are non-existent. Prospects for success were very low, and the consequences of rebelling were very grave.[189] But this is not to suggest that large revolts did not exist at all, especially when many enslaved adult men were concentrated in a specific area. A short-lived revolt took place in 135 or 134 BCE in Sicily. Around 100 BCE, Athenian slaves in the Laurium mines of Attica rose up and killed their guards, seizing the town of Sunium and ravaging the countryside before the revolt was put down.[190] Enemy invasions also prompted resistance. When Syracuse was invaded by Athens in 414 or 413 BCE, enslaved people within Syracuse refused orders. They demanded to fight as hoplites and to receive equal rations. Hunt notes that this was recorded because the

180 Vlassopoulos (2009) 358.
181 Vlassopoulos (2021) 101.
182 Hunt (2017) 142; Justinian (1998) 21.1.17.14.
183 Xenophon (2014) ch 20, sections 16–21.
184 Columella (1941) Vol I, Book I, 7.6.
185 Hunt (2017) 143.
186 Hunt (2017) 143; Arnaoutoglou (2004) 136.
187 Hunt (2017) 147.
188 Hunt (2017) 148.
189 Vujčić (2023).
190 Vujčić (2023) 229.

Syracusans defused the mutiny by seizing and killing the leaders of the revolt during a conference to discuss their terms.[191]

There were also runaway communities. On the island of Chios in the third century BCE, a slave revolt was led by a man called Drimacus. Large numbers of enslaved people fled their masters and congregated in an isolated, mountainous part of the island, and successfully resisted attempts to enslave them.[192] Eventually the enslaved people reached an agreement with the islanders, where the community would cease violent actions in exchange for agreed amounts of food and goods. This is paralleled by the Maroon communities in the Caribbean. In Jamaica, Maroon leaders led by Captain Cudjoe reached an agreement with the colonial government that had provisions matching the Chiot agreement with Drimacus.[193]

Large-scale revolts and rebellions tend to occur under a specific set of circumstances. Hunt, in explaining the lack of explicit revolts in the ancient Greek world, draws a comparison to the enslaved population on the Caribbean islands during the eighteenth and nineteenth centuries. There, enslaved people may have accounted for 80 to 90 per cent of the entire population. This meant revolts were more likely. In the Greek city states, the enslaved population was between one-quarter and one-half of the overall population. The population was also heterogeneous relative to other enslaved populations throughout history, making it hard to unite and collaborate.[194] A heterogeneous population led to more people staying and accepting their fate or trying to escape.[195] The 'fugitive slave' appears to be a chronic issue in the Greek city states. Moses Finley cites Thucydides' estimate that more than 20,000 Athenian slaves fled in the final decade of the Peloponnesian War, after encouragement from Spartans. Many were skilled workers.[196]

Where enslaved people outnumbered their masters, and had a relatively homogenous population, the likelihood of revolts and even wars increased.[197] Around 464 BCE, the helots of Sparta rose up and conducted a rebellion which lasted for years.[198] The helots outnumbered the Spartans and were brutally oppressed.[199] Theresa Urbainczyk describes them as an indigenous people who had been subjugated, and had a shared history, language, culture and even a memory of freedom.[200] After the revolt, a group of the enslaved

191 Hunt (2017) 156.
192 Finley (1998) 181.
193 Vujčić (2023) 230–5; Finley (1998) 182.
194 Hunt (2017) 157.
195 de Ste Croix (1981) 146.
196 Finley (1959) 159.
197 Lewis (2018) 125–46.
198 Urbainczyk (2008) ch 7; Hunt (2017) 157–61.
199 Hunt (2017) 168.
200 Urbaincyzk (2008) 93.

were permitted to escape to Athens.[201] This combination also appeared in the late Roman Republic, as we will see in the next chapter. Great concentrations of unattended and unguarded enslaved people in Italy and Sicily, including many gladiators, led to rebellions that started during periods of societal turmoil.[202]

What do these examples show us? The enslaved person was a liminal figure, existing at the threshold of free and unfree. Enslaved people were also constantly resisting in various forms. Whilst Aristotle provided Western European thought a justification for slavery, individuals were carving out forms of life by undermining, subverting or playing with legal forms and classifications. From the ancient Greeks, we have been given ideas of belonging, politics and freedom which still shape our world today. Yet these ideas required the exclusion of forms of life like enslaved people. Our attention should be paid to those forms of life and how they imagined and lived freedom, living their lives as a form. As we shall see, this form-of-life continues to show itself throughout history, whenever a person attributed with humanity comes face to face with a human being denied theirs.

Conclusion

This chapter considered one of three main interlocutors for Agamben – Aristotle. Aristotle's philosophical defence of slavery provided the basis for Agamben's argument that the use of the body of the enslaved is a form-of-life. Aristotle bequeathed to Western European thought certain forms of political belonging and freedom. Aristotle, like Agamben, uses an anthropological machine in his thought. Aristotle's *polis* is only available for those recognised as human beings by the machine, which excludes the enslaved. Aristotle's natural slavery provided Western political and legal thought with a justification for chattel slavery. There exist forms of life that are incomplete humans who can be enslaved and complete free men who can never be enslaved.

Coloniality repeated this division. Aristotle's work provided the basis for race to become an epistemology of domination. Despite 'race' not existing in the Greek city states as modernity would understand it, Aristotle lived in a time of imperial expansion, and there was an ethnic division in ancient Greece between citizens and barbarians. The idea of beings whose nature means they deserve to be enslaved can also be found today in debates surrounding robots (itself a word meaning 'forced labour') and artificial intelligence. For Aristotle and authors in antiquity, machines remained extensions of the master (just like enslaved people) and could replace the enslaved human. But this approach still repeats paradigms of colonialism and an anthropological

201 Finley (1959) 157–8.
202 Finley (1959) 158.

machine that bases political belonging on the exclusion from the *polis* of certain types of life. The existence of human automata is interpreted for its effects on 'us' rather than in terms of what the chattels know, feel and experience. Since sustaining one's humanity requires actualising a set of arbitrary human qualities, and the suspension of animality, philosophy's response to this has been to attempt to redefine the political community to include more people within it.

I have also outlined Agamben's reading of Aristotle, which is based on the use of the slave's body. This deactivates the machine, opening the possibility of a different form of the human being, without a vocation. This figure of the slave is designed to help us imagine a different form of politics for the future. Agamben's reading of Aristotle is partial, omitting several key elements of Aristotle's writings on slavery, including the discussion of the slave's soul and that soul's relationship to the master's soul. Agamben's references to Aristotle also omit wider references to how slavery operated in the Greek city states.

This chapter also explored how no enslaved person can be without a voice. Enslaved people resisted both actively and passively all the time. There is limited evidence of individual forms of resistance and revolt, but evidence does exist. The status of enslaved people was indeterminate. The enslaved person was difficult to distinguish from the free man and the citizen. It is in these actions and activities, as tenuous and perilous as they were, that Agamben's conception of the enslaved person as a form-of-life should be found.

Reference List

Agamben, G (1998) *Homo Sacer: Sovereign Power and Bare Life,* Heller-Roazen, D (trans.), Stanford: Stanford University Press.

Agamben, G (2004) *The Open: Man and Animal*, Attell, K (trans.), Stanford: Stanford University Press.

Agamben, G (2016) *The Use of Bodies*, Kotsko, A (trans.), Stanford: Stanford University Press.

Aristotle (1984a) 'Magna Moralia' in *The Complete Works of Aristotle, Volume Two*, Barnes, J (ed.), Princeton: Princeton University Press.

Aristotle (1984b) 'Nicomachean Ethics' in *The Complete Works of Aristotle, Volume Two*, Barnes, J (ed.), Princeton: Princeton University Press.

Aristotle (1984c) 'On the Soul' ('*De Anima*') in *The Complete Works of Aristotle, Volume One*, Barnes, J (ed.), Princeton: Princeton University Press.

Aristotle (1984d) 'Politics' in *The Complete Works of Aristotle, Volume Two*, Barnes, J (ed.), Princeton: Princeton University Press.

Aristotle (1984e) 'Rhetoric' in *The Complete Works of Aristotle, Volume Two*, Barnes, J (ed.), Princeton: Princeton University Press.

Arnaoutoglou, I (2004) 'Fear of Slaves in Ancient Greek Legal Texts', *Rethymon 4–7 November*, 133–34.

Brace, L (2018) *The Politics of Slavery,* Edinburgh: Edinburgh University Press.

Brunstetter, D and Zartner, D (2011) 'Just War against Barbarians: Revisiting the Valladolid Debates between Sepúlveda and Las Casas', *Political Studies*, 59, 733–52.
Bull, M (1998) 'Slavery and the Multiple Self', *New Left Review*, 231, 94–131.
Campbell, M (1974) 'Aristotle and Black Slavery: A Study in Race Prejudice', *Race*, 15, 283–301.
Cartledge, P (1993) '"'"Like a Worm i' the Bud?" A Heterology of Classical Greek Slavery', Greece and Rome, 40, 163–80.
Christiaens, T (2018) 'Aristotle's Anthropological Machine and Slavery', *Epoché: A Journal for the History of Philosophy*, 23, 239–62.
Clemens, J (2018) 'As Fire Burns: Philosophy, Slavery, Technology', *Crisis & Critique*, 6, 130–45.
Columella (1941) *De Re Rustica (On Agriculture)*, Cambridge: Harvard University Press.
Cuffel, V (1966) 'The Classical Greek Concept of Slavery', *Journal of the History of Ideas*, 27, 323–42.
de Boer, Y (2023) 'The Figure of the Slave as an Ethical Paradigm in the Work of Agamben', *Netherlands Journal of Legal Philosophy*, 52, 227–41.
de la Durantaye, L (2012) 'The Paradigm of Colonialism' in Bignall, S and Svirsky, M (eds.), *Agamben and Colonialism*, Edinburgh: Edinburgh University Press, 229–38.
de Las Casas, B (1583) *The Spanish -Colonie: Or Briefe Chronicle of the Acts and Gestes of the Spainardes in the West Indies, Called the Newe World, for the Space of xi yeeres*, London: William Broome.
de Ste Croix, G E M (1981) *The Class Struggle in the Ancient Greek World: From Archaic Age to the Arab Conquest*, Ithaca: Cornell University Press.
Devecka, M (2013) 'Did the Greeks Believe in Their Robots?', *The Cambridge Classical Journal*, 59, 52–69.
Dietz, M (2012) 'Between Polis and Empire: Aristotle's Politics', *The American Political Science Review*, 106, 275–93.
Ehrenberg, V (1969) *The Greek State*, 2nd edn, London: Methuen & Co.
Finley, M I (1959) *Was Greek Civilisation Based on Slave Labour?*, Historia: Zeitschrift für Alte Geschichte, 8, 145-64.
Finley, M (1981) *Economy and Society in Ancient Greece*, London: Chatto & Windus.
Finley, M (1998) *Ancient Slavery and Modern Ideology*, Princeton: Markus Wiener Publishers.
Fisher, N R E (1993) *Slavery in Classical Greece*, London: Bristol Classical Press.
Foster, W (2010) *Gender, Mastery and Slavery*, Basingstoke: Palgrave Macmillan.
Fusco, G-G (2023) *Form of Life: Agamben and the Destitution of Rules*, Edinburgh: Edinburgh University Press.
Hall, E (1989) *Inventing the Barbarians: Greek Self-Definition through Tragedy*, Oxford: Clarendon Press.
Hanke, L (1959) *Aristotle and the American Indian: A Study in Race Prejudice in the Modern World*, London: Hollis & Carter.
Homer (1992) *Iliad*, Knox, B (ed.), Fagles, R (trans.), London: Penguin.
Homer (2003) *Odyssey*, Rieu, E V and Rieu, D C H (trans.), London: Penguin.

Hunt, P (2016) 'Violence against Slaves in Classical Greece' in Reiss, W and Fagan, G (eds.), *The Topography of Violence in the Greco-Roman World*, Ann Arbor, University of Michigan Press, 136–61.
Hunt, P (2017) *Ancient Greek and Roman Slavery*, Hoboken: Wiley-Blackwell.
Justinian (1998) *The Digest of Justinian, Volume 1*, Watson, A (ed.), Philadelphia: University of Pennsylvania Press.
Kopytoff, I (1986) 'The Cultural Biography of Things: Commoditization as Process' in Appadurai, A (ed.), *The Social Life of Things: Commodities in Cultural Perspective*, Cambridge: Cambridge University Press, 64–91.
LaGrandeur, K (2011) 'The Persistent Peril of the Artificial Slave', *Science Fiction Studies*, 38, 232–52.
LaGrandeur, K (2020) 'Artificial Slaves in the Renaissance and the Dangers of Independent Innovation' in Cave, S, Dihal, K and Dillon, K (eds.), *AI Narratives: A History of Imaginative Thinking about Intelligent Machines*, Oxford: Oxford University Press, 95–118.
Lenoir, T (2002) 'Makeover: Writing the Body into the Posthuman Technoscape. Part One: Embracing the Posthuman', *Configurations*, 10, 203–20.
Lewis, D (2018) *Greek Slave Systems in their Eastern Mediterranean Context, c. 800-146 BC*, Oxford: Oxford University Press.
Mayor, A (2018) *Gods and Robots: Myths, Machines, and Ancient Dreams of Technology*, Princeton: Princeton University Press.
Millett, P (2007) 'Aristotle and Slavery in Athens', *Greece and Rome*, 54, 178–209.
Monoson, S S (2011) 'Navigating Race, Class, Polis and Empire: The Place of Empirical Analysis in Aristotle's Account of Natural Slavery' in Alston, R, Hall, E and Proffitt, L (eds.), *Reading Ancient Slavery*, London, Bristol Classical Press, 133–51.
Nyquist, M (2013) *Arbitrary Rule: Slavery, Tyranny and the Power of Life and Death*, Chicago: University of Chicago Press.
Patterson, O (1991) *Freedom, vol 1: Freedom in the Making of Western Culture*, New York: Basic Books.
Patterson, O (2007) 'The Ancient and Medieval Origins of Modern Freedom' in Mintz, S and Stauffer, J (eds), *The Problem of Evil: Slavery, Freedom, and the Ambiguities of American Reform,* Amhurst and Boston: University of Massachusetts Press, 31–66.
Plato (2005a) 'Meno' in *The Collected Dialogues, Including the Letters*, Hamilton, E and Cairns, H (eds.), Princeton: Princeton University Press.
Plato (2005b) 'Republic' in *The Collected Dialogues, Including the Letters*, Hamilton, E and Cairns, H (eds.), Princeton: Princeton University Press.
Robinson, C (2001) 'The Inventions of the Negro', *Social Identities*, 7, 329–61.
Robinson, D (1971) *Slavery in the Structure of American Politics*, New York: Harcourt Publishers.
Rosivach, V (1999) 'Enslaving "Barboroi" and the Athenian Ideology of Slavery', *Historia: Zeitschrift für Alte Geschichte*, 48, 129–57.
Schofield, M (1999) *Saving the City: Philosopher Kings and Other Classical Paradigms*, London: Routledge.
Shaw, B (1998) "A Wolf by the Ears': M. I. Finley's Ancient Slavery and Modern Ideology in Historical Context' in Finley, M, *Ancient Slavery and Modern Ideology*, Princeton: Markus Wiener, 3–53.

Smallwood, S (2004) 'Commodified Freedom: Interrogating the Limits of Anti-Slavery Ideology in the Early Republic', *Journal of the Early Republic*, 24, 289–98.
Sohn-Rethel, A (2020) *Intellectual and Manual Labour: A Critique of Epistemology*, Leiden: Brill.
Sorentino, S-M (2019) 'Natural Slavery, Real Abstraction, and the Virtuality of Anti-Blackness', *Theory & Event*, 22, 630–73.
Thomas, Y (2002) 'Le corps de l'esclave et son travail à Rome. Analyse d'une dissociation juridique', in Mreau, P (ed.), *Corps romains. Actes de la table ronde organisée par la Société française d'anthropologie de la Rome antique en janvier 1999*, Grenoble: Jérôme Milion, 225–50.
Thomson, G (1955) *The First Philosophers: Studies in Ancient Greek Society*, London: Lawrence & Wishart.
Urbainczyk, T (2008) *Slave Revolts in Antiquity*, London: Routledge.
Veyne, P (1997) *The Roman Empire*, Goldhammer, A (trans.), Cambridge: Belknap Press.
Vlassopoulos, K (2009) 'Slavery, Freedom and Citizenship in Classical Athens: Beyond a Legalistic Approach', *European Review of History*, 16, 347–63.
Vlassopoulos, K (2021) *Historicising Ancient Slavery*, Edinburgh: Edinburgh University Press.
Vujčić, N (2023) 'Large Scale Slave Revolts in Ancient Greece: An Issue of Absence of an Absence of Issue?', *Athens Journal of History*, 9, 225–48.
Walsh, M (1997) 'Aristotle's Conception of Freedom', *Journal of the History of Philosophy*, 35, 495–507.
Williams, E (1994) *Capitalism & Slavery*, Chapel Hill: University of North Carolina Press.
Xenophon (2014) *The Economist*, Dakyns, H (trans.), Scotts Valley: CreateSpace.
Xenophon (2017) *The Old Oligarch: Pseudo-Xenophon's Constitution of the Athenians*, Osborne, R (trans.), Cambridge: Cambridge University Press.
Zelnick-Ambramowitz, R (2005) *Not Wholly Free: The Concept of Manumission and the State of Manumitted Slaves in the Ancient Greek World*, Leiden and Boston: Brill.
Ziarek, E (2008) 'Bare Life on Strike: Notes on the Biopolitics of Race and Gender', *South Atlantic Quarterly*, 108, 89–106.

Chapter 4

St Paul, messianic time and the power of the example

Introduction

St Paul is an intermediary figure between Aristotle and Hegel in Agamben's thought. Paul wrote of slavery in a way distinct from Aristotle and Hegel. Both Paul and Aristotle write of the *doulos*. Agamben does not theorise the connection between the two. The slave (*doulos*) as an 'animate instrument' (in Aristotle) cannot be reconciled with Paul's messianism exemplified in the slave (*doulos*). Paul's writings reflect a form of radical equality that is not found in Aristotle. I consider the historical realities of slavery in Paul's Roman world. Roman law made a human being into a thing. The legal limits to the lives of enslaved people counter Agamben's claim that the sexual use of the body of the enslaved was not perceived as an abuse in any way. Yet what we see in Roman slavery are enslaved people, through small and seemingly insignificant actions, trying to carve out their own modes of freedom.

Paul's messianism is based on the 'as not', the revocation of every vocation, and the deactivation of every apparatus. Using Furio Jesi's work I explain how this deactivation affects machines of control, be they mythological or anthropological. I use this as the springboard for considering the nature of time and the difference between *chronos* and *kairos*. *Chronos* represents the idea of time running in a straight line with direction and purpose, a homogeneous continuum. This forms a chronopolitics which naturalises the effects of colonialism and the way entire populations are labelled as 'timeless' and outside of humanity.

Agamben, following Paul, states that we must reconceive time as *kairos*. Central to Paul's writings on the slave, and his messianism, is a conception of time as *kairos*. *Kairos* is fulfilled time, the time of the now, concerned not with the future but the present. It represents a form of action where life is fulfilled in the moment. Decolonial thought also develops alternative ways of relating to time and community. For example, the work of John Mbiti (in a manner similar to *kairos*) sees the present as serving the past, which in turn gives purpose to the present. Time has a crucial communal dimension, created through communal events, and experienced through hyper-hermeneutic

DOI: 10.4324/9781003303534-5

gestures to become real for people. Form-of-life lives in *kairological* time. Examples of this time can be found scattered through the Western cultural tradition. *Kairological* time can be placed in a decolonial register in order to think about the world anew. In the final part of the chapter, using the figure of Spartacus, I apply Jesi's and Agamben's writings on time and messianism. I argue that the *example* of the 'slave' operates as a figure of emancipation for future political struggles, connecting back to *kairos* and the way the past can be grasped to inform present political action. The time of the now cannot be separated from what has gone before, and the coming politics involves an excavation of the past.

Aristotle, the Pauline Epistles and radical equality

Aristotle's theory of slavery is incompatible with the use and invocation of slavery in Paul's New Testament writings, an incompatibility that Agamben is silent about. The slave is central to Paul, but in a different way to Aristotle's animate instrument. Paul calls for a form of radical equality between slave and free. Paul's slave is invested with the messianic vocation, and an ability to live as a form-of-life. Aristotle's use of the body should be moved into a messianic register.

The Greek word *doulos*, slave, appears 47 times in the Pauline Epistles. Paul's *doulos* is used to express how juridical and social conditions are neutralised by the messianic event. Paul refers to himself as a slave on more than one occasion.[1] At the time of Paul's ministry, there was little questioning of the propriety of slavery. His references to transitional moments in the enslaved person's life are similar to concerns raised by his contemporaries.[2] Paul was not alone. Jesus's teachings routinely mentioned the figure of the slave. The Matthean parables understood the moral purpose of the enslaved person being to forward the slaveholder's interests.[3]

In contrast, Aristotle's *Politics* presents the household's organisation as occurring spontaneously, whereas the city needs deliberate construction. Politics in the city involves equality and contestation; the household displays a harmonious hierarchical order.[4] The inspiration for bare life comes from the same passages of the *Politics* where Aristotle set out his theory of natural slavery.[5] The Greek city-state was based on a series of exclusions.[6] For Aristotle the slave is very much a figure of the economic realm, and not

1 Rom 1:1; Phil 1:1; 2 Cor 4:5.
2 Glancy (2002) 99.
3 Glancy (2002) 129.
4 Kotsko (2018) 67.
5 Kotsko (2018) 49; Fiskesjo (2012) 163.
6 Aristotle (1984b) 1283a.

completely human.[7] Centuries later White slave masters similarly claimed to find in the Black body an inherent capacity to be enslaved.[8] The roots of today's systems of political domination and chattel slavery are found in the attempt to move from 'human economies' of personal relations to impersonal market systems founded on predatory violence.[9] In ancient Athens, the household, including the enslaved people that resided in it, represents the beginnings from which the human community grows.[10]

Aristotle's political and economic system is based on a hierarchy of human lives. In contrast, Mika Ojakangas points to elements in Paul's writings pointing to the absolute equality of all humans before God, enslaved and free.[11] Early Christianity provided a language for criticising various forms of coercion.[12] The freedom that came to the Christian through surrender to the absolute power of God (spiritual re-enslavement) did not imply an abandonment of the negative freedom guaranteed by the salvific blood of Christ.[13] Everybody is owned by God by whose grace we are what we are.[14] Those who live in Christ (the Pauline metaphor for the righteous living together) live in peace and in mutual understanding.[15]

The figure of the slave is central to Paul's Epistles. The royal Saul that becomes Paul on the road to Damascus witnesses the becoming given that in Latin *paulus* signifies minor. The one who lives in Christ becomes weak and enslaved.[16] This is the perspective to understand Paul's statement that power is made perfect in weakness and his claim that "when I am weak, then I am strong".[17] The enslaved person and the weak are excluded from all communities, making them able to be the foundation of a community that does not exclude anyone, which is shown when Paul says that "God chose what is low and despised in the world".[18] In Christ there is no exclusion or violence between human beings, no sin, for sin is "enmities, strife, jealousy, anger, quarrels, dissensions, factions, envy".[19]

In his letter to the Galatian Christians, Paul makes reference to a baptismal formula to remind his readers their new identity in Christ dissolves the claims of other statuses:

7 Badiou (2017) 35.
8 Kotsko (2018) 72.
9 O'Connell Davison (2015) 198.
10 Trott (2017) 127.
11 Ojakangas (2011) 19; Rom 2:11; Rom 3:22.
12 Patterson (2007) 31.
13 Patterson (2007) 36.
14 Ojakangas (2011) 19; 1 Cor. 15:10.
15 Ojakangas (2011) 20–1; 1 Cor. 12:14–19.
16 Ojakangas (2011) 22; 1 Cor. 9:19–22.
17 Ojakangas (2011) 22; 2 Cor. 12:10.
18 Ojakangas (2011) 22; 1 Cor. 1:27.
19 Ojakangas (2011) 20; Gal. 5:19.

> There is neither Jew nor Greek; there is neither slave nor free; there is no 'male and female'; for all of you are One in Christ Jesus.[20]

In the Greek speaking world of the first century CE, there was a clear legal distinction between free (*eleutheros*) and slave (*doulos*). *Doulos* specifically meant an enslaved person in whom one had property rights. But while the English word 'slave' can refer to a male or female slave, *doulos* is grammatically masculine. Jennifer Glancy notes that contemporary scholars erroneously assume the majority of enslaved people were men and overlook the gendered nature of slavery.[21] Pauline and post-Pauline Christianity centred on the model of the slaveholding family.[22] The development of Christian ideology, especially in the last quarter of the fourth century CE, had as its template the patriarchal family with a slaveholding 'lord' at its head, and an image of the discipline of the whip.[23]

In the fourth chapter of the Epistle to the Galatians, Paul acknowledges differences between the enslaved and free. He dismisses the categories 'male' and 'female', but Glancy explains the tropes of slavery and freedom Paul uses in the Epistle are gendered.[24] For Paul the legitimating power of the spirit means those formerly enslaved by the law are manumitted from slavery and adopted as sons.[25] This evokes the Roman practice where a patriarch could decide whether a small child is adopted as a son or raised as enslaved.[26] This also invoked the fact that, at the time, the status of the child followed the status of the mother.[27] The identities of these indeterminate bodies depended upon a man's decision to label himself 'father' or 'owner' to a body born of a woman.[28] Slavery was understood in corporeal terms in the Roman Empire. In this way, Paul promises to suspend the categories of male and female and slave and free within Christian communities. But Paul's rhetoric insists on consigning bodies to places in society defined by those same categories.[29]

For Paul, the somatic dangers of physical slavery are subordinated to the pitfalls of spiritual enslavement. In the Epistle to the Colossians Paul commands masters to give their slaves "justice and equality",[30] and warns against masters ignoring the repercussions of wrongs they do to the enslaved here on

20 Gal. 3:27–28; Glancy (2002) 34.
21 Glancy (2002) 16.
22 Shaw (1998) 51.
23 Shaw (1998) 51.
24 Glancy (2002) 34.
25 Gal. 4:7.
26 Glancy (2002) 36.
27 Glancy (2002) 36.
28 Glancy (2002) 37.
29 Glancy (2002) 38.
30 Col. 4:1.

earth, as they also have a master in heaven.[31] In the same way, the enslaved should obey their earthly masters as they would obey Christ.[32] This is illustrated clearly in the Book of Philemon. Philemon is the owner of Onesimus, an enslaved man who has left him, was baptised by Paul and is with Paul.[33] Paul intercedes for Onesimus and introduces him as a new believer.[34] Paul notes that although Onesimus was formerly useless to Philemon, he is now useful, both to Philemon and to Paul.[35] Paul attempts to make Philemon treat Onesimus as "no longer as a slave, but better than a slave, as a dear brother".[36] Treating Onesimus as "a beloved brother" should occur "in the flesh", in everyday life. One's earthly status is irrelevant in the fellowship of Christ's body.[37] Here Philemon also owes a debt or obligation as a believer to be a brother to the other brothers and sisters in the Lord.[38] This is a debt to receive Onesimus for what he had become, a believer, not for being enslaved.[39]

Slavery in Rome and Roman law

Missing from Agamben's work on Paul is a detailed consideration of slavery in Roman Law in the later Roman Republic and early Empire. Kostas Vlassopoulos contends that the term 'Roman slavery' should cover the parts of the world under Roman authority, temporally bounded from the early republican period to no later than the early imperial period.[40] Slavery as an institution means an organisation of roles that include conduct, and a system of practices and ideas that are socially sanctioned.[41] By the fifth century BCE enslaved and free were distinguished in law, and enslaved people could be bought and sold in Rome.[42] By the late first century BCE, probably 20–30 per cent of the population of Roman Italy were enslaved.[43]

Orlando Patterson states that it was in Rome that the new legal concept of the idea of an absolute ownership of things appeared.[44] Roman slavery involved the combination of the widespread use of enslaved people by elite

31 Col. 3:25–4:1.
32 Col. 3:22–24.
33 Taylor (2012) 277–88.
34 Donfried and Marshall (1993) 177–9.
35 Glancy (2020) 17; Philemon 11.
36 Philemon 16.
37 Taylor (2012) 284.
38 Taylor (2012) 2856; Petersen (1985) 78.
39 Petersen (1985) 295.
40 Vlassopoulos (2021) 167.
41 Joshel (2010) 10–11.
42 Joshel (2010) 54.
43 Joshel (2010) 56.
44 Patterson (1982) 28.

households in both rural and urban settings,[45] and the middle classes' use of small-scale employment of enslaved people.[46] Most Roman writers and jurists tended to cast into the shadows the experience of those they dominated.[47] The laws of slavery are the most characteristic intellectual product of Rome.[48] The Roman law of slavery outlasted the Empire. It was applied in the State of Louisiana, with provisions for manumission remaining close to what was prescribed in the Code of Justinian.[49]

Patterson explains that the Roman legal system invented the legal fiction of absolute ownership, or *dominium*. *Dominium* emphasised the categories of *res* (thing) and *persona* (owner). It also made a distinction between corporeal and incorporeal things, with the aim of ensuring there would be no question as to what was and was not legally property.[50] This legal paradigm, made up of *persona*, *res* and *dominium*, was modelled on the elements of the master-slave relationship, namely master, slave and enslavement.[51]

To be free and enslaved in the Roman Empire

For Ulpian, human beings living in a world of natural law (*ius naturale*) are just "men" – slavery is unknown, and all are free.[52] However, the law of nations (*ius gentium*) identifies three classes of persons – free men, freedmen and enslaved people.[53] Human beings live under that law of nations. A free person was anyone not legally a slave.[54] The *liber homo* had a concrete set of negative liberties and positive privileges.[55] In Roman law two elements were held to be necessary for full legal personality: freedom from slavery (*libertas*) and citizenship (*civitas*). The loss of either of these elements involved loss of status.[56]

All freeborn Romans were citizens of the state. Where two parents were citizens, the child was a citizen. Roman citizenship was a privilege.[57] Paul discovered his Roman citizenship could protect him from the brutalities of Roman governance.[58] Male citizens had the right to vote, to control property,

45 Harper (2011) 144–200.
46 Harper (2011) 100–43.
47 Joshel (2010) 14.
48 Buckland (2010) iv.
49 Vetter (2005) 375–84; Miller (1999) 90.
50 Patterson (1982) 31.
51 Patterson (1982) 31.
52 Joshel (2010) 30.
53 Shumway (1901) 642.
54 Patterson (2007) 37.
55 Patterson (2007) 50.
56 Shumway (1901) 636.
57 Lewis (2015) 169.
58 Acts 22:25; Lewis (2015) 169–70.

to marry and to have legitimate children who were also citizens.[59] Female citizens could have a proper Roman marriage and have children who were citizens.[60] Joshel states that on the death of the *paterfamilias* the citizen was legally independent and in charge of their own life and property (including enslaved people). Paternal power passed down the generations, securing a legitimate place in society for fathers and sons. Freeborn people had physical integrity, with protections from summary execution, flogging, chaining, imprisonment and torture.[61] Social standing was limited by birth and property, and the distribution of wealth in Roman society was unequal, along with the distribution of prestige.[62]

Subordination was a permanent feature of Roman social and legal life. Only a few male Roman citizens possessed full legal rights in both private and public life.[63] Citizenship could be lost if the citizen became enslaved.[64] If a freed woman sustained illicit relations with an enslaved person against the master's protest, she became that master's slave.[65] The enslaved was an outsider, *res*, a thing, property, an object. They could be lent, sold, mortgaged, given away or bequeathed in a will.[66] The master could rule his subjects as he saw fit.[67] Despite lacking capacity an enslaved person could act on behalf of their master, managing his property and creating commercial obligations on his behalf. To the Roman lawyer, slavery was a perpetual extension of the moment of imminent death over a defeated foe.[68]

The master's right to coerce and abuse their legal slaves was generally absolute. Compensation for the death of an enslaved person or for mutilation by third parties was to be paid not to the victim but to the master.[69] The children of enslaved people were owned by the master. Not every child was lucky enough to grow up in a household with their biological parents.[70] An average enslaved person was sold for around five years' salary for the average labourer.[71] This meant abuse against the enslaved, while serious, often did not end in death.[72] The vulnerability of enslaved bodies was inscribed in law. For example, Roman law specified that injuries inflicted by a slave were

59 Joshel (2010) 33; Shumway (1901) 644.
60 Joshel (2010) 32–3.
61 Joshel (2010) 34.
62 Joshel (2010) 37.
63 Lewis (2015) 151.
64 Shumway (1901) 644.
65 Shumway (1901) 641.
66 Shumway (1901) 637.
67 Vlassopoulos (2021) 115; Cassius Dio Cocceianus (1990) 54.23.
68 Lenski (2016) 275.
69 Lenski (2016) 285.
70 Rawson (1966) 71–83, quoted in Glancy (2002) 5.
71 Harper (2011) 206–38.
72 Lenski (2016) 283.

serious, as the insult caused is greater than if the injury was inflicted by a free man. In such a case then the enslaved person can be brought to court by the slave owner to be whipped as punishment. If an enslaved person inflicted an injury by the order of their master, and more importantly, if that could be proved, the master could be sued.[73] The buying and selling of enslaved people at a Roman marketplace was dehumanising.[74] In a manner evocative of the Atlantic slave trade, enslaved people were displayed on a raised platform and could be asked to jump or undress by potential buyers.[75] They were physically scrutinised, reduced to the status of an object without any dignity.[76]

Manumission was a type of 'social re-birth',[77] and an enslaved person could be released by their master.[78] Once freed a formerly enslaved person could marry, buy property, make a contract and have legal capacity. Freedom could be given by enrolling an enslaved person's name on the census – a list of citizens.[79] Freedom could also be granted through a legal process in the praetor's court, the *Vindicta*. Shumway explains that the enslaved person had a friend assert their fictional liberty. The slave owner, in response to this legal fiction, would not challenge the claim. The court had to declare the enslaved person was free.[80] The enslaved population blended into the larger population in Rome. The high manumission rate meant ethnicity was useless as a tool for identifying enslaved people.[81] A servile past was a social stigma – the lack of a socially acknowledged father dishonoured the ex-slave.[82] The former master was a 'patron' and remained a sort of parent to the child of the freed slave. Patrons had a claim to their ex-slaves' labour.[83] Those who gained their freedom from their masters might in certain circumstances have this freedom revoked for ingratitude.[84] If an enslaved person did not show proper *obsequium* to their ex-master, they could lose their freedom.[85]

Sexual relations and agency

As part of his study of the slave and the use of the body, Agamben turns to the matter of sexual relations in the ancient world. For Agamben the sexual

73 Justinian (1998b) 47.10.17.3–10.
74 Brace (2018) 29.
75 Brace (2018) 29; Bradley (1992) 129.
76 Bradley (1992) 129.
77 Joshel (2010) 42.
78 Lewis (2015) 154.
79 Shumway (1901) 647.
80 Shumway (1901) 648.
81 Patterson (1982) 58.
82 Joshel (2010) 43.
83 Joshel (2010) 46.
84 Cornelius Tacitus (1939) 13.26.
85 Joshel (2010) 45–6.

relation made up an integral part of the use of the body of the enslaved and "was not in any way perceived as an abuse".[86] He states that the use of the body of the enslaved includes the use of his sexual parts. The two bodies became indeterminate, with the "serviceable" hand of the master is equivalent to the service of the enslaved. Agamben notes that this leads to a 'striking promiscuity' that defines the relationships of masters with servants, including the masters bathing the servants, clothing them and combing their hair without this being driven by necessity.[87]

The evidence does not support this claim. Agamben cites Kyle Harper's study, *Slavery in the Late Roman World*, to support his argument, but Harper says something different to Agamben's reading. Harper explains that Roman society (and Roman law) accepted dalliances between married men and enslaved people they owned. Enslaved people were completely sexually available.[88] The power of the individual master over the enslaved person was central to the institutionalised sexual use of the enslaved and sex workers.[89] Roman law recognised that raping someone else's enslaved person might be an assault on the owner's proprietary interests.[90] Masters cared greatly about the sexual behaviour of their enslaved women. Once enslaved people had been purchased, sex became a domestic service, and sexual access was part of the master's proprietary rights.[91] The Roman sexual aesthetic sanctioned heterosexual and homosexual sex between the master and the enslaved, provided the enslaved person was the pathic partner.[92] A male slave could have their appearance (long hair) and body (castration) altered for sexual purposes. The physical vulnerability expressed in the enslaved person's sexual use and abuse dishonoured the victim.[93] Roman society was based on monogamous marriage, which needed a free and honourable woman. For women, sex was confined to marriage, and women were expected to be virgins at marriage.[94] Sexual exclusiveness is the mark of female honour, so female slaves live with a state of perpetual shame.[95] For female slaves, sex work was a likely endpoint, and sex workers were dishonoured, even when they were not enslaved.[96]

86 Agamben (2016) 17.
87 Agamben (2016) 18.
88 Harper (2011) 282–3.
89 Harper (2011) 284.
90 Harper (2011) 294.
91 Harper (2011) 295.
92 Lenski (2016) 281.
93 Joshel (2010) 40.
94 Harper (2011) 287.
95 Saller (1998) 85–91.
96 Treggiari (1975) 400–1.

Enslaved people were available without restriction in ancient Greece and Rome and were sexually exploited by their masters and their masters' families and friends.[97] There remained a double standard – for men sex was not confined to marriage. Augustan laws made *stuprum*, illicit sexual violation, an indeterminate crime. It covered unmarried *matres familias*, women possessing social honour, who were mainly widows and virgins from decent families.[98] *Stuprum* was undefined legally – it was sex with honourable women, though a woman's sexual availability measured her honour. The determination of honour was left to judges and lawyers. Sexual crime against enslaved people you owned or against sex workers was impossible by definition. The law propped up systemic sexual exploitation.[99] This did not mean men could act without consequence. Slaveholders' sexual relations with their own enslaved people could disrupt the families and love affairs of the enslaved. The law patrolled men's sexual treatment of other owners' enslaved people but put few limits on an owner's relations with his own enslaved people.

How does this relate to Paul's writings? Kyle Harper notes that Christian sexuality was rooted in Pauline scripture.[100] I follow Harper's analysis here. Harper explains that for Paul, the sexual alternatives for a man were celibacy, marriage and *porneia*. *Porneia* referred to casual sex permitted in Roman culture. Harper says *porneia* refers to a culture of sexuality in which male sexuality was given free rein to exploit dishonoured women, including sex workers and enslaved people.[101]

Glancy develops this line of thought. Paul's claim was that membership in the body of Christ removed barriers between enslaved and free.[102] Yet Paul did also promote an instrumental attitude towards women.[103] For example, Paul advised that a man, to control his sexual urges, should "obtain his own vessel", which could include enslaved people in his household.[104] This is despite Paul not explicitly making reference to slaveholders having sexual relations with their slaves.[105] The Pauline doctrine of marriage helped assimilate the Christian religion into Mediterranean society. This is why early Christian texts were silent on the matter of sex with enslaved people, and the early Church did not oppose the sexual exploitation of enslaved people.[106] It was only when Christianity became the state religion in the fourth

97 Finley (1998) 163–4.
98 Harper (2011) 289.
99 Harper (2011) 290.
100 Harper (2011) 322.
101 Harper (2011) 322.
102 1 Cor. 12:13; Gal. 3:28.
103 Glancy (2002) 61.
104 Glancy (2002) 62.
105 Glancy (2002) 64–5.
106 Harper (2011) 322.

century that complete silence on the master's sexual power over an enslaved person became impossible, and systematic critiques of the sexual exploitation of enslaved people arose.[107] What is not clear is how this relates to Agamben's claim that the Church lost the messianic experience of time that marked the early Christian communities. The same early Church, existing in Paul's time and soon thereafter, was riven with a contradiction that had a gendered nature.[108]

Glancy explains that for Paul, enslaved sex workers were excluded from being members of the Christian body. They had no control over their slaveholder's decision to profit from their bodies, but Paul's insistence that sexual activity only take place within a marriage presented enslaved people with a conundrum. What should they do if their masters insisted on having sexual relations with them?[109] It was not acceptable behaviour for an enslaved person to resist sexual overtures sanctioned by their masters, regardless of whether they were a man or a woman.[110] By insisting that sex work was incompatible with the Christian community, Paul left sex workers outside of that community. Paul even used slave trading as a metaphor to warn the early Christian community not to visit sex workers. Christians should instead express concern for the involuntary sexual use of the bodies of enslaved people, even in sex work.[111]

To live as an enslaved person in the Roman Empire was to be surrounded by violence and uncertainty. Many enslaved people made the best life possible within this system of slavery, resisting the oppression they were subjected to.[112] Most resistance was based on cunning. As Harriet Jacobs put it centuries later:

> Who can blame slaves for being cunning? They are constantly compelled to resort to it. It is the only weapon of the weak and oppressed against the strength of their tyrants.[113]

Phaedrus drew up a genealogy of the fable, or *fabella*, which is a cunning attempt by enslaved people to say what they cannot say without incurring punishments and whippings. With made-up jokes it escapes accusations (*calumnia*), the false, lethal accusation that hangs over everyone, particularly the weak and insecure, who are inclined to allow themselves to be accused

107 Harper (2011) 322–3.
108 Agamben (2012) 3.
109 1 Cor. 7; Glancy (2002) 50; Fee (1987) 259–60.
110 Glancy (2002) 53.
111 Glancy (2002) 67.
112 Hunt (2017) 138–9; Joshel (2010) 153.
113 Jacobs (1987) 100–1.

and even to accuse themselves.[114] Gossip by enslaved people could impact the social standing of masters.[115] Irritation at gossip, or the fear of its effects, finds parallels in other times in the ancient world.[116]

Some enslaved people removed themselves from their owner's power by killing themselves.[117] Enslaved persons also fled their masters.[118] References to runaways are ubiquitous.[119] The problem for enslaved people was where to hide or how to disguise themselves as free people.[120] Enslaved people left their owner's control temporarily without the intention of fleeing permanently. As an *erro* the enslaved person indulges in aimless roaming and returns home at a late hour.[121] Enslaved people in the cities spend their time idling, gambling or visiting the public square, the circus, theatres, taverns or brothels.[122] Given the chance, enslaved people were lazy, loitering, time-wasting, and slept away the day. Some feigned illness, others were insolent.[123] Roman lawyers and writers complained about petty theft by enslaved people, often not worth public attention.[124] Enslaved people also externalised their anger, revulsion and violent urges by attacking and even killing their masters.[125] Other more subtle forms of agency were common. Enslaved people writing in Latin used all the freeborn terms for family relations – wife/husband, father, mother, sister, brother – despite the legal and social denial of the legitimacy of their family ties.[126] There are no direct testimonies from enslaved persons in the Roman Empire. But however *we* interpret enslaved people's behaviour, slave resistance was part of the everyday relations of slave owners and the enslaved – part of the slave system itself.[127] Even a comfortable slavery was seen as bondage: better hunger, rain, snow and a hard life in the woods than a full belly, if it means chains and no freedom to go where you like.[128] This is a paradigmatic example of trying to live one's life as a form, beyond any personal identity or status that we are assigned by the law.

114 Agamben (2023c) 38–9, citing Phaedrus (1984) Book III, The Prologue.
115 Cornelius Tacitus (1939) 15.54–55; Cornelius Tacitus (1964) 1.2.
116 Hunt (2017) 144.
117 Justinian (1998a) 21.1.17.4 and 6, 21.1.23.3.
118 Justinian (1998a) 21.1.17.10; Joshel (2010) 153.
119 Hunt (2017) 148; Marcus Porcius Cato (1998), 2.2–3.
120 Joshel (2010) 154.
121 Justinian (1998a) 21.1.17.14.
122 Columella (1941) 1.8.2.
123 Columella (1941) 1.7.6, 1.8.2; Joshel (2010) 155.
124 Justinian (1998b) 48.19.11.1; Joshel (2010) 154.
125 Lenski (2016) 293.
126 Joshel (2010) 141.
127 Camp (2004) 2.
128 Joshel (2010) 160.

Paul, the messianic and the decolonial

Paul and the messianic 'as not'

Central to Paul's writings is a different conception of time that allows one to live 'as not', or *hōs mē*. To live one's life 'as not' means the revocation of every vocation. This revocation is a deactivation and transformation of existing vocations and traditions, opening them for a new use.[129] The emphasis on deactivation is crucial. In our culture, an anthropological machine defines the human by suspending and capturing within itself the irrational animal and produces the human by "stubbornly circumscribing the speaking human being".[130] The machine seeks to dominate and domesticate the animal:

> Only if I exclude it from my life as a human being and nevertheless implicate and capture it in that life, can I know and dominate the animal that I am.[131]

Similarly, what Jesi called a *mythological machine* produces narratives that structure the world in which we live. The machine never provides the truth, but versions of the truth in the form of mythologies. Humankind participates simultaneously in myth and historical time.[132] The speaking being lies in the same place as the mythological machine.[133] It is only through deactivating these machines that human beings can live in the now. In his later work, Jesi sought to deactivate myth by emptying the subjectivising machine of Western politics of its power to wrench us outside of ourselves.[134] This provided the model for Agamben's gestures identified with the *hōs mē*.[135] Machines, be they mythological or anthropological, purport to contain inaccessible realities that we are forced to live by. Destroying these machines would only leave them to reform like the Hydra.[136] Deactivation and the suspension of time is the key.[137]

The substance of the reading of the *hōs mē* is derived from Martin Heidegger's reading of 1 Corinthians. 1 Corinthians 7:21 tackles institutional slavery.[138] Michael Flexsenhar points out that Paul is using a hypothetical

129 Agamben (2012) 13–18; Whyte (2010).
130 Agamben (2023c) 179.
131 Agamben (2023c) 181.
132 Agamben (2019a) 1052; Jesi (2014) 157–8.
133 Agamben (2019a) 1052.
134 Noronha (2019) 1086; Jesi (2001) 106–7, 109–20.
135 Aarons (2023) 48.
136 Agamben (2019a) 1055.
137 Agamben (2019a) 1056.
138 Flexsenhar (2015) 72.

argument about manumission for instructional purposes.[139] But the theological consensus is that Paul is speaking to enslaved Corinthians who were concerned about their social and legal status, encouraging them they do not have to remain in their slavery calling.[140] Heidegger read 1 Corinthians and suggested a slave should remain a slave, as in enacting a Christian life, "something remains unchanged and yet is radically changed".[141] For Heidegger, what is decisive is a way of being in an unchanged, yet radically changed, world.[142] Agamben states Heidegger's interpretation of the Christian way of life is determined not by the content of worldly relations, but by the way in which these inauthentic, or improper, relations are "appropriated in their very impropriety".[143]

As van der Heiden argues, Agamben sees the notion of use as introduced in relation to the enslaved person in 1 Corinthians 7:21.[144] Use is therefore found in the account of the slave in both Aristotle and Paul. The enslaved person is a starting point to contemplate what it means to use the body absent compulsive praxis.[145] Paul's advice to the enslaved members of the baptised community in Corinth is that if they have a chance at freedom they should "rather use".[146] The *hōs mē* is an example of a messianic form-of-life that is not based on a vocation but instead 'used'.[147] With this argument, Agamben can deprive messianic calling of any form of identity:

> To be messianic, to live in the Messiah, signifies the expropriation of each and every juridical-factical property (circumcised/uncircumcised; free/slave; man/woman) under the form of the *as not*. This expropriation does not, however, found a new identity.[148]

The 'use of self' is "a new figure of human praxis".[149] To use one's calling as an enslaved person means you do not possess or dominate your own life or that of another.[150] van der Heiden cautions that we must avoid the possibility that in certain uses, the user is in fact enslaved by the thing used.[151]

139 Flexsenhar (2015) 72.
140 Harrill (2003) 575–607.
141 Heidegger (2004) 85.
142 Heidegger (2004) 75.
143 Agamben (2005b) 34.
144 van der Heiden (2020b) 312; Agamben (2016) 3–23.
145 Agamben (2016) 65.
146 Glancy (2020) 13; 1 Cor. 7:21.
147 van der Heiden (2020a) 70; Agamben (2005b) 23–7.
148 Agamben (2005b) 26.
149 Brophy (2021) 196; Agamben (2016) 30.
150 van der Heiden (2020b) 312.
151 van der Heiden (2020a) 73.

The primordial use requires the human to *become a subject that uses as not abusing.*[152]

Paul, chronos and the colonial

Every culture is first of all a particular experience of time. Here we must distinguish time from temporality. Temporality is materially constructed by memory practices and is the experience and perception of time.[153] Time is socially constructed and cognitive, representing the objective attempt to quantify, measure and mark temporality.[154] For Agamben, no new culture is possible without an alteration to time (and, I would add, a focus on temporality). Genuine criticism changes time.[155] As Thanos Zartaloudis explains, the dominant conception of time in Western culture is one of a precise and homogeneous continuum.[156] This empty homogeneous time sees the past as irrevocable, and 'progress' promises a brighter future ahead.[157]

Agamben notes that the Greco-Roman conception of time is conceived specifically as essentially circular and continuous and as having no direction other than unceasingly returning back on itself.[158] Agamben then turns to Aristotle's *Physics* to find the "fundamental character of the Greek experience of time":

> Aristotle thus defines time as "quantity of movement according to the before and after", and its continuity is assured by its division into discrete instants [*tò nŷn*, the now], analogous to the geometric point [*stigmē*]. The instant in itself is nothing more than the continuity of time [*synécheia chrónou*], a pure limit which both joins and divides past and future.[159]

The fleeting instant divides time yet also unites past and future and ensures continuity.[160] This sense of time is ahistorical, not able to be mastered. Modernity is a provisional selective universalisation of a particular linear and singular sorting of time.[161] This is *chronos*, and it empties human time of all content.[162] The fleeting now appears as a 'dead time' compared to a

152 van der Heiden (2020a) 73.
153 Adébísí (2023) 109; Ortiz (2021) 792.
154 Grabham (2016) 16, 34–5.
155 Agamben (2007a) 99.
156 Zartaloudis (2010) 295.
157 Benjamin (2003) 394–5.
158 Agamben (2007a) 100–11.
159 Agamben (2007a) 101.
160 Aristotle (1984a) 222a34–b8.
161 Latour (1993) 76.
162 Zartaloudis (2010) 296; Agamben (2007a) 105.

history of continuous, infinite progress.[163] I connect this to coloniality, which relies on certain approaches to time and temporality to give itself meaning. Coloniality does this through focusing on linearity and mono-temporality (in other words, a *chronopolitics*), which presuppose the inevitability of progress in ways which naturalise the effects of colonialism.[164]

This privileges "the historically specific legal and political infrastructure of European capitalism".[165] Pierre Bourdieu describes this as the exercise of absolute power, manifested through manipulating time to deny alternative possibility to others and grant endless possibility to self.[166] Chronopolitics subsumes bodies and spaces into a single measurement of time, making the contrived and conceived seem natural.[167] Linear time erased other understandings of time in the colonial encounter. This fiction erases the significance of race to the modern state, including how race is used to define who is 'inside' and 'outside' the state.[168] The overlapping of racialisation with modernity ties civilisation to populations marked 'White', erasing any advancement outside of that marking.[169] The times of Indigenous, racialised and colonised peoples became labelled as 'timeless', outside of the developmental process of humanity.[170]

For Agamben, *chronos* is a nullified experience of time and does not allow us to attain authentic history. This splits the human being between being-in-time as an elusive flow of instants and being-in-history as the originary dimension of man, a twofold nature that never coincides in time.[171] This is analogous to Frantz Fanon's writing that colonialism distorts, disfigures and destroys the past of "the oppressed people".[172] This linearity makes invisible the ongoing violence enacted through erasure of othered bodies. It allows 'decolonisation' to be framed as a matter of seeking justice for past wrongs rather than a concern for the future and making the world anew. The colonial-enslavement project appears as a fixed past event rather than an ongoing structure affecting present and future.[173]

Agamben states that we must reconceive time by critiquing the dominance of the *instant* point of time.[174] This different conception of time can be found

163 Agamben (2007a) 106.
164 Adébísí (2023) 109.
165 Tzouvala (2020) 4.
166 Bourdieu (2000) 228.
167 Adébísí (2023) 110.
168 Adébísí (2023) 115.
169 Bell (2020) 389.
170 Alcoff (2007) 84.
171 Agamben (2007a) 109.
172 Fanon (2005) 149.
173 Adébísí (2023) 109.
174 Zartaloudis (2010) 296; Agamben (2007a) 112.

"among the folds and shadows of the Western cultural tradition".[175] One such place is in Paul's writings.[176] This point becomes more resonant if we remember Fanon's charge that Europe is "literally the creation of the Third World".[177] The folds and shadows of Europe's cultural tradition hide many decolonial stories. I view Agamben's thought as capable of being reinvented to this end. I follow Paul Gilroy who compiled an "odd collection of humanist and antihumanist voices" (including Agamben) who:

> [H]ave been bold enough … to approach the metaphysical potency of racism, and to become engaged by what the history of its expressions shows about the constitution of sovereign power, the diminution of justice, and the functional articulation of rationality with irrationality.[178]

Agamben's reading of Paul starts with the first few verses of the Letter of the Romans. Agamben's study aims to place a new meaning on the text that Paul did not intend. This is a Paul of cultural memory, rather than the Paul of historical study.[179] Agamben's Paul is trying to bring about a world which does not yet exist but is a demand – the kingdom of heaven is *here* and *now* for those who are farthest from it.[180]

Agamben's is a "postsecular" reading of Paul that both restores Paul's messianism and remains relevant to the modern era.[181] Paul's writing on slavery is closely connected to the law, and specifically its fulfilment in the messianic moment.[182] The Messiah's arrival brings about the fulfilment, deactivation and inoperativity of the law – the law is fulfilled and gains another use.[183] This affects every juridical and social condition.[184] The enslaved person is invested with the messianic vocation.

Messianic time is a time divided by the messianic event. To live "the time that remains" means a radical transformation of our experience of time.[185] It is a space that escapes the grasp of power and its laws.[186] This is also influenced by Walter Benjamin, who advocated for a relation between the present and the past, in which the struggles of the past are seized and re-actualised in

175 Agamben (2007a) 110.
176 Agamben (2007a) 110.
177 Fanon (2005) 58.
178 Gilroy (2010) 73, 189n29.
179 Wright (2015) 311.
180 Agamben (2018) 32, 34.
181 Agamben (2005b) 1; Frey (2008) 52.
182 Agamben (1999b) 160.
183 Agamben (1999b) 163; Agamben (2005a) 64.
184 Agamben (2005b) 13; Bikundo (2022) 7.
185 Agamben (2012) 9.
186 Agamben (2005b) 27.

the "time of the now" (*Jetztzeit*),[187] which is akin to Paul's term for the messianic event – *ho nun kairos*, "the time of the now".[188] The memory Benjamin focuses on is the memory of "the struggling, oppressed class" and he seeks to re-actualise the hopes, defeats and promises of past generations to transform the present.[189] This time is experienced in authentic revolutions which have been lived as a halting of time and an interruption of chronology.[190] To experience this messianic time implies an integral transformation of ourselves and of our ways of living.[191]

Kairos *and decolonial time*

Decolonisation seeks an escape from coloniality's time and temporality.[192] Time is a fundamental spirit of freedom and its fair distribution the ultimate justice.[193] The task of a genuine revolution is not just to change the world, but to change time.[194] *Kairos* is an idea of time in which life is fulfilled in the moment.[195] *Kairos* works and transforms *chronos* from within,[196] conveying the experience of a singular event that produces an effect not possible in chronological time.[197] Agamben articulates this time as a moment to be taken hold of, to be 'seized'.[198] It is about grasping the potentialities of our current situation to help shape future forms of life.[199] We can understand *kairos* as a rupture in the existing state of affairs that means a:

> [N]ew order becomes possible, in which new possibilities for life, knowledge and the whole of human conduct open up, but it is also a time in which new misfortunes become possible.[200]

This is why experiencing messianic time implies an integral transformation of ourselves and of our ways of living.[201] This interpretation of *kairological time*

187 Benjamin (2003) 394–5.
188 Agamben (2005b) 61.
189 Benjamin (2003) 394.
190 Agamben (2007a) 115.
191 Agamben (2012) 12–13; 1 Cor. 7:29–31; Kerekes (2015) 27–53.
192 Adébísí (2023) 124.
193 Shippen (2014) 3–7.
194 Agamben (2007a) 99.
195 Zartaloudis (2010) 297; Agamben (2007a) 110–11.
196 Agamben (2005b) 67f.
197 Smith (1969) 1–13.
198 Agamben (2005b) 67ff.
199 Agamben (2012) 59.
200 Ó Murchadha (2013) 7.
201 Agamben (2012) 12–13.

emphasises non-synchronised moments and multiple temporal dimensions.[202] This is in the same sense that destitution involves the desire to tear down, dismantle and cancel prevailing political representations and institutions.[203] Such destituent politics and its use of messianic time is a creative movement.[204] In approaching the continuing coloniality of the modern world, decolonisation seeks the abolition of the ongoing and evolving structures of violent exploitation including the epistemologies that keep them in place.[205] It is a historical process of complete disorder.[206] Decolonisation must unseat colonially produced structures of power and technologies of permanent dispossession and dehumanisation.[207] There is power and possibility in dehumanised bodies, spaces and temporalities.[208]

I want to draw a parallel between Agamben's use of *kairos* and the work of Mbiti, who wrote on particularly African notions of time, which he sees as event-orientated.[209] These have been declared as 'out of time' by Western coloniality. Whereas Western notions of time are abstract, Mbiti is concerned with past events, which serve as markers for, and of, time.[210] This evokes Agamben who states that the only place in which the past can live is the present,[211] and the 'now' is a contraction of past and present, and especially of past events.[212] Mbiti explains:

> The linear concept of time in western thought, with an indefinite past, present and indefinite future is practically foreign to African thinking. The future is virtually absent because events which lie in it have not taken place, they have not been realized and cannot, therefore, constitute time … *Actual time* is therefore what is present and what is past. It moves "backward" rather than "forward"; and people set their minds not on future things, but chiefly on what has taken place.[213]

Time has a long past, a present and virtually no future.[214] Mbiti's understanding of time relies heavily on the Kiswahili world, and the concepts of *Zamani*

202 Lindroos (1998) 12.
203 Tarì (2021) 13; Invisible Committee (2017) 76.
204 Aarons (2020) 51.
205 Adébísí (2023) 15.
206 Fanon (2005) 36.
207 Adébísí (2023) 33.
208 Adébísí (2023) 35.
209 Mbiti (1969) 15–28.
210 Cilliers (2018) 114; Booth (1993) 84, quoting Mbiti.
211 Agamben (2019b) 2.
212 Agamben (2005b) 77–8.
213 Mbiti (1969) 17.
214 Mbiti (1969) 16.

and *Sasa*. *Zamani* is part of the Akamba conception of history.[215] *Zamani* is the beginning and end of everything. *Zamani* indicates a point that nothing can go beyond. Here, all time and all events halt.[216] *Sasa* is used by Mbiti to conceive of the present, but *Sasa* (like *Zamani*) is embedded in the 'past'.[217] *Zamani* and *Sasa* are different dimensions of time, but they are reciprocal notions and they also cannot be separated. For example, the ancestors are not absent today but are contemporary.[218]

Johan Cilliers explains that time moves from present (*Sasa*) to past (*Zamani*), and not in a linear movement from past, to present to future. *Sasa*, when used to think of the present, is a complete dimension of time. It has a short future, a dynamic present and a past which is experienced.[219] In that short future, *Sasa* is concerned with what is of immediate concern for people.[220] The present does not influence the future. Rather, it serves the past, and the past gives purpose to the present.[221] On this reading, Western chronopolitics has a 'future' that extends much further than the future in the African notions of time explored by Mbiti.[222] Mbiti's view of time is the 'mirror opposite' of the West.[223] Time does progress linearly in one dimension, but there is a crucial communal dimension. Time is 'created' by events within the community.[224] Events must be experienced to be real:

> Time has to be experienced in order to make sense or to become real … Since what is the future has not been experienced, it does not make sense; it cannot, therefore, constitute part of time, and people do not know how to think about it – unless, of course, it is something which falls within the rhythm of natural phenomena.[225]

On this reading, *Sasa* as actual, present time (the 'now') is intimately connected to the past, which is the idea of *Zamani*. The now is also connected to the future as potential time.[226] 'Now' is the symbolic value of an event, an experience determined by sharing and communality.[227] The values and traditions of a group are handed down from generation to generation through

215 Booth (1993) 83, quoting Mbiti.
216 Cilliers (2019) 205.
217 Cilliers (2019) 204.
218 Mbiti (1969) 23; Cilliers (2019) 204.
219 Cilliers (2018) 116.
220 Cilliers (2019) 204.
221 Cilliers (2018) 116–17.
222 English (2006) 54.
223 Cilliers (2018) 117; Booth (1993) 84, quoting Mbiti.
224 Cilliers (2018) 118.
225 Mbiti (1969) 17.
226 Cilliers (2019) 209.
227 Cilliers (2019) 209.

recalling life's experiences. This can be done through song, dance or stories.[228] The present, or the 'now', is the experience of the event of actual time.[229] Cilliers connects this to fulfilled time, or *pleroma*. Experiencing actual time involves the experiencing of the fullness, the *pleroma*, of a given time in a given place.[230] This is speaking the same language of messianic time as Agamben. The *pleroma* of encounters makes the here and now worthwhile.[231] Cilliers further connects this *pleroma* to *kairos*, which emphasises the communal and relational dimension of experiencing time.[232] Achille Mbembé makes a similar point when he explains that in ancient African traditions, the point of departure for the questioning of human existence (which is lived temporally) is one of relation and mutual implication. Identity is not a matter of substance but plasticity. History, from this point of view, unties and reties the knots and potentials of situations.[233]

How can we conceive of this life of shared experiences? From the asymmetry of messianic time within history flows an *asymmetrical model of conflict*.[234] Agamben speaks of a 'remnant', which he holds stands for a *people* who embody resistance to the prevailing systems.[235] This indicates that grasping messianic time does transform our way of living, but this grasping is not a solitary activity.[236] We must seek a genuinely autonomous premise for collective life, and the *gestures* that permit us to inhabit it.[237]

Form-of-life dwells together and is structured by its reference to others.[238] A dwelling life is a life of continuity, with life's various moments (the past and the present especially) being "infinitely connected".[239] One is free to use one's own existence and all its contingent characteristics and callings, including a life with others.[240] Being-thus always means being with. This is reflected in *Nudities* when Agamben admits the centrality of relations with others to humanity:

> The desire to be recognised by others is inseparable from being human. Indeed, such recognition is so essential that, according to Hegel, everyone is ready to put his or her own life in jeopardy in order to obtain it. This is

228 Cilliers (2018) 120.
229 Cilliers (2018) 123.
230 Cilliers (2019) 211.
231 Cilliers (2018) 124.
232 Cilliers (2018) 130.
233 Mbembé (2019) 28.
234 Aarons (2020) 82.
235 Agamben (2005b) 57.
236 Agamben (2005b) 54–5.
237 Agamben (2000) 59–114; Aarons (2020) 82.
238 Agamben (2023b) 295.
239 Agamben (2023b) 309–10.
240 van der Heiden (2020b) 312; Agamben (2005b) 26.

> not merely a question of satisfaction or self-love; rather, it is only through recognition by others that man can constitute himself as a person.[241]

Agamben's *kairos* can be read as relying on a communal experience of past events, and a refusal to live one's life according to chronopolitics:

> For history is not, as the dominant ideology would have it, humans' servitude to continuous linear time, but their liberation from it: the time of history and the *cairós* in which humans, by this initiative, grasp favorable opportunity and choose their own freedom in the moment. Just as the full, discontinuous, finite and complete time of pleasure must be set against the empty, continuous and infinite time of vulgar historicism, so the chronological time of pseudo-history must be opposed by the *cairological* time of authentic history.[242]

What is most proper to every creature is its substitutability, its being in any case in the place of the other.[243] This notion of substitution effects the transition to a messianic community as the site in which the displacement of each is the condition of possibility by which things might be displaced and novel.[244]

Messianic *kairos* can be read as decolonial. The use of the slave for Paul means seizing the 'now' and stepping out of the homogeneity of time as *chronos*. Hyper-hermeneutic gestures are messianic in the sense that they transform an existing vocation into a new use, and are modes of living to be followed. This reading of Paul allows us to consider how and why the choice of using one's life differently is a form of freedom lived in the moment. Gestures can disrupt the idea of time as endless progress. Living in the 'now' means living for yourself but also with others, deactivating colonial apparatuses through actions that become examples that impact future gestures. In the remainder of this chapter, I use the figure of Spartacus, and the writings of Jesi, to show how past events can shape political action in the 'now' of *kairos*.

The Spartacist revolt

The example of revolts by enslaved people has had an enduring influence and informed the communal understanding of time, connecting the past to the present and future. The Spartacist revolt is such an example. Badiou viewed it as an example of an 'event', which demonstrated "the real political

241 Agamben (2010a) 46.
242 Agamben (2007a) 115.
243 Agamben (2007b) 23; Karmy Bolton (2023) 168.
244 Agamben (2007b) 1.

subjectivity of the slave".[245] Major Roman revolts by the enslaved were primarily a feature of the late Republic (133–30 BCE). The civil wars were caused due to Roman conquests in the Mediterranean, and the massive influx of enslaved people into the Roman system.[246] The Romans constantly feared such revolts. Roman slaveholders had a saying – you have as many enemies as you have slaves.[247] The first of these famous slave wars was the first Sicilian slave war, which carried on until the late 130s BCE. The Spartacist revolt finished in 71 BCE.[248] Hunt puts it bluntly – Rome's resources and determination were immense. Crassus was given ten legions to defeat Spartacus. If Crassus failed, Pompey had been given a large army in Spain. In the event, Pompey's forces killed the soldiers of Spartacus who had escaped Crassus.[249]

Spartacus's revolt was not just a slave revolt. Although Spartacus and his generals were gladiators, and although there were enslaved people in his army, this was not a slave war but a nationalist conflict of Italians against Roman rule.[250] Plutarch noted that Spartacus's fighters were not criminals deserving of their death.[251] Spartacus used Roman funeral rites for his generals. Florus saw Spartacus as a would-be Roman. Spartacus died fighting in the front line, like a true Roman general.[252] The enslaved put on gladiatorial games using 400 Roman prisoners.[253] Large concentrations of Italian peasants and enslaved people in Italy deserted to the rebels, especially in areas where there were large concentrations of enslaved people and few free people.[254]

We do not know exactly what the rebels wanted. The idea that Spartacus was a prophet with a social message opposing slavery has been doubted in recent scholarship.[255] The nature of the revolt took on different interpretations by readers, in a similar way to the ways the judgment in *Somerset* was interpreted by enslaved people. The rise of Christianity led to the nature of the rebellion being rewritten. Christians assimilated the attitudes of their classical ancestors, sometimes changing narratives and histories to better connect to their religion.[256] Augustine saw Spartacus as having divine help, given the strength of Rome at the time.[257] In the 1760s, Spartacus became a

245 Badiou (2009) 51–4; C Wright (2013).
246 Urbainczyk (2008) 103.
247 Joshel (2010) 64.
248 Urbainczyk (2008) 102.
249 Hunt (2017) 164.
250 Piccinin (2004) 198; Rubinsohn (1971) 290–9.
251 Plutarch (1859) 8.1.
252 Florus (1960) 2.8.14; Urbainczyk (2008) 109.
253 Orosius (2010) 5.24.3.
254 Hunt (2017) 169.
255 Urbainczyk (2008) 101–2; Griffith (1981) 64–70.
256 Urbainczyk (2008) 113.
257 Augustine (2003) 4.5; Burnell (1993) 184–5.

symbol of resistance to oppression and of the struggle for liberty and freedom. The figure of Spartacus the 'rebel slave' was hailed as a romanticised ideology of resistance in the past that was tied to debates about the freedom of the citizens in the nation states in the present.[258] The 'Spartacus ideology' was closely intertwined with ideological battles.[259]

The way Spartacus came to serve as an icon for modern Western contemplations of liberty is a warning that there is no aspect of the study of ancient slavery that is exempt from the effects of ideological abuse.[260] Against these concerns, I wish to view Spartacus as an example, a paradigm. Our present is intelligible as the past of the object. Past forms-of-life provide a model, or a structure of behaviour, for the present. Spartacus stands as an example which was used in the immediate aftermath of the Great War in Germany for others seeking to seize the time of the 'now'.

The Spartakusbund

The *Spartakusbund* was a radical-left group operating in Germany during the Great War, gathered around Rosa Luxemburg and Karl Liebknecht.[261] It was at the centre of the January 1919 Berlin uprising. Spartacus was deliberately invoked by the group. This was done in part because Luxemburg had predicted that capitalist accumulation would slow and lead to crisis and war.[262] Using mythical figures from antiquity was not unusual. Marx referred to Rome in his use of the Roman *proletarii* to conceptualise the modern working class and even described Spartacus as a "genuine representative of the ancient proletariat".[263]

Jesi saw the Berlin uprising, with its invocation of Spartacus, as a messianic event. *Spartakus* is an effort to work through the defeat of a mass uprising.[264] The present was conceived of as an anticipation.[265] The use of the name of Spartacus was a political operation, an invocation of the mythical time of the slave revolt,[266] as well as the perceived commonalities between the slave revolt and the modern class struggle.[267] The late Roman Republic was seen as a historical moment where class antagonism had a disruptive force.[268]

258 Shaw (1998) 50.
259 Shaw (1998) 50–1.
260 Shaw (1998) 51.
261 Noronha (2019) 1082.
262 Noronha (2019) 1095; Luxemburg (1951) 446.
263 Noronha (2019) 1083; Marx and Engels (1985) 264–5.
264 Aarons (2019) 1020.
265 Scholem (1971) 3.
266 Jesi (2014) 40.
267 Noronha (2019) 1087.
268 Noronha (2019) 1091.

Enslaved people were exploited and commodified in a manner similar to the German working class at the time.[269] Spartacus inflicted two years of military defeats against the greatest power of the time. The fact that he was only presumed dead (his body was never identified), contributed to the myth surrounding him.[270]

Ricardo Noronha makes clear that the memory of Spartacus persisted as he opened a briefly glimpsed horizon of possibilities which then almost completely vanished. He was a symbol of unfulfilled collective emancipation.[271] 'Bolshevism' acquired a status of promising collective emancipation after the October Revolution.[272] The history of Roman antiquity also seemed to mirror the German ruling classes' attempts at foreign conquest and forcing foreign prisoners of war into labour.[273] Waves of strikes and mass demonstrations in November 1918 led to the Kaiser's abdication.[274] In December, in messianic language, Luxemburg foresaw the final battle in the continuation or abolition of exploitation.[275] Luxemburg repeated this apocalyptic tone in the programme drafted for the German Communist Party (KDP), declaring that only a world revolution can bring order to chaos.[276]

On 5 January 1919 there was a "Spartacist week", a putsch. Noronha explains that several hundred armed men occupied buildings in Berlin, in anticipation of the decisive moment. For Jesi, this insurrection led the *Spartakusbund* to act as a "flag for revolt", a symbol of fighting against unfavourable odds.[277] The choice of label is vital. Jesi distinguishes revolts from revolutions. Both seek to seize power, but they have different experiences of time. Jesi called 'revolts' those actions that suspend historical time. In contrast, revolutionary subjectivity is identified with and sustains historical time.[278] This is because revolution has a longer-term strategic horizon.[279] Revolt cannot be understood through the ideological and material factors that conditioned its emergence. Its event-like structure effects a symbolic transformation like a mythic epiphany. Aarons explains further: a revolt overturns any link between revolutionary strategy and historical forces; it has its own internal logic and rhythm that is irreducible to the reasons the

269 Noronha (2019) 1092; Schiavone (2013) 66–7.
270 Jesi (2014) 139; Shaw (2001) 44–50.
271 Noronha (2019).1092–3.
272 Noronha (2019) 1093.
273 Noronha (2019) 1095–6.
274 Noronha (2019) 1097–8.
275 Kuhn (2012) 114; Noronha (2019) 1096.
276 Luxemburg (1971) 366–7.
277 Noronha (2019) 1099; Jesi (2014) 56.
278 Jesi (2014) 46, 51–2; Aarons (2023) 51.
279 Aarons (2019) 1022; Jesi (2014) 58.

participants may have offered for their involvement.[280] Jesi acknowledges the role of the past as an example or paradigm to influence the present:

> To represent, *to repeat*, is a gesture that cannot be genuinely carried out unless one takes into account the profound contrast, or better yet the radical opposition, between remembrance and survival, memory and duration.[281]

During the Spartacist revolt, as an armed clash became inevitable, the experience of time changed in Berlin. Every hour had become an hour of waiting, instants in a greater wait for victory. Everything that happened seemed to happen forever.[282] The messianic time that gripped the revolution was underpinned with the figure of an enslaved person, rebelling against the catastrophe underway.[283] Revolt crystallises a shared horizon of partisan experience, generating a distinct 'common'.[284] In a revolt a human being determines their self-realisation as part of a collective.[285] It is only in revolt that the city becomes your *own* city because it belongs to you and the 'others'. In the hour of revolt, one is no longer alone in the city.[286]

Like Spartacus's rebellion, the *Spartakusbund* was doomed to fail. They were opposed by the heavily armed *Freikorps*, and the remaining reliable units of the German Army. Jesi argues that the Spartacist revolt failed as it served the very power it attacked. The suspension of historical time proved indispensable for the holders of power who sought to restore the 'normal times' which they had suspended during the Great War.[287]

Decolonial thought against the machine

The example of the *Spartakusbund* for Jesi shows that challenging the mythological machine requires more than revolt or revolution.[288] In a post-mythological age, mythic violence does not disappear but reasserts itself in negative forms.[289] This means revolt can be captured by counter-revolutionary mytho-symbolic forms, as it was in Berlin.[290] Agamben also notes the urgency of

280 Aarons (2023) 49.
281 Jesi (2014) 119.
282 Jesi (2014) 46–7.
283 Noronha (2019) 1101.
284 Aarons (2019) 1024.
285 Jesi (2014) 53.
286 Jesi (2014) 54–5.
287 Jesi (2014) 60–1.
288 Jesi (2019) 1015.
289 Aarons (2019) 1018.
290 Aarons (2023) 52.

overcoming the opposition between revolt and revolution.[291] We require a gesture that elicits a 'nonknowledge' of what the mythological (or anthropological) machine offers. This gesture is a destituent 'as not', and the idea that another time can make itself present in this world.[292]

The acts of the *Spartakusbund*, much like the acts of the Franciscan Order, point the way to a new world, and show how examples from the past can shape the present, even if they did not succeed in deactivating systems of control. In this sense, destituent potential "welcomes non-Being".[293] Non-Being, a sterile and arid region,[294] is where authentic (but fragile) upheaval can be born, and time as *kairos* given effect through events.[295] Decolonisation's key register is anticolonial – a refusal.[296] This refusal is important. Destituent events are political as they involve a revocation of representation and identities. The central problem is a question of understanding how our own lives came to be neutralised or "suspended", as if our very existence were "put in parentheses".[297]

Agamben sees a refusal as "the strongest objection to the principle of sovereignty".[298] An individual's ability to refuse is a key register of resistance and can open up (in Agamben's terms) future possibilities for living one's life as a form. Our present refusals are real possibilities for our future. This means that past actions will also inform the present and the future, in the sense of actual time mentioned by Mbiti.[299] The messianic community is not a factual event or state that occurs at a given moment but names the experiential process through which time is actively seized upon and constructed from fragment to fragment.[300] There will be a small displacement that establishes a new world.[301]

Each of us is living out the "absurdity of individual existence", but this is the precursor to a new form of life.[302] The focus must be on messianic gestures which seek to decolonise time and seize the now. These gestures will be evental, and actions will be linked to the past to (re)define the understanding of the present and the future. In doing so, these gestures will create forms of life.[303] Such gestures and events will escape from this chronopolitics, halting

291 Aarons (2023) 68, translating Agamben (1996).
292 Aarons (2023) 66–7; Agamben (1999b):
293 Agamben (1999a) 182.
294 Fanon (1970) 2.
295 Fanon (1970) 10.
296 James (2001) 362.
297 Agamben (2023a) 15–16.
298 Agamben (1998) 48.
299 Agamben (2023b) 321.
300 Aarons (2020) 82–3.
301 Agamben (2007b) 53.
302 Agamben (2007b) 65.
303 Invisible Committee (2017) 70.

the machine that divides life and point towards possible forms of agency and belonging.

Conclusion

This chapter has placed the writings of Paul as an intermediary between Aristotle and Hegel in Agamben's own philosophy. I have used Paul's writings on the radical equality of a slave to distinguish his approach from Aristotle. We must think about the use of the body in messianic terms. Paul's messianism 'deactivates', in the sense that it revokes all legal and social labels and categories, and every vocation. It deactivates machines and apparatuses of control, be they mythological or anthropological. It is through deactivation, not revolution, that form-of-life will find space to live. Paul's notion of time as *kairos* is also crucial here. *Kairos* is distinct from *chronos*, which is the idea of time running in a homogeneous continuum or progress. *Chronos* is the time of colonialism. *Kairos* is the time of the now, a life fulfilled in the moment. This is connected to decolonial approaches to time. For example, Mbiti. For Mbiti, the present serves the past, and the past gives purpose to the present. Time is a communal experience of events. For me, this indicates that form-of-life lives *kairologically*, as part of a community of others. There are examples of this time throughout our cultural history. Spartacus is one such example.

The action of the Spartacist revolt was an example of emancipation that influenced the actions of the *Spartakusbund* in Germany in 1919. The past actions of enslaved people thus shape political activity in the now. The coming politics will involve an excavation of the past. The *Spartakusbund*, despite failing, shows how shards of messianic time can point towards what it means to live a life as a form. In the next chapter, this point is developed in relation to Hegel's master-slave dialectic, and Alexander Kojève's interpretation of Hegel. Hegel's dialectic, so crucial to Western philosophy, cannot be separated from early modern colonial slavery. The figure of the slave gains a crucial destiny in the philosophical anthropology of the West, but one which ignores the lives of enslaved people.

Reference List

Aarons, K (2019) 'Cruel Festivals: Furio Jesi and the Critique of Political Autonomy', *Theory & Event*, 22, 1018–46.

Aarons, K (2020) 'Destitution and Creation: Agamben's Messianic Gesture', *Journal of Italian Philosophy*, 3, 51–89.

Aarons, K (2023) '"A Dance without a Song": Revolt and Community in Furio Jesi's Late Work', *South Atlantic Quarterly*, 122, 47–72.

Adébísí, F (2023) *Decolonisation and Legal Knowledge: Reflections on Power and Possibility*, Bristol: Bristol University Press.

Agamben, G (1996) 'Il talismano di Furio Jesi' in Jesi, F, *Lettura del 'Bateau ivre' di Rimbaud*, Rome: Quodlibet.
Agamben, G (1998) *Homo Sacer: Sovereign Power and Bare Life*, Heller-Roazen, D (trans.), Stanford: Stanford University Press.
Agamben, G (1999a) 'On Potentiality' in *Potentialities: Collected Essays in Philosophy*, Heller-Roazen, D (trans.), Stanford: Stanford University Press, 177–84.
Agamben, G (1999b) 'The Messiah and the Sovereign: The Problem of Law in Walter Benjamin' in *Potentialities: Collected Essays in Philosophy*, Heller-Roazen, D (trans.), Stanford: Stanford University Press, 160–74.
Agamben, G (2000) *Means Without End: Notes on Politics*, Binetti, V and Casarino, C (trans.), Minneapolis: University of Minnesota Press.
Agamben, G (2005a) *State of Exception*, Attell, K (trans.), Chicago: University of Chicago Press.
Agamben, G (2005b) *The Time That Remains: A Commentary on the Letter to the Romans*, Dailey, P (trans.), Stanford: Stanford University Press.
Agamben, G (2007a) *Infancy and History: On the Destruction of Experience*, Heron, L (trans.), London: Verso Books.
Agamben, G (2007b) *The Coming Community*, Hardt, M (trans.), Minneapolis: University of Minnesota Press.
Agamben, G (2010a) *Nudities*, Kishik, D and Pedatella, S (trans.), Stanford: Stanford University Press.
Agamben, G (2010b) *The Sacrament of Language: An Archaeology of the Oath*, Kotsko, A (trans.), Stanford, Stanford University Press.
Agamben, G (2012) *The Church and the Kingdom*, de la Durantaye, L (trans.), London: Seagull Books.
Agamben, G (2016) *The Use of Bodies*, Kotsko, A (trans.), Stanford: Stanford University Press.
Agamben, G (2018) *What Is Philosophy?*, Chiesa, L (trans.), Stanford: Stanford University Press.
Agamben, G (2019a) 'On the Impossibility of Saying "I": Epistemological Paradigms and Poetic Paradigms in the Work of Furio Jesi', *Theory & Event*, 22, 1047–57.
Agamben, G (2019b) *Creation and Anarchy: The Work of Art and the Religion of Capitalism*, Kotsko, A (trans.), Stanford: Stanford University Press.
Agamben, G (2023a) 'Destituent Potentiality and the Critique of Realization', *The South Atlantic Quarterly*, 112, 9–17.
Agamben, G (2023b) *Hölderlin's Madness: Chronicle of a Dwelling Life, 1806–1843*, Price, A L (trans.), Chicago, University of Chicago Press.
Agamben, G (2023c) *Pinocchio: The Adventures of a Puppet, Doubly Commented Upon and Triply Illustrated*, Kotsko, A (trans.), Calcutta: Seagull Books.
Alcoff, L M (2007) 'Mignolo's Epistemology of Coloniality', *CR: The New Centennial Review*, 7, 79–101.
Aristotle (1984a) 'Physics' in *The Complete Works of Aristotle, Volume One*, Barnes, J (ed.), Princeton: Princeton University Press.
Aristotle (1984b) 'Politics' in *The Complete Works of Aristotle, Volume Two*, Barnes, J (ed.), Princeton: Princeton University Press.
Augustine (2003) *City of God*, London: Penguin.
Badiou, A (2009) *Logic of Worlds*, Toscano, A (trans.), London: Continuum.

Badiou, A (2017) 'Hegel's Master and Slave', *Crisis and Critique*, 4, 34–47.
Bell, D (2020) *Dreamworlds of Race: Empire and the Utopian Destiny of Anglo-America*, Princeton: Princeton University Press.
Benjamin, W (2003) 'On the Concept of History' in *Walter Benjamin, Selected Writings, Volume 4: 1938–1940*, Jennings, M (ed.), Cambridge: Harvard University Press, 389–400.
Bikundo, E (2022) 'Follow Your Leader – I Prefer Not to: Slavery, Giorgio Agamben and Herman Melville', *Law, Culture and the Humanities*, 18, 4–19.
Booth, N (1993) 'Time and African Beliefs Revisited' in Olupona, J and Nyang, S (eds.), *Religious Plurality in Africa: Essays in Honour of John S Mbiti*, Berlin and Boston: De Gruyter, 83–94.
Bourdieu, P (2000) *Pascalian Meditations*, Stanford: Stanford University Press.
Brace, L (2018) *The Politics of Slavery,* Edinburgh: Edinburgh University Press.
Bradley, K (1992) '"The Regular Daily Traffic in Slaves": Roman History and Contemporary History', *The Classical Journal*, 87, 125–38.
Brophy, S (2021) 'A Politics Like No Other: Agamben, Fanon, and the Colonial Fracture' in Norris, M and Dickinson, C (eds.), *Agamben and the Existentialists*, Edinburgh: Edinburgh University Press, 191–211.
Buckland, W (2010) *The Roman Law of Slavery: The Condition of the Slave in Private Law from Augustus to Justinian*, New York: Cambridge University Press.
Burnell, P (1993) 'The Problem of Service to Unjust Regimes in Augustine's *City of God*', *Journal of the History of Ideas*, 54, 177–88.
Camp, S (2004) *Closer to Freedom: Enslaved Women and Everyday Resistance in the Plantation South*, Chapel Hill: The University of North Carolina Press.
Cassius Dio Cocceianus (1990) *The Augustan Settlement: Roman History Books 53.1–55.9*, Rich J (ed.), Warminster: Art & Phillips.
Cilliers, J (2018) 'The *Kairos* of *Karos*: Revisiting Notions of Temporality in Africa', *Stellenbosch Theological Journal*, 4, 113–32.
Cilliers, J (2019) *Timing Grace: Reflections on the Temporality of Preaching*, Stellenbosch: SUN PReSS.
Columella (1941) *De Re Rustica (On Agriculture)*, Cambridge: Harvard University Press.
Cornelius Tacitus (1939) *The Annals of Tacitus*, London: Methuen & Co Ltd.
Cornelius Tacitus (1964) *The Histories*, London: Penguin.
Donfried, K and Marshall, I H (1993) *The Theology of the Shorter Pauline Letters*, Cambridge: Cambridge University Press.
English, P (2006) 'Kalumba, Mbiti, and a Traditional African Concept of Time', *Philosophia Africana*, 9, 53–6.
Fanon, F (1970) *Black Skin, White Masks*, Markmann, C (trans.), London: Paladin.
Fanon, F (2005) *The Wretched of the Earth*, Farrington, C (trans.), New York: Grove Press.
Fee, G (1987) *The First Epistle to the Corinthians*, Grand Rapids: Eerdmans.
Finley, M (1998) *Ancient Slavery and Modern Ideology*, Princeton: Markus Wiener Publishers.
Fiskesjö, M (2012) 'Outlaws, Barbarians, Slaves: Critical Reflections on Agamben's Homo Sacer', *HAU: Journal of Ethnographic Theory*, 21, 161–80.

Flexsenhar III, M (2015) 'Recovering Paul's Hypothetical Slaves: Rhetoric and Reality in 1 Corinthians 7:21', *Journal for the Study of Paul and his Letters*, 5, 71–88.

Florus (1960) *Epitome of Roman History*, Cambridge: Harvard University Press.

Frey, C (2008) 'χλῆ̂σις/Beruf: Luther, Weber, Agamben', *New German Critique*, 105, 35–56.

Gilroy, P (2010) *Darker than Blue: On the Moral Economies of Black Atlantic Culture*, Cambridge: Harvard University Press.

Glancy, J (2002) *Slavery in Early Christianity*, Oxford: Oxford University Press.

Glancy, J (2020) 'On Agamben's Slave without Slavery', *Diacritics*, 38, 4–27.

Grabham, E (2016) *Brewing Legal Times: Things, Form, and the Enactment of Law*, Toronto: University of Toronto Press.

Griffith, J G (1981) "Spartacus and the Growth of Historical and Political Legends' in Fol, A (ed.), *Spartacus: Symposium Rebus Spartaci Gestis Dedicatum 2050*, Sofia: Editions de l'Académie Bulgare de Sciences, 64–70.

Harper, K (2011) *Slavery in the Late Roman World*, Cambridge: Cambridge University Press.

Harrill, J A (2003) 'Paul and Slavery' in Sampley, P (ed.), *Paul in the Greco-Roman World: A Handbook*, Harrisburg: Trinity Press International, 575–607.

Heidegger, M (2004) *The Phenomenology of Religious Life*, Fritsch, M and Gosetti-Ferencei (trans.), Bloomington: Indiana University Press.

Hunt, P (2017) *Ancient Greek and Roman Slavery*, Hoboken: Wiley-Blackwell.

Invisible Committee (2017) *Now*, Hurley, R (trans.), Los Angeles: Semiotext(e).

Jacobs, H (1987) *Incidents in the Life of a Slave Girl: Written by Herself*, Yellin, J (ed.), Cambridge: Harvard University Press.

James, C L R (2001) *The Black Jacobins: Toussaint L'Ouverture and the San Domingo Revolution*, London: Penguin.

Jesi, F (2001) *Materiali Mitologici. Mito e Antropologia nella Cultura Mitteleuropea*, Torino: Einaudi.

Jesi, F (2014) *Spartakus. The Symbology of Revolt*, Toscano, A (trans.), Chicago: Chicago University Press.

Jesi, F (2019) 'A Reading of Rimbaud's 'Bateau ivre'', *Theory & Event*, 22, 1003–17.

Joshel, S (2010) *Slavery in the Roman World*, Cambridge: Cambridge University Press.

Justinian (1998a) *The Digest of Justinian, Volume 2*, Watson, A (ed.), Philadelphia: University of Pennsylvania Press.

Justinian (1998b) *The Digest of Justinian, Volume 4*, Watson, A (ed.), Philadelphia: University of Pennsylvania Press.

Karmy Bolton, R (2023) 'The Absolute Gift: Martyrdom as Destituent Power', *South Atlantic Quarterly*, 122, 157–70.

Kerekes, E (2015) 'The Figure of the Apostle Paul in Contemporary Philosophy (Heidegger, Badiou, Agamben, Žižek)', *Journal for the Study of Religions and Ideologies*, 14, 27–53.

Kotsko, A (2018) *Neoliberalism's Demons: On the Late Political Theology of Late Capital*, Stanford: Stanford University Press.

Kuhn, R (2012) *All Power to the Councils! A Documentary History of the German Revolution of 1918–1919*, Oakland: PM Press.

Latour, B (1993) *We Have Never Been Modern*, Cambridge: Harvard University Press.

Lenski, N (2016), 'Violence and the Roman Slave', in Reiss, W and Fagan, G (eds.), *The Topography of Violence in the Greco-Roman World*, Ann Arbor: University of Michigan Press, 275–98.

Lewis, A (2015) 'Slavery, Family, and Status' in Johnston, D (ed.), *The Cambridge Companion to Roman Law*, Cambridge: Cambridge University Press, 151–74.

Lindroos, K (1998) *Now-Time, Image-Space: Temporalization of Politics in Walter Benjamin's Philosophy of History and Art*, Jyvăskylă: University of Jyvăskylă: SoPhi.

Luxemburg, R (1951) *The Accumulation of Capital*, London: Routledge.

Luxemburg, R (1971) *Selected Political Writings*, New York: Monthly Review Press.

Marcus Porcius Cato (1998) *De agricultura*, Blackawton: Prospect Books.

Marx, K and Engels, F (1985) *Collected Works, Volume 41*, London: Lawrence & Wishart.

Mbembé, A (2019) *Necropolitics*, Durham: Duke University Press.

Mbiti, J (1969) *African Religions and Philosophy*, London: Heinemann.

Miller, F (1999) 'The Greek East and Roman Law. The Dossier of M. Cn. Lucinius Rufinus', *Journal of Roman Studies*, 89, 90–108.

Noronha, R (2019), 'The Myth of Spartacus and the Tradition of the Oppressed', *Theory & Event*, 22, 1082–1104.

Ó Murchadha, F (2013) *The Time of Revolution: Kairos and Chronos in Heidegger*, London: Bloomsbury.

O'Connell Davison, J (2015) *Modern Slavery: The Margins of Freedom*, Basingstoke: Palgrave Macmillan.

Ojakangas, M (2011) 'Becoming Whosoever: Reexamining Pauline Universalism', *The Bible & Critical Theory*, 7, 17–26.

Orosius (2010) *Seven Books of History Against the Pagans*, Fear, A (trans.), Liverpool: Liverpool University Press.

Ortiz, P L (2021) 'Against the Mythological Machine, Towards Decolonial Revolt', *Theory & Event*, 24, 787–815.

Patterson, O (1982) *Slavery and Social Death: A Comparative Study*, Cambridge: Harvard University Press.

Patterson, O (2007) 'The Ancient and Medieval Origins of Modern Freedom' in Mintz, S and Stauffer, J (eds.), *The Problem of Evil: Slavery, Freedom, and the Ambiguities of American Reform,* Amhurst and Boston: University of Massachusetts Press, 31–66.

Petersen, N (1985) *Rediscovering Paul: Philemon and the Sociology of Paul's Narrative World*, Philadelphia: Fortress Press.

Phaedrus (1984) *Babrius and Phaedrus*, Perry, B E (trans.), Cambridge: Harvard University Press.

Piccinin, P (2004) 'Les Italiens dans le Bellum Spartacium', *Historia*, 53, 173–99.

Plutarch (1859) *Plutarch's Lives: Translated from the Original Greek, with Notes, Critical and Historical, and a Life of Plutarch*, New York: Derby & Jackson.

Rawson, B (1966) 'Family Life among the Lower Classes at Rome in the First Two Centuries of the Empire', *Classical Philology*, 61, 71–83.

Rubinsohn, W Z (1971) 'Was the Bellum Spartacium a Servile Insurrection?', *Rivista di filologia e d'instruzione classica*, 99, 290–99.

Saller, R (1998) 'Symbols of Gender and Status Hierarchies in the Roman Household' in Joshel, S and Murnaghan, S (eds.), *Women and Slaves in Greco-Roman Culture: Differential Equations*, New York: Routledge, 85–91.
Schiavone, A (2013) *Spartacus*, New Haven: Harvard University Press.
Scholem, G (1971) *The Messianic Idea in Judaism And Other Essays on Jewish Spirituality,* New York: Schocken Books.
Shaw, B (1998) "A Wolf by the Ears': M. I. Finley's Ancient Slavery and Modern Ideology in Historical Context' in Finley, M, *Ancient Slavery and Modern Ideology*, Princeton: Markus Wiener, 3–53.
Shaw, B (2001) *Spartacus and the Slave Wars. A Brief History with Documents,* Boston: Bedford/St. Martins.
Shippen, N (2014) *Decolonizing Time: Work, Leisure, and Freedom*, New York: Springer.
Shumway, E (1901) 'Freedom and Slavery in Roman Law', *The American Law Register (1898–1907)*, 49, 636–53.
Smith, J (1969) 'Time, Times and the "Right Time": Chronos and Kairos', *The Monist*, 53, 1–13.
Tarì, M (2021) *There Is No Unhappy Revolution: The Communism of Destitution*, Richard Braude (trans.), Brooklyn: Common Notions.
Taylor, W (2012) *Paul: Apostle to the Nations, An Introduction*, Minneapolis: Fortress Press.
Treggiari, S (1975) 'Family Life among the Staff of the Volusii', *Transactions of the American Philological Association*, 105, 393–401.
Trott, A, (2017) 'Nature, Action and Politics: A Critique of Arendt's Reading of Aristotle', *Ancient Philosophy*, 37, 113–28.
Tzouvala, N (2020) *Capitalism as Civilisation: A History of International Law*, Cambridge: Cambridge University Press.
Urbainczyk, T (2008) *Slave Revolts in Antiquity*, London: Routledge.
van der Heiden, G-J (2020a) 'Exile, Use, and Form-of-Life: On the Conclusion of Agamben's *Homo Sacer* Series', *Theory, Culture & Society*, 37, 61–78.
van der Heiden, G-J (2020b) 'On Use and Care: A Debate between Agamben and Heidegger', *International Journal of Philosophy and Theology*, 81, 310–27.
Vetter, B (2005) 'Another Legal Transplant: The Application of the Roman Law of Slavery in the United States – The Unique Case of the State of Louisiana', *Fundamina*, 11, 375–84.
Vlassopoulos, K (2021) *Historicising Ancient Slavery*, Edinburgh: Edinburgh University Press.
Whyte, J (2010) "A New Use of the Self': Giorgio Agamben on the Coming Community', *Theory & Event*, 13.
Wright, C (2013) *Badiou in Jamaica: The Politics of Conflict*, Melbourne: Re-Press.
Wright, N T (2015) *Paul and His Recent Interpreters: Some Contemporary Debates*, London: SPCK.
Zartaloudis, T (2010) *Giorgio Agamben: Power, Law and the Uses of Criticism*, Abingdon: Routledge.

Chapter 5

The master-slave dialectic and the enslaved

Introduction

This chapter considers G W F Hegel's master-slave dialectic. It is through the dialectic that the figure of the slave gains a crucial destiny in the philosophical anthropology of the West, which shaped subsequent understandings of political belonging. Hegel is a key thinker in considering the importance of the enslaved person for Agamben's form-of-life. Both assign the slave a "constitutive anthropological function".[1] But Agamben's writings on the slave go further than Hegel, who uses the slave in an abstract form to think about the preconditions of the truly human.[2] Agamben sees the community of use between the master and slave as having the potential for a new figure of human praxis, which is further connected to Alexander Kojève's concept of the 'workless slave'.

Agamben's 'slave' combines Aristotle's 'use of the body' with Paul's messianic conception of time as *kairos* that can deactivate apparatuses of control, rendering them inoperative. This is connected to Hegel through the dialectic, which Agamben sees as a basis for theories of recognition and a life with others, and is influenced by both Luther and Paul. Specifically, Agamben connects Hegel's 'sublation' to Paul's use of *katargēsis* or inoperativity. In this sense, Hegel's thought is read messianically. But Agamben's Hegel is also Kojève's Hegel. Kojève's concept of *désoeuvrement* is also, on Agamben's argument, a translation of the Pauline *katargein*. The workless slave ends the dialectic of history through non-dialectical means and inoperative praxis.

But any consideration of the master-slave dialectic must understand that Hegel's account cannot be separated from early modern colonial slavery. Race is the historical limitation to the master-slave dialectic in Hegel. In a similar vein, Agamben's consideration of slavery needs to engage with intersections

1 Agamben (2016) 36.
2 Glancy (2020) 10.

DOI: 10.4324/9781003303534-6

of race, gender and the histories of enslaved populations to ameliorate it.[3] This sets the stage for the remaining chapters of this book.

This chapter has three sections. Firstly, I examine the Hegelian dialectic and the connections between the treatment of slavery in Aristotle and the treatment of the enslaved person in Hegel. Drawing on Malcolm Bull's work, I show how for Hegel, slavery creates the conditions for freedom. I outline the meaning of the dialectic, which seeks to explain self-consciousness and is the model for the mutual recognition of all by all. The master and the slave are the *outcomes* of the struggle for recognition. In recognising oneself in the other, each human being is both different and the same. Recognition is about freedom. Freedom is a claim. Only in making a claim (and establishing a social relation) can my deeds be considered as truly free. Agamben reads Hegel's dialectic as abstract and internal to the individual, a process within consciousness that leads to self-consciousness. This allows me to conclude by considering the influence of Luther on Hegel's work and the connections between Hegel and Paul's messianic thought.

The second section connects Hegel's thought to slavery. I draw on Susan Buck-Morss to argue that the master-slave dialectic was heavily influenced by the successful rebellion in Saint-Domingue (Haiti). Contrary to Aristotle, Hegel admitted that free men could be enslaved and that the enslaved may become free, exemplified through the experience of Haiti. But Hegel moved away from the radicality of his writings on slavery towards a racist and derogatory view of Africa and Africans, which reflected the view of the slave-owning classes of the time.

In the final section, I view how Agamben follows Kojève's interpretation of the master-slave dialectic through the concept of 'work'. For Agamben, Hegel sees the intimate relation between the master and the figure of the slave as a use of the body. The 'workless slave' deactivates the master-slave distinction and is a form-of-life. This inoperativity is an originary feature of the human condition and the world in which it lives. I turn to examples of these workless slaves in the remaining chapters of the book.

The Hegelian dialectic

Hegel's slave, Aristotle's slave

My starting point is anthropological. Agamben claims that Aristotle developed his idea of the human being starting from the paradigm of the free man, even if the figure of the slave was the free man's condition of possibility. Agamben claims that Aristotle could have developed an "entirely different

3 Glancy (2020) 5.

anthropology" if he had taken account of the slave.[4] Aristotle's (ancient) paradigm can be connected to Hegel's (modern) conception of recognition. Bull has written that slavery was a natural focus for Hegel. His master-slave dialectic has been called "the most profound analysis of slavery ever written".[5] Bull contends Hegel's dialectic is an attempt to focus on the ambiguous condition of the figure of the slave in Aristotle. In Aristotle, the enslaved person is both a separate being and a part of the master.[6] Hegel considered the self as simultaneously double or multiple rather than single. He is by no means alone.[7] W E B Du Bois wrote of the 'double consciousness' of the African American who led a double life, with double thoughts and double social classes, a conflict between what was 'African' and what was 'American'.[8] Bull explains that double consciousness stretches back to the beginnings of Western philosophy.[9] Hegel saw the servile obedience in ancient Greece and ancient Rome as forming the beginning of freedom. To become free all nations must undergo the discipline of subjection to the master. True freedom results from the servile self-consciousness freeing itself from the individuality of the master and also from its own individuality. In this way the slave can grasp what is rational and universal.[10]

Bull explains: Aristotle's argument that there was a clear division between slave and free was not compatible with the realities of late eighteenth- and early nineteenth-century slavery in Hegel's time. The backdrop here was a growing abolitionist movement in Western Europe. For Aristotle, natural slavery meant certain people were, by nature, slaves. Slavery has a natural hierarchy.[11] It would be contradictory to speak of these slaves being emancipated. This would mean the emancipated were not slaves to begin with.[12] Hegel was writing at the time of the Haitian Revolution, when enslaved people had formed a state. Hegel's approach was different – free beings could be enslaved; enslaved people could become free.[13] True freedom is not about status, but the capacity to abstract from one's particular interests.[14] For Hegel, Aristotle's division of barbarians and Greeks was not a natural fact, but a result of uneven development.[15]

4 Agamben (2016) 20.
5 Davis (1999) 558.
6 Bull (1998) 103.
7 Bull (1998) 94.
8 Du Bois (2008) 165; Bruce Jr (1992) 301.
9 Bull (1998) 98–9.
10 Hegel (1991a) 175–6.
11 Smith (1992) 102.
12 Bull (1998) 116; Aristotle (1984) 1280a32.
13 Bull (1998) 116–17.
14 Oquendo (1999) 437.
15 Bull (1998) 107.

Bull connects Aristotle and Hegel's writings on slavery, via the late eighteenth-century German translation of Aristotle's *Politics* by philosopher Christian Garve. Bull notes that Garve usually translates Aristotle's *doulos* into both *Sklave* and *Knecht*. However, where the slave is directly contrasted to the master, the two terms are translated as *Knecht* and *Herr*.[16] Garve explains the master as *despotés* is the Greek word for *Herr*, and the master rules over slaves. *Doulos* signified servitude.[17] Bull argues that Garve shows *Herr* and *Knecht* were taken to be the German equivalents of Aristotle's master and slave.[18] Bull explains that Hegel developed an insight from Garve's translation in his account of the slave's self-recognition through work. For Aristotle slaves have virtue when they need it to perform their masters' orders. Free artisans have their virtue derived from carrying out orders. Virtue comes from the master directing tasks.[19] Garve's translation opened up space for those enslaved persons to exercise autonomy. For example, a craftsman remains free while they work, which has the potential to overturn the normal social hierarchy.[20] Garve suggests this is why the craftsman's work was transferred from enslaved people to free men, removing the chance an enslaved person could experience freedom through work.[21]

The question of how and why labour can lead to freedom forms part of Hegel's dialectic. In fashioning the thing, the bondsman realises that he exists and in his own right, acquiring a mind of his own. [22] Work is a site of transformation. Hegel sees slavery and tyranny as a necessary historical stage.[23] For Hegel, without slavery a transition to a truly ethical order, an order in which freedom can flourish, would not be possible.[24] Slavery created the conditions for the first experiment in freedom. The initial understanding and experience of freedom evolved to a place in which there is no need for slavery. Almost counter-intuitively (and mirroring a conclusion also reached by Orlando Patterson), the institution of slavery was central to setting this process in motion.[25] Hegel, like Agamben, sees in the enslaved person a kernel of possibility, of freedom. But Hegel's slave remains an abstract form that he uses to think about what a truly human consciousness involves.[26] Bull concludes that Aristotle's theory of slavery was used as justification

16 Bull (1998) 104; Aristotle (1799–1802) I, 14, 18, 58.
17 Bull (1998) 104; Aristotle (1799–1802) II, 69.
18 Bull (1998) 104.
19 Bull (1998) 104; Aristotle (1984) 1260a34–1260b5.
20 Bull (1998) 105; Aristotle (1799–1802) II, 142–3.
21 Bull (1998) 105; Aristotle (1799–1802) II, 143.
22 Hegel (1977) 118–19.
23 Bull (1998) 106.
24 Oquendo (1999) 440.
25 Oquendo (1999) 445.
26 Glancy (2020) 10.

for the institution by generations of slaveholders in Europe; Bull also notes that the Hegelian dialectic appealed to individuals and groups struggling for liberation.[27]

The dialectic of self-consciousness

The *Phenomenology of Spirit* endowed slavery with a full philosophical significance.[28] Hegel asks how self-consciousness can show itself as more than a mere part of the world. Self-consciousness exists for itself when it exists for another. It exists for another when it is acknowledged by another self-consciousness.[29] Self-consciousness is the desire for self-preservation.[30] The master-slave dialectic is a dialectic of self-consciousness, but it also describes the process of recognition and explains how actions and lives can be considered as free. There is a double movement of two mirrored self-consciousnesses, the 'I' and the 'other'.[31] The 'I' is certain of itself, but not of the other self, which it views as an unessential object.[32] Each self-consciousness recognises themselves through mutually recognising each other.[33] This can only be brought about by both parties.[34]

The struggle for recognition comes from each seeking the death of the other, and each staking their own life in the process.[35] It is only through staking one's life that freedom is won.[36] The battle for recognition does not give either combatant what they want. If one party kills the other, their freedom cannot be externally recognised. The struggle can only end through a recognition that risking one's life to achieve self-consciousness is self-defeating – self-consciousness requires you to be alive. The fear of death makes everything that appears stable and solid appear not to be. We do not know what we can do or change (or not do or not change) until we are faced with necessity. The fear of death makes the slave surrender all desires and needs to stay alive, which is needed for self-consciousness to be achieved. The experience of fear becomes a settled disposition – the master-slave relation, which is both the master giving the fear of death form, and the beginning of wisdom and knowledge.[37] For those that survived the struggle, there are two unequal

27 Bull (1998) 125–6.
28 Timofeeva (2017) 431.
29 Hegel (1977) 111; Rae (2012) 24.
30 Hegel (1977) 110.
31 Bull (1998) 110.
32 Hegel (1977) 113.
33 Hegel (1977) 112.
34 Riley (1981) 22.
35 Hegel (1977) 113–14; Rae (2012) 36.
36 Hegel (1977) 114.
37 Hegel (1977) 114.

and opposed shapes of consciousness, the outcomes of a struggle for recognition: an independent consciousness whose nature is to be for itself, the lord; and a consciousness whose nature is to live or be for another, the bondsman. The lord is the power over the bondsman, holding the bondsman in subjection.[38] To be a slave is to give up all your natural desires and only to act on the desires of another.

Buck-Morss explains that Hegel understands the position of the master in both political *and* economic terms.[39] The lord relates to the object of desire, the thing, through the bondsman, and enjoys it.[40] The slave can make his master's wishes come true,[41] but the master is deprived of the chance to labour on things to externalise the self.[42] The bondsman only works on the thing, which is really the action of the lord. The lord achieves his recognition through another consciousness, and the recognition is one-sided and unequal.[43] However, Laura Brace explains that the lord cannot truly enslave the bondsman. To do that he would have to control the bondsman's actions and motivations, which would require the lord to become the bondsman's self-consciousness. This would mean the lord would become the bondsman.[44]

Through working on the object, the bondsman acts for himself, someone existing on his own account and in his own right,[45] acquiring a mind of his own.[46] This means lordship is the reverse of what it wants to be, as the lord is dependent on the bondsman. Servitude also turns into the opposite of what it immediately is and becomes a truly independent consciousness. The slave achieves self-consciousness by showing they are a subject who can transform material nature.[47] The bondsman has experienced the fear of death, "the absolute Lord".[48] The structure of slavery engenders a structure that leads to the desire for independence, or mastery.[49] Slavery transforms chaotic activity into work and intelligent activity, and slaves can work their way to freedom.[50] As Louis Althusser summarised:

38 Hegel (1977) 115.
39 Buck-Morss (2009) 53.
40 Timofeeva (2017) 434.
41 Bird-Pollan (2012) 248.
42 Brace (2018) 102; Lloyd (1988) 90.
43 Hegel (1977) 116; Lloyd (1988) 90.
44 Brace (2018) 101.
45 Hegel (1977) 118.
46 Hegel (1977) 119.
47 Buck-Morss (2009) 54.
48 Hegel (1977) 117.
49 Bird-Pollan (2012) 248.
50 Hegel (1977) 118; Hutchings (2003) 75.

> The triumph of freedom in Hegel is not the triumph of any freedom whatever: it is not the mightiest who prevails in the end; history shows, rather, that human freedom is engendered by the slave.[51]

Hegel, Agamben, Luther, Paul

Bull argues that as the institution of slavery is a function of human progress in history, the Hegelian dialectic is an account of how that progress can be achieved.[52] There is an underlying religious dimension of Hegel's thought, connecting lordship (*Herrschaft*) and bondage (*Knechtschaft*) not to domination and oppression, but the 'Lord' (*Herr*) and 'servant' or 'slave' (*Knecht*) of the Bible. Hegel's dialectic can be read as a secularisation of Christian theology. Christianity, not labour, could be seen as the cause of the transition from slave-holding antiquity to modernity.[53] Ever since Luther, *Herrschaft* and *Knechtschaft* have been central to German Protestant theology.[54] German allows for these terms to be given a political and theological interpretation. Hegel's attempt to reconcile this ambiguity is central to the breadth of his perspective.[55] Lordship and bondage are reciprocal or complementary terms. The existence of one term implies the existence of the second term of the pair.[56]

Abraham Rotstein explains that the rhetoric of transfiguration between lordship and bondage is found in the Old and New Testament. In the Old Testament, the Mosaic Covenant refers to the bondage of the Israelities to the Egyptian Pharaoh.[57] God replaces Pharaoh's tyrannical lordship with a lordship of righteousness and justice, transforming the Jewish people from oppressed slaves in Egypt to God's exalted slaves.[58] Rotstein notes that the Hebrew word *eved* is used to describe both forms of slavery, but its meaning is changed from overwhelming oppression to total salvation.[59] Rotstein continues: the New Testament speaks of the bondage of the Christian to the body, sin and death. The Greek *doulos* replaces the Hebrew *eved* but is inverted in the same way.[60] The 'slaves' of Christ become 'lords' or joint heirs of Christ,[61] and the Christian becomes "lord of all".[62] The former slaves

51 Althusser (2014) 172.
52 Bull (1998) 110.
53 Smith (1992) 99–100.
54 Rotstein (1979) 76.
55 Rotstein (1979) 76.
56 Rotstein (1979) 77.
57 Rotstein (1979) 77; Deuteronomy 6:21.
58 Rotstein (1979) 77; Leviticus 25:55.
59 Rotstein (1979) 77.
60 Rotstein (1979) 77–8; Romans 6:16; Ephesians 6:6.
61 Romans 8:17.
62 Rotstein (1979) 78; Galatians 4:1.

create a new community with God that resolves the original antithesis of lordship and bondage.[63] For Luther, scripture speaks through antithesis, the same relation that exists between lordship and bondage. Everything that is opposed to Christ reigns in him.[64] Luther's theology was preserved in Hegel's work. In the Hegelian dialectic, the slave or bondsman evokes Paul (and Luther) writing about slavery.[65]

Agamben seeks to connect Paul, Luther and Hegel. van der Heiden notes that in 1 Corinthians 1:28, Paul uses a particular verb, *katargein*, to express what happens to the things that are after the messianic event. Agamben draws our attention to the importance of the verb *katargein* and its noun *katargēsis*.[66] The verb is etymologically connected to *argōs*, inoperativity.[67] Messianic *katargēsis* deactivates things and brings them to fulfilment. Agamben then connects Hegel's sublation to Paul's *katargēsis*.

In the English translations of Hegel, *Aufhebung* is usually translated as 'sublation'. *Aufheben* is the German verb and *Aufhebung* the noun related to the verb. *Aufheben* carries a double meaning of abolishing and conserving (*aufbewahren* and *aufhören lassen*) used by Hegel as a foundation for his dialectic.[68] In Hegel's dialectic, the form of logic has three moments.[69] The first moment is the moment of the understanding in which forms have a stable definition or determination.[70] The second moment is the dialectical. This is a moment where the determination that was fixed in the first moment passes into its opposite.[71] This negation preserves and endows upon the negated both content and form.[72] This process is described by Hegel in terms of 'sublation'. The third 'speculative' moment is the unity of the opposition between the first two determinations. It is the positive result of the disintegration and transition of the determinations and unifies those distinct determinations.[73] For Hegel, sublation is the motor of all dialectical logic, the "fundamental determination" of its movement, which repeatedly occurs throughout the whole of philosophy.[74] Hegel's *Aufhebung* means the coexistence of two

63 Rotstein (1979) 78.
64 Rotstein (1979) 79.
65 Rotstein (1979) 84; Galatians 4:3.
66 van der Heiden (2016) 179; Agamben (2005) 93–107.
67 Agamben (2005) 95; van der Heiden (2016) 180.
68 Agamben (2005) 99.
69 Hegel (1991b) §79.
70 Hegel (1991b) §80.
71 Hegel (1991b) §81.
72 Timofeeva (2017) 428–9.
73 Hegel (1991b) §82.
74 Hegel (1969) 107.

opposites of unequal value in a unity, one of which also functions as the unifying concept.[75] The sublation of a contradiction drives the dialectic.[76]

Agamben connects Hegel's *Aufhebung* to Pauline *katargēsis*, via Luther's translation of *katargein* as *aufheben*.[77] Luther was aware of the *aufheben*'s double meaning of abolishing and conserving. The term acquires its particular facets through the translation of the Pauline letters, leaving Hegel to pick it up and develop it, which was a "delight" for "speculative thought".[78] But Agamben argues we need to focus on this messianic element of the dialectic. Agamben states that for Hegel, consciousness is a dialectical process internal to the individual. The dialectic is not a struggle between two individuals, but an inner doubling within consciousness that leads to self-consciousness.[79] More importantly, for Alysia Garrison, this means self-consciousness's relation to itself is always self-sundering, a splitting apart within the self.[80] As a result, consciousness "can never grasp itself as an entirety, but is whole only in the total process of its becoming". This means that the negative experience of death structures the human being.[81] Experience becomes unattainable except as an abstraction of the total social process.[82]

Hegel's end of history is "genuinely messianic", but Hegel thinks the time of the end in terms of a global process rather than each instant's relation to the Messiah.[83] In the Western tradition, a metaphysical concept, which focuses on the moment of foundation and origin, coexists with a messianic concept, which focuses on a moment of fulfilment.[84] Agamben states:

> What is essentially messianic and *historic* is the idea that fulfilment is possible by retrieving and revoking foundation, by coming to terms with it.[85]

When the messianic and the historic are separated, we are left with a foundation which is part of an infinite task. If we drop the messianic and only focus on the moment of foundation or origin, we are left with empty signification and history as infinite deferment.[86] On Agamben's reading, time in the dialectic is experienced as a continuum of negative fleeting instants,

75 Brinkmann (2010) 123.
76 Brinkmann (2010) 132.
77 van der Heiden (2016) 180; Agamben (2005) 99.
78 Agamben (2005) 99; Hegel (1969) 107.
79 Agamben (2007) 34; Kelly (1966) 784.
80 Garrison (2017) 139.
81 Agamben (2007) 34.
82 Agamben (2007) 34.
83 Agamben (2005) 101.
84 Agamben (2005) 103.
85 Agamben (2005) 103–4.
86 Agamben (2005) 104.

capturing human experience and happiness.[87] Hegel's experience of time, like Aristotle's, does not allow human beings to attain an authentic history. Time is split between an elusive flow of instants and history as the originary dimension of man. Man is therefore unable to take possession of his own historical nature.[88]

The answer is time as *kairos*.[89] *Kairos* liberates man from servitude to time as *chronos*. The true revolutionary remembers history as he would remember his own home, and brings this memory to everything, exacting this promise from each instant.[90] Agamben claims the *Aufhebung*, like Paul's *katargēsis*, renders things inoperative, allowing human beings, who are ungrounded, to repeat their own ungroundedness, abandoning themselves to themselves.[91] This speculative interpretation of Hegel allows Agamben to contend that Hegel used a weapon against theology furnished by theology itself and that this weapon is genuinely messianic.[92] What is presupposed by Agamben's reading of *Aufhebung* is not eliminated but persists, is lifted and is preserved.[93] *Aufhebung* implies that this preservation is taken up in a new identity, a new unitary figure of the subject.[94] In focusing on this messianic reading of Hegel, we must connect the dialectic to its influence from colonial slavery and the actions of enslaved people who were trying to become free.

Hegel, Haiti and Colonialism

Hegel's writing on the master-slave dialectic was published in 1807 when slavery had become the "root metaphor of Western political philosophy, connoting everything that was evil about power relations".[95] In all large-scale slaveholding societies, there existed a large group of free non-slaveholding persons. Even the poorest free person was proud of not being enslaved.[96] This view of freedom underwrote the West's economic system, "facilitating the global spread of the very Enlightenment ideals that were in such fundamental contradiction to it".[97]

Hegel's dialectic has been read in diverse ways. In Patterson's reading, the dialectic is moved from involving two individuals to representing the

87 Agamben (2007) 107.
88 Agamben (2007) 109.
89 Zartaloudis (2010) 296–7.
90 Agamben (2007) 115.
91 Agamben (1999) 134.
92 Agamben (2005) 100.
93 Agamben (2005) 100; Hegel (1969) 107.
94 van der Heiden (2016) 181.
95 Buck-Morss (2009) 21; Brace (2018) 97.
96 Patterson (1982) 99.
97 Buck-Morss (2009) 21.

institution of slavery as a whole. Here, Patterson reads slavery as an enduring social process, which was opposed to manumission.[98] In Patterson's dialectic, freedom is not born in the consciousness of the master but in the reality of the slave's condition as a slave. Only control matters to the master. For the slave, freedom is creative, the consciousness of the negation of their social death and a new life.[99] Paul Gilroy argues that the relationship between master and enslaved is modern. For Gilroy, the 'universality' and 'rationality' of enlightened Europe and America did not eradicate the racial difference inherited from pre-modernity. Instead, that order of racial difference was sustained and relocated.[100] Gilroy, much like Agamben, pushes back against the notion of time as *chronos* and progress.[101]

Plantation slavery and Caribbean sugar production founded new economic, social and political relations, moving slavery to a public, global stage.[102] The production of sugar required endless supplies of enslaved people and produced fantastic wealth for European nations.[103] The Caribbean slaveholding class dropped any claims to culture and civilisation and abused enslaved people physically and sexually. In this very real 'trial by death', Patterson argues that the slave (if they survived) emerged with the need for dignity and honour, with a voice that allowed that dignity to surface.[104]

The Revolution's influence on Hegel

The master-slave dialectic was heavily influenced by the successful rebellion in the French colony of Saint-Domingue, today's Haiti. During this period, there were many revolts in the colonial Americas, common to all societies with slaves.[105] Buck-Morss argued Hegel's original intent was to focus on uprisings and rebellions by enslaved people. Those who once acquiesced to slavery demonstrate their humanity when they are willing to risk death rather than remain subjugated.[106] Hegel is not alone in being symbolically and materially influenced by the Haitian Revolution, and in this section, I primarily focus on this symbolism.

On 22 August 1791, representative enslaved people from nearby plantations gathered to participate in a secret ceremony. The ceremony is considered to be the start of the Revolution, which involved tens of thousands of

98 Patterson (1982) 100.
99 Patterson (1982) 98.
100 Gilroy (1993) 49.
101 Gilroy (1993) 55.
102 Brace (2018) 98.
103 Buck-Morss (2009) 29.
104 Patterson (1982) 100.
105 Patterson (1982) 173.
106 Buck-Morss (2009) 55.

enslaved people. It demonstrated an optimism for what the future had to offer.[107] Cora Kaplan is effusive in stating that the Haitian Revolution was a moment in which enslaved people secured an equal status in the human race.[108] Laurent Dubois claims that the Revolution granted all people freedom and citizenship, transformed the world, helped destroy slavery in the Americas and was a crucial moment in the history of democracy and the struggle for human rights.[109] Dubois continues:

> If we live in a world in which democracy is meant to exclude no one, it is in no small part because of the actions of those slaves in Saint-Domingue who insisted that human rights were theirs too.[110]

Their actions and successes showed that the French Revolution was "world-historical in its implications",[111] laying bare the social and economic foundations not just of the colony of Saint-Domingue, but the world.[112] As Buck-Morss explains:

> Conceptually, the revolutionary struggle of slaves, who overthrow their own servitude and establish a constitutional state, provides the theoretical hinge that takes Hegel's analysis out of the limitlessly expanding colonial economy and onto the plane of world history, which he defines as the realization of freedom – a theoretical solution that was taking place in practice in Haiti at that very moment.[113]

Robin Blackburn has argued that the Haitian Revolution became an abolitionist theme in Europe and North America, a torch of freedom sustaining new communities and values and vanquishing slavery in the New World.[114]

Haitian independence was achieved on 1 January 1804, but the road to be travelled was unmarked and undefined on the eve of the rebellion.[115] By the end of 1791, the rebellion's leaders had to come to terms with the colonial authorities. Fick explains that the rebel leadership offered an apology, stating that the insurrection was a result of the tyranny of their masters and their enslavement. They asked for an amnesty for all participants in the revolt, an

107 Casimir (2020) 288.
108 Kaplan (1998) 49.
109 Dubois (2004) 6–7.
110 Dubois (2004) 3.
111 Buck-Morss (2009) 39.
112 Fick (1998) 1.
113 Buck-Morss (2009) 10–12.
114 Blackburn (2006) 672–4.
115 Fick (1998) 2.

amelioration of their treatment and freedom for the revolt leaders.[116] The Colonial Assembly refused their demands. The struggle could only be won by force.[117]

Two years of sustained insurrectionary activity was required before emancipation could be achieved.[118] In 1794, France had to acknowledge the abolition of slavery in Saint-Domingue, an abolition then applied to all other French colonies.[119] Across 13 years, the struggle adapted pragmatically, involving warfare, revolution, foreign occupation and popular insurrections, all the time breaking new ground.[120] General emancipation was reached in stages and in different circumstances in different parts of the country.[121] In 1804, the first ruler of an independent Haiti, Jean-Jacques Dessalines, declared independence from France and became the first state to guarantee liberty to all its inhabitants.[122]

Buck-Morss's reading of Hegel starts with his view that the enslaved person is responsible for their own lack of freedom by choosing life over liberty:

> But if someone is a slave, his own will is responsible, just as the responsibility lies with the will of a people if that people is subjugated. Slavery occurs in the transitional phase between natural human existence and the truly ethical condition; it occurs in a world where a wrong is still right. Here, the wrong is *valid*, so that the position it occupies is a necessary one.[123]

In the *Phenomenology* Hegel makes clear through the dialectic that freedom is not handed from above but reached through the struggle for recognition where one's life is staked.[124] Tony Burns suggests that for Hegel, failure to recognise others as you wish to be recognised is unjust. This extends to enslaved people. If people with the status of slaves are not acknowledged as human beings, they are being treated unjustly.[125]

Buck-Morss sees Hegel as the first philosopher to describe the de-territorialised, world market of the European colonial system,[126] not least because he

116 Fick (1998) 4.
117 Fick (1998) 5.
118 Fick (2000) 15.
119 Buck-Morss (2009) 37.
120 Brace (2018) 81.
121 Fick (1998) 6.
122 Brace (2018) 79–80.
123 Hegel (1991a) 88.
124 Hegel (1977) 113–14.
125 Burns (2006) 96.
126 Buck-Morss (2009) 7–8.

was well-informed about Caribbean slavery and the events in Haiti.[127] Events in Saint-Domingue, the richest colony in the Western hemisphere,[128] were frequently mentioned in contemporary German newspapers.[129] Because of this, Buck-Morss reaches the conclusion that Hegel knew about enslaved people successfully revolting against their masters. The dialectic was deliberately elaborated with this background in mind.[130]

Why is there not more explicit discussion of Haiti in his texts? Buck-Morss suggests this is due to his connections with Freemasonry, and the habit of those members to keep silent about his sources of documentation and information.[131] When Hegel completed the *Phenomenology*, he was 36 and his life was a mess. He had no money, no real paying job, and a child by a woman who was married to someone who had abandoned her, Hegel's landlord.[132] He would not include in his first major publication explicit references to Haiti. This would likely upset the German authorities at the time, as well as Napoleon Bonaparte, who was responsible for Toussaint L'Ouverture's death and was invading Hegel's city, Jena. Hegel did not want to risk arrest.[133]

For Buck-Morss, Hegel has the potential in his thought to rescue the idea of universal human history from the uses to which White dominion has put it.[134] The project of universal freedom must be redeemed and reconstituted.[135] There was no explicit connection made between the dialectic and enslaved people in Haiti.[136] Sibylle Fischer notes Hegel retreated into silence at the very moment revolutions led by enslaved people occurred.[137] These discontinuities, gaps and silences show that there was not a continuous historical progress. Instead, they are analogous to moments of now-time, representing conflicting projects of emancipation.[138] Saint-Domingue involved "multiple revolutionary moments" in a history full of repetitions.[139] Enslaved people showed they were willing to enter into a life and death struggle to achieve recognition, rather than remain enslaved.[140]

127 Buck-Morss (2009) 36.
128 Buck-Morss (2009) 36.
129 Brace (2018) 99; Buck-Morss (2009) 44.
130 Buck-Morss (2009) 50.
131 Buck-Morss (2009) 17–19.
132 Pinkard (2000) 230.
133 Buck-Morss (2009) 19–20; Pinkard (2000) 228, 230.
134 Buck-Morss (2009) 74.
135 Buck-Morss (2009) 74–5.
136 Fischer (2004) 28.
137 Fischer (2004) 32; Fischer (2010) 168.
138 Fischer (2004) 37; Brace (2018) 108.
139 Fischer (2004) 133; Brace (2018) 108.
140 Brace (2018) 84; Buck-Morss (2009) 54.

Hegel did not maintain this form of revolutionary radicalism.[141] Laura Brace notes that in 1822, in his lectures of what would form *The Philosophy of History*, Hegel cut Africa adrift from history and favoured a gradual, rather than an immediate, abolition of slavery.[142] Slavery is recognised as an injustice by Hegel. But for him, every intermediary stage between an unjust society and a rational State would contain injustice, and slavery is a mode of advancement from isolated sensory existence and allows a being to become a participant in a higher morality. As such, man must be matured for freedom.[143] Hegel wrote of 'the African':

> This distinction between himself as an individual and the universality of his essential being, the African in the uniform, undeveloped oneness of his existence has not yet attained; so that the Knowledge of an absolute Being, an Other and a Higher than his individual self, is entirely wanting.[144]

Buck-Morss notes Robert Bernasconi's analysis of Hegel's lectures during the 1820s and compares them with the sources on Africa that he consulted, demonstrating how Hegel ignored counterevidence that did not fit his formula for progress.[145] Hegel described sub-Saharan Africa as 'Africa proper', which was isolated. This was obviously not the case. Hegel also described 'Africa proper' as unhistorical, static and unchanging in time.[146] Bernasconi states:

> An examination of Hegel's sources shows that they were more accurate than he was and that he cannot be so readily excused for using them as he did.[147]

Buck-Morss explains that Hegel embellished stories of cannibalism and human sacrifice. He distorted and exaggerated to fit the scheme of the developmental process of the State.[148] Hegel spoke of the King of Dahomey's 3,333 wives being massacred and the bonds of society loosened upon the monarch's demise. The wives, we are told, regarded their death as a necessity.[149] Africa and African peoples and cultures were presented as inferior in relation to superior Christian spirituality.[150] Africans had not yet attained

141 Buck-Morss (2009) 67.
142 Brace (2018) 107.
143 Hegel (2022) 99.
144 Hegel (2022) 93.
145 Bernasconi (1998) 41–63; Buck-Morss (2009) 116.
146 Bernasconi (1998) 43; Buck-Morss (2009) 116.
147 Bernasconi (1998) 63.
148 Buck-Morss (2009) 117.
149 Hegel (2022) 98.
150 Buck-Morss (2009) 117; Bernasconi (1998) 51–8.

a consciousness of their freedom and were no more than a mere thing, an object of no value.[151]

Hegel argued that the slavery that existed in Africa was worse than the Atlantic slave trade. In 'Africa proper' moral sentiments were non-existent. Parents sold their children into slavery; children sold their parents into slavery. Polygamy was used to produce children that would be sold as slaves.[152] By taking Africans out of Africa as slaves (mere chattel), Europeans had released them from a bare human existence, an improvement even if they were not free.[153] To remain in Africa was to remain in a condition that could not be developed and had no culture.[154] For Hegel, Africans had a want of regard for life.[155] Bernasconi states:

> So even when Blacks revolt against slavery, as they did successfully in Haiti, this would seem, in Hegel's view, to be because they have come in contact with European views about freedom.[156]

At this point, Hegel declares that "we leave Africa, not to mention it again".[157] Hegel's schema provided "a potent justification" for the later exploitation of the African continent by Europeans. Bernasconi inferred from this that Hegel believed 'civilised' peoples could interfere legitimately with those who were judged not to be as developed. Africa and Africans therefore had to submit to colonialism.[158] Because of this, he was seen as an ally to slave owners in the United States.[159]

After the Revolution

Despite Hegel's move away from the dialectic and its Haitian influence, this does not detract from the fact that the dialectic can be read as a method of attaining freedom from enslavement.[160] Along with enslaved people, new forms of worship appeared in the Americas – Vodou incorporated elements of Catholicism, African religions, and traditions of local indigenous peoples.[161]

151 Hegel (2022) 96.
152 Hegel (2022) 96.
153 Bernasconi (1998) 58.
154 Hegel (2022) 98.
155 Hegel (2022) 96.
156 Bernasconi (1998) 61.
157 Hegel (2022) 99.
158 Bernasconi (1998) 59.
159 Bernasconi (1998) 58.
160 Buck-Morss (2009) 138.
161 Timofeeva (2017) 441–2.

Buck-Morss is correct to state that the Haitian Revolution is seen as a triumph for universal history in our imaginations only.[162] Haitian political leaders persecuted Vodou priests even before independence and many were killed on the grounds that their own definition of the insurrection threatened the state's monopoly of power.[163] Vodou was seen as a way to manipulate the peasantry and a source of power for politicians of every persuasion.[164] Inter-ethnic conflict among formerly enslaved peoples did not disappear. Leaders of the enslaved fought against and betrayed each other.[165] For instance, Dessalines was assassinated in 1806. Joan Dayan explains that the assassination was ordered by a clique of mulattoes and Blacks from the west and south, including his friend General Alexandre Pétion.[166]

The Revolution experienced existential uncertainties and moral ambiguities. The leaders of Haitian independence aimed to reproduce the modern, secular, imperial Eurocentric state.[167] The colonial approach to using labour was maintained.[168] The 1801 Constitution declared freedom from slavery, but did not claim sovereignty for the people or declare independence.[169] The slave trade supplied Haiti with workers,[170] but these workers were bonded to their plantations, working under slave-like conditions for the benefit of the elites, with no option to change either their estate or their occupation.[171] The plantation system was enforced by military inspectors, imposing a forced labour regime. A huge gap grew between the people and the elites who controlled the plantations and the state.[172] Labour codes connected the private morality of the family with order and economic progress. This was deliberate, to get the family to act as an encouragement for ex-slaves to move away from peasant farming toward engaging in the plantation system.[173] Divorce was prohibited and Catholicism was made the state religion.[174] The labourer was made into a second-class citizen.[175] Elizabeth Colwill notes that the narratives of freedom and the logic of citizenship were both gendered.[176] The Haitian Constitution of 1804 confirmed the end of slavery and declared

162 Buck-Morss (2009) 148–51.
163 Buck-Morss (2009) 138.
164 Buck-Morss (2009) 138.
165 Buck-Morss (2009) 144.
166 Dayan (2010) 367.
167 Casimir (2020) 39.
168 Casimir (2020) 37; Dubois (2004) 4.
169 Fischer (2004) 229; Ferrer (2012) 50.
170 James (2001) 215.
171 Brace (2018) 83.
172 Brace (2018) 83–4; Fick (1998) 12.
173 Brace (2018) 82; Garrigus (2007) 148.
174 Aristide (2008) 48.
175 Casimir (2020) 285.
176 Colwill (2009) 115.

all citizens as "Black", but this imagined a unity that did not exist.[177] This Constitution made a gap between leaders and masses that became virtually unbreachable.[178]

Ada Ferrer explains that the country split in two in 1806. A southern republic, headed by Pétion, and a northern kingdom ruled by Henri Christophe. Both men were committed to ensuring legal slavery and European colonialism would never return. The northern kingdom retained large-scale landholdings, producing sugar through the labour of formerly enslaved people, and worker mobility was limited. The southern republic had dismantled the old plantation system and distributed modest plots, with larger pieces of land going mostly to the military.[179] Ferrer sees the Republic's constitution of 1816 as a product of a thorough intellectual engagement with longstanding and emerging principles of freedom and rights.[180] In 1817 the southern Haitian Republic granted legal protection, freedom from slavery and Haitian citizenship to seven Jamaican slaves who escaped their bonds and sailed to the country. The Republic's constitution allowed all persons who came to reside in the country their freedom. Pétion, president of the Republic, refused to return the men to the British colonial authorities.[181] Such citizenship was also offered to those who arrived in Haiti on their own initiative.[182] Haiti's Black identity functioned as a national myth that was in tension with the idea of universal emancipation to which the revolution had given birth.[183] Despite this, the "spirit of the thing" cannot be tied down and dragged off as a war trophy or bought by the highest bidder.[184]

But to narrate Haiti's history as good versus evil stunts our capacity for moral judgment. Only a distorted history is morally pure.[185] We must salvage the historical facts about freedom for our own time. As Gilroy declared – the "time has come for the primal history of modernity to be reconstructed from the slaves' point of view".[186] How? Gilroy reads Frederick Douglass's conflict with a slave breaker, Edward Covey, as an example of Hegel's dialectic of recognition becoming a narrative of emancipation.[187] Covey's brutal regime led Douglass to flee and stand up in his own defence to Covey.[188] For Gilroy,

177 Buck-Morss (2009) 145.
178 Fick (1998) 13.
179 Ferrer (2012) 44; Lacerte (1978) 449–59.
180 Ferrer (2012) 55.
181 Ferrer (2012) 42–3.
182 Ferrer (2012) 57–9.
183 Buck-Morss (2009) 145–6.
184 James (2001) 391.
185 Buck-Morss (2009) 138.
186 Gilroy (1993) 55.
187 Gilroy (1993) 60.
188 Douglass (1855) 170.

the enslaved person actively prefers the possibility of death to the inhumanity of plantation slavery.[189] Gilroy opposes this 'choice' of death to the Hegelian dialectic which represents modern Western thinking. While the bondsman may prefer bondage, actual enslaved people in the Americas prefer the negativity of death.[190]

Gerard Aching argues that viewing the work of enslaved people only as an activity by which the master physically subjugates them only accounts for part of their struggle to be free.[191] Aching describes Hegel's bondage as showing how subjects emerge and persist in various forms of subjection, which accounts for the enslaved person's obstinate attachment to life. Gilroy privileges the symbolism of individual acts of bravery over methods of enduring bondage.[192] Enslaved people evidenced a "stubborn willingness to survive slavery", adopting a range of strategies in response to the coercion they experienced.[193] Douglass himself explained that more enslaved people have not escaped because they would be leaving behind "strong cords of affection that bind them to their friends".[194]

This is not to downplay the importance of symbolism or examples. Leonard Cassuto contends that slave narratives show that if a person can be equated with a thing, this human/thing can become a full-fledged person again.[195] These narratives form a "culture of resistance", nothing less than "an alternative way of conceiving human history",[196] what I have been developing here as *kairos*. The master-slave dialectic is not a life and death struggle ending with the liberation of the slave but "describes moments of freedom made possible by the unsettling work of reflection that constitutes the ground zero of resistance".[197] The dialectic speaks to a radical focus on the consciousness and action of the enslaved, their conception of time, the use of their body, where such subtle actions form the basis of form-of-life, and a recognition of living one's life as a form. It is in the figure of the workless slave that Agamben identifies such potential.

189 Gilroy (1993) 63.
190 Gilroy (1993) 68.
191 Aching (2012) 913.
192 Aching (2012) 914.
193 Aching (2012) 917.
194 Douglass (1855) 102.
195 Cassuto (1996) 231.
196 Said (1993) 216.
197 Aching (2012) 916.

The workless slave

The nexus between messianism and the new subject is found in the master-slave dialectic, re-emerging in Hegel in the problem of the end of history.[198] The most influential of commentaries on Hegel's master-slave dialectic is Kojève's *Introduction to the Reading of Hegel*. This is a controversial treatment, making the dialectic the key to the whole of Hegel's thought.[199] Kojève's reading of Hegel has been described as one-dimensional, only focusing on social or anthropological aspects.[200] The basis for this critique is that slavery is a moral and psychological problem as well as a social and political one.[201] However, Agamben's interpretation of Hegel has been heavily shaped by Kojève's writings. Agamben contends the concept of *désoeuvrement* – a translation of the Pauline *katargein* – first appears in twentieth-century philosophy in Kojève. It appears in his definition of the post-historical condition of man, the *voyou désoeuvré* as the "shabbat of man",[202] is enough to prove that the connection here to the messianic has not yet been completely neutralised.[203] *Désoeuvrement* is translated by Agamben as 'inoperativeness', the figure of the fullness of man at the end of history.[204]

Agamben's development of the workless slave is a rejoinder to the structural role of the slave in Hegel.[205] The 'workless slave' lives through paradigmatic gestures which allow them to live their life as a form. Inverting Hegel's reasoning, and moving away from Kojève's end of history, we need to search for forms of action which render inoperative the dominant forms of political control, and the ideas of mastery which underpin Eurocentric conceptions of freedom and political agency. The use of the 'workless slave' means the subject doing something in which they are interested.[206] The workless slave shows another figure of human praxis, in which the roles of enjoyment and labour, central to the Hegelian dialectic, cannot be assigned.[207]

Kojève's Hegel

Kojève interprets the 'life and death' struggle of the dialectic, claiming that Master and Slave are two different people, rather than two parts of the same

198 Agamben (2005) 101.
199 Riley (1981) 5.
200 Kelly (1966) 782.
201 Smith (1992) 99.
202 Kojève (1952) 387–97.
203 Agamben (2005) 101.
204 Agamben (1998) 61–2.
205 Glancy (2020) 5.
206 Agamben (2016) 29; Glancy (2020) 10.
207 Agamben (2016) 37.

self-consciousness.[208] The life and death struggle between two people raises their certainty of being for themselves to truth by recognising the other and themselves as self-conscious. Kojève's dialectic states human society and the historical process begin when people want to risk their lives in this fight to the death for recognition. The Master negates his natural being by risking his life and overcoming his antagonist, who is reduced to the role of the Slave.[209] For Kojève, Hegel sees man as nothing less than the desire for recognition. For Hegel, on the other hand, man *is* recognition.

Kojève sees history as understood in terms of 'negating action' through fight and work, of which only human beings are capable.[210] In other words, only human beings find the *end* of history meaningful.[211] Work (which is the labour of the Slave in the service of the Master) is 'negating action' for the Slave, which transformed the natural world into a historical world that human beings live in, negating the present into the past.[212] This negating action quite literally *destroys* the existing world in the Master's service,[213] and the Master takes the result of this negating action created by the destruction as an object for their enjoyment.[214] Kojève calls the Master's 'existential impasse' the moment when the Master, having achieved lordship, realises that he has become dependent on the Slave.[215] By working for the Master, the Slave represses a desire to consume the fruits of his activity, instead civilises and educates himself.[216] Whereas the Master remains static through the historical process, for Kojève the Slave becomes through his negating action. Through transforming the world through work, the Slave transforms themselves, creating the conditions that allow them to renew their fight for recognition.[217] In so doing, the Slave overcomes his initial fear of death and becomes a "free Worker".[218] In this way. Kojève's Slave drives the dialectic through his work, creating the world that he will inherit after killing the Master and attaining the freedom he has been deprived of throughout the historical process.[219]

208 Timofeeva (2017) 436.
209 Kojève (1969) 29–30; Prozorov (2009) 527.
210 Prozorov (2014) 130.
211 Prozorov (2014) 153.
212 Kojève (1969) 23; Prozorov (2014) 130.
213 Kojève (1969) 29.
214 Kojève (1969) 98.
215 Kojève (1969) 19.
216 Prozorov (2009) 526; Kojève (1969) 24.
217 Kojève (1969) 29–30.
218 Kojève (1969) 57.
219 Prozorov (2014) 131.

The final fight is non-dialectical. The Master is killed and dies as Master.[220] The Slave therefore achieves the synthesis of Master and Slavery.[221] There is no longer anyone left to be Master.[222] This is the last project of realising the future by negating the present into the past.[223] But slavery is not historically complete until men choose their own work and become citizens of a Hegelian state. Until this point, history is a history of slave ideologies by which slaves conceal their slavery from themselves.[224] Oxana Timofeeva argues that as long as humanity affirms its human nature and freedom at the expense of another there will exist those who are denied recognition of their humanity.[225] As long as there is slavery – to men or to capital – man will never be truly free.[226] The completely free man is the Slave who has 'overcome' his slavery.[227]

Agamben's workless slave

Kojève's life and death struggle is motivated by a human motive, namely the desire for pure prestige. The struggle also provides the necessary condition for the emergence of the only sort of being who can have that motive. The battle for recognition both explains the emergence of the human and provides an account of something that is already completely human – the desire for recognition. Kojève's desire for recognition plays two roles, both explaining the human and constituting the human.

Agamben suggests that Kojève's theme of inoperativity, or *désoeuvrement*, is inadequately developed. Kojève's overcoming of the master-slave dialectic leaves the presuppositional structure of the dialectic intact.[228] *Désoeuvrement* is a "good translation of Pauline *katargein*", and remains messianic, but ultimately confuses the messianic (*kairos*) with the idea of a post-history, an eschatology.[229] This therefore connects Luther, Paul, Hegel and Kojève to Agamben's messianic thinking. The key difference is that Agamben's messianism, the basis for form-of-life, invokes the need to think of the end of the state and the end of history at the same time.[230] The other face of this eschatological end of history is seen in the totalitarianisms of the twentieth

220 Kojève (1969) 225, n.22.
221 Prozorov (2014) 141.
222 Kojève (1969) 231.
223 Prozorov (2014) 141.
224 Riley (1981) 7–8.
225 Timofeeva (2017) 438.
226 Riley (1981) 8.
227 Kojève (1969) 20.
228 Agamben (1998) 61.
229 Agamben (2005) 101.
230 Agamben (2000) 111.

century.[231] There is no post-history or eschatology to *kairos*. Time is not deferred, but seized in the now, in the paradigmatic gesture.[232]

To this end, Agamben imagines a 'workless slave', someone who suspends his work without taking up the fight for recognition.[233] In Kojève's work, a true man only exists where there is a Slave and a Master.[234] But Agamben's workless slave is distinct from the figure of the Master, and the "autonomous Self-Consciousness" of the Slave that mastered history and produced a world in which they can become free.[235] The workless slave is analogous to the body of the anthropophorous (man-like) animals, which bears the human being, in the sense that humanity takes bodily form within it.[236] To render the dialectic inoperative in Agamben's sense means:

> [M]an will therefore mean no longer to seek new – more effective or authentic – articulations, but rather to show that the central emptiness, the hiatus that – within man – separates man and animal, and to risk ourselves in this emptiness: the suspension of suspension.[237]

This is a different end of history, one that suspends, rather than completes the dialectical historical process of negating action as Kojève intended.[238] It is non-dialectical. In this manner, it is analogous to the operation of the paradigmatic circle. Just as the paradigm resolves the aporia of the hermeneutic circle, the non-dialectical workless slave resolves the circularity of the dialectic. Just as we considered how paradigmatic gestures rendered inoperative the self-referential nature of the hermeneutic circle, opening the proper sphere of that which is human,[239] the workless slave suspends the dialectic.

Whereas race was the limit for Hegel's dialectic, race remains repressed in Agamben's discourse and in the figure of the workless slave. Agamben's argument is at the limits of *racialisation*.[240] This requires a correction of some of his claims, as well as an appreciation of the connection between form-of-life and its *world*. Agamben sees the post-Cold War period as involving a transformation of global politics into a 'society of the spectacle', in which the political and legal categories of previous eras (sovereignty, right, nation, people, democracy) no longer have anything to do with what they used to

231 Agamben (2004) 76.
232 Agamben (2005) 100–1.
233 Prozorov (2014) 131.
234 Kojève (1969) 43.
235 Kojève (1969) 29–30.
236 Agamben (2004) 12.
237 Agamben (2004) 92.
238 Prozorov (2014) 154; Kojève (1969) 200.
239 Agamben (2000) 57.
240 Carter (2013) 77.

designate.[241] But to speak of racialisation is to speak of a much longer history. Racialisation questions how the colonial relation of 'European/non-European' was created, maintained, reproduced and repressed.[242] The slave ship and the Caribbean plantation are much more relevant here than the Berlin Wall.[243] Just as bare life is produced as a remainder of the operation of the relationship between living beings and apparatuses that create subjects, 'non-Europeanisation' is repressed in producing Europeanisation as a racialised and colonised substance.[244] To undergo non-Europeanisation is to become bare life. It is to be marginalised or denied a place in the order of the world, just as Hegel treated Africa in his turn away from the dialectic. 'Whiteness' is a will toward lordship, which requires a non-European bondsman.[245]

Bringing the colonised under control is what Fanon called the part and parcel of the pacification and transformation of the landscape. This landscape concerns the living being in an essential way.[246] Speaking of Algeria, Fanon says the colonised are made part of:

> [T]he *natural* background to the human presence of the French … colonization is a success when all this indocile nature has finally been tamed. Railways across the bush, the draining of swamps and a native population which is non-existent politically and economically are in fact one and the same thing.[247]

Control of the world means control of living beings. To live one's life as a form is to change one's relationship with the landscape. The human world is opened through a landscape, an outstanding form of use and inoperativity. Looking at a landscape involves a contemplation of the world and all the elements that make it. Landscape is where use-of-oneself and use of the world correspond without a remainder. Agamben states:

> Landscape is a dwelling in the inappropriable as form-of-life, as justice. For this reason, if in the world the human being was necessarily thrown and disoriented, in landscape he is finally at home.[248]

241 Agamben (2000) 111; Prozorov (2014) 127–8.
242 Carter (2013) 77.
243 Carter (2013) 85–6.
244 Carter (2013) 81.
245 Carter (2013) 82.
246 Agamben (2016) 89.
247 Fanon (2005) 250.
248 Agamben (2016) 91.

What was so important about the Haitian Revolution was that enslaved people lived their lives without remainder, but also introduced a new relationship with the landscape surrounding them. The Haitian peasantry continued to do this even as the leadership of the newly freed country attempted to reintroduce the slave trade and the plantation economy. To think of form-of-life as a new figure of the human must involve a challenge to Eurocentric modes of thought and relationships with the world. This will accept that apparatuses in the modern world are producing *homo racialis*.[249]

Despite the talk of the end of history in Kojève, contemporary society is still constructed on a base of an invisible, anonymous mass of slaves (rather than a mass of enslaved people), deprived of their status as human beings. Timofeeva explains that these slaves are literally below ground, in basements, illegal houses of sex workers or gambling, and factories using slave labour. Through these illegal, secret spaces, contemporary capitalism spreads its roots.[250] Aristotle saw enslaved people are guaranteeing those citizens of the *polis* the freedom they needed to govern themselves democratically.[251] The black market of enslaved people is not incompatible with the idea of democracy being founded on freedom. Today, after the formal abolition of slavery, everyone is a master. Who works in modernity if all are masters? Those who are unrecognised and are not fully human.[252]

Conclusion

The workless slave is a figure of form-of-life. Aristotle's use of the body, Paul's writings on time as *kairos*, not *chronos*, and the Hegelian dialectic which underpins the importance of the figure of the slave in Western philosophical thought share a commonality. Agamben's thought seeks to trace a messianic connection from Hegel, via Luther, to Paul. This messianic inoperativity that deactivates apparatuses of control is further connected via Hegel and Kojève to the Pauline Epistles. The idea of time as *kairos*, in contradistinction to the representation of time in Aristotle and Hegel, is also analogous to decolonial approaches to time. All of this means that Agamben's reflections on the body of the slave in Aristotle's *Politics* actually have a crucial messianic property. It is possible to live one's life as a form and deactivate apparatuses of control that create and sustain bare life. In the past three chapters, I have also sought to show that enslaved people as forms-of-life have been creating new and alternative forms of freedom throughout recorded history; in the Greek city states, the late Roman Republic and throughout the Atlantic slave trade.

249 Carter (2013) 86.
250 Timofeeva (2017) 427.
251 Timofeeva (2017) 430.
252 Timofeeva (2017) 441.

The actions of enslaved people have been individual and communal, and have acted as paradigmatic examples, not vested in a notion of chronological progress.

This chapter has sought to show the limitations but also the radicality to the Hegelian dialectic. It is the dialectic that shows the centrality of recognition to human belonging and self-consciousness. Unlike Paul's radical equality between slave and free, Hegel's dialectic makes a key distinction between the figures of lord and bondsman through the struggle for recognition. Only in making a claim (and establishing a social relation) can my deeds be considered as truly free. Despite choosing submission over death, in Hegel's schema, the bondsman actually gains an experience of freedom, and the lord realises that they cannot exist without the bondsman's labour in the world. I have followed Buck-Morss's argument in showing that the Hegelian dialectic was heavily influenced by the successful Haitian Revolution. The bondsman had its equivalent in the enslaved Haitians, enacting a life-and-death struggle in the richest European colony in the world. But race operates as a historical limitation to the dialectic; doubly so given Hegel's move away from this revolutionary potential to views steeped in coloniality.

Despite this, the Hegelian dialectic, which seeks to explain self-consciousness, is the model for the mutual recognition of all by all. The move to Kojève by Agamben is important here. The community of use between the master and slave has the potential for a new figure of human praxis, ending the dialectic of history through non-dialectical means (here we can see the importance of the idea of 'inoperativity' in bringing these different strands of theological and philosophical thought together). This can be connected to the manner of paradigmatic gestures and their shaping of form-of-life.

Reference List

Aching, G (2012) 'The Slave's Work: Reading Slavery through Hegel's Master-Slave Dialectic', *PMLA*, 127, 912–17.

Agamben, G (1998) *Homo Sacer: Sovereign Power and Bare Life,* Heller-Roazen, D (trans.), Stanford: Stanford University Press.

Agamben, G (1999) '*Se: Hegel's Absolute and Heidegger's *Ereignis*' in *Potentialities: Collected Essays in Philosophy*, Heller-Roazen, D (trans.), Stanford: Stanford University Press, 116–37.

Agamben, G (2000) *Means Without End: Notes on Politics*, Binetti, V and Casarino, C (trans.), Minneapolis: University of Minnesota Press.

Agamben, G (2004) *The Open: Man and Animal*, Attell, K (trans.), Stanford: Stanford University Press.

Agamben, G (2005) *The Time That Remains: A Commentary on the Letter to the Romans*, Dailey, P (trans.), Stanford: Stanford University Press.

Agamben, G (2007) *Infancy and History: On the Destruction of Experience*, Heron, L (trans.), London: Verso Books.

Agamben, G (2016) *The Use of Bodies*, Kotsko, A (trans.), Stanford: Stanford University Press.

Althusser, L (2014) *The Spectre of Hegel: Early Writings*, Goshgarian, G M (trans.), New York: Verso.

Aristide, J-B (2008) *Toussaint L'Ouverture: The Haitian Revolution*, London: Verso.

Aristotle (1799–1802) *Die Politik des Aristotles, 2 vols*, von Garve, C (trans.), Breslau: W G Korn.

Aristotle (1984) 'Politics' in *The Complete Works of Aristotle, Volume Two*, Barnes, J (ed.), Princeton: Princeton University Press.

Bernasconi, R (1998) 'Hegel at the Court of the Ashanti' in Barnett, S (ed.), *Hegel after Derrida*, London: Routledge, 41–63.

Bird-Pollan, S (2012) 'Hegel's Grounding of Intersubjectivity in the Master-Slave Dialectic', *Philosophy and Social Criticism*, 38, 237–56.

Blackburn, R (2006) 'Haiti, Slavery, and the Age of Democratic Revolution', *The William and Mary Quarterly*, 63, 643–74.

Brace, L (2018) *The Politics of Slavery*, Edinburgh: Edinburgh University Press.

Brinkmann, K (2010) 'The Dialectic of the Inverted World and the Meaning of *Aufhebung*' in Limnatis, N (ed.), *The Dimensions of Hegel's Dialectic*, London: Continuum, 123–39.

Bruce Jr, D (1992) 'W E B Du Bois and the Idea of Double Consciousness', *American Literature*, 64, 299–309.

Buck-Morss, S (2009) *Hegel, Haiti and Universal History*, Pittsburgh: University of Pittsburgh Press.

Bull, M (1998) 'Slavery and the Multiple Self', *New Left Review*, 231, 94–131.

Burns, T (2006) 'Hegel, Identity Politics and the Problem of Slavery', *Culture, Theory and Critique*, 47, 87–104.

Carter, J K (2013) 'The Inglorious: With and Beyond Giorgio Agamben', *Political Theology*, 14, 77–87.

Casimir, J (2020) *The Haitians: A Decolonial History*, Dubois, L (trans.), Durham: The University of North Carolina Press.

Cassuto, L (1996) 'Frederick Douglass and the Work of Freedom: Hegel's Master-Slave Dialectic in the Fugitive Slave Narrative', *Prospects*, 21, 229–59.

Colwill, E (2009) 'Gendering the June Days: Race, Masculinity, and Slave Emancipation in Saint Domingue', *Journal of Haitian* Studies, 15, 103–24.

Davis, D B (1999) *The Problem of Slavery in the Age of Revolution, 1770–1823*, Oxford: Oxford University Press.

Dayan, J (2010) 'Haiti, History, and the Gods' in Howe, S (ed.), *The New Imperial Histories Reader*, London: Routledge, 359–77.

Douglass, F (1855) *My Bondage and My Freedom*, New York and Auburn: Miller, Orton and Mulligan.

Du Bois, W E B (2008) *The Souls of Black Folk*, Oxford: Oxford University Press.

Dubois, L (2004) *Avengers of the New World: The Story of the Haitian Revolution*, Cambridge: Belknap Press.

Fanon, F (2005) *The Wretched of the Earth*, Farrington, C (trans.), New York: Grove Press.

Ferrer, A (2012) 'Haiti, Free Soil, and Antislavery in the Revolutionary Atlantic', *The American Historical Review*, 117, 40–66.

Fick, C (1998) 'Dilemmas of Emancipation: From the Saint Domingue Insurrections of 1791 to the Emerging Haitian State', *History Workshop Journal*, 46, 1–16.
Fick, C (2000) 'Emancipation in Haiti: From Plantation Labour to Peasant Proprietorship', *Slavery and Abolition*, 21, 11–40.
Fischer, S (2004) *Modernity Disavowed: Haiti and the Cultures of Slavery in the Age of Revolution*, Durham, NC and London: Duke University Press.
Fischer, S (2010) 'History and Catastrophe', *Small Axe*, 14, 162–73.
Garrigus, J (2007) '"To Establish a Community of Property": Marriage and Race before and During the Haitian Revolution', *The History of the Family*, 12, 142–52.
Garrison, A (2017) 'Georg Wilhelm Freidrich Hegel' in Kotsko, A and Salzani, C (eds.), *Agamben's Philosophical Lineage*, Edinburgh: Edinburgh University Press, 138–45.
Gilroy, P (1993) *The Black Atlantic: Modernity and Double Consciousness*, London: Verso.
Glancy, J (2020) 'On Agamben's Slave Without Slavery', *Diacritics*, 38, 4–27.
Hegel, G W F (1969) *Science of Logic*, Miller A V (trans.), Amherst: Humanity Books.
Hegel, G W F (1977) *The Phenomenology of Spirit*, Miller, A V (trans.), Oxford: Oxford University Press.
Hegel, G W F (1991a) *Elements of the Philosophy of Right*, Nisbet, H B (trans.), Cambridge: Cambridge University Press.
Hegel, G W F (1991b) *The Encyclopaedia Logic: Part I of the Encyclopaedia of the Philosophical Sciences with the Zustze*, Geraets, T F, Suchting, W A and Hariis, H S (trans.), Indianapolis: Hackett.
Hegel, G W F (2022) *The Philosophy of History*, Sibree, J (trans.), Milton Keynes: Legare Street Press.
Hutchings, K (2003) *Hegel and Feminist Philosophy*, Cambridge: Polity Press.
James, C L R (2001) *The Black Jacobins: Toussaint L'Ouverture and the San Domingo Revolution*, London: Penguin.
Kaplan, C (1998) 'Black Heroes/White Writers: Toussaint L'Ouverture and the Literary Imagination', *History Workshop Journal*, 46, 32–62.
Kelly, G A (1966) 'Notes on Hegel's "Lordship and Bondage"', *Review of Metaphysics*, 19, 780–802.
Kojève, A (1952) 'Les Romans de la sagesse', *Critique*, 8, 387–97.
Kojève, A (1969) *Introduction to the Reading of Hegel: Lectures on the Phenomenology of Spirit*, Nichols Jr, J (trans.), Ithaca: Cornell University Press.
Lacerte, R (1978) 'The Evolution of Land and Labor in the Haitian Revolution, 1791–1820', *The Americas*, 34, 449–59.
Lloyd, G (1988) *The Man of Reason*, London: Routledge.
Oquendo, A (1999) 'Hegel's Account of Ancient Slavery', *History of Philosophy Quarterly*, 16, 437–65.
Patterson, O (1970) 'Slavery and Slave Revolts: A Socio-Historical Analysis of the First Maroon War Jamaica, 1655–1740', *Social and Economic Studies*, 19, 289–325.
Patterson, O (1982) *Slavery and Social Death: A Comparative Study*, Cambridge: Harvard University Press.
Pinkard, T (2000) *Hegel: A Biography*, Cambridge: Cambridge University Press.
Primera, G (2019) *The Political Ontology of Giorgio Agamben: Signatures of Life and Power*, London: Continuum.

Prozorov, S (2009) 'Giorgio Agamben and the End of History: Inoperative Praxis and the Interruption of the Dialectic', *European Journal of Social Theory*, 12, 523–42.

Prozorov, S (2014) *Agamben and Politics: A Critical Introduction*, Edinburgh: Edinburgh University Press.

Rae, G (2012) 'Hegel, Alienation, and the Phenomenological Development of Consciousness', *International Journal of Philosophical Studies*, 20, 23–42.

Riley, P (1981) 'Introduction to the Reading of Alexandre Kojève', *Political Theory*, 9, 5–48.

Rotstein, A (1979) 'Lordship and Bondage in Luther and Marx', *Interpretation: A Journal of Political Philosophy*, 8, 75–102.

Said, E (1993) *Culture and Imperialism*, New York: Knopf.

Smith, S (1992) 'Hegel on Slavery and Domination', *Review of Metaphysics*, 46, 97–124.

Timofeeva, O (2017) 'Freedom Is Slavery', *Crisis & Critique*, 4, 425–45.

van der Heiden, G-J (2016) 'The Dialectics of Paul: On Exception, Grace, and Use in Badiou and Agamben', *International Journal of Philosophy and Theology*, 77, 171–90.

Zartaloudis, T (2010) *Giorgio Agamben: Power, Law and the Uses of Criticism*, Abingdon: Routledge.

Chapter 6

Racial capitalism and decoloniality

Introduction

Agamben's form-of-life is an invocation for a coming politics to be lived in the contemporary world. The biopolitical apparatuses Agamben seeks to deactivate exist today. These remaining chapters use the enslaved person to theorise the end of this world. This is an expression of a self-evident need. Today's world (of which Agamben writes and to which his coming politics seeks to apply) is shaped by racial capitalism, colonialism, coloniality and enslavement. The colonial matrix of power (CMP) has held sway since 1500. The examples of bare life in modernity focused upon by Agamben occur in its shadow. The camp occurs in the same modern world as the slave ship. The biopolitical body is structured by colonial and racial logic.

Agamben is a Eurocentric thinker. This in itself is not a criticism of his work and thought. Yet any future politics must be decolonial in order to counter the colonial heritage of Europe. Quoting Slavoj Žižek (who in turn was paraphrasing Antonio Gramsci): "the old world is dying, and the new world struggles to be born: now is the time of monsters".[1] I draw upon elements of decolonial theory and writings to develop Agamben's writings on the enslaved person, and my own conception of hyper-hermeneutics. This is done to consider the potential of the form-of-life embodied by the enslaved person.

This chapter aims to show the centrality of race, coloniality and enslavement to the modern world and modern epistemologies (including Agamben's thought). The position of the slave in the legal and political thought of Europe is both *materially* and *symbolically* significant. To explore this, we must speak of racial capitalism and its broader connotations. Eurocentrism remains contingent on anti-Blackness. The CMP demonstrates the way that colonial logics have been produced and reproduced through conceptions of personhood and racialising or dehumanising narratives to support capitalist

1 Žižek (2010) 95.

DOI: 10.4324/9781003303534-7

accumulation. I discuss the way the concept of 'domination' relates to the figure of the slave to structure Western conceptions of freedom, both in terms of the body and what is permitted speech. Central to modern racial capitalism and coloniality is the Atlantic slave trade, and the transformation of human life into an object of economic transaction. Transatlantic slavery *is* modern slavery.[2] The triangular trade forms the basis for today's forms of oppression and domination, which I develop using examples from Afropessimism and the resistance of female bodies.

The next section of the chapter uses decolonial themes and ideas to show how the CMP can be challenged. How can Agamben's thought reach beyond Eurocentrism? We must interrogate the coloniality that has shaped the modern world. In this way, form-of-life can be removed from a reading that restricts it to a liberal Western juridical subject. There is power and possibility in dehumanised bodies, spaces and temporalities. This has been occurring throughout the epoch of the CMP. We must look for bodies unseen by the death zone, in the silence after the disturbed waters and in desolate and sunken places. There remains a surplus which escapes all attempts at capture within a social or legal status.

I then turn to Agamben's writing on sadomasochism. Agamben states sadomasochism is a ritualised re-creation of Hegel's master-slave relation, and an insufficient attempt to render inoperative the dialectic between master and slaves. References to sadomasochism abound in Agamben's work. An abstract and rather benign sadomasochism is posited, and I connect this to the historical connections between unfree labour and abuse. To provide a decolonial 'correction' to Agamben's writings on sadomasochism, I draw on the work of Alexander Weheliye. Weheliye connects sadomasochism to what he terms 'pornotroping'. For Weheliye, despite race's connection to human physiology, potential libidinal currents slumber in all acts of political domination, of which slavery is one.

Racial capitalism and coloniality

Beginnings

Capitalism is an ideology that assigns variable values to human beings and their labour. Racial capitalism explains how racialism merged with capitalism and highlights the coercion in capital investment and forms of exchange. To racialise means to naturalise: to turn history into biology, cultural differences to dissimilarities of essence.[3] Race presents itself as stable, but history compromises this fixity.[4] Capitalism is a momentous, historical force,

2 O'Connell Davidson (2015) 19.
3 Wacquant (2022) 78.
4 Robinson (2021) 330.

providing substantially the character of the present industrial world.[5] Cedric Robinson argued that racialism permeated European civilisation, its intellectual thought, its proletariat, its revolutions.[6] Robinson traces a lineage of European racialism from the formative period of Aristotle, the medieval world, via the Islamic domination of Mediterranean culture, through to the period of colonisation and plantation slavery that formed the basis for industrial labour.[7] This is not to state that Robinson's argument is uncontested.

Loïc Wacquant provides a strong objection to the concept of 'racial capitalism', and sees the term being used as an oratorical gesture.[8] Wacquant notes that Robinson does not elaborate on what he means by 'racialism'. Robinson uses the adjectives ethnic, national, regional, tribal, linguistic and immigrant to characterise the subalterns of Europe's interior.[9] This allows him to claim that race was the epistemology of domination, its ordering principle and structure, its moral authority, the template of which was Aristotle's 'natural law'. From the twelfth century, European ruling orders reiterated and embellished this.[10] But Wacquant does question what makes Aristotle's work 'racial' and 'Western'. Other ancient civilisations inferiorised women and ethnic outsiders.[11] In addition, *Western* capitalism is not the only type of capitalism on the planet. Capitalism is not a single homogeneous entity across the European span and through the centuries.[12] The idea of a unified European civilisation is a scholastic concept.[13]

Wacquant also argues that slavery is historically not a racial institution.[14] No iron law of capitalism mandated its association with enslavement. Slavery spawned race when it became strategic to deploy to divide the enslaved and prevent rebellions.[15] Others would agree, including Eric Williams, who said: "Slavery was not born of racism: rather, racism was the consequence of slavery".[16] Chance, rather than design, led to the transatlantic slave trade becoming as profitable as it did.

For Wacquant, racial capitalism erases historical variations, interludes and contingencies to replace them with monolithic depiction and mechanical

5 Robinson (2021) 65.
6 Robinson (2021) 28.
7 Robinson (2021) 67.
8 Wacquant (2023b) 160.
9 Wacquant (2023b) 155; Robinson (2021) 10.
10 Robinson (2021) li.
11 Wacquant (2023b) 155.
12 Wacquant (2023a) 185.
13 Subrahmanyam (2023).
14 Wacquant (2023b) 159–60; Patterson (1982) 176.
15 Wacquant (2023a) 186.
16 Williams (1994) 7.

necessity. Wacquant states that we cannot assume that racial division, colonial or metropolitan, is functional to capitalism across all lands and epochs.[17] Race as an essentialist principle of classification and stratification is not a monopoly of Western traditions and empires.[18] Race goes beyond slavery, impacting bonded labour and indentured servitude, which contributed to colonialism and capitalist accumulation, as well as imperial, communist and despotic regimes.[19]

But to observe Wacquant's criticism in isolation is to ignore the way that the pursuit of European rational utopias is only possible because of the historical material and epistemological violence of colonialism.[20] Colonialism is not an event (colonisation), but an interruption and reordering of human interactions and relations with the planet.[21] Whether we accept Robinson's larger timeline stretching back to Aristotle, he was correct to contend that capitalism as we understand it first appeared in the fifteenth century, an extension of the feudal social relations into the larger tapestry of the modern world.[22] 'Racial identity' became the basis for capitalist exploitation.[23]

Coloniality remains the "darker side" of modernity.[24] Here we return to the CMP and the way colonial logics continue to be produced and reproduced. The CMP is the era of the Westernisation of the planet, political and economic unilaterality, and epistemic and aesthetic universality.[25] As Quijano notes:

> [I]t is very clear that the large majority of the exploited, the dominated, the discriminated against, are precisely the members of the 'races', 'ethnics', or 'nations' into which the colonized populations, were categorized in the formative process of that world power, from the conquest of America and onward.[26]

The coloniality of power permanently structures the old ideas of superiority of the colonisers, and the inferiority of those dominated under European colonialism.[27] At first, European culture was placed out of reach for subaltern peoples – "[t]hen European culture was made seductive: it gave access to

17 Wacquant (2023a) 187.
18 Wacquant (2022) 69.
19 Wacquant (2022) 83.
20 Brayson (2021) 74.
21 Adébísí (2023) 21.
22 Robinson (2021) 10.
23 Leong (2013).
24 Mignolo (2011).
25 Mignolo (2021) ix–x.
26 Quijano (2007) 168–9.
27 Quijano (2007) 169.

power. After all, beyond repression, the main instrument of all power is its seduction".[28]

Central to modernity is the Atlantic slave trade, and the transformation of human life into an object of economic transaction. Atlantic slavery combined the old cruelties of other forms of enslavement with the brutal logic of a commodities market.[29] After 1492, the triangular trade transformed the Atlantic into an entangled economy connecting Africa, the Americas, the Caribbean and Europe.[30] The invasion and violent settlement of the Americas, including the extermination and enslavement of Indigenous populations, came with the globalisation of the extra-spatial "Europe as idea" and a European dominated market.[31] The Columbian expedition to what was termed the 'New World' would not have been possible without the inauguration of the Atlantic slave trade.[32] By the sixteenth century the relative truth of natural slavery was accepted.[33]

Ian Baucom makes the connection that today's hyper-financialised world repeats the earlier world of Atlantic slavery, intensifying it, expanding it.[34] Pocock described how the financial revolution of the eighteenth century was driven by a system of public credit that replaced a system of hegemonic sovereign power with a complex system of debt entanglement.[35] Slaves became a commodity available for exchange or credit acquisition.[36] The enslaved African was *at the same time* a 'commodified' source of labour power *and* a 'thingified' labouring body,[37] active subjects owned by others and deprived of their own names and languages.[38]

Baucom explains that the slave trade was a trade in financial instruments. Slave cargoes, on reaching the 'New World', would be assigned a sales agent, who would sell the slaves, deduct a commission, and 'remit' the proceeds of the sale in an interest-bearing bill of exchange. The bill guaranteed the payment of the full amount with interest, after a set period.[39] The market in enslaved Africans benefitted European nations by forging economic connections predicated on wealth gained from racialised enslavement and exploitative colonisation.[40] Insurance made sure that the commodity's value was a

28 Quijano (2007) 169.
29 Scanlan (2020) 18.
30 Mbembé (2017) 14.
31 Glissant (1992) 2; Hickel (2017) 58–63.
32 Garba and Sorentino (2020) 775.
33 Sorentino (2019) 632.
34 Baucom (2005) 21, 26.
35 Pocock (1985) 110.
36 Baucom (2005) 90.
37 Shilliam (2012) 593.
38 Mbembé (2017) 3.
39 Baucom (2005) 60–1.
40 Bhambra (2020) 307–22.

product of imagination and agreement. The real test of something's value did not occur at the point of exchange, but at the moment of loss or damage.[41] This allowed finance capital to speculate and profit from these imaginary markets and imaginary valuations.[42] Insurance was crucial to stimulating investment (by reducing risk) and providing speculators with another industry to invest in.[43] The slave trade fed the insurance industry which nourished the financial revolution.[44]

On symbolism

Sylvia Wynter explains that the position of the slave in the legal and political thought of Europe was *symbolically* significant, not just materially. There was material significance in the sense that the reification of Africans as the only "legitimately enslavable population" enabled the emerging discourses of republicanism and civil humanism and sutured the "moral and philosophical foundations of post-1492 polities".[45] The symbolic structures of slavery helped to produce space and its meanings.

Slavery was recognised as *internal* to the structure of Western civilisation.[46] In *The Future of an Illusion*, Freud commented that it is impossible for every civilisation to do without control of the masses through coercion.[47] It is necessary to produce an identity of the suppressed class or classes with the class that rules or exploits them.[48] Saidiya Hartman evokes both Aristotle and Hegel in her point that the slave is a fungible metaphor, a vessel through which the master regenerates their position:

> The dispossessed body of the enslaved is the surrogate for the master's body since it guarantees his disembodied universality and acts as a sign of his power and dominion.[49]

To be subject to the status of slave means to be a dominated thing, a body with natural movements but lacking reason, an existence entirely absorbed in another.[50] Coloniality and domination are reflected in falsified and misleading

41 Baucom (2005) 95.
42 Baucom (2005) 96.
43 Dickson (1967) 6.
44 Baucom (2005) 99.
45 Wynter (1995) 35.
46 Blackburn (1988).
47 Freud (1961) 7.
48 Freud (1961) 13.
49 Hartman (1997) 21.
50 Wallon (1879) 409.

terms exalting the coloniser and humbling the colonised.[51] This has symbolic significance. As we have seen, the bondsman's struggle for freedom and emancipation became a radical insight taken from Hegel's thought.[52] Mbembé explains that 'slave' is the name we give to a person whose body can be degraded, whose life can be mutilated, whose work and resources can be squandered with impunity.[53] Slaves were wild animals with human characteristics which could be domesticated for the economic benefit of the colonial power.[54]

The concepts of domination and slavery are central for the history of political philosophy and for contemporary political discourse.[55] European feminists drew analogies between their situation and that of 'slaves', in order to denounce their position of dependence, in the sense of being minors-for-life:

> Within the antislavery repertoire of bodily metaphors, the predominant one was the scourged body of the bondswoman, an image that symbolized the slave's utter debasement.[56]

Yet in focusing on the figure of the slave, they erased the central elements of enslavement, appropriating through analogy a condition that was not theirs.[57]

Quentin Skinner and Philip Pettit proposed that domination and servitude, and the injustice they involved, was to experience dependence on another person's will. This is to be vulnerable to an arbitrary power possessed by that person. Slavery is still used as a metaphor for political tyranny.[58] In *Liberty before Liberalism*, Skinner found that the seventeenth-century English parliamentarians were inspired by the discussion of slavery and freedom in the Code of Justinian, and the political writings of ancient Rome. This led them to define injustice in a political sphere as a state of dependence on the will of a ruler: enslaved people existed in this state, and so freedmen should not.[59] The parliamentarians argued that when a king possessed any discretionary or prerogative powers (even if these powers were never exercised), his subjects ceased to be free and were instead reduced to slavery. This allowed Charles I's opponents to attack his claim to have the right to veto any legislation put to him by Parliament: if the King's will were able to determine the law

51 Mpofu and Steyn (2021) 12–13; Mammi (1974) 123.
52 Patterson (1982) 98.
53 Mbembé (2001) 235.
54 Mbembé (2001) 236–7.
55 Skinner (1998); Pettit (1999).
56 Stanley (1998) 25.
57 Verges (2021) 28.
58 O'Connell Davidson (2015) 20.
59 Skinner (1998) 36–41.

in this way, then his subjects were enslaved.[60] In a similar vein, Pettit sees 'domination' and 'servitude' as synonymous. For Pettit, a just political dispensation is one of 'non-domination', which he understands to mean one in which people are immune from others' arbitrary or discretionary power.[61] This use of slavery does not focus on the condition of enslaved people, but rather is a polemic that signals the values which are cherished in the political arena.[62] This political arena was exclusionary. A view of extending rights to one group as also entailing the erosion of the rights of others represents a mentality that puts us in competition for resources defined as scarce.[63]

We can see the implications of these positions in relation to the 'right' to free speech. Free speech activism has been co-constituted with racialised state formation and empire since the 1800s.[64] Darcy Leigh has shown how John Stuart Mill saw free speech as the main motor of progress of liberal states and societies, through the discovery and dissemination of the truth.[65] Mill argued that if ideas could be debated freely in the marketplace of ideas, then speech would lead to truth.[66] This would be underpinned by the invisible hand of Enlightenment rationalism.[67] But the doctrine of liberty only applied to humans with mature faculties,[68] a qualifier that did not include indigenous peoples, who were akin to children.[69] To be immature was to be unable to live without direction from another, and be unqualified for exercising freedom.[70] To be colonised was to lack social development, and be subject to despotic government.[71] Civilisation is opposed to such savagery and barbarism.[72] This lack of development or humanity is shown through the assumption that non-White minds and rationality lack self-knowledge.[73] Mill's marketplace of ideas justifies colonisation[74] and is a regime of regulation that excludes, assimilates and stratified non-White speech as part of enslavement and racial capitalism.[75]

60 Skinner (1998) 28–9.
61 Pettit (1999) 21–3.
62 Nyquist (2013) 5.
63 Fraser (2000) 107–20.
64 Leigh (2022) 7.
65 Leigh (2022) 9; Mill (1901) 15–52.
66 Mill (1901) 50.
67 Mill (1901) 9–10.
68 Leigh (2022) 9.
69 Mill (1901) 9–10.
70 O'Connell Davidson (2015) 83; Kant (2009) 2.
71 Leigh (2022) 9; Mill (1901) 9–10.
72 Mill (1901) 120–2.
73 Leigh (2023) 770; Jackson (2020), 5.
74 Leigh (2022) 9.
75 Leigh (2022) 11.

Coloniality, race and the socially dead

The proper human is repressed by the limits of his own world, a world where that being cannot control its ontological foundation and a world that must constitute them.[76] In a manner analogous to Agamben, Afropessimism contends that the ontological basis of the modern world is based on a division of life, developing Orlando Patterson's concept of social death, making it clear that the fungible Slave remains a necessary foil for constructing the socially alive Human.[77] Slaveness is modernity's origin.[78] Colonial violence oversaw the entrenchment of subjugation by force, and violence was lived by the colonial subject, forcing them to contemplate the reality of a truly animal existence.[79] It is a violence that never goes into remission, and operates as a concurrent history, not a past event.[80]

Life is granted value against Blackness.[81] Blackness is unmappable in the cartographic logic of what is called the modern world.[82] Agamben never talks about Blackness.[83] The attribute *human* is wielded – given and taken away from 'weaker peoples', creating a climate of fear.[84] Mbembé stated that to produce Blackness is to produce a subjected body of extraction, from which great effort is made to extract the most profit.[85] He goes on: "To be Black is to be stuck at the foot of a wall with no doors, thinking nonetheless that everything will open up in the end".[86] For the Black Man to be identified as such, a veil must have already been placed over his face, making it "bereft of all humanity".[87] Mbembé goes on to explain that the power of race means that people we decide not to hear or see cannot exist for themselves or speak for themselves. When they do speak, what they say cannot be deciphered, and another must always speak for them.[88]

Whiteness became a *property*: a status property that confers rights denied to others and entails a right to exclude.[89] The racialisation of 'the human' is underscored by the dehumanisation of Blackened figures.[90] Their oppression

76 Mason (2020) 170.
77 Wilderson (2021) 41; Sorentino (2016).
78 Wilderson (2020) 219–20.
79 Mbembé (2012) 22.
80 Wilderson (2020) 224.
81 Wilderson (2010) 43.
82 Moten (2018) 207.
83 Mason (2020) 169.
84 Soyinka (2004).
85 Mbembé (2017) 18.
86 Mbembé (2017) 151–2.
87 Fanon (2005) 420.
88 Mbembé (2017) 111.
89 Harris (1993).
90 Wynter (2003).

is not morally wrong given their deficiencies,[91] and the African belongs to a world we cannot penetrate.[92] Africa, the very figure of the strange, serves as an argument for Europe's desire to assert its difference from the rest of the world.[93]

Afropessimism claims that it is epistemologically impossible to imagine an alternative Human world as the relationality which underpins our politics is predicated on an 'anti-Blackness',[94] on which Eurocentrism remains contingent.[95] The world remains ready for certain kinds of bodies, and bodies remember such histories, even when we forget them.[96] Mbembé sees the legacies of this process of destruction everywhere:

> Racial capitalism is the equivalent of a giant necropolis. It rests on the traffic of the dead and human bones.[97]

'Euro-modernity' was born in Western Europe in the seventeenth century, and this was a vehicle for the 'capitalist-colonial-enslavement' project.[98] Eurocentrism subsumes and subordinates any epistemology or entity considered to be non-European, and it inscribes White supremacy as a longstanding political project.[99] Frantz Fanon argued that colonial practices deprive the colonised individual of a meaningful past (of a meaningful *time*), especially where there is dignity, glory and sobriety there.[100] This allows the coloniser's history (a chronopolitics) to ignore the horrors of imperial history.[101] The racist structure of colonial violence was invisible.[102] Weheliye notes that colonial policies and discourses are grounded in racial distinctions, meaning the colonised subject cannot experience their nonbeing except through the dominant ideology that 'Western Man' as the only recognised type of human.[103]

Capitalist development also began with a war on women – the European witch-hunts of the sixteenth and seventeenth centuries destroyed the female subjects, practices and knowledge standing in the way of capital.[104] Saidiya Hartman speaks of the slave ship as a womb and an abyss, and the planta-

91 Mamdani (2013).
92 Mbembé (2001) 2.
93 Mbembé (2001) 3.
94 Wilderson (2021) 40.
95 Adébísí (2023) 18; Williams (1994) 306.
96 Ahmed (2006) 111.
97 Mbembé (2017) 136–7.
98 Adébísí (2023); Mignolo, Delgado and Romero (2000) 29.
99 Adébísí (2023) 19; Mills (1999) 3, 7, 11–12.
100 Fanon (2005) 148.
101 Gilroy (2004) 108, 111.
102 Gordon (1995) 38.
103 Weheliye (2014) 26.
104 Federici (2018) 47–9.

tion is the belly of the world, with the modern world following the belly. Gestational language is key to describing the world-making and world-breaking capacities of racial slavery.[105] Maria Lugones explained that colonial capitalism imposed the ideology of heteropatriarchy. What Lugones calls the colonial/modern gender system ordered White bourgeois lives and constituted the meanings of gender and compulsory heterosexuality. Colonised people were expected to aspire to bourgeois gender. Genders that did not fit the Western binary were violently eradicated.[106]

Even after the formal abolition of slavery, coloniality retains a close connection to property. The law reports of all common law jurisdictions contain judicial statements rejecting the property status of human bodies, corpses and bodily materials.[107] Yet it is the case (as Brenna Bhandar explains) that the production of modern property laws happens alongside that of racial subjects, stating that the two "share conceptual logics and are articulated ... [and] produced through one another in the colonial context".[108] Bhandar argues that:

> [T]o study modern property laws ... without accounting for the significance of the colonial scene to their development is to disaffiliate the development of modern law from its deep engagements with colonial sites.[109]

For Bhandar, race and property are bound and articulated at key historical junctures, and "articulations of race and property ... do not emerge in a consistent, linear, or even fashion. The temporalities of colonialism are multiple and uneven".[110]

The use and abuse of Black women's reproductive labour did not end with formal abolition. In 1951, Henrietta Lacks was being treated for cervical cancer at Johns Hopkins University Hospital. Cells were taken from Henrietta without her consent and formed the source of the first immortal cell line, known as HeLa. Unlike other human cells, they did not die after a few divisions.[111] These cells could be grown in a laboratory and used for many experiments. The total weight of all the HeLa cells grown exceeds 50 million metric tonnes.[112] The HeLa cell line helped develop the polio vaccine and improve cancer treatment, in vitro fertilisation and gene mapping. Much work was done at Tuskegee University, Alabama. Black scientists and

105 Hartman (2016) 166.
106 Lugones (2008) 1–17.
107 Pila (2020) 808–39.
108 Bhandar (2018) 8.
109 Bhandar (2018) 3.
110 Bhandar (2018) 23.
111 Truog, Kesselheim and Joffe (2012) 37–8.
112 Skloot (2010) 94.

technicians, many of them women, used Henrietta's cell line to help save the lives of millions of Americans, most of them White.[113] This occurred on the same campus as the Tuskegee syphilis study, where hundreds of Black Americans were enrolled in a study to investigate the natural course of syphilis. The study patients were denied treatment and the study, started in 1932 and scheduled to last six months, only stopped in 1972 after a public outcry.[114]

Decolonial destitution

Achille Mbembé critiques messianic thinkers like Agamben, who he sees as not concerned about the fate of the enslaved.[115] For messianism to be meaningful, Mbembé contends that it must be about more than mere survival. It must bring about a community.[116] Becoming human requires affirming a different form of humanity, "the possibility of reconstituting the human after humanism's complicity with colonial racism".[117] This is not a form of politics based on the State. The key to the coming politics is not that of a struggle to control the State or between new or old social subjects, or between hegemonic or counter-hegemonic forms. It will be a struggle between the State and the non-State (humanity), between singular beings and the organisations of the State.[118] These social forms of sovereign or governmental power have always sought to pervert what has always been inoperative and free.

The concept of the 'state' was developed as part of a unique modern European model of power over the last several hundred years.[119] As Peter Skalník explains, the nation state legitimates state power by appealing to reason and by the representation of all citizens in decision-making bodies.[120] The *ius publicum Europaeum* provided the framework for the emergence of states and the elements of proper international behaviour for the new nations. When the *ius publicum Europaeum* travelled with European powers to the periphery, the jurisdictional practices by which the colonies could be ordered accorded to a Eurocentric national logic.[121] The Eurocentric state was 'found' (or imposed) wherever there was hierarchy, stratification or

113 Skloot (2010) 97.
114 Tobin (2022) 1145–58.
115 Mbembé (2019) 106.
116 Mbembé (2019) 107. There have been attempts to read Agamben's work in the form of the 'Black messianic', although this goes beyond the scope of my argument. See Kaplan (2021); Kaplan (2019).
117 Mbembé (2021) 54.
118 Agamben (2000) 88.
119 Skalník (1987) 301.
120 Skalník (1987) 302.
121 Eslava and Pahuja (2020) 119–20.

centralisation of executive functions. This opposed states to 'stateless' societies lacking those centralised features.[122]

Non-European peoples organised themselves in a variety of ways prior to colonisation in original, unmediated forms.[123] Skalník (writing in the 1980s) complained that the "often lamented instability" of modern African states can be explained by a struggle between the Western-imposed state system and Indigenous social and political institutions. Skalník argued that those Indigenous institutions "show the world that without the state a society could function quite well, even better than with it".[124] The studies of politics in Indigenous Africa began only when those institutions had been 'tamed' and incorporated into colonial regimes.[125] The result of formal decolonisation was that the new states could only exist within the confines of the nation-state form, and often according to pre-established colonial boundaries that enclosed in single national formations highly disparate ethnic groups and incongruous geographical spaces.[126]

Agamben emphasises "we Europeans" and European history in his thought.[127] This must, borrowing Agamben's own terms, be corrected or, at least, completed.[128] Susan Brophy argues that Agamben's reading of *homo sacer* relies on an idiosyncratic Westernism.[129] Brophy cautions that Agamben's form-of-life remains a politics fit for a narrowly conceived liberal Western juridical subject, at best.[130] Europe's history is the history of the CMP and Euro-modernity. We need to move away from any perspective on Europe that does not meaningfully engage with Europe's responsibility for the 'capitalist-colonial-enslavement' project. As Fred Moten explains:

> Perhaps the world the slaveholders made is the text of impossible origins. The Bible and the Greeks are the world the slaveholders made. ... The Bible and the Greeks. These texts are Europe. Europe is Man.[131]

Man is made by and belongs to the polity, and the polity is made by Man's indebtedness to it. The polity only exists in Man's European capitalist ontology.[132] Complicity in what Fanon called the stasis of Europe is complicity

122 Skalník (1987) 303.
123 Skalník (1983) 25.
124 Skalník (1983) 25.
125 Skalník (1996) 109–22.
126 Eslava and Pahuja (2020) 121.
127 Agamben (2019) 1.
128 Agamben (1998) 9.
129 Brophy (2021) 192; Said (1993) 268.
130 Brophy (2021) 205.
131 Moten (2018) 31.
132 Mason (2020) 173.

in the coloniser's logic, that is, the logic of non-relation that is a condition of not having to see or be seen.[133] The world is a multitude of singularities. To rehabilitate singularity and difference is to affirm that the world cannot be reduced to Europe, and to avoid equating the universal with Europe.[134] The historical contextualisation of the experience of the fractured self does matter.[135] Opposing reductivist mentions of the "Third World",[136] we must broaden our philosophical horizons. This is even more pressing today. As Walter Mignolo explains, the CMP as a 'nomos of the earth', which inaugurated a hegemonic planetary European narrative, came to a close in 2000, slowly being replaced (in his view) by a multiplicity of the world and a pluriversity of knowledge where people decolonially take their destinies into their own hands.[137] This is despite colonial control continuing.[138]

I aim to show how Agamben's thought can be read as concerned with the enslaved.[139] Agamben's philosophy *destitutes*. Destitution is a form of revolt, seeking to change time. Decoloniality also destitutes and disrupts the legacies of racial, gender and geopolitical inequalities, and delinks from the CMP,[140] seeking new ways of living, thinking and being in the world. There is power and possibility in dehumanised bodies, spaces and temporalities.[141]

To this end, I wish to draw another connection between Agamben's thought and Afropessimism. Afropessimist thinkers like Frank Wilderson have commented that Agamben's analysis of the *Muselmann* and Auschwitz was not so much wrong as it was 'late'.[142] Wilderson's correction to Agamben's Eurocentrism is to state that Auschwitz was not unprecedented, given the singular nature of the Middle Passage's horrors. But he notes that while Jews remained Jews both before and after Auschwitz, Africans went into the slave ships and exited as 'Blacks'.[143] Kieran Aarons explains that the way forward cannot involve transforming dominant structures of signification, because these structures (even if changed) will still be based on the exclusion of the Black body.[144] What are perceived as liberatory discourses – Marxism, feminism, even strands of decoloniality – presuppose a grammar of suffering that

133 Brophy (2021) 205–6; Fanon (2005) 316.
134 Mbembé (2017) 157–8.
135 Brophy (2021) 206.
136 Agamben (1998) 180.
137 Mignolo (2021) 494.
138 Hall (2017) 24.
139 See also Kaplan (2019); Kaplan (2021).
140 Mignolo (2011) xxvii–xxviii.
141 Adébísí (2023) 35.
142 Wilderson (2010) 36.
143 Wilderson (2010) 38; Aarons (2016).
144 Aarons (2016).

both does not apply to the position of the Black-Slave and is also parasitic on the Black-Slave's incommensurable grammar of suffering.[145]

Whereas Fanon advocated decolonial revolt as an injunction,[146] a struggle for a world free of the burden of race, a world which all would have a right to,[147] destitution is not necessarily violent. Destitution also rejects any politics which seeks to institute a new constituent order. Destitution is also not anarchy. The Invisible Committee points out that anarchy is steeped in the Western European political tradition, focusing on individual self-expression, freedom, and so on. The figure of the anarchist represents the most extreme point of Western civilisations, where the hard-line affirmation of Western fictions (the individual, free will, justice, democracy) coincides with their declamatory negation.[148] Afropessimism seeks to abolish, refusing to validate, affirm, or strengthen the forms of subjectivity produced under racial capitalism and White supremacy.[149] This includes existing conditions of oppression *and* the identities that those conditions produce.[150] It is an ontological challenge to the being of the world.[151]

Likewise, Agamben's coming politics is a freeing of the beings who already exist in this world.[152] These ethical moments are a political refusal of 'ordinary' politics, and a revocation of given representations and identities. Of course, in seeking abolition, hyper-hermeneutic gestures will face a three-dimensional violence of coloniality.[153] But my focus is on the living being and its choice to live its life as a form. Even modest actions can carve out forms of life which are separate from the state and the colonial order (and live separate from our current identities). To destitute means to unseat colonially produced structures of power and technologies of permanent dispossession and dehumanisation, which must include 'ordinary' politics[154] and organisations that appropriate singular activity.[155] Aarons explains the stakes of this destitution. Fighting a common enemy does not mean there is a common *experience* of that enemy. The coming politics must reject the idea of solidarity based on 'common interests'. The struggle is one for ungovernable forms of life. These struggles may create solidarity in parallel lines, but not

145 Wilderson (2010) 79.
146 Crowley (2015) 23–37.
147 Mbembé (2012) 24.
148 Invisible Committee (2013); Aarons (2016).
149 Aarons (2016).
150 Aarons (2016).
151 Wilderson (2021) 38.
152 Mason (2020) 167.
153 Fanon (2018) 654.
154 Adébísí (2023) 33.
155 Colectivo Situaciones (2011) 47.

convergent lines. The task is to assault the conditions that enforce identities and constitute the self.[156]

Following Agamben's logic of the paradigm, we are dealing with the radical singularity of the example.[157] The singularity of the paradigm means that every case (every gesture that seeks to destitute) is an *exemplar* of a general rule that can never be stated a priori.[158] The paradigm is also an *exemplum* which allows statements and discursive practices to be gathered into a new intelligible ensemble and in a new problematic context.[159] Form-of-life is therefore both a way of living that is not based on a remainder, whether labelled as bare life or the excluded Black body, and it is also a model.[160] The actions and behaviours of forms-of-life in the past can provide a model, or a structure of behaviour, for the present. But they are not connected through common interests. They retain the potential to abolish the hermeneutics that structure the world, and in this sense these paradigms are hyper-hermeneutic.

Agamben's paradigm locates itself at the crossing of diachrony and synchrony. This makes our present as intelligible as the past of the object.[161] In looking to the past, we are cleaving open a chronological archive to produce a paradigm and make the whole archive legible.[162] Searching for past actions and gestures which sought to abolish and destitute can help inform our actions and choices today. Our commonality lies in what we wish to negate in ourselves that frees the way for us to find something more powerful.[163] Maurice Blanchot showed us that when our identities and accepted subjectivities become absent, life is opened up to its own passivity, exposing it to an unknown.[164] This is a life lived as a form. It is what Wilderson termed a 'gratuitous freedom', or a life lived without negative presuppositions.[165]

What world do we want to emerge beyond coloniality, and on the other side of our necropolitical world? What lies beyond Euro-modernity involves looking through bodies unseen by the death zone, in the silence after the disturbed waters, and in desolate and sunken places.[166] Escaping this darkness does not involve trying to remake this world shaped by coloniality. The master's tools will not dismantle the master's house.[167] Genuine change requires

156 Aarons (2016)
157 Agamben (2009) 19, 31.
158 Fusco (2023) 17; Agamben (2009) 22.
159 Agamben (2009) 18.
160 Frost (2014) 219.
161 Agamben (2009) 32.
162 Agamben (2009) 32.
163 Aarons (2016).
164 Blanchot (1995) 63.
165 Wilderson (2020) 249.
166 Adébísí (2023) 64.
167 Lorde (2007) 112.

a flight from the present. Even small gestures can represent a flight. To grasp gratuitous freedom is to grasp the invitation of social death embodied in Black beings.[168] The condition of possibility of a politics of destitution and refusal, and an acceptance of living a life as a form, involves us embracing the disorder of the dance of social death, and allowing oneself to be elaborated by it.[169]

Whilst past paradigms as examples can serve as models for the present, it is important to state that there is a scarcity of individual African narratives of captivity and enslavement.[170] This is because the slave condition is a triple loss. Loss of a 'home', loss of rights over the body, and loss of political status.[171] Human dignity was destroyed, names were removed, and groups disbursed so that there would be no common language amongst the slaves.[172] Mignolo states that individuals' single stories can be dangerous as the storyteller assumes that there is only one place to start the story.[173] But Hartman makes clear that in re-telling stories she displaces the received or authorised account, jeopardising the status of the event. The aim is to make visible disposable lives and to describe the resistance of the subject-made-object.[174] Mbembé sees acts of historical reconstruction as a necessary act of "moral imagination".[175] Counter-histories of slavery connect to the past and help us write our present, accepting that it is formed by past events.[176]

Mbembé claims that there is an *uneliminable surplus* that escapes all attempts at capture within a social or legal status. Even death cannot interrupt it.[177] This is inspired by Fanon's injunction that the human being remains a human being, despite all of the efforts of slavery and colonisation to make them think that they are not one.[178] Analogously, I can claim that what is present in hyper-hermeneutic paradigms is something that remains in surplus to power and *dispositifs* of control. This is form-of-life. In thinking apart from the concept of the state or governance, which is irredeemably contaminated with coloniality, there remains the potential for the living being to be thus. To live is to exist, and to exist is a triumph for life.[179]

168 Wilderson (2020) 249.
169 Wilderson (2020) 249–50.
170 Hartman (2008) 3.
171 Mbembé (2003) 21.
172 hooks (1981) 19.
173 Mignolo (2020) vii.
174 Hartman (2008) 11–12; Moten (2003) 14.
175 Mbembé (2017) 28–9.
176 Hartman (2008) 4.
177 Mbembé (2017) 46.
178 Fanon (1970) 45; Mbembé (2017) 46.
179 Fanon (2005) 308.

Mbembé's approach is instructive here. Form-of-life is plastic, allowing it to become other than the legal or political categories to which they are reduced and enable them to live their life as a form. This becoming can occur even when the human is constrained to loss, destruction or even annihilation.[180] This can create a rag-human, a figure with human characteristics but so disfigured that it is at once outside and within the human, as an infrahuman. But something remains. This could be speech or the ability to act.[181] Enslaved people made use of both, refusing the radical abdication of the subject (which for Agamben is the result of the action of *dispositifs* on living beings) that was demanded of them.[182] Mbembé goes on:

> [T]he work for life consists in distancing oneself time and time again from memory and tradition at the very moment that one depends on them to negotiate the twists and turns of life.[183]

This multiplicity offers possibilities – the marginalised now have the potential to burst open in altered forms.[184] Mbembé states:

> [A]s long as the retreat from humanity is incomplete, there is still a possibility of restitution, reparation, and justice. These are the conditions for the collective resurgence of humanity. Thinking through what must come will of necessity be a thinking through of life, of the reserves of life, of what must escape sacrifice. It will of necessity be *a thinking in circulation, a thinking of crossings, a world-thinking*.[185]

One of the possibilities of destituent potentiality is found by Agamben in sadomasochism.

Sadomasochism and the use of bodies

On sadomasochism and privacy

For Agamben, sadomasochism is a ritualised re-creation of Hegel's master-slave relation, and an 'insufficient attempt' to render the master-slave dialectic inoperative, by parodically finding in it the traces of a freer and fuller use of bodies which modernity has lost all access to.[186] The importance of the

180 Mbembé (2017) 132.
181 Mbembé (2017) 135.
182 Mbembé (2017) 48.
183 Mbembé (2017) 149.
184 Mignolo (2021) 509; Quijano (2016) 10.
185 Mbembé (2017) 179.
186 Agamben (2016) 35–6.

dialectic is underscored by Jürgen Habermas's explanation that Hegel was the first philosopher for whom modernity became a problem.[187] The final section of this chapter considers Agamben alongside the work of Weheliye to show how potential libidinal currents of destitution slumber in all acts of political domination.

In the master-slave dialectic, the bondsman works and the lord enjoys the fruits of that work. In sadomasochism, the two roles are reversed. Enjoyment and labour are unassignable in another figure of human praxis. Agamben views the Hegelian dialectic as a dialectical process internal to the individual, an inner doubling within consciousness that leads to self-consciousness.[188] In *Remnants of Auschwitz*, sadomasochism appears as a bipolar system in which:

> [A]n infinite receptivity – the masochist – encounters an equally infinite impassivity – the sadist – and in which subjectification and desubjectification incessantly circulate between two poles without properly belonging to either.[189]

Sadomasochism is not a result of a struggle of life and death, but an interminable process through which the two subjects exchange their roles. The masochistic subject only gets pleasure through the master, and the sadistic subject only recognises himself through transmitting pleasure to the slave via instruction and punishment:

> But since the masochistic subject enjoys his cruel training by definition, what was to be the instrument of the transmission of knowledge – punishment – is instead the instrument of pleasure; and discipline and apprenticeship, teacher and pupil, master and slave become wholly indistinguishable.[190]

In sadomasochism, the one who uses the body of the other can be used by the other for his own pleasure. The sadist and the masochist reciprocally use their bodies.[191] This is why Agamben draws a parallel to his discussion of the use of the slave's body in the thought of Aristotle. But this use of bodies is precisely what the *dispositifs* of control (including the structures of the state) cannot allow. The master and slave are in a community of life, and the originary form of property is the capture of the use of those bodies in the juridical

187 Habermas (1990) 43.
188 Agamben (2007a) 34.
189 Agamben (2002) 108.
190 Agamben (2002) 108–9.
191 Agamben (2016) 35.

order.[192] Nonstate formations cannot be permitted to exist. Living beings must be made into subjects.

Sadomasochism is presented as a doorway through which a life can live a form-of-life. No form of life or domain of existence is true in terms of its content.[193] This is representative of the use of bodies, and sadomasochism is one element of a banal site of lifestyle, including all acts involving "nutrition, digestion, urination, defecation, sleep and sexuality" that are labelled as 'private'.[194] Sergei Prozorov highlights that Agamben sees this use of bodies as containing a "genuinely political element" within "the opacity of our clandestine lifestyle".[195] Prozorov summarises that the truth of a form of life is its form-of-life and that means it cannot be contained within the form itself.[196] Form-of-life is life as it is lived: the tastes, habits, manners or styles that comprise the subject's forms of life.[197] This is the only ethical experience, the experience of being one's own potentiality. The only evil consists in not undertaking this experience.[198]

I follow Prozorov in interpreting Agamben's writings on sadomasochism as invoking us to make a different, common and political use of the everyday and intimate.[199] This action – a common or different use of the everyday – has been evidenced by enslaved people throughout the recorded history of enslavement in Western Europe and its colonies. All that was available to many enslaved people was to adopt a different perspective on something familiar and banal, to live otherwise than they (or we) have done before.[200] In other words:

> [I]t is not justice or beauty that moves us but the mode that each one has of being just or beautiful, of being affected by her beauty or her justice. For this reason, even abjection can be innocent, even "something slightly disgusting" can move us.[201]

192 Agamben (2016) 36.
193 Prozorov (2017) 157.
194 Agamben (2016) xx.
195 Agamben (2016) xxi; Prozorov (2017) 150.
196 Prozorov (2017) 158.
197 Agamben (2016) 231; Watkin (2021) 212; Prozorov (2017) 153.
198 Agamben (2007c) 44.
199 Prozorov (2017) 150; Agamben (2007b) 77–91.
200 Prozorov (2017) 153.
201 Agamben (2016) 232.

In this sense, the everyday and the intimate are not aesthetic issues, but ontological issues.[202] Intimacy is being held in relation with an inappropriable zone of non-consciousness.[203]

Agamben makes a further claim, which is that in modernity 'privacy' transforms form-of-life into another attribute of our identity as a subject, or simply an aspect of human capital.[204] Privacy is a crucial aspect of the modern subject, a modern *dispositif* that captures living beings and is defined first by being able to regulate access to one's intimacy. Intimacy selectively regulates access to the self, and privacy comes to replace the use of bodies. In a society formed of individuals, the transformation of use-of-oneself into a 'jealous possession' has, for Agamben, a political significance which remains "stubbornly hidden".[205] If the sovereign subject is sovereign over their own body, and if intimacy (as the use-of-oneself as inappropriable) becomes the fundamental biopolitical substance, this means that every individual has a right to share their liking of the other's inappropriable.[206]

This again connects use to inoperativity. Inoperativity is not a new practice or a new way of life but rather coincides with living a life.[207] Inoperativity allows us to understand how 'use' relates to those 'forms of production' which exist in any given epoch, including our present. For every form of production there is a corresponding form of inoperativity that allows for a new use of those works. For Agamben, an inoperative society is a classless society. But this is a society that currently exists in the here and now of racial capitalism, just like shards of messianic time are present in infamous and visible forms.[208] How does this commentary relate to enslaved people? How can we rectify what Paul Gilroy describes as the banishment of slave experience from accounts of modernity?[209]

Habeas viscus

Alexander Weheliye notes that Agamben's ideas are frequently invoked without scrutinising the foundations upon which they are constructed. This is a charge I agree with, and one I have been trying to remedy in this study. Agamben's bare life neglects and also actively disputes the existence of alternative modes of life alongside the violence, subjection, exploitation and

202 Prozorov (2017) 150; Agamben (2016) 231.
203 Agamben (2016) 91.
204 Agamben (2016) 230.
205 Agamben (2016) 92.
206 Agamben (2016) 92–3.
207 Agamben (2016) 277.
208 Agamben (2016) 94.
209 Gilroy (1993) 54.

racialisation that define the modern human.[210] In the Atlantic slave trade, race became pinioned to human physiology. Weheliye's main reference point is Hortense Spillers's conception of "the flesh".[211] Elliot C Mason notes that the flesh is antecedent to the body, beginning as an object of European Being in the Middle Passage but preceding it.[212]

The flesh exists at society's points of vulnerability. Becoming flesh means to be dominated over time, and having your political voice effaced. The CMP wounds, sears, divides and rips apart the flesh.[213] Spillers terms the "hieroglyphics of the flesh" the process that turns slaves into flesh. Creating flesh involves "the calculated work of iron, whips, chains, knives, the canine patrol, the bullet".[214] Flesh is fundamentally a racialising and a (de)gendering possibility, marked by fungibility.[215] Race intersects with gender and sexuality, so that we can speak of a racialised gendered sexuality.[216] Gender is a possible 'blind spot' within mainstream decolonial scholarship, which needs focusing upon to provide us with a comprehensive understanding of the foundations which need to be uprooted.[217] Any discussion of a new use of the body, beyond current borders, must understand that the borders we seek to free ourselves from are a construct of enslavement and coloniality.[218]

Weheliye speaks of '*habeas viscus*' (you shall have the flesh), a compound of the flesh and *habeas corpus*. *Habeas viscus* shows how the flesh excavates the social afterlife of bare life. Weheliye reads Agamben's bare life as posing an indivisible biological substance that exists prior to the racialisation of that substance. Weheliye sees Agamben's strengths as his weaknesses. Bare life can be transposed to many different contexts because Agamben does not place race at the forefront of his analyses, which overlooks the way race creates hierarchies between those who do and do not belong.[219]

Weheliye argues that bare life should not be read as prior to race.[220] Weheliye questions Agamben's focus on the concentration camp to the displacement of racial slavery, colonialism and indigenous genocide.[221] This is a pertinent question, given the *Muselmann* of the Nazi death camps, a paradigmatic figure of bare life, was a racial category.[222] Suffering caused by political

210 Weheliye (2014) 1–2.
211 Spillers (1987) 67.
212 Mason (2020) 174.
213 Spillers (1987) 67–8.
214 Spillers (1987) 67.
215 Mason (2020) 175.
216 Tamale (2020) 105.
217 Tamale (2020) 3–4.
218 Gordon (1995) 76.
219 Weheliye (2014) 4.
220 Weheliye (2014) 6–7.
221 Weheliye (2014) 36.
222 Weheliye (2014) 55.

violence has functioned as a hallmark of humane sentience and inhuman brutality.[223] Paul Gilroy saw the concentration camp as a space where 'normal' rules were set aside, and it was colonial societies that provided the context in which the camp emerged.[224]

Habeas viscus is a parallel to my interpretation of form-of-life and hyper-hermeneutics. Weheliye focuses on deformations of freedom that are possible in the absence of resistance. These are common and political uses of the everyday and intimate. There are manifold occurrences of freedom, "miniscule movements, glimmers of hope, scraps of food, the interrupted dreams of freedom found in those spaces deemed devoid of full human life".[225] Categories can be challenged and remade, sometimes from within.[226] The key is building our own houses of thought, which will mean that colonial mastery itself will cease to maintain its imperial status.[227] These lines of flight can be read in parallel to Robinson's invocation of the Black Radical Tradition, a "revolutionary consciousness" proceeding from the historical experience of Black people.[228] As Fred Moten has stated: "The history of blackness is testament to the fact that objects can and do resist".[229] In opposing ourselves to the world of nonhumans, we oppose ourselves.[230] We must try and sustain 'reservoirs of life', reanimating beings and things that may appear lifeless.[231] The signs of the world-to-come can be found in the present, in fragile forms.[232]

I now turn to Weheliye's concept of 'pornotroping'. This was a term coined by Spillers meaning the enactment of Black suffering for a shocked and titillated audience. The humanity found in oppressed peoples and individuals shows us what being 'human' means in modernity.[233] Political oppression often produces a sexual dimension, but this is a dimension that is not controllable by the forces that produced it.[234] Pornotroping is the name given to the 'becoming-flesh' of the (Black) body, and it is a primary process in transforming individuals into bare life.[235]

223 Weheliye (2014) 75.
224 Gilroy (2002) 60.
225 Weheliye (2014) 12.
226 Mbembé (2017) 48.
227 Gordon and Gordon (2006) ix.
228 Robinson (2021) 169.
229 Moten (2003) 1.
230 Mbembé (2017) 180.
231 Mbembé (2017) 181.
232 Mbembé (2017) 177.
233 Weheliye (2014) 12.
234 Weheliye (2014) 90.
235 Weheliye (2014) 91.

The power relations and knowledge that continually reproduce hierarchies of race, gender and geopolitics must be dismantled.[236] Weheliye expands on the 'flesh':

> The idea of the flesh ... constitutes a liminal zone comprising legal and extralegal subjection, violence, and torture as well as lines of flight from the world of Man in the form of practices, existences, thoughts, desires, dreams, and sounds.[237]

Liminality is key here. It is in liminality that form-of-life can dwell, at the limits of *dispositifs* of control, and at the limits of coloniality and state power's operation. Pornotroping ignites the libidinal currents slumbering in all acts of political domination and as part of modern sexuality. Weheliye sees such a libidinal current in the way sadomasochism shadows Agamben's work.[238] Whereas for Agamben sadomasochism is the technique of sexuality by which the bare life of a sexual partner is brought to life,[239] in pornotroping, the political acts as producing a sexual remainder feeding back into the power dynamic.[240] Pornotroping moves from a space of negativity defined by the total lack of agency and subjectivity toward something more elusive.[241] The body is vulnerable to abuse, but it is also the most powerful means of self-expression, and histories of oppression and rebellion can be read through bodies.[242] This necessitates us reappropriating the body and rediscovering its capacity for resistance.[243]

On the resistance of the body

Women's bodies are absent from Agamben's writings.[244] Colby Dickinson views this as deliberate. He goes on to claim that theories of gender and sexuality limit our ability to embrace those forms of life lived beyond the borders within which we are typically inscribed.[245] On one level this is true. But living beyond the borders we are inscribed within does not mean ignoring gender and its role in constructing the figure of the slave.

236 Maldonado-Torres (2011).
237 Weheliye (2014) 132.
238 Weheliye (2014) 108.
239 Agamben (1998) 134.
240 Weheliye (2014) 108.
241 Weheliye (2014) 110.
242 Federici (2020) 53.
243 Federici (2020) 123–4.
244 Deutscher (2008) 59.
245 Dickinson (2015) 167.

Catherine Mills sees a 'gender-blindness' throughout Agamben's work,[246] with him being part of a long philosophical tradition of casting women as the privileged figures of ephemerality. These figures cannot access the universal, but they are also instrumental in ensuring men have access to it. Agamben's writings on gender suffer from their brevity, and internal contradictions. Agamben mentions "the woman" as one of many social-juridical entities that supersede "the Marxian scission between man and citizen".[247] He also mentions the "two essential figures of femininity" being "woman (or mother) and girl (or virgin)",[248] and refers to feminine figures as being the threshold between animal and man (and god).[249] Gender is not analysed as part of his figurations of sexual fulfilment and happiness. Rosi Braidotti has opposed this type of figuration of the woman as a sign for the repressed or irrational other of rationality identified as male.[250]

Despite this, in his attempts to see the body beyond its inscribed borders,[251] Agamben speaks of the "glorious body", which:

> [I]s not another body, more agile and more beautiful, more luminous and more spiritual: it is the same body, within the act where idleness freed from enchainment and open to a new common usage is possible.[252]

For Agamben, bodies are not given over to stereotypical pronouncements on our 'gendered being'.[253] Agamben's approach ignores the way in which women were victims of sexual abuse and mistreatment that could *only be inflicted on women*. It also repeats the slaveholders' logic in the CMP. Slavers would terrorise the Black woman so thoroughly she would submit passively to the will of the White master.[254] Fanon understood this when he explained that the coloniser must first of all "conquer the women" to destroy the structure of the colonised society.[255]

Spillers uses the concept of "ungendering" to refer to the particular effects on the body and on society at the intersection of being racialised and gendered away from normativity ('White' being 'normal'). Ungendering produces a body that is open to be violated by all, in all ways.[256] Not all women have the

246 Mills (2008) 114.
247 Agamben (2000) 6–7.
248 Agamben and Ferrando (2014) 3.
249 Agamben and Ferrando (2014) 44.
250 Braidotti (1991) 39.
251 Dickinson (2015) 179.
252 Agamben (2010) 103.
253 Agamben (2007c) 48.
254 hooks (1981) 20.
255 Fanon (2003) 44.
256 Spillers (1987) 77.

same gender because of their lived experiences that are inflected by factors like race, geography and class.[257] Ungendering does not remove gender. The quintessential slave is female.[258] Women specifically could be exploited and repressed in ways that locked them into their female roles.[259] This was a daily drama, enacted through innumerable anonymous encounters with abusers who were convinced their acts were only natural.[260] Jennifer Morgan coined the phrase 'porno-tropical writing' to describe conventional early modern European travel literature that portrayed people from the tropical world as hypersexual and exotic.[261]

Silvia Federici explains that the history of the body can only be told by weaving together the histories of those who were enslaved, colonised, turned into wage workers or unpaid housewives and the histories of the children, whilst recognising these are not mutually exclusive classifications.[262] The body was 'enclosed' by the development of capitalism, and women suffered a double process of mechanisation, most brutally by slavery. Women were subject to the discipline of paid and unpaid work in plantations, factories and homes, and also turned into sexual objects and breeding machines.[263] Women became the arms, the hands, the genitals, and the womb: parts cut off from a body as the "atomizing of the captive body".[264]

The body resisted. Enslaved people were never *merely* victims of the Atlantic slave trade; they resisted servitude with all their might and fought back against their oppressors. On the African coast, resistance began before the slave ships sailed. Slaves would try to make a dash for freedom at the very point of sale, and there were frequent uprisings, both by those locked up awaiting shipment,[265] and those already embarked.[266] Life on the lower decks of slave ships in the Middle Passage was collective and insurgent, forming new bonds of community, a site of creative resistance for those who discovered themselves to be "black folks".[267]

Resistance continued in the living hell of the 'Middle Passage'. Resistance was cultural, and this cultural insurgence was associated with women, including singing, dancing, drumming (the ship itself was wooden and a percussive

257 Brown (1992) 298.
258 Spillers (1987) 73.
259 Davis (2019) 4–5.
260 Davis (2019) 159.
261 Morgan (2021) 46.
262 Federici (2020) 11.
263 Federici (2020) 13–14.
264 Spillers (1987) 67.
265 Wax (1966) 9–10.
266 Mannix and Cowley (1963) 108–11.
267 Rediker (2007) 307; Youngquist (2011) 14.

instrument) and storytelling.[268] Few voyages were ever completed without the discovery or threat of a slave conspiracy.[269] Slave owners understood slave women as embodying a pacifying influence on enslaved populations,[270] but Rebecca Hall has shown that the majority of slave revolts on slave ships on the Atlantic and in British North America during the eighteenth century were led by women.[271]

Every possible precaution was taken to prevent the slaves from revolting. Guards were always posted to insure against the crew's being taken by surprise. The vessels were carefully searched to make sure that no pieces of iron, wood or other weapons were within reach of the slaves.[272] Upon boarding, both men and women were chained below decks until the ship left African waters. Once the ship left the coast the women and children were unchained and brought up on deck. Keeping women accessible would be a 'benefit' for the crew. Rape and sexual violence were tools for domination and control. The women used their relative mobility and access to weapons to plan and initiate revolts. Women were kept on deck, unchained, and near the weapons. Slave ship crews remained oblivious to the agency of enslaved women.[273]

Women redefined the imagined identities created for them by slave owners by effecting a fusion between African-derived cultural beliefs and powerful resistance strategies that undermined the slave system.[274] Enslaved women resisted through a variety of single or collective acts including malingering, feigning illness, shirking work, lying, stealing and even open defiance.[275] Slave owners found women, especially pregnant women, the most difficult to manage, as they often sought exemptions from working in the fields.[276] Sasha Turner has shown how enslaved mothers fought to preserve their privacy and their rights to their children; slaveholders grasped for the labour and capital that enslaved children represented.[277] Women's rejection of plantation violence took many forms, including the use of clothing as a bulwark against commodification, and taking pleasure in their own bodies, to deny that they were only, or mainly, worth the prices their owners placed on them.[278]

Women actively rejected slave owners' efforts to turn them into breeders, situating their decisions as "made consciously and with full awareness of the

268 Rediker (2007) 278; Youngquist (2011) 15.
269 Craton (1982) 24; Scanlan (2020) 51.
270 Morgan (2021) 212.
271 Hall (2021).
272 Greene (1944) 347.
273 Hall (2021).
274 Bush (2001) 116.
275 Bush (1990) 45, 53.
276 Thomson (1820) 112.
277 Turner (2017).
278 Camp (2004) 83.

potential political and economic ramifications involved".[279] The oppression of the plantation influenced slave women's responses to childbirth and infant rearing consciously and unconsciously.[280] Caribbean planters frequently accused women of procuring abortions and frustrating their attempts to increase the slave population.[281] There were accusations of slave women pretending to have miscarried to get time off work.[282] Loretta Ross contends that abortion and infanticide were acts of desperation, motivated not by a desire to avoid birth or the burdens of parenting, but by a commitment to resist the oppressive conditions of slavery.[283] As Hartman describes, enslaved women yearned for radically different ways of being in the world.[284] In attending to familial or corporeal pleasures, enslaved women (and men) enacted a critique of the edifices of their containment.[285] This was a use of the body as a site of pleasure and resistance, to counter the appropriation of their bodies through domination.[286]

This is what Audre Lorde sees as the 'erotic', a resource within each of us that lies in a deeply female and spiritual plane, rooted in the power of unexpressed or unrecognised feeling.[287] The erotic is the opposite of pornography, an internal sense of satisfaction which, once experienced, becomes an aspiration.[288] To be utilised, erotic feelings must be recognised, and are all too often characterised by looking away, and calling them something else. Misnaming the erotic means it cannot be experienced.[289] This experience requires community.[290] These were forms of life, enslaved people, carving out communities from beneath the abyssal plane, in unedifying places. They were, through small and large acts, refusing the logics of coloniality and enslavement and showing how life could exist and be lived according to its own terms.

Everyday behaviour and living in networks and communities made it clear a form of life persisted.[291] In that community, the performance of drudgery helped those communities survive.[292] As Hartman reminds us, the pastoral plays a crucial role in understanding Black performance because it articulates the complex relations in which the performance of everyday life, especially

279 Hine (1979) 126.
280 Bush-Slimani (1993) 83.
281 Reverend Henry Beame, cited in Craton, Walvin and Wright (1976) 141.
282 Thomson (1820) 112–13.
283 Ross (1992) 276; Perrin (2001) 255–74.
284 Hartman (2016) 167.
285 Morgan (2021) 219.
286 Camp (2004) 66–8.
287 Lorde (2007) 53.
288 Lorde (2007) 54–5.
289 Lorde (2007) 58–9.
290 Lorde (2007) 112.
291 Gutman (1976) 356–7.
292 Davis (1971) 6.

under enslavement, has been understood and bound up: "the pastoral renders the state of domination as an ideal of care, duty, familial obligation, gratitude, and humanity".[293]

Cultural negotiation took place in the African disapora and the Caribbean between Black and White, creole and African-born and slaves taken from different parts of Africa. Links were forged through resistance.[294] Black identity was lived as a coherent (if not always stable) experiential sense of self, an outcome of practical activity, language, gesture, bodily significations and desires.[295] Cultural struggles involved powerful resistance to White-constructed identities of slave women. They facilitated the negotiation of new identities rooted in women's 'African' memory which enabled them to reclaim their own destinies.[296]

Conclusion

This chapter has turned to the way in which the enslaved person can be used to theorise the end of the CMP. Form-of-life is an invocation for the coming politics, in the face of the CMP. We need to theorise the end of the world in which we live. Race, coloniality and enslavement have constructed the modern world. This is in part due to the figure of the slave being *materially* and *symbolically* significant to European thought, including in relation to feminist thought, the growth of finance capitalism, and critiques of capitalism.

In this chapter I have discussed the importance of racial capitalism to the formation of the modern world. Here, racialism joined with capitalism, and shaped capital exchange and investment. This has married with coloniality and its production of certain accepted notions of belonging and personhood. Central to modern racial capitalism and coloniality is the Atlantic slave trade, and the transformation of human life into an object of economic transaction. The growth of industrial capitalism and modern technology is impossible to understand without colonialism and its technologies of race and power. The slave (as a legal and political category) was a technology used to produce and create wealth.

I have also considered what a decolonial approach to challenging the CMP would involve. Such an approach also allows us to extend Agamben's thought beyond the Eurocentric horizons that often circumscribe his thought. Form-of-life can be removed from a reading that restricts it to a liberal Western juridical subject. I considered how Afropessimism can assist in this task.

293 Hartman (1997) 53.
294 Bush (2001) 123.
295 Gilroy (1993) 102.
296 Bush (2001) 135.

There is power and possibility in dehumanised bodies, spaces and temporalities. This decolonial praxis has been occurring throughout the epoch of the CMP. There remains a surplus (form-of-life, the bare fact of living) which escapes all attempts at capture within a social or legal status. This surplus is developed through reference to Agamben's exploration of sadomasochism, Alexander Weheliye's conceptions of *habeas viscus* and pornotroping, and the example of resistance in the body (and especially in the female body) through the CMP, the Atlantic slave trade and against colonial forms of domination. This explores how potentially libidinal currents slumber in all acts of political domination, and how form-of-life can exist and live its life as a form even in desolate and sunken places.

Reference List

Aarons, K (2016) 'No Selves to Abolish: Afropessimism, Anti-Politics and the End of the World', *MetaMute* (29 February 2016) http://www.metamute.org/editorial/articles/no-selves-to-abolish-afropessimism-anti-politics-and-end-world.

Adébísí, F (2023) *Decolonisation and Legal Knowledge: Reflections on Power and Possibility*, Bristol: Bristol University Press.

Agamben, G (1998) *Homo Sacer: Sovereign Power and Bare Life,* Heller-Roazen, D (trans.), Stanford: Stanford University Press.

Agamben, G (2000) *Means Without End: Notes on Politics*, Binetti, V and Casarino, C (trans.), Minneapolis: University of Minnesota Press.

Agamben, G (2002) *Remnants of Auschwitz: The Witness and the Archive*, Heller-Roazen D (trans.), New York: Zone Books.

Agamben, G (2007a) *Infancy and History: On the Destruction of Experience*, Heron, L (trans.), London: Verso Books.

Agamben, G (2007b) *Profanations*, Fort, J (trans.), Princeton: Princeton University Press.

Agamben, G (2007c) *The Coming Community*, Hardt, M (trans.), Minneapolis: University of Minnesota Press.

Agamben, G (2009) *The Signature of All Things: On Method*, D'Isanto, L and Attell, K (trans.), New York: Zone Books.

Agamben, G (2010) *Nudities*, Kishik, D and Pedatella, S (trans.), Stanford: Stanford University Press.

Agamben, G (2016) *The Use of Bodies*, Kotsko, A (trans.), Stanford: Stanford University Press.

Agamben, G (2019) *Creation and Anarchy: The Work of Art and the Religion of Capitalism*, Kotsko, A (trans.), Stanford: Stanford University Press.

Agamben, G and Ferrando, M (2014) *The Unspeakable Girl: The Myth and Mystery of Kore*, de la Durantaye, L and Wyman, A (trans.), East Peoria, Seagull Books.

Ahmed, S (2006) *Queer Phenomenology*, Durham: Duke University Press.

Baucom, I (2005) *Spectres of the Atlantic: Finance Capital, Slavery, and the Philosophy of the Atlantic*, Durham and London: Duke University Press,

Bhambra, G (2020) 'Colonial Global Economy: Towards a Theoretical Reorientation of Political Economy', *Review of International Political Economy*, 28, 307–22.

Bhandar, B (2018) *Colonial Lives of Property: Law, Land and Racial Regimes of Ownership*, Durham: Duke University Press.

Blackburn, R (1988) *The Overthrow of Colonial Slavery, 1776–1848,* London: Verso.

Blanchot, M (1995) *The Writing of the Disaster*, Smock, A (trans.), Lincoln: University of Nebraska Press.

Braidotti, R (1991) *Patterns of Dissonance*, Cambridge: Polity Press.

Brayson, K (2021) 'Generating Comparison-in-Law: Embodied Epistemologies, For the Love of Knowledge', *Critical Analysis of Law*, 8, 52–86.

Brophy, S (2021) 'A Politics Like No Other: Agamben, Fanon, and the Colonial Fracture' in Norris, M and Dickinson, C (eds.), *Agamben and the Existentialists*, Edinburgh: Edinburgh University Press, 191–211.

Brown, E B (1992) ''What Has Happened Here': The Politics of Difference in Women's History and Feminist Politics', *Feminist Studies*, 18, 295–312.

Bush, B (1990) *Slave Women in Caribbean Society, 1650–1832*, Bloomington: Indiana University Press.

Bush, B (2001) 'From Slavery to Freedom: Black Women, Cultural Resistance and Identity in Caribbean Plantation Society' in Bremer, T and Fleischmann, U (eds.), *History and Histories in the Caribbean*, Madrid: Iberoamericana, 115–59.

Bush-Slimani, B (1993) 'Hard Labour: Women, Childbirth and Resistance in British Caribbean Slave Societies', *History Workshop Journal*, 36, 83–99.

Camp, S (2004) *Closer to Freedom: Enslaved Women and Everyday Resistance in the Plantation South*, Chapel Hill: The University of North Carolina Press.

Colectivo Situaciones (2011) *Nineteen and Twenty: Notes for a New Social Protagonism*, Nate Holdren (trans.), New York: Minor Compositions.

Craton, M (1982) *Testing the Chains: Resistance to Slavery in the British West Indies*, Ithaca & London, Cornell University Press.

Craton, M, Walvin, J and Wright, D (1976) *Slavery, Abolition and Emancipation: Black Slaves and the British Empire: a Thematic Documentary*, London: Longman.

Crowley, P (2015) 'Fanon: Religious Language, Messianic Time and the New Man', *Nottingham French Studies*, 54, 23–37.

Davis, A (1971) 'Reflections on the Black Woman's Role in the Community of Slaves', *The Black Scholar*, 3, 2–15.

Davis, A (2019) *Women, Race & Class*, London: Penguin Books.

Deutscher, P (2008) 'The Inversion of Exceptionality: Foucault, Agamben and "Reproductive Rights"', *South Atlantic Quarterly*, 107, 55–70.

Dickinson, C (2015) 'The 'Absence' of Gender' in *Agamben's Coming Philosophy: Finding a New Use for Theology*, Dickinson, C and Kotsko, A, London: Rowman & Littlefield International, 167–82.

Dickson, P G M (1967) *The Financial Revolution in England: A Study in the Development of Public Credit, 1688–1756,* New York: St Martin's.

Eslava, L and Pahuja, S (2020) 'The State and International Law: A Reading from the Global South', *Humanity: An International Journal of Human Rights, Humanitarianism, and Development*, 11, 118–38.

Fanon, F (1970) *Black Skin, White Masks*, Markmann, C (trans.), London: Paladin.

Fanon, F (2003) *Decolonization: Perspectives from Now and Then*, Prasenjit Duara (ed.), New York: Routledge.

Fanon, F (2005) *The Wretched of the Earth*, Farrington, C (trans.), New York: Grove Press.

Fanon, F (2018) *Alienation and Freedom*, Khalifa, J and Young, R (eds.), Corcoran, S (trans.), London: Bloomsbury.
Federici, S (2018) *Witches, Witch-Hunting and Women*, Oakland: PM Press.
Federici, S (2020) *Beyond the Periphery of the Skin: Rethinking, Remaking, and Reclaiming the Body in Contemporary Capitalism*, Oakland: PM Press.
Fraser, N (2000) 'Rethinking Recognition', *New Left Review*, 3, 107–20.
Freud, S (1961) *The Standard Edition of the Complete Psychological Works of Sigmund Freud, Vol. XXI (1927–1931)*, London: The Hogarth Press.
Frost, T (2014) 'Thinking Relationality in Agamben and Levinas', *Griffith Law Review*, 23, 210–31.
Fusco, G-G (2023) *Form of Life: Agamben and the Destitution of Rules*, Edinburgh: Edinburgh University Press.
Garba, T and Sorentino, S-M (2020) 'Slavery Is a Metaphor: A Critical Commentary on Eve Tuck and K. Wayne Yang's "Decolonization Is Not a Metaphor"', *Antipode: A Radical Journal of Geography*, 52, 764–82.
Gilroy, P (1993) *The Black Atlantic: Modernity and Double Consciousness*, London: Verso.
Gilroy, P (2002) *Against Race: Imagining Political Culture Beyond the Color Line*, Cambridge: Harvard University Press.
Gilroy, P (2004) *After Empire: Melancholia or Convivial Culture?* Abingdon: Routledge.
Glissant, E (1992) *Caribbean Discourse: Selected Essays*, Charlottesville: University of Virginia Press.
Gordon, L (1995) *Fanon and the Crisis of European Man: An Essay on Philosophy and the Human Sciences*, New York: Routledge.
Gordon, L and Gordon, J (2006) 'Introduction: Not Only the Master's Tools' in Gordon, L and Gordon, J (eds.), *Not Only the Master's Tools: African-American Studies in Theory and Practice*, Boulder: Paradigm.
Greene, L (1944) 'Mutiny on the Slave Ships', *Phylon*, 5, 346–54.
Gutman, H (1976) *The Black Family in Slavery and Freedom, 1750–1925*, New York: Pantheon Books.
Habermas, J (1990) *The Philosophical Discourse of Modernity: Twelve Lectures*, Lawrence, F (trans.), Cambridge: MIT Press.
Hall, R (2021) *Wake: The Hidden History of Women-Led Slave Revolts*, New York: Simon & Schuster.
Hall, S (2017) *Familiar Stranger*, Durham: Duke University Press.
Harris, C (1993) 'Whiteness as Property', *Harvard Law Review*, 106, 1707–91.
Hartman, S (1997) *Scenes of Subjection: Terror, Slavery, and Self-Making in Nineteenth-Century America*, Oxford: Oxford University Press.
Hartman, S (2008) 'Venus in Two Acts', *Small Axe*, 12, 1–14.
Hartman, S (2016) 'The Belly of the World: A Note on Black Women's Labors', *Souls: A Critical Journal of Black Politics, Culture, and Society*, 18, 166–73.
Hickel, J (2017) *The Divide: A Brief Guide to Global Inequality and Its Solutions*, London: Random House.
Hine, D (1979) 'Female Slave Resistance: The Economics of Sex', *The Western Journal of Black Studies*, 3, 123–27.
hooks, bell (1981) *Ain't I a Woman: Black Women and Feminism*, Boston: South End Press.

Invisible Committee (2013) 'Spread Anarchy, Live Communism' in Blumenfeld, J, Bottici, C and Critchley, S (eds.), *The Anarchist Turn*, London: Pluto Press, 224–34.

Jackson, Z I (2020) *Becoming Human: Matter and Meaning in an Antiblack World*, New York: New York University Press.

Kant, I (2009) *An Answer to the Question: What Is Enlightenment?*, Ferrer, D (trans.), London: Penguin.

Kaplan, A S (2019) 'Notes Toward (Inhabiting) the Black Messianic in Afro-Pessimism's Apocalyptic Thought', *The Comparatist*, 43, 68–89.

Kaplan, A S (2021) 'On the *Annihilation* of the Human's Fundamental Fantasy of Life: Toward an Anagrammatical Liturgy of Black Messianic Death', *The Comparatist*, 45, 41–63.

Leigh, D (2022) 'The Settler Coloniality of Free Speech', *International Political Sociology*, 16, 1–18.

Leigh, D (2023) 'From Savages to Snowflakes: Race and the Enemies of Free Speech', *Review of International Studies*, 49, 763–79.

Leong, N (2013) 'Racial Capitalism', *Harvard Law Review*, 126, 2151–226.

Lorde, A (2007) *Sister Outsider*, Berkeley: Crossing Press.

Lugones, M (2008) 'The Coloniality of Gender', *Worlds & Knowledges Otherwise*, 2, 1–17.

Maldonado-Torres, N (2011) 'Thinking Through the Decolonial Turn: Post-Continental Interventions in Theory, Philosophy, and Critique – An Introduction', *Transmodernity: Journal of Peripheral Production of the Luso-Hispanic World*, 1. http://dx.doi.org/10.5070/T412011805.

Mamdani, M (2013) *Define and Rule: Native as Political Identity*, Johannesburg: Wits University Press.

Mammi, A (1974) *The Colonizer and the Colonized*, New York: Routledge.

Mannix, D and Cowley, M (1963) *Black Cargoes: A History of the Atlantic Slave Trade 1518–1865*, London: Longmans.

Mason, E (2020) 'Thing: A fugitive in( )operation", *Journal of Italian Philosophy*, 3, 163–89.

Mbembé, A (2001) *On the Postcolony*, Chicago: University of Chicago Press.

Mbembé, A (2003) 'Necropolitics', *Public Culture*, 15, 11–40.

Mbembé, A (2012) 'Metamorphic Thought: The *Works* of Frantz Fanon', *African Studies*, 71, 19–28.

Mbembé, A (2017) *Critique of Black Reason*, Dubois, L (trans.), Durham: Duke University Press.

Mbembé, A (2019) *Necropolitics*, Durham: Duke University Press.

Mbembé, A (2021) *Out of the Dark Night: Essays on Decolonization*, Daniela Ginsburg (trans.), New York: Columbia University Press.

Mignolo, W (2011) *The Darker Side of Western Modernity: Global Futures, Decolonial Options*, Durham: Duke University Press.

Mignolo, W (2020) 'Foreword: Thinking Decoloniality beyond One Nation – One State' in Casimir, J, *The Haitians: A Decolonial History*, Dubois, L (trans.), Durham: The University of North Carolina Press, vii-xvi.

Mignolo, W (2021) *The Politics of Decolonial Investigations*, Durham: Duke University Press.

Mignolo, W, Delgado, L and Romero, R (2000) 'Local Histories and Global Designs: An Interview with Walter Mignolo', *Discourse*, 22, 7–33.
Mill, J S (1901) *On Liberty*, London: The Walter Scott Publishing Co Ltd,
Mills, C (1999) *The Racial Contract,* Ithaca and London: Cornell University Press.
Mills, C (2008) *The Philosophy of Agamben*, Stocksfield: Acumen Publishing.
Morgan, J (2021) *Reckoning with Slavery: Gender, Kinship, and Capitalism in the Early Black Atlantic*, Durham: Duke University Press.
Moten, F (2003) *In the Break: The Aesthetics of the Black Radical Tradition*, Minneapolis: University of Minnesota Press.
Moten, F (2018) *The Universal Machine*, Durham: Duke University Press.
Mpofu, W and Steyn, M (2021) 'The Trouble with the Human' in Steyn, M and Mpofu, W (eds.), *Decolonising the Human: Reflections from Africa on Difference and Oppression*, Johannesburg: Wits University Press, 1–24.
Nyquist, M (2013) *Arbitrary Rule: Slavery, Tyranny and the Power of Life and Death*, Chicago: University of Chicago Press.
O'Connell Davison, J (2015) *Modern Slavery: The Margins of Freedom*, Basingstoke: Palgrave Macmillan.
Patterson, O (1982) *Slavery and Social Death: A Comparative Study*, Cambridge: Harvard University Press.
Perrin, L (2001) 'Resisting Reproduction: Reconsidering Slave Contraception in the Old South', *Journal of American Studies*, 35, 255–74.
Pettit, P (1999) *Republicanism: A Theory of Freedom and Government*, Oxford: Oxford University Press.
Pila, J (2020) 'Property in Human Genetic Material: An Old Legal Question for a New Technological Age' in Orentlicher, D and Hervey, T (eds.), *The Oxford Handbook of Comparative Health Law*, Oxford: Oxford University Press, 808–39.
Pocock, J G A (1985) *Virtue, Commerce, and History: Essays on Political Thought and History, Chiefly in the Eighteenth Century*, Cambridge: Cambridge University Press.
Prozorov, S (2017) 'Living *à la mode*: Form-of-life and democratic biopolitics in Giorgio Agamben's *The Use of Bodies*', *Philosophy and Social Criticism*, 43, 144–63.
Quijano, A (2007) 'Coloniality and Modernity/Rationality', *Cultural Studies*, 21, 168–78.
Quijano, A (2016) 'Bien Vivir – Between Development and the De/Coloniality of Power', *Alternautas*, 3, 1–23.
Rediker, M (2007) *The Slave Ship: A Human History*, New York: W W Norton.
Robinson, C (2021) *Black Marxism: The Making of the Black Radical Tradition*, London: Penguin Books.
Ross, L (1992) 'African-American Women and Abortion: A Neglected History', *Journal of Health Care for the Poor and Underserved*, 3, 274–84.
Said, E (1993) *Culture and Imperialism*, New York: Knopf.
Scanlan, P (2020) *Slave Empire: How Slavery Built Modern Britain*, London: Robinson.
Shilliam, R (2012) 'Forget English Freedom, Remember Atlantic Slavery: Common Law, Commercial Law and the Significance of Slavery for Classical Political Economy', *New Political Economy*, 17, 591–609.

Skalník, P (1983) 'Questioning the Concept of the State in Indigenous Africa', *Social Dynamics*, 9, 11–28.
Skalník, P (1987) 'On the Inadequacy of the Concept of the Traditional State - Illustrated with Ethnographic Material on Nanun, Ghana', *Journal of Legal Pluralism and Unofficial Law*, 25, 301–26.
Skalník, P (1996) 'Authority Versus Power: Democracy in Africa Must Include Original African Institutions', *Journal of Legal Pluralism and Unofficial Law*, 37, 109–22.
Skinner, Q (1998) *Liberty before Liberalism*, Cambridge: Cambridge University Press.
Skloot, R (2010) *The Immortal Life of Henrietta Lacks*, New York: Crown Publishers.
Sorentino, S-M (2016) 'The Sociogeny of Social Death: Blackness, Modernity, and its Metaphors in Orlando Patterson', *Rhizomes: Cultural Studies in Emerging Knowledge, 29.*
Sorentino, S-M (2019) 'Natural Slavery, Real Abstraction, and the Virtuality of Anti-Blackness', *Theory & Event*, 22, 630–73.
Soyinka, W (2004) *Climate of Fear*, London: Profile Books.
Spillers, H (1987) "Mama's Baby, Papa's Maybe': An American Grammar Book', *Diacritics*, 17, 64–81.
Stanley, A D (1998) *From Bondage to Contract: Wage Labor, Marriage, and the Market in the Age of Slave Emancipation*, Cambridge: Cambridge University Press.
Subrahmanyam, S (2023) 'Revisiting 'Racial Capitalism'', *European Journal of Sociology*, 64, 173–81.
Tamale, S (2020) *Decolonization and Afro-Feminism*, Ottawa: Daraja Press.
Thomson, J (1820) *A Treatise on the Diseases of the Negroes as They Occur in the Island of Jamaica, with Observations on the Countries Remedies*, Jamaica: Alexander Aikman.
Tobin, M (2022) 'Fiftieth Anniversary of Uncovering the Tuskegee Syphilis Study: The Story and Timeless Lessons', *American Journal of Respiratory and Critical Care Medicine*, 205, 1145–58.
Troug, R, Kesselheim, A and Joffe, S (2012) 'Paying Tissue Donors: The Legacy of Henrietta Lacks', *Science*, 337, 37–8.
Turner, S (2017) *Contested Bodies: Pregnancy, Childbearing and Slavery in Jamaica,* Philadelphia: University of Pennsylvania Press.
Verges, F (2021) *A Decolonial Feminism*, Bohrer, A (trans.), London: Pluto Press.
Wacquant, L (2022) 'Resolving the Trouble with 'Race'', *New Left Review*, 133/4, 67–88.
Wacquant, L (2023a) 'Racial Capitalism Decoupled: A Rejoinder and Reformulation', *European Journal of Sociology*, 64, 183–93.
Wacquant, L (2023b) 'The Trap of "Racial Capitalism"', *European Journal of Sociology*, 64, 153–62.
Wallon, H (1879) *Histoire de l'escavage dans l'antiquité*, Paris: Hachette.
Watkin, W (2021) 'Agamben's Impotentiality: Separation, Nonrelationality, and Destituent Potential in *The Use of Bodies*', *Italian Studies*, 76, 200–14.
Wax, D (1966) 'Negro Resistance to the Early American Slave Trade', *Journal of Negro History*, 51, 1–15.
Weheliye, A (2014) *Habeas Viscus: Racializing Assemblages, Biopolitics, and Black Feminist Theories of the Human*, Durham: Duke University Press.

Wilderson III, F (2010) *Red, White & Black: Cinema and the Structure of US Antagonisms*, Durham: Duke University Press.

Wilderson III, F (2020) *Afropessimism*, New York: Liversight Publishing.

Wilderson III, F (2021) 'Afropessimism and the Ruse of Analogy: Violence, Freedom Struggles, and the Death of Black Desire' in Jung, M-K and Helion, C V J (eds.), *Antiblackness*, Durham: Duke University Press, 37–59.

Williams, E (1994) *Capitalism & Slavery*, Chapel Hill: University of North Carolina Press.

Wynter, S (1995) '1492: A New World View' in Hyatt, V L and Nettleford, R (eds.), *Discourse, and the Origin of the Americas*, Washington: Smithsonian Institution Press, 5–57.

Wynter, S (2003) 'Unsettling the Coloniality of Being/Power/Truth/Freedom: Towards the Human, after Man, Its Overrepresentation – an Argument', *The New Centennial Review*, 3, 257–337.

Youngquist, P (2011) 'The Mothership Connection', *Cultural Critique*, 77, 1–23.

Žižek, S (2010) 'A Permanent Economic Emergency', *New Left Review*, 64, 85–95.

Chapter 7

The gestures of the body

Introduction

Our capitalist world is structured by coloniality and lived through time conceived as *chronos*, linear progression from the past to the future. In contrast, form-of-life is a life lived through paradigmatic gestures. I have sought to connect an example of this form-of-life in the actions and lives of enslaved people. These examples are found throughout the ancient and modern worlds. As philosophy was using slavery as a device to consider what it meant to be free, there lived people who were carving out their own modes of living, separate from dominant political orders.

These forms-of-life are lived in the moment, grasping time as *kairos*, the 'now'. This is a moment to be seized,[1] a rupture in the existing state of affairs in which new possibilities open up.[2] This is a form of life that dismantles prevailing politics, without proposing an alternative replacement.[3] Decolonial politics conceives of time as *kairos*, seeking the abolition of existing structures of exploitation. The present 'now' is inseparably linked to both the past and the future. Singular examples can operate just as they are, and as models and forms of life that show us the world can be otherwise than it is. As Johan Cilliers has explained, the recalling of life's experiences take place by means of song, dance, stories, conserving the values and traditions of the group and passing them down to future generations.[4]

What is a life of shared experiences? The enslaved person is an embodied individual within capitalism, but one who is dominated and expelled from humanity altogether. We must search for a 'remnant', a people embodying resistance to the existing political hegemony through their gestures and way

1 Agamben (2005) 67ff.
2 Agamben (2012) 59.
3 Invisible Committee (2017) 76.
4 Cilliers (2018) 120.

DOI: 10.4324/9781003303534-8

of being.[5] This grasping of *kairos* is not solitary.[6] Form-of-life is structured by its reference to others, and recognition by others.[7] The recalling of the experiences of life is a communal, shared experience of past events, akin to a decolonial refusal.[8] The gestures of the body can disrupt coloniality and transform this world into a new use.

In this chapter I show how paradigmatic acts and gestures of enslaved people in the colonial matrix of power (CMP) point towards new forms of political belonging not based on the divided subject. Living in the 'now' means deactivating apparatuses through actions that become examples impacting the future. Enslaved people in Caribbean societies transformed the colonial order by maintaining an alternative perspective towards time, work and self. Enslaved people took gestures, languages and instruments and made them into performances, showing the way human beings can create bonds through music and the body.[9] Enslaved people acted (in small ways) against the very institution which enchained them and challenged the dominant legal order. Our lives, although precarious, are always in-the-making. Caribbean Maroon societies were composed of enslaved people who had escaped the plantations and are examples of communities outside of the European colonial state who refused to give up their humanity, carving out new ways of belonging in the world with others. These 'workless slaves' show how a life can be lived as a form, gesturally.

This chapter revisits the aftermath of the Haitian Revolution. In contrast to the way the Revolution has been used symbolically to underscore the importance of human rights, I use the work of Jean Casimir to explore how the struggle in Haiti was between the workers and the oligarchs who ran the country. The lives of what Casimir terms the 'captives' were lived as a form, examples of a radically different political imaginary. Women played a key role in founding a new Haitian community that destroyed the slave system. These types of acts have led to new forms of life. One such form is found in the figure of the 'zombii', a life that renders inoperative the relationship between subject and object, and which points towards a life in contact with one another, beyond the control of necropolitical capitalism. Forms of resistance against dominant and totalising power are tenuous, but they do exist, and they point the way towards conceptions of belonging which are just, just as they are.

5 Agamben (2005) 57.
6 Agamben (2005) 54–5.
7 Agamben (2010) 46.
8 Agamben (2007a) 115.
9 Mbembé (2003) 22.

Culture, marronage and (the) Quashee(s)

Edwin Bikundo argued that the figure of the slave had become a 'lazy scapegoat', opposed to modernity, liberal freedom and Western civil and political rights.[10] Roberto Esposito's genealogy of the 'person' separates slaves (*servi*) from free men (*liberi*). Free men are further divided into free men born free (*ingenui*) and those manumitted from legal slavery (*liberti*). Bikundo argues that liberal Western thought's conceptions of rights is based on the *liberti*, a legal device representing a free person who was manumitted from legal slavery.[11] Bikundo summarises that the basis of all legal and political rights is projected onto an artificial legal personality. The subject of rights is as abstract as the figure of the slave, the very figure used to measure our freedoms materially, historically and legally.[12]

We must look beyond the figure of the slave. Coloniality generates images of the world that prevent us from seeing what is in front of us.[13] There have been no real social, ideological and political alternatives to racial capitalism.[14] Slavery and colonialism separated what they deemed useful from what they labelled as waste. This economy of waste production is connected to the production of human beings as 'waste'.[15] Arendt saw modern capitalism producing an economy of waste, within which things are devoured and thrown away almost as quickly as they have been created.[16]

This waste must be disposed of without being seen by those who are entitled to enjoy a good life. Françoise Verges notes that, according to the World Bank's own figures, the global production of material waste rose in 2016 to 1.3 billion tonnes per year. This cleaning must remain *invisible*. The person doing the cleaning disappears, and the violence and disdain they encounter on the job are legitimised.[17] Verges continues:

> An entire humanity is condemned to undertake invisible and overexploited work to create a world suitable for hyper-consumption and maintaining institutions. For those people: the dirt, the pollution, the non-potable water, the uncollected garbage, the plastics that invade everything, the gardens where plants die from lack of maintenance, the sewers that do not work, the polluted air. For others: the clean city, the gardens, the flowers, the serene wandering. The world is segregated through a division of the

10 Bikundo (2022b) 63.
11 Esposito (2012) 22.
12 Bikundo (2022b) 65.
13 Mignolo (2020) xiv.
14 Robinson (2021) 316.
15 Verges (2021) 77.
16 Arendt (1998) 134.
17 Verges (2021) 81.

clean and the dirty, which rests on a racial division of urban space and the environment, a division that also exists in the Global South.[18]

Our starting point must be this waste, from which we can retrieve the living being.[19] 'Slave pedagogy' is the strategies and practices that help articulate a vision of the humanity of the enslaved person and the affirmation of their life against the physical and ontological violences of dehumanisation. Songs, stories and rituals all played a role in forging a community outside of the confines of the state. Today's nation-state form of governance has failed.[20] State sovereignty can only affirm itself by producing bare life.[21] This culture resists being turned into bare life, waste.[22]

Just as in the ancient world, enslaved people resisted in myriad ways. Acts of nearly invisible defiance included false compliance, feigned ignorance and sabotage.[23] Enslaved people were seen as sullen,[24] and would do as little work as possible.[25] They would feign illness, inflict injuries on themselves and sometimes kill themselves either individually or in groups.[26] Countless slaves ran away.[27] Thousands of acts of overt resistance included the destroying of plantation property, killing owners and engaging in revolt and rebellions.[28]

Enslaved people and communities invented their own literature, music and ways of celebrating the divine,[29] created out of the debris within which they lived.[30] Despite the body of the enslaved being owned by another, that same body could be used to create human bonds.[31] The body retained and sustained the potential for a radical insurgency, or as Mbembé puts it poetically, the body was akin to "a silt deposited at the confluence of half-worlds produced by the dual violence of race and capital". [32] This involved an alternative perspective towards time, work and self.[33] Those subjected to these barbarous systems:

18 Verges (2021) 77.
19 Mbembé (2019) 158–9.
20 Mignolo (2020) xv.
21 Agamben (2000) 11.
22 Haymes (2006) 202; Mbembé (2019) 159–60.
23 Scott (1985) 39.
24 Walvin (2019) 81.
25 Fryer (2021) 85.
26 Fryer (2021) 85–6.
27 Craton & Greenland (1978) 245.
28 Craton (1982) 335–9.
29 Mbembé (2017) 48.
30 Mbembé (2019) 160–1.
31 Mbembé (2003) 22; Abrahams (1992).
32 Mbembé (2017) 36–7.
33 Mbembé (2019) 75.

> [P]roduced ways of thinking and languages that were truly their own. They had to know how and when to become like everybody else, how and when to be nobody, when to be alone, when to hide.[34]

Music is its own embodiment of resistance, aiming to change and transform.[35] Music is embedded in sociocultural, historical and political contexts, and 'non-Western' music is often seen as savage and exotic. Universalising music falsely romanticises it and its interactions with different societies around the world.[36] *Mousike*, or music "marks the splitting between man and his language, between the voice and the *logos*",[37] and, in doing so, shows that the primary opening of man to the world is not logical but musical. *Mousike's* essential link to language and to poetry was audible to the archaic ear. Poetry "originates within the experience of *mousike*".[38] Philosophy is today possible only as a reformation of music. Music is "the origins and taking place of the word", and "music expresses and governs the relation the living being has with the event of the word".[39] Language itself can also be redeployed, as Glissant explains in relation to the development of Creole and when it started to be used as a communication medium between enslaved and slaveowner:

> For Caribbean man, the word is first and foremost sound. Noise is essential to speech. Din is discourse. ... Since speech was forbidden, slaves camouflaged the word under the provocative intensity of the scream. It was taken to be nothing but the call of a wild animal. This is how the dispossessed man organized his speech by weaving it into the apparently meaningless texture of extreme noise.[40]

The experience of language is always conditioned musically. Every discourse is always already museically tuned. For this reason, in every age, living beings are always more or less intentionally educated to politics and prepared for it through music, even before this happens through traditions and precepts that are transmitted by means of language.[41] For communities whose past involved subjection and humiliation, religious and artistic creation has represented a form of defence against dehumanisation and death. The primary

34 Mbembé (2019) 160.
35 Ghadery (2022) 32.
36 Ghadery (2022) 39.
37 Agamben (2018b) 100.
38 Zartaloudis (2018) 344.
39 Agamben (2018b) 97; Zartaloudis (2018) 359.
40 Glissant (1992) 123–4.
41 Agamben (2018b) 101.

function of the work of art redoubles the original object, deforming it, distancing itself from it and conjuring with it.[42]

Sylvia Wynter names the plantation as the origin of capitalist modernity. Land became a resource from which to extract crops.[43] The relationship between the earth and human beings changed from one of food cultivation for sustenance to one of crop cultivation for exchange on the market. This removes any sociality and meaning linking land, food and people.[44] Dillon explains that the plantation disentangled a plant (sugar) from its native world and alienated and disentangled the peoples trafficked across the Atlantic from their land and lifeworlds.[45] The sugar plantation forced enslaved people to relate to each other and to their owners in new ways, structured by contemporary ideas about time, progress, property and freedom.[46]

Jamaica had a profound plantation system (like Haiti). But Jamaica (and Haiti) also hosted a 'proto-peasant' economy involving enslaved people who cultivated food in mountains and on backlands.[47] Slices of land were allocated to enslaved people (or taken through squatting) to grow provisions – the 'provision ground'. In many colonies in the slave empire, the provision grounds were fertile enough that enslaved people produced surpluses, which they sold in colonial markets. Provision grounds came to feed both enslaved people and colonists.[48] Wynter states that the provision ground was a focus of resistance to the market system and market values:

> For African peasants transplanted to the plot all the structure of values that had been created by traditional societies of Africa, the land remained the Earth – and the Earth was a goddess; man used the land to feed himself; and to offer first fruits to the Earth; his funeral was the mystical reunion with the earth.[49]

This led to a contradiction. For example, in British colonies enslaved people did not have legal personality or legal rights. They were legally property. In practice, enslaved people routinely had money, in particular from the sale of crops from provision grounds. People who were property by law *owned* property by custom.[50]

42 Mbembé (2017) 173.
43 Wynter (1971) 95.
44 Dillon (2019) 634.
45 Dillon (2019) 635.
46 Scott (2004) 128.
47 Besson (1999) 38–9.
48 Scanlan (2020) 98.
49 Wynter (1971) 99.
50 Scanlan (2020) 99.

A parallel can be drawn between the provision grounds and the Franciscan notion of 'use'. In use the Franciscan monks only have a natural right to use things in cases of necessity.[51] If form-of-life vests in the use of the body, here we have the body using land. Miguel Vatter draws a parallel between this use of land and the operation of a trust, the recognition of a group personality.[52] Vatter states that in a trust forms-of-life-in-common generate the rights and duties of its members, which designate the space of the common. In this community, these rights and duties are not produced by the state, nor by the state of nature.[53]

Ultimately, these ideas of the use of land, the development of animative materiality, and the non-state community find their confluence in the Maroons. The Caribbean Maroon communities show how *marronage* can shut down the system. Enslaved people in the 'New World' rejected every part of their experience. They did not want to transform the Western project of coloniality and enslavement. They did not want to overthrow capitalism. Maroon communities were made of escaped slaves, legally 'things'.[54] They ran away and tried to return home, even at the risk of their lives.[55] Enslaved people transgressed the law that placed them in a continual state of flight marked by the ongoing threat of re-enslavement.[56] Running away or *marronage* was not mere resistance. Marx saw this as a rejection of the "barbaric horrors of slavery".[57] Maroons were attempting to establish autonomous free societies as an alternative to the colonial enslavement project.[58] In this manner, 'fugitivity' can create possibilities.[59] This is an embodiment of what Agamben sees as the task of a genuine revolution – to change time.[60] If rebellion was not possible, Robinson notes that "the people prepared themselves" through fostering beliefs, myths and messianic visions, to enable the captives to one day attempt the impossible.[61]

Colonial powers passed many laws and introduced many punishments to prevent *marronage*, but enslaved people found ways to escape the plantations. One example is the 'underground maritime' route set up from the Danish West Indies to Spanish Puerto Rico. These involved stages of migration. Slaves would escape into the cane fields and live there for a while (cane

51 Vatter (2017) 240.
52 Vatter (2017) 249.
53 Vatter (2017) 250.
54 Maitland and Pollock (1898) 2:472.
55 Robinson (2021) xiv.
56 Hartman (1997) ch 2.
57 Marx (1990) 345; Marx (1971) 111.
58 Roopnarine (2010) 90.
59 Harvey and Moten (2013) 97.
60 Agamben (2007a) 99.
61 Robinson (2021) 310.

marronage), move to safer and secure grounds, and then ultimately migrate to Spanish Puerto Rico and other distant Caribbean islands.[62] The treatment of slaves in Puerto Rico was relatively mild. Slaves were mobilised to work on the plantations for a year and then granted freedom and even given a plot of land.[63]

Not all Caribbean islands and colonies experienced *marronage* at the same rate. Jean Casimir distinguished *marronage* in Haiti from that in Barbados. In the latter "classic plantation society", generations of captives lived on plantations owned by the same family. Barbadian society was dense and cohesive, in contrast to Haiti.[64] But Barbadian society experienced both *petit* and *grand* marronage. Many of these Maroon bands were short-lived, due to the small size of the island and the lack of forests. But these enslaved people perceived their actions as a way to stay free to the limit of human resistance.[65] In Haiti, the masters were unable to impose on those kidnapped from Africa – two-thirds of the population – the spectacle of a lifestyle which, from generation to generation, ended up seeming natural and normal to both dominators and the dominated.[66] This allowed the Haitian captives free reign to organise their own society, constituted by their accumulated experience.[67]

Jamaican Maroons were in open war against the British for the first part of the eighteenth century. Jamaica's Leeward Maroons, under the leadership of Kojo (Cudjoe),[68] forced the British to treaty in 1739.[69] In Accompong Town (in St. Elizabeth, Jamaica, the oldest persisting corporate Maroon society in the Americas), rebel slaves and their descendants wrested land from the colonial regime through squatting and transformed that land into a sacred landscape rooted in common land.[70] While the colonial regime thought ceding land rights to a wilderness would confine the rebel slaves, the Maroons embraced this common land.[71] These were lives that constituted a gesture of refusal of existing in the colonial and enslaved order. In many cases, these Maroon communities continued the day-to-day communal activities they conducted as slaves.

The Maroon is a form of a 'workless slave'. The workless slave lives through paradigmatic gestures that render dominant forms of control inoperative. This is a messianic ending of the state and the end of history. This does

62 Bulstrode (2023); Hall (1985) 476–98.
63 Dookhan (1974) 164.
64 Casimir (2020) 369.
65 Handler (1982) 12.
66 Dubois (2004) 42.
67 Casimir (2020) 369–70.
68 Brown (2020) 90–2.
69 Bilby (1997) 655–89.
70 Besson (1999) 32.
71 Besson (1999) 40.

not mean seeking new forms of politics, but rather, seeking to live through paradigms of gestures.[72] Bikundo turns to Marx, who saw in the Maroons human beings who did not give up their humanity and who valued idleness, not work.[73] The slave in Marx was enmeshed in a set of exchange relations, even when celebrating armed insurgency by enslaved people against the slave owning classes.[74] But Marx noted the importance of the way that formerly enslaved people, when they ceased to be slaves, did not become wage labourers, but peasants living sustainably.[75] Maroon communities were forms-of-life. Marx drew on a letter written by a post-emancipation owner named 'Expertus' who was highly critical of the free Black communities in Jamaica. Expertus named this community "Quashees", treating this as a generic term for a formerly enslaved person; Marx "the Quashees".[76]

The Ghanaian Quashee, Quasie, Kwesi, Kwasi or Akwesi are male names, and Quasheeba, Quasheba, and Kwasiba are female names, referring to a child born on a Sunday.[77] The Quashees were made up of Black Jamaicans from many places and of many varied experiences. These political communities were hard won through negotiation across different languages, practices and conceptual frameworks.[78] The Maroon, a freed slave, no longer allows another to put into use their body (even for money). The only use of the body is to do what is necessary to sustain them.[79] Bikundo admits that this model may be difficult to follow. However, Quashee communities illuminate the potentialities of resistance. These are through acts and gestures which constitute a community that is not defined through a shared essence, other than dwelling as forms-of-life. These are hyper-hermeneutic gestures, dwelling in the now, deactivating apparatuses of control through a withdrawal from the colonial and enslavement system of control and a use of the body. These workless slaves show us how to refuse work,[80] and how to reclaim the dream of laziness once and for all.[81]

72 Agamben (2004) 92.
73 Bikundo (2022b) 58.
74 Ralph & Singhal (2019) 860, citing Marx (1849).
75 Marx (1973) 251–2.
76 Marx (1973) 250–1; Bikundo (2022b) 66.
77 DeCamp (1967) 139–49.
78 Brown (2020) 85–128.
79 Bikundo (2022b) 66–7.
80 Marx and Engels (1976) 5.
81 Bikundo (2022b) 59.

The decolonial Haitian Revolution

The counter-plantation culture

We return to the Haitian Revolution. Today's Haitian state is considered autocratic, the promise of the Revolution long since washed away.[82] The Revolution gave Haitians a form of citizenship and social freedom, from 1821, rooted in a unified state. But this state was ineffective, unable to intervene in the lives of the peasantry due to having limited civic participation.[83] Timofeeva speaks about Haiti when making the point that the Atlantic slave trade formed the modern capitalist world in which we live:

> [W]e must once again place real slavery front and center, this time the contemporary kind, existing in Haiti, incidentally, on a colossal scale ... over 200,000 people are currently living in slavery there, most of them children. It appears that after the revolution everything took a turn for the worse, as usual: slavery led not to freedom, but to lordship. Former slaves became masters and themselves took slaves. History began all over again.[84]

Does this mean the Revolution was a failure? Haitian history has been written by the imperialists, who were all men (colonisers and colonised).[85] Focusing on the *consequences* detracts from the gesture of revolt. To adopt the language and approach of consequentialism judges the nature of the act through future events, repeating the logic of colonial, linear time.

Likewise, privileging race in analyses of the Haitian Revolution incorporates the colonial perspective that enabled plantation owners to erase the ethnicities of the captives and make them homogenised colonial labourers. These interpretations erase a variety of life experiences that existed before, during and after enslavement.[86] This helped create a Black ruling class in a state where no distinctions of rank were meant to exist.[87] The oligarch class incorporated modern racism into their thinking, and aimed to 'civilise' those persons in Haiti deemed to carry exotic forms of thinking and acting.[88] But even this civilising mission did not destroy the cultural dynamism of the enslaved.[89]

82 Fatton (2006); Fatton (2007); Maingot (1986).
83 Blackburn (2006) 671.
84 Timofeeva (2017) 441.
85 Dayan (2010) 373.
86 Casimir (2020) 14–15.
87 Brace (2018) 83; Fick (1998) 11; James (2001) 201.
88 Casimir (2020) 39–41.
89 Bush (2001) 146.

The Haitian people also never stopped resisting slavery and domination. All forms of social reproduction imposed by enslavement and international commerce were refused until the American occupation of the country in 1915.[90] By the beginning of the nineteenth century, *marronage* was seen as a threat to the security of Haiti's internal stability.[91] By the end of that century, imperial capitalism had fixed Haiti in its sights. The American occupation destroyed any resistance to the political order in the rural population.[92]

A decolonial reading of the Revolution is grounded in the experiences and shared memories of the people, the captives and the way their daily praxis of living and building a community *in spite of politics*, and not because of it.[93] The Revolution was made up of many events, some violent or dramatic, some subtle and forgotten. It was the result of many forms of life focusing on *how* they live their lives.[94] The benefits of liberation were not available to the majority of Haitians. The 1 January 1804 Declaration of Haitian Independence prioritised stable, republican governments, entrusting the future of the country to the Creoles. The minority of *freed* slaves (usually Creoles and less than one-tenth of the population) had never lived in a society without merchant slavery and rushed to take advantage of the successes of the Haitian Revolution. In Haiti, there lived freed Blacks, the part of the population that took power. The Creole slaves were born in the colony of Saint Domingue. A third group, the *bossales*, were slaves who were born in Africa.[95] The Haitian state after 1804 involved an urban sector that tried to reproduce colonial society.[96] After independence, the oligarchs sought to maintain the status quo. Toussaint L'Ouverture saw the enslaved people who rebelled and deserters as outlaws.[97] The former slaves, called *Africans* or *cultivators*, were placed at the bottom of the social ladder.[98] The labour market was replaced by legal mechanisms of coercion.[99]

Later on 1 January 1804, a proclamation to the people of Haiti aimed to guarantee an empire of liberty, and it was the approach of this proclamation that "was put into practice by peasant society".[100] Jean Casimir distinguishes 'captive' from 'slave'. A 'slave' is a word naming an entity. That word also

90 Casimir (2020) 3.
91 Eddins (2022) 234.
92 Casimir (2020) 133; Schmidt (1995).
93 Mignolo (2020) ix; Casimir (2020) 23.
94 Agamben (2016) 231; Agamben (2018b) 27.
95 Casimir (2020) 256.
96 Casimir (2020) 192.
97 Casimir (2020) 135.
98 Casimir (2020) 140–1.
99 Casimir (2020) 180.
100 Casimir (2020) 16.

creates an ontology for that entity that fits a certain meaning of the world.[101] Haiti was a project of re-existence. It was a project built in the face of adverse conditions and sought to occupy a social and cultural place of dignity, re-existing with others in radically distinct terms.[102] The captives behaved as if they were free.[103] The majority of the Haitian population escaped politics,[104] creating new forms of knowledge to resist coloniality.[105] This included a different relationship to the land, holding that land in ways that did not alarm the owners or provoke a hostile reaction from them.[106] The familial piece of lane is where spirits dwell. It is sacred and cannot be given away, divided or sold. It marks the spiritual heritage of the group.[107] The plantation structure had fallen into disrepair, causing Toussaint to impose heavy obligations on formerly enslaved people.[108] In some areas, when the plantations were abandoned, provision grounds were created and the freed slaves took land for their own use, expanded cultivated plots, gathered wood and used animals to take their goods to market.[109] The working population exercised their sovereignty in isolation.[110] Garden plots cultivated on plantations were a foundation for reconstructing private lives outside of the dominant system.[111]

Preferring not to participate involved rejecting the colonial enslavement system as such.[112] Demanding recognition and inclusion leads to a limited notion of personhood as property that focuses on one type of subjugation and not others. Recognising minority groups into the class of 'human' is done at the cost of newly disposable populations.[113] The living of life as a form *must* be brought about and is generated by its manner of being, through its gestures.[114] Humanity-in-creation is the product of a gesture that makes a relationship with the others in my position possible.[115] Haitians lived their lives through the most modest of gestures.[116] Gesture is pure mediality and is

101 Mignolo (2020) xiv.
102 Achinte (2012) 30.
103 Casimir (2020) 96.
104 Casimir (2020) 35.
105 Casimir (2020) 71–2.
106 Casimir (2020) 57.
107 Dayan (2010) 371.
108 Blackburn (2006) 666.
109 Fick (1998) 7.
110 Casimir (2020) 137.
111 Casimir (2020) 329.
112 Bikundo (2022a) 12.
113 Weheliye (2014) 81.
114 Agamben (2016) 224, 231.
115 Fanon (2018) 219.
116 Casimir (2020) 15–16.

never a means to an end for the one who carries it out.[117] Becoming-human-in-the-world is a matter of transfiguration, meaning the individual:

> [E]mbrace the broken up part of its own life; that it compel itself to take detours and sometimes improbable connections; that it operates in the interstices if it cares about giving a common expression to things that we commonly dissociate.[118]

Humanity arises only when a gesture is possible that allows oneself to be affected by a being-with others, and when that gesture is related to a silence-breaking language.[119] A community was built first through the Kreyol (or Creole) language, the language of the 'sovereign people'. The sovereignty of the people emerged from knowledge oriented toward taking charge of oneself, one's community and one's family.[120] Here we can refer back to Agamben's work on 'contact' in his philosophy. For Agamben, two bodies are in contact when no medium can be inserted between them – when they are unmediated. Contact is not representation. A relation of representation between two things, like subject and object or master and slave, does not mean that they are in contact. Contact is unrepresentable. Only if there is a failure of representation can things be in contact. What is touched is not just the object, but also the flesh that is moved or moved by it. In contact, we touch our own sensitivity and are affected by our own receptivity.[121] *Marronage* was the core tradition (or contact) of resistance that created spaces of escape from capitalist economic processes. This involved taking advantage of events to carve out spaces of freedom.[122] The captives sculpted a new character through behaviours and habits which exceeded the Western colonial project, influenced by the fact that at the start of the Revolution, at least two-thirds of the captives had been born in Africa.[123]

Though enslaved, the sovereign people were never captive or enslaved in the sphere of language or spirituality. African languages and belief systems were captured and transported to the 'New World', building a memory. The enslaved person was forged into a new form of life through the oppressed community in which they lived, and through participating in the practices of Vodou.[124] This counter-plantation system included gender relations, family,

117 Agamben (2007b) 87; Agamben (2018a) 80–1.
118 Mbembé (2019) 187.
119 Mbembé (2019) 176.
120 Casimir (2020) 333.
121 Agamben (2021).
122 Eddins (2022) 222; Scott (2018).
123 Casimir (2020) 15; Dubois (2004) 42.
124 Casimir (2020) 256.

Vodou temples, garden-towns, leisure, crafts and the arts.[125] The complex interpenetrations of different cultural traditions re-humanised the captives, reclaiming their heritage and their connection to the land.[126] The struggle in Haiti drew sustenance from the memories of the smallest victories, nourishing the power of their communities to surpass the present. Haitians simultaneously invented a nation, the conditions for its social and economic existence, and the institutions that would guarantee its survival.[127] Casimir states:

> Indivisible family property, the Kreyol language, Vodou spirituality, the calendar and rhythm of communal life, leisure, dance, music – all these were controlled by the decisions of the sovereign people.[128]

The Creole language was a defence against the loss of an identity. It preserved the rich linguistic structures of Africa, had rich nuance and cutting satire that challenged oppression, and remained central to a new identity.[129] The *bossales* survived as they carried the memory that somewhere a family survived, in a proud, strong and prosperous nation. These memories were the backdrop for the ordeals experienced. 'Fictive kin' was established to replace lost families.[130] Their innovations in surviving opened up a precarious future not imposed on mourning for a degraded nature and culture. The *bossales* survived by creolising themselves, carrying a consciousness of their suffering. Their forms of mutiny shaped the experiences of the subjugated.[131]

Women played a key role in founding a new community that destroyed the slave system, using *marronage* to travel across the colony, smuggling weapons and food.[132] Women helped the enslaved community survive materially and psychically and engaged in cultural struggles that challenged coloniality and enslavement.[133] Through circumstance, women were at the centre of enslaved communities, and were essential to the community's survival.[134] Survival requires the oppressed to know the system's rules. Knowledge was reinvented, an indispensable element of resistance based on social groups formed through solidarity. These forms-of-life both compromised with or respected the rules and resisted them in a struggle for self-emancipation.[135]

125 Casimir (2020) 351.
126 Gilroy (1993) 48; Eddins (2022) 223.
127 Casimir (2020) 4.
128 Casimir (2020) 304.
129 Bush (2001) 142.
130 Bush (2001) 135.
131 Casimir (2020) 278.
132 Casimir (2020) 4.
133 Bush (2001) 151.
134 Davis (1971) 7.
135 Casimir (2020) 275.

Women's cultural defiance was expressed through language and song. On slave plantations, women were often the leading singers.[136] Such singing, typically African in structure, made work less burdensome, accompanied all important events and provided entertainment. Plays were popular and combined music and dance.[137] Female 'folk' knowledge was transmitted through 'women's culture', and this made connections between different generations. This included knowledge related to childbirth, child-rearing and contraception,[138] and participation in the informal economy centred on provision-grounds.[139] This form of life reinforces a form of solidarity in the face of oppression and misfortune, and the ability to create a stable life for themselves. Casimir explicitly engages with the language of 'use', claiming that the captive and sufferer both *use* the dominant system without altering their deepest being.[140]

The Revolution was a now-time event which disrupted the inevitable future of colonialism and coloniality. The slave owner's monopoly of knowledge created a form of invisibility for the captive. The captive produced and reproduced a knowledge of how to live, gained through experiences in their daily lives, and lived in solidarity with others.[141] This was a 'fragile' lifeline, finding a new way to live in a hostile world, choosing what was needed from the traditions inherited by their ancestors. Groups became linked by common habits,[142] exploiting fractures and lines of flight in systems of domination.[143] These private spaces were intimate, a space inaccessible to the masters which could be found in the interstices of plantation life, in which forms of life could sovereignly reject or escape Western propositions.[144] Much like the Haitian captives, to live our life as a form we need to make a different, common and political use of the everyday and intimate.[145] It involves adopting a different perspective on something familiar and banal, to live otherwise than we have done before.[146] The everyday and the intimate are ontological issues.[147]

Casimir argues that this private life was the only place where it was not possible to establish an order not built on any presupposition. It excluded all that was historical and was a radical reinvention.[148] This life could not be

136 Bush (2001) 142.
137 Bush (2001) 143.
138 Bush (2001) 140.
139 Bush (2001) 117.
140 Casimir (2020) 273.
141 Casimir (2020) 292–3.
142 Casimir (2020) 294–5.
143 Casimir (2020) 300.
144 Casimir (2020) 301.
145 Prozorov (2017) 150; Agamben (2007b) 77–91.
146 Prozorov (2017) 153; Agamben (2016) 232.
147 Prozorov (2017) 150; Agamben (2016) 231.
148 Casimir (2020) 327.

seized by the colonists or the state. The captive took care of this life, reproducing it every day, preventing an absorption into plantation society.[149] Once the Revolution occurred, it became a past event, but a past event which is able to shape the present. Just as successful runaways served as an inspiration to other slaves seeking freedom,[150] Vincent Brown, in his work on Tacky's Revolt, points out that historians often overlook the ways that enslaved people "channelled slave revolt across generations".[151] Enslaved people in Jamaica knew about previous revolts in Barbados and Guiana, they knew about the Haitian Revolution, they remembered the history of their parents and grandparents.[152]

The zombi(e)

The world of the people did not integrate into the world of the state. The world of the people did not aim to overthrow or change the state. The two worlds were in contact, reciprocally manipulating each other. Because the world of the people was repugnant to international capital, the oppressive Haitian state was sponsored by them.[153] The Haitian lifeworld destituted the state due to its non-engagement and contact with it. A key part of this world was Vodou. Vodou was a vehicle for revolution, an organisational tool for resistance, part of the land purified by a spirit of liberation.[154] Dayan notes that the *lwa* (god, image or spirit) most invoked by today's Vodou practitioners does not originate in Africa but was born during the revolution.[155]

The dispossession accomplished by slavery was the model for Vodou possession, making a man not into a thing but into a spirit.[156] The figure of the zombi points toward the figure of the workless slave. The zombie (or Haitian 'zombi') reveals much about the way we code inferior subjects as unworthy of life.[157] As with other myths, the zombi has evolved and now signifies the empowerment of the Haitian people and has been remade to respond to Haiti's contemporary struggles.[158] Today the zombi, whether thought of as a type of evil spirit or a reanimated body, remains our most powerful symbol of loss, anonymity and apathy.[159] Following Paul Veyne, the essence of myth

149 Casimir (2020) 328.
150 Paton (2004) 27.
151 Brown (2020) 238.
152 Scanlan (2020) 274.
153 Casimir (2020) 358.
154 Lauro (2015) 55.
155 Dayan (2010) 365,
156 Dayan (2010) 371.
157 Lauro and Embry (2008) 87.
158 Lauro (2015) 115.
159 Dayan (2010) 372.

is not that everyone knows it, but that it is supposed to be known and is worthy of being known by all.[160] This can be further connected to enslavement. The master does not inculcate an ideology in the slave. The master only needs to show they are more powerful. The slave will react, creating an imaginary truth for themselves.[161]

The link between zombi and slave is not borne out by the contemporary discourse on the Haitian Revolution. The figure of the zombi scarcely appears in contemporary texts on the Revolution.[162] The secularised definition of the Haitian zombi at the time by colonists and missionaries was a body that is a victim of poisoning in the guise of sorcery.[163] Horror and terror are associated with the zombie from its inception, but it is only with the US occupation of Haiti that the Haitian zombi became the American 'zombie', different from other monsters because the body is resurrected and retained: only consciousness is permanently lost.[164] Sarah Juliet Lauro and Karen Embry explain that there are connected fears or terrors associated with the 'zombie'. There is a fear or being eaten or devoured by a zombie, which threatens the body. There is also a fear that in becoming a zombie, one's consciousness will be lost, and the individual will simply become another zombie in a horde of monsters.[165] As Dayan explains, our contemporary views of 'zombification' grew out the twentieth-century history of forced labour, victimisation and denigration during the American occupation of Haiti. American writers and directors invented the zombie of popular culture: a soulless slave without consciousness directed by a zombie master.[166] Haitians were forced to build roads, thousands of peasants were brutalised and massacred, and tales of zombies proliferated in the United States.[167] The second half of the twentieth century saw the idea develop that the zombie committed a social infraction and that their removal from the community is a benefit to the whole.[168]

In other Caribbean cultures shaped by enslavement and resistance, similar figures emerged. Dayan explores this further. In Jamaica, slaves were construed as things without thought, with no attention paid to their souls. *Duppies*, the unquiet dead, returned in various forms. The scraps of bodies bought, bartered and sold as if they were animals or pieces of furniture return as ancestor spirits, but these spirits are caught in the very evil that created them in the first place. In the Anglophone or Francophone Caribbean or the

160 Veyne (1988) 45.
161 Veyne (1988) 91.
162 Hoermann (2017) 156.
163 Davis (1985); Lauro (2015) 37.
164 Lauro and Embry (2008) 89.
165 Lauro and Embry (2008) 89–90.
166 Hoermann (2017) 158–9.
167 Dayan (2010) 372.
168 Lauro (2015) 10.

American South, these demonic spirits took vengeance as vampires or *lou-gawou*, suckers or *soucriants*, shapeshifters that shed skin and suck blood. Condemned to wander the earth in the form of pigs, cows, cats or dogs, these vile spirits, known in Haiti as *baka* and in Jamaica as *rolling calf* or *roaring calf*, are the surfeit of an institution that turned humans into chattels.[169]

The origins of the zombi, like other myths, are unclear. In Haitian folklore *zombi* meant "a body without a soul" and "a soul without a body".[170] The Haitian concept of the soul is dualistic, and this is derived from Central and West African communities.[171] The idea of a body separated from its soul came to Haiti from Africa with the captives, but the word 'zombi' was not connected to this idea until the eighteenth century when it was introduced by French authors.[172] There is also a potential historical, rather than spiritual, origin for the word. In 1804, during Dessalines' massacre of the French, a man named Jean Zombi, a mulatto hailing from Port-au-Prince, earned a reputation for brutality.[173] On Dessalines' order, he massacred the most Whites during the liberation of Haiti from French colonialism.[174]

Regardless of origins, there are two types of zombis: a material zombi of the body, and an immaterial zombi of the soul. In its history and metaphors the zombi is most often a slave. It is a figure that helps us understand how the 'other' is subjugated and oppressed, and the importance of moving toward an 'antisubject' to resolve the contradictions of political belonging and exclusion.[175] Embodied and disembodied zombis both represent the slave in certain circumstances and the rebel in others.[176] The zombi known today in Vodou originates as the material presence of the living death of slavery.[177] The zombi was a body raised from the dead through Vodou rituals by a witch doctor to labour in the fields at night.[178] Elizabeth McAlister explains that in Afro-Haitian religious thought, after death, part of the individual's spirit immediately goes to God. But another part lingers on earth for a period of time. This lingering part of the spirit is able to be captured and made to work.[179]

169 Dayan (2011) 130.
170 Cohen (1972) 59.
171 Ackermann and Gaulthier (1991) 469.
172 Lauro (2015) 41.
173 Dayan (2010) 371.
174 Dayan (2010) 372.
175 Lauro and Embry (2008) 87.
176 Ackermann and Gaulthier (1991) 467.
177 Dillon (2019) 626–7.
178 Ott (1973) 47; Lauro and Embry (2008) 98.
179 McAlister (2012) 468–9.

A sorcerer can put this spirit in a bottle and put it to work. A zombi is an instance of and a figure for social reproduction on the plantation.[180] This figure retains certain bodily functions that enable it to carry out simple comments, such as working on sugar-cane plantations during the night. This meant that the original meaning of the zombi was forced labour, not a type of impersonal evil.[181] Daniel Cohen writes (using the label 'zombie') that:

> [T]he zombie is sort of a slave's nightmare. For the slave the only hope of release was death and the possible promise of a blissful afterlife. But if a dead slave's body was reanimated for labor as a zombie, then the slave existence would continue even after death.[182]

In this reading we have a soulless, animated corpse that is "not inherently evil, like a vampire; it is merely a servant".[183] The horrific figure of the zombi aims to prevent workers and slaves from rebelling against their masters by equating the anti-colonist revolution with zombification, terror and death.[184] But it is true that unlike the American zombies, slaves remained "invincibly human beings", a resilience that is a precondition for the Haitian Revolution.[185] The figure of the American zombie risks depriving the enslaved of revolutionary agency,[186] and can be read as a deeply anti-revolutionary trope.[187]

In Lauro's reading, however, the figure of the zombi represents either the history of a people's enslavement or their fierce resistance to oppression.[188] Subject and object are obliterated. The figure of the zombi is simultaneously slave and slave rebellion. In its origins, the zombi is raised to labour in the fields as a slave. The zombie metaphor reveals our irrevocable enslavement to our bodies. The zombi metaphor is also slave rebellion. Lauro and Embry see zombification as representing slavery for life *and* after life as well.[189]

The Haitian Declaration of Independence in 1804 slogan was 'Freedom or Death!'. This takes on different meaning here,[190] indicating that slaves had nothing to fear from a literal death.[191] Death would mean a return to the ancestral homeland. Slaves would (if killed in rebellion) be free from the

180 Dillon (2019) 638.
181 Timofeeva (2017) 442.
182 Cohen (1972) 60.
183 Cohen (1972) 60.
184 Hoermann (2017) 159.
185 James (2001) 9.
186 Hoermann (2017) 163.
187 Hoermann (2017) 166.
188 Lauro (2015) 29.
189 Lauro and Embry (2008) 90.
190 Timofeeva (2017) 442.
191 Lauro (2015) 51.

curse of living death and would reawaken in Africa.[192] The zombi is a cultural form that transmutes a history of death and terror under slavery into religious life.[193] The insurgents' battle cry was "We have no mother, no child; What is death?"[194] The slave who perceives themselves as dead, transported to a foreign land and forced to work for others, is resistive.[195] To die in battle and return to Africa was a different form of the Hegelian 'trial by death' but one which restored the subject to 'life', or at least, to ownership of themselves in their death.[196] Reports of the slaves rebelling in Haiti painted them as not human but almost supernatural: "fanatic and insensate hordes of blacks rose as a single body to overwhelm the more 'rational' white troops".[197]

Lauro and Embry argue the figure of the zombi is inextricably linked from the very beginning with capitalism and the construction of a working subject. Lauro and Embry turn to Hannah Arendt to show how the zombi and slave are subject to necessity. Arendt saw in the ancients an attempt to win freedom only through the domination of those enslaved persons, who were subjected to necessity by force.[198] The slave is performing another's labour; the zombi labours for no-one and only produces more zombis. A free man can shift the burden of necessity on to the slave. The figure of the infectious, consuming zombi represents humanity's attempt to transfer the burden of necessity onto others. Today, no appetite is satisfied, and all become slaves.[199]

But capitalism relies on the ability of individuals not to develop a revolutionary collective, but to promote the attitude that drives capital – everyone for themselves. But it is not the case that the individual has always been implicated in capitalism's colonial history.[200] The records of enslaved people who lived their lives as a form, show how to transgress the line between object and subject. When the enslaved Haitian took up arms, they rejected their legal status as chattel and object and claimed a place as subjects. In overcoming imperialism, the individual asserted their own agency.[201] The zombi undermines the idea of stable subject and object positions, as it is simultaneously occupying a body that is both living and dead. This creates a dilemma for power relations and risks destroying existing social dynamics.[202] The zombi is a line of flight, marking an instance of cultural creativity,

192 Lauro (2015) 52.
193 McAlister (2012) 468–9.
194 Davis (1988) 20.
195 Lauro (2015) 52–3.
196 Lauro (2015) 53.
197 Davis (1988) 20.
198 Arendt (1998) 64.
199 Lauro and Embry (2008) 99–100.
200 Lauro and Embry (2008) 106.
201 Lauro and Embry (2008) 107.
202 Lauro and Embry (2008) 95.

produced from within social death.[203] The omnipresence of death in the colony was the source of rich cultural creativity, shaping key aspects of social life.[204] The zombi tells the story of the insistence of life and sociality under the regime of social death.[205] Today, as our global system of capitalism tries to prevent any attempt to withdraw from its system, our only viable option becomes deactivating the system itself and the individuals that it created.[206]

Lauro and Embry propose the 'zombii' as a subject that is not a subject, an interminable boundary between subject and object, much like Agamben defines contact as existing without a representation of relation between subject and object.[207] The zombii does not advocate a new model for humanity but nullifies the subject's position. Lauro and Embry present this in terms of the 'posthuman', but I wish to recast their argument in terms of form-of-life, jettisoning the posthumanism, and focusing on the implications for capitalist coloniality. The zombii disrupts the system and is presented as an "analogy for humanity as it exists today", as well as foreboding a "monstrous future".[208] This is a form of destituent politics, dismantling without proposing an alternative. Such a figure would exist in contact with others, which is first of all contact with ourselves. We have an experience of ourselves for the first time when, touching another body, we also touch our own flesh. To abolish all contact is to lose any immediate experience of ourselves.[209]

The zombii is a workless slave, a messianic figure that suspends work without seeking recognition as a subject. Like the Maroon, and the Haitian captive living on a provision ground away from oligarchical control, the zombii does not seek new articulations for living, but shows the emptiness of the relation that holds man and animal, subject and object together. History is ended through the living of their lives, not the violent overthrow of an oppressive system, which would only reproduce what it seeks to end. This workless slave suspends history through opening a sphere of that which is human, unmediated by the state or *dispositifs* of control. This is a positive affirmation of a communal way of living and a positive relationship to one's landscape.[210]

The lives of enslaved people throughout history provide numerous examples of form-of-life, which show how lives can be lived in abyssal or even hadal zones. What does this mean for the present day and the future? Agamben's paradigm locates itself at the crossing of diachrony and synchrony, making

203 Dillon (2019) 636.
204 Brown (2010).
205 Dillon (2019) 638.
206 Lauro and Embry (2008) 107–8.
207 Agamben (2021).
208 Lauro and Embry (2008) 95.
209 Agamben (2021).
210 Agamben (2000) 57; Agamben (2018a) 84–5.

our present intelligible as the past of the object.[211] If we view the enslaved person as a form-of-life, then the actions and behaviours of forms-of-life in the past can provide a model, or a structure of behaviour, for the present. In seeking to comprehend the present, human beings find themselves compelled to interrogate the past.[212] Throughout this book, I have attempted to show how chronological archives can be "cleaved open to produce a paradigm" to make the whole archive legible.[213] These paradigms allow for a constellation of phenomena (such as the lives and actions of enslaved people) to be understood.[214] This archive shows that capitalism, coloniality and oppression are not totalising, and form-of-life is not dependent on violence or a revolutionary overturning of the dominant political form. Gestures as paradigms are revolutionary through their subtlety and everydayness.

Conclusion

This chapter has developed the argument that the actions and gestures of enslaved persons can contribute towards an alternative conception of agency and belonging in the Western European legal and political tradition. The enslaved person is an embodied individual within the development of capitalism. Despite this, there always exists small acts and gestures by enslaved people that create new forms of political belonging, separate from the CMP and logic of coloniality. These examples (paradigms) from the past can inform living in the present and the future. I have explored examples from the Atlantic slave trade, including the enslaved persons who rebelled in Haiti against French dominion, and the Maroon communities whose culture and resistance enabled them to create their own communities in spite of enslavement and colonial policies, analogous to the community of Franciscans which Agamben sees as examples of form-of-life. Form-of-life is found in unedifying places and is very tenuous. Forms of resistance against dominant and totalising power always are. But they do exist, and they do point the way towards conceptions of belonging which are just, just as they are.

Reference List

Abrahams, R (1992) *Singing the Master: The Emergence of African American Culture in the Plantation South*, New York: Pantheon.

Achinte, A A (2012) 'Epistemes "otras" ¿Epistemes Disruptivas?', *KULA. Antropólogos del Atlántico Sur*, 6, 22–34.

211 Agamben (2009) 32.
212 Agamben (2019) 1.
213 Agamben (2009) 32.
214 Agamben (2009) 27–8.

Ackermann, H-W and Gauthier, J (1991) 'The Ways and Nature of the Zombi', *The Journal of American Folklore*, 104, 466–94.
Agamben, G (2000) *Means Without End: Notes on Politics*, Binetti, V and Casarino, C (trans.), Minneapolis: University of Minnesota Press.
Agamben, G (2004) *The Open: Man and Animal*, Attell, K (trans.), Stanford: Stanford University Press.
Agamben, G (2005) *The Time That Remains: A Commentary on the Letter to the Romans*, Dailey, P (trans.), Stanford: Stanford University Press.
Agamben, G (2007a) *Infancy and History: On the Destruction of Experience*, Heron, L (trans.), London: Verso Books.
Agamben, G (2007b) *Profanations*, Fort, J (trans.), Princeton: Princeton University Press.
Agamben, G (2009) *The Signature of All Things: On Method*, D'Isanto, L and Attell, K (trans.), New York: Zone Books.
Agamben, G (2010) *Nudities*, Kishik, D and Pedatella, S (trans.), Stanford: Stanford University Press.
Agamben, G (2012) *The Church and the Kingdom*, de la Durantaye, L (trans.), London: Seagull Books.
Agamben, G (2016) *The Use of Bodies*, Kotsko, A (trans.), Stanford: Stanford University Press.
Agamben, G (2018a) *Karman: A Brief Treatise on Action, Guilt and Gesture*, Kotsko, A (trans.), Stanford: Stanford University Press.
Agamben, G (2018b) *What Is Philosophy?*, Chiesa, L (trans.), Stanford: Stanford University Press.
Agamben, G (2019) 'On the Impossibility of Saying "I": Epistemological Paradigms and Poetic Paradigms in the Work of Furio Jesi', *Theory & Event*, 22, 1047–57.
Agamben, G (2021) 'A Philosophy of Contact', Braude, R (trans.), *Ill Will*, https://illwill.com/philosophy-of-contact.
Arendt, H (1998) *The Human Condition*, 2nd edn, Chicago: University of Chicago Press.
Besson, J (1999) 'Folk Law and Legal Pluralism in Jamaica: A View From the Plantation-Peasant Interface', *Journal of Legal Pluralism*, 43, 31–56.
Bikundo, E (2022a) 'Follow Your Leader – I Prefer not to: Slavery, Giorgio Agamben and Herman Melville', *Law, Culture and the Humanities*, 18, 4–19.
Bikundo, E (2022b) 'Metaphor, Marx, Agamben and International Law: The Jamaican Quashee/Quasheeba, the Necessity of Labour, and the Subjectivity of Emancipated Slaves', *Law, Text, Culture*, 26, 58–72.
Bilby, K (1997) 'Swearing by the Past, Swearing to the Future: Sacred Oaths, Alliances, and Treaties Among the Guianese and Jamaican Maroons', *Ethnohistory*, 44, 655–89.
Blackburn, R (2006) 'Haiti, Slavery, and the Age of Democratic Revolution', *The William and Mary Quarterly*, 63, 643–74.
Brace, L (2018) *The Politics of Slavery*, Edinburgh: Edinburgh University Press.
Brown, V (2010) *The Reaper's Garden: Death and Power in the World of Atlantic Slavery*, Cambridge: Harvard University Press.
Brown, V (2020) *Tacky's Revolt: The Story of an Atlantic Slave War*, Cambridge: Harvard University Press.

Bulstrode, J (2023) 'Black Metallurgists and the Making of the Industrial Revolution', *History and Technology*, 39, 1–41.
Bush, B (2001) 'From Slavery to Freedom: Black Women, Cultural Resistance and Identity in Caribbean Plantation Society' in Bremer, T and Fleischmann, U (eds.), *History and Histories in the Caribbean*, Madrid: Iberoamericana, 115–59.
Casimir, J (2020) *The Haitians: A Decolonial History*, Dubois, L (trans.), Durham: The University of North Carolina Press.
Cilliers, J (2018) 'The *Kairos* of *Karos*: Revisiting Notions of Temporality in Africa', *Stellenbosch Theological Journal*, 4, 113–32.
Cohen, D (1972) *Voodoo, Devils, and the Invisible World*, New York: Dodd, Mead and Company.
Craton, M & Greenland, G (1978) *Searching for the Invisible Man: Slaves and Plantation Life in Jamaica*, Cambridge & London: Harvard University Press.
Craton, M (1982) *Testing the Chains: Resistance to Slavery in the British West Indies*, Ithaca & London, Cornell University Press.
Davis, A (1971) 'Reflections on the Black Woman's Role in the Community of Slaves', *The Black Scholar*, 3, 2–15.
Davis, W (1985) *The Serpent and the Rainbow*, New York: Simon & Schuster.
Davis, W (1988) *Passage of Darkness: The Ethnobiology of the Haitian Zombie*, Chapel Hill: University of North Carolina Press.
Dayan, C (2011) *The Law Is a White Dog: How Legal Rituals Make and Unmake Persons*, Princeton: Princeton University Press.
Dayan, J (2010) 'Haiti, History, and the Gods' in Howe, S (ed.), *The New Imperial Histories Reader*, London: Routledge, 359–77.
DeCamp, D (1967) 'African Day-Names in Jamaica' *Language*, 43, 139–49.
Dillon, E M (2019) 'Zombie Biopolitics', *American Quarterly*, 71, 625–52.
Dookhan, I (1974) *A History of the Virgin Islands of the United States*, Kingston: Canoe Press.
Dubois, L (2004) *Avengers of the New World: The Story of the Haitian Revolution*, Cambridge: Belknap Press.
Eddins, C (2022) 'Maroon Movements Against Empire: The Long Haitian Revolution, Sixteenth-Nineteenth Centuries', *Journal of World-Systems Research*, 28, 219–41.
Esposito, R (2012) 'The *Dispositif* of the Person', *Law, Culture and the Humanities*, 8, 17–30.
Fanon, F (2018) *Alienation and Freedom*, Khalifa, J and Young, R (eds.), Corcoran, S (trans.), London: Bloomsbury.
Fatton Jr, R (2006) 'Haiti: The Saturnalia of Emancipation and the Vicissitudes of Predatory Rule', *Third World Quarterly*, 27, 115–33.
Fatton Jr, R (2007) *The Roots of Haitian Despotism*, Boulder: Lynne Rienner Publishers.
Fick, C (1998) 'Dilemmas of Emancipation: from the Saint Domingue Insurrections of 1791 to the Emerging Haitian State', *History Workshop Journal*, 46, 1–16.
Fryer, P (2021) *Black People in the British Empire*, London: Pluto Press.
Ghadery, F (2022) 'Beyond International Human Rights Law – Music and Song in Contextualised Struggles for Gender Equality', *Transnational Legal Theory*, 13, 31–58.
Gilroy, P (1993) *The Black Atlantic: Modernity and Double Consciousness*, London: Verso.

Glissant, E (1992) *Caribbean Discourse: Selected Essays*, Charlottesville: University of Virginia Press.
Hall, N A T (1985) 'Maritime Maroons: 'Grand Marronage' from the Danish West Indies', *The William and Mary Quarterly*, 42, 476–98.
Handler, J (1982) 'Slave Revolts and Conspiracies in Seventeenth-Century Barbados', *New West Indian Guide/Nieuwe West-Indische Gids*, 56, 5–42.
Hartman, S (1997) *Scenes of Subjection: Terror, Slavery, and Self-Making in Nineteenth-Century America*, Oxford: Oxford University Press.
Harvey, S and Moten, F (2013) *The Undercommons: Fugitive Planning & Black Study*. New York: Minor Compositions.
Haymes, S (2006) 'Pedagogy and the Philosophical Anthropology of African-American Slave Culture' in Gordon, J and Gordon, J A (eds.), *Not Only the Master's Tools: African-American Studies in Theory and Practice*, Boulder: Paradigm, 173–204.
Hoermann, R (2017) 'Figures of Terror: The "Zombie" and the Haitian Revolution', *Atlantic Studies: Literary, Historical and Cultural Perspectives*, 14, 152–73.
Invisible Committee (2017) *Now*, Hurley, R (trans.), Los Angeles: Semiotext(e).
James, C L R (2001) *The Black Jacobins: Toussaint L'Ouverture and the San Domingo Revolution*, London: Penguin.
Lauro, S J (2015) *The Transatlantic Zombie: Slavery, Rebellion, and Living Death*, New Brunswick: Rutgers University Press.
Lauro, S J and Embry, K (2008) 'A Zombie Manifesto: The Nonhuman Condition in the Era of Advanced Capitalism', *Boundary* 2, 35, 85–108.
Maingot, A (1986) 'Haiti: Problems of a Transition to Democracy in an Authoritarian Soft State', *Journal of Interamerican Studies and World Affairs*, 28, 75–102.
Maitland, F W and Pollock, F (1898) *The History of English Law Before the Time of Edward I, 2 vols*, Cambridge: Cambridge University Press.
Marx, K (1849) 'Wage Labour and Capital', *Neue Rheinische Zeitung*, April.
Marx, K (1971) *The Poverty of Philosophy*, Quelch, H (trans.), New York: International Publishers.
Marx, K (1973) *Grundrisse: Foundations of the Critique of Political Economy*, Nicolaus, M (trans.), Harmondsworth: Penguin.
Marx, K (1990) *Capital: A Critique of Political Economy, Vol. 1*, Moore, S and Aveling, E (trans.), Harmondsworth: Penguin.
Marx, K and Engels, F (1976) *The German Ideology*, Moscow: Progress Publishers.
Mbembé, A (2003) 'Necropolitics', *Public Culture*, 15, 11–40.
Mbembé, A (2017) *Critique of Black Reason*, Dubois, L (trans.), Durham: Duke University Press.
Mbembé, A (2019) *Necropolitics*, Durham: Duke University Press.
McAlister, E (2012) 'Slaves, Cannibals, and Infected Hyper-Whites: The Race and Religion of Zombies', *Anthropological Quarterly*, 85, 457–86.
Mignolo, W (2020) 'Foreword: Thinking Decoloniality beyond One Nation – One State' in Casimir, J, *The Haitians: A Decolonial History*, Dubois, L (trans.), Durham: The University of North Carolina Press, vii–xvi.
Ott, T (1973) *The Haitian Revolution, 1789–1804*, Knoxville: University of Tennessee Press.
Paton, A (2004) *No Bond But the Law: Punishment, Race, and Gender in Jamaican State Formation*, Durham: Duke University Press.

Prozorov, S (2017) 'Living *à la mode*: Form-of-Life and Democratic Biopolitics in Giorgio Agamben's *The Use of Bodies*', *Philosophy and Social Criticism*, 43, 144–63.
Ralph, M and Singhal, M (2019) 'Racial Capitalism', *Theory & Society*, 48, 851–81.
Robinson, C (2021) *Black Marxism: The Making of the Black Radical Tradition*, London: Penguin Books.
Roopnarine, L (2010) 'Maroon Resistance and Settlement on Danish St Croix', *Journal of Third World Studies*, 27, 89–108.
Scanlan, P (2020) *Slave Empire: How Slavery Built Modern Britain*, London: Robinson.
Schmidt, H (1995) *The United States Occupation of Haiti, 1915–1934*, New Brunswick: Rutgers University Press.
Scott, D (2004) *Conscripts of Modernity*, Durham: Duke University Press.
Scott, J (1985) *Weapons of the Weak: Everyday Forms of Peasant Resistance*, New Haven: Yale University Press.
Scott, J (2018) *The Common Wind: Currents of Afro-American Communication in the Era of the Haitian Revolution*, London: Verso.
Timofeeva, O (2017) 'Freedom Is Slavery', *Crisis & Critique*, 4, 425–45.
Vatter, M (2017) 'Law and Life Beyond Incorporation: Agamben, Highest Poverty and the Papal Legal Revolution' in *Agamben and Radical Politics*, McLoughlin, D (ed.), Cambridge: Cambridge University Press, 234–62.
Verges, F (2021) *A Decolonial Feminism*, Bohrer, A (trans.), London: Pluto Press.
Veyne, P (1988) *Did the Greeks Believe in their Myths? An Essay on the Constitutive Imagination*, Wissing, P (trans.), Chicago: University of Chicago Press.
Walvin, J (2019) *Resistance, Rebellion & Revolt: How Slavery Was Overthrown*, London: Robinson.
Weheliye, A (2014) *Habeas Viscus: Racializing Assemblages, Biopolitics, and Black Feminist Theories of the Human*, Durham: Duke University Press.
Wynter, S (1971) 'Novel and History, Plot and Plantation', *Savacou*, 5, 95–102.
Zartaloudis, T (2018) *The Birth of Nomos*, Edinburgh: Edinburgh University Press.

Chapter 8

The way forward

To end, a division

This final chapter concludes my study. Today slavery is illegal and utterly inimical to the values of the modern world,[1] yet slavery still dwells in that world's centre.[2] In the words of Frederick Douglass: "the determination of slavery to perpetuate itself ... due to the folly of endeavouring to retain the new wine of liberty in the old bottles of slavery".[3] But Agamben's critique of modernity has been criticised as being limited to the concentration camp and the city, and of the contemporary citizen and the figure of bare life.[4] I have sought to respond to this point of view.

This study has focused on the enslaved person. Agamben uses the figure of the slave as an example, or a paradigm, of a potential form of future political existence. For Agamben, apparatuses of control divide the living being, deciding what is counted as human and what is counted as not human.[5] Subjects are produced through this operation, which produces a remainder, bare life, a figure cast out from the *polis*.[6] Starting with Aristotle, there exist persons with incomplete humanity who can be enslaved and complete humanity who are able to enslave others. The figure of the slave became a non-normative remainder which cannot be accounted for and yet is necessary to the operation of a divided humanity. The human being's possibility is always falling back into animality.[7] The human being can find itself only by presupposing the not-truly-human. Political action is based on the inclusive exclusion of the use of the body and the inoperativity of the slave.[8] Freedom

1 O'Connell Davidson (2015) 13.
2 Timofeeva (2017) 429.
3 Douglass (2018) 488.
4 Campbell (2011) 44.
5 Agamben (2004) 15.
6 Agamben (1998) 181.
7 Agamben (2016) 188.
8 Agamben (2016) 45.

DOI: 10.4324/9781003303534-9

is double, and slavery is freedom's necessary counterpoint. The claiming of rights requires the exclusion of others from those rights, through the social death that is slavery. The figure of the slave becomes the ideal human tool, a dominated thing, an instrument for the master.[9]

Afropessimism reads this figure as a Black body, with modernity marked by devalued Black lives driven "by a racial calculus and a political arithmetic that were entrenched centuries ago".[10] The colonial matrix of power (CMP) has exported this division globally and can be traced to the figure of the slave. Blackness and race have constituted the foundation of the modern project of knowledge and governance.[11] Colonisation and the CMP have led to the destruction of extraordinary possibilities of culture, institutions, religions and art, all torn away from individuals.[12]

My focus has been on the realities of enslaved people living their lives. The enslaved person is a form-of-life that points toward an alternative way of political belonging. Form-of-life ceaselessly surpasses and overtakes what we call 'life' in our political theory.[13] It is a life totally concerned with its own exemplarity.[14] Agamben's thought and work focuses on the possibilities available to us now and is a clarion call to seize them. This is a *destituent* politics, a politics which puts into question the current ways and strategies of politics.[15] Destituent power cannot resolve itself into a constituted power,[16] and is never instrumental.[17] Central to the story of form-of-life are the populations deemed surplus and expendable, and those who have stood in the path of death yet remain alive.[18] This is why Saidiya Hartman speaks of the need to "imagine what cannot be verified", and to reckon the precarious lives visible only as they disappeared.[19] The lived realities of enslaved people have carved out forms of agency and political belonging through their lives, their actions and their gestures. This is often a life lived in the shadow of racialisation, and domination created and compounded through gendered politics, as well as the denial of political rights.

I have connected destituent politics to strands of decolonial theory, looking at 'refusal' as a commonality between them. Refusal is a form of 're-existence', which seeks to build projects of society and life in the face of

9 Patterson (1982) 335.
10 Hartman (1997) 6.
11 Mbembé (2017) 2.
12 Césaire (1973) 43.
13 Agamben (2016) 191.
14 Agamben (2016) 259.
15 Agamben (2023a) 9.
16 Agamben (2016) 268.
17 Agamben (2016) 269.
18 Mbembé (2019) 36.
19 Hartman (2008) 12.

adverse conditions, and ultimately seek to occupy a social and cultural place of dignity, re-existing with others in radically distinct terms.[20] I associated this to what I term hyper-hermeneutics. This conveys Agamben's attempt to create a *paradigmatic circle* by breaking free of the hermeneutics that have structured the CMP. Our interpretation and understanding of the world only acquires its true meaning from within a paradigmatic method. Paradigms are actual historical phenomena but "constitute and make intelligible a broader historical-problematic context".[21] A term, once taken as a paradigm, is 'deactivated' from its normal use.[22] The paradigm is therefore able to offer singular examples of alternative forms of political belonging. Form-of-life is hyper-hermeneutic, constructed through singular paradigmatic examples. These paradigms are gestural.[23] These gestures are coterminous with a form generated by living itself, a style of living.[24] Such hyper-hermeneutic gestures are 'pure means' without any connection to an end or result, an exposition of humankind's creative semi-indifference to any task.[25] Such gestures open up an existence beyond the frame of racial capitalism and the CMP, new forms of political intervention.[26]

The enslaved, whilst being treated as a mere instrument of production, in fact (through acts of culture, music and the body) acted against the very institution that enslaved them. These are examples of living one's life as a form. The enslaved also tried to create a world of their own, sometimes against the world of their masters. We must, to paraphrase Achille Mbembé, open the singular being up to the possibility of becoming a human form of being rather than a thing.[27] Ours is a time of planetary *entanglement*.[28] Entanglement asks us to probe intimacies between histories of violence, injury and loss, to acknowledge alliances forged beyond specific times and spaces in the pursuit of justice. The time of entanglement is "not a series but an interlocking of presents, pasts, and futures that retain their depths of other pasts, presents, and futures".[29] It is an emerging time, a time that is appearing. To think of time as entanglement is to attend to history's vitality, its pulse, its ruptures, its untimely returns. It is "to seize hold of a memory as it flashes up at a moment of danger".[30] All resistance is an accumulated and accumulating

20 Achinte (2012) 30.
21 Agamben (2009a) 9.
22 Agamben (2009a) 18.
23 Agamben (2009a) 27.
24 Agamben (2016) 220–3.
25 Agamben (2000) 141–2.
26 Agamben (2007b) 77.
27 Mbembé (2021) 51.
28 Mbembé (2019) 93.
29 Mbembé (2001) 83–4.
30 Benjamin (1999) 247.

commitment to act for the hope of the future.[31] Those enslaved persons who 'prefer not to' appear to point to the nucleus of a form-of-life (and freedom) that deactivates the institution of slavery which has captured and divides life.

In the first section of the chapter I discuss how slavery operates as a metaphor in Marxist and anarchist critiques of capitalism. This then leads on to a discussion of how life in the modern world, structured by the Anthropocene and the CMP, is populated by hyper-exploited outsiders who are necessary for the functioning of the economy. I go on to discuss how debt helps reinforce an 'unfreedom' at the heart of the neoliberal economy, considering the role of debt. I contend that a non-Statist anarchism can be problematic in repeating the logics of coloniality.

The second section of the chapter argues that technology is not the answer to the problems of slavery. Agamben argues that the slave is an ancient category of technology, and today's dependence on technology is akin to the ancient dependence on slavery. I read this claim in light of Martin Heidegger's essay on technology, arguing that technology operates as an apparatus of control. I draw on Donna Haraway's work on the 'cyborg' and Maurizio Lazzarato's writing on 'machinic enslavement' to show how technology is built on the same colonial, Euro-modern and anti-Black bases as the world is. Our approach to technology repeats Aristotle's idea that some people are natural slaves, and the slave owners control the means of production.

Ultimately, Agamben's politics is optimistic, but his anarchistic tendencies remain born of Eurocentrism and coloniality. I end the chapter, and the book, by returning to my decolonial 'correction' of Agamben's thought, noting that his non-Statist politics cannot be a form of anarchism with its basis in Western European colonial logics. The form-of-life of the enslaved person points toward a form of politics able to deactivate the apparatuses of control that exist around the world but were born of the CMP.

The infernal economy and the figure of the slave

The figure of the slave in Marxism and anarchism

The figure of the slave has operated as the foundation of a critique of capitalism in both Marxist and anarchist traditions. The symbolic figure of the slave helped shape Marx's critique of capitalism. The issue of slave labour was woven into Marx's social formations (ancient and modern) and was inextricably intertwined with his treatment of wage labour.[32] In *Capital*, Marx wrote that the wage-labourers of Europe existed in a 'veiled slavery', compared to the 'unqualified slavery' of the Atlantic slave trade.[33] The unqualified slavery

31 Verges (2021) 5.
32 Foster, Holleman and Clark (2020) 97.
33 Marx (1990) 925.

of the Atlantic slave trade was the pedestal for the veiled slavery of Europe.[34] The figure of the slave critiques the structure of capitalist economics.

The wage-labourer's freedom is double. This encompasses a positive freedom, which means the wage-labourer can dispose of their labour-power as a commodity, in effect 'selling' it to employers. There is also a negative freedom, which is a freedom from being dependent.[35] This double freedom exists because labourers in a capitalist society can freely offer their labour power to whoever they want, and on whatever terms they can negotiate. These were new impersonal relations of dependence individuals owed to things in the market.[36] The worker was also unfree because the wage worker has to give up their labour power to the capitalist in order to live.[37] 'Free' wage-labour does not mean an absence of coercion.[38] Free means the wage-labourer is divorced from the means of production.[39] 'Wage slavery' means that the worker is nothing less than a contemporary form of an enslaved person.[40]

There is a debate surrounding the precise meaning of this veil and pedestal metaphor. It has been argued that the real meaning of this metaphor was structural and spatial: the naked, unqualified slavery in Marx's analysis was significant only insofar as it pointed to the 'veiled slavery' of wage labour, which attained supreme importance.[41] Oxana Timofeeva argues that Marx forgets real slavery in favour of metaphorical slavery, as he thought of history in terms of successive economic formations and saw slavery as archaic.[42] Sorentino contends that Marx's metaphor downgraded the reality of New World slavery.[43] Sorentino goes on to point out that Marx could only appropriate Aristotle's idea of natural slavery because of the conjunction of anti-Blackness and slavery.[44] Cedric Robinson identifies Marx's failure to fully realise that the human cargo crossing the Atlantic were human beings with different African cultures, cultural mixes, languages, habits, beliefs and moralities. These cargoes were made up of human beings who brought their pasts with them.[45] Fred Moten sees Black sociality as on the map but at the same time unmappable, unusable in a modal ontology as it is already shared.[46] There is an ethic of restitution and reparation that implies the recognition of

34 Foster, Holleman and Clark (2020) 99; Marx (1990) 719.
35 Marx (1990) 273.
36 Marx (1973) 158.
37 Shilliam (2012) 604.
38 Sorentino (2019b) 20.
39 Banaji (2010) 13.
40 Sorentino (2019b) 27.
41 Johnson (2004) 306.
42 Timofeeva (2017) 441.
43 Sorentino (2019b) 17.
44 Sorentino (2019a).
45 Robinson (2021) 121–2.
46 Mason (2020) 183; Moten (2018) 202.

the other's share. This share is not ours, but it is something that we are the guarantor for.[47]

Marx did pay close attention to New World slavery, suggesting there was more to his analysis than a straightforward metaphor.[48] Marx was making a literal argument about slavery being foundational to capitalism, with the plantation economy being an integral part of the historical development of capitalism.[49] 'Direct slavery' was a pivot of industrialisation. This slavery gave value to the colonies, which in turn created world trade, which in turn created large-scale machine industry.[50] The slave variant of capitalism existed only as it was an integral part of a larger capitalist system rooted in wage labour. Slaveowner capitalism grafted the method of production on to slavery.[51] Any persistence of slavery into capitalism would be the result of a stubborn persistence on slavery's part.[52] For Marx, slavery took the form of continual violence and perpetual fear of torture and premature death. Enslaved people were worked to death, and this was of little significance because they were easily replaceable. This led Marx to view the slave in his writings as both capital assets and labour.[53] Under slave production it was possible to work slaves more intensively, exploiting them, which you could not do with wage labour.[54] Slavery under capitalism was more brutal than anything seen before in human history.[55] As we have seen in relation to Maroon communities in the previous chapter, Marx was aware of slave revolts, as well as the existence of runaways who banded together, determined to resist the "barbaric horrors of slavery".[56]

However, Marx made clear that whilst New World plantation slavery was capitalist in form and carried out by capitalists, the primary form of capitalism was the exploitation of wage labour.[57] The capitalist mode of production was explored through examples of industry in England. The metaphor of slavery was structured according to the logic of the CMP. Marx removed the slave from the historical development of capitalism.[58] The dialectic of double freedom applied to the English servant, but never worked for enslaved people. Freedom would not be manifested because the enslaved person entered

47 Mbembé (2017) 182–3.
48 Marx (1990) 915–24.
49 Marx (1971) 111.
50 Marx to P V Annenkov, Brussels, 28 December 1846 in Marx (1971) 188.
51 Foster, Holleman and Clark (2020) 104; Marx (1968) 302–3.
52 Marx (1973) 891.
53 Foster, Holleman and Clark (2020) 101.
54 Blackburn (1997) 339–40.
55 Marx (1990) 377.
56 Marx (1990) 345; Marx (1971) 111.
57 Marx (1973) 464, 513.
58 Shilliam (2012) 604.

the commercial world market as commodified labour and a politically unfree thing.[59] Shilliam concludes that Marx's dialectic could never bear the weight of that ultimate alienated labourer in commercial law, the enslaved African.[60]

Work is not an organic principle for the slave.[61] Because slavery was based on force and compulsion, it could only be effectively employed in producing certain things,[62] like centralised large-scale production in gangs on monoculture plantations.[63] Timofeeva notes that there was no *structural* difference between the slave and wageworker, as labour for money was as coercive as enslavement.[64] But the free wage worker has no value itself (there was value in the worker's labour power). In contrast the slave was a capital asset, forming the basis of fictitious or speculative capital.[65]

The figure of the slave also played a key role in anarchist thought, which is further connected to the idea of domination. To be a slave is to be dominated. To be free is not to be dominated. This idea of domination is something that can be found in both modern anarchism and republican political theory.[66] Anarchists honed the language of domination and slavery in the late nineteenth century, shaped by debates about the abolition of slavery and serfdom.[67] Pierre-Joseph Proudhon conjoined property with slavery, considering property to be 'theft'.[68] Private title in things facilitated the theft of property and value from those who produced it. Under capitalism, labourers work to produce, but the title to the capital and the exclusive domain over property ensures that the product of labour never remains with the labourer, and that the labourer remains as dependent on the master as the slave had been prior to emancipation.[69] Proudhon argued that the transformation of slavery, from chattel to wage labour, and the theft of the product of labour resulted from the legal appropriation of property as an exclusive right of dominion: "the emancipated slave, and, a few centuries later, the enfranchised serf, without means of existence, was obliged to become a tenant and pay tribute".[70] Mikhail Bakunin saw the worker's life as a "continuous and dismaying succession of terms of serfdom".[71] Voluntary servitude, contract

59 Shilliam (2012) 604.
60 Shilliam (2012) 604–5.
61 Wilderson (2003) 230.
62 Marx (1990) 1014, 1016, 1033–4.
63 Foster, Holleman and Clark (2020) 108.
64 Timofeeva (2017) 438–9; Marx (2007) 23, 81.
65 Marx (1990) 377; Marx (1973) 288–9.
66 Kinna and Prichard (2019) 221–2.
67 Kinna and Prichard (2019) 224.
68 Proudhon (1994) 13.
69 Kinna and Prichard (2019) 226.
70 Proudhon (2011) 523.
71 Bakunin (1964) 188.

slavery, is central to the capitalist labour market.[72] Proudhon's argument was that the exercise of domination, experienced as dependency on a master by chattel and wage slaves alike extended from the exclusive right to private property.[73] We are all slaves to the logic of property and the market.[74]

This is why anarchist politics does not take place within the framework of the State. The state is a violent instrument of domination. Anarchism aims to make clear the contingency and arbitrariness of the way society is constructed. Agamben evokes this claim when he states that the capitalist economy has no foundation on which to rest.[75] For anarchism, our social arrangements are established through multiple dominations and exclusions.[76] This is why human mobility threatens the state's authority. As O'Connell Davison maintains, human mobility undercuts the control of a sovereign power, which is spatially limited to territories. If sovereign power can be evaded, this also means that the social order imposed by that sovereignty can also be subverted.[77]

An anarchist politics does require organisation however: the building and defending of autonomous, collective spaces outside of the state; an experimentation with alternative forms of democratic decision-making and egalitarian forms of exchange; even a form of discipline (which is voluntary and non-coercive).[78] This is why Simon Critchley proposes an "an-archic metapolitics" that distances itself from the State, making demands on it while working independently of it. This works in the interstices of state power, constructing spaces beyond its grasp.[79] On this reading it is not possible to overcome power completely, as every overcoming is the imposition of another regime of power. Freedom is to be found by working within this world.[80]

Anarchy is based on an essentially optimistic conception of human nature, precluding the need for the State. Man is essentially cooperative, and the State has a negative impact on these natural social relations.[81] Anarchists obey the authority of 'natural laws' that are not external to man but determine the world in which we live.[82] For Bakunin, the ideas of 'justice' and 'the good' are human constructs, and, like all other human constructs, have their

72 Kinna and Prichard (2019) 229.
73 Kinna and Prichard (2019) 227.
74 Bakunin (1964) 188.
75 Agamben (2019) 76.
76 Newman (2010b) 64.
77 O'Connell Davidson (2015) 113.
78 Newman (2010a).
79 Critchley (2007) 111–114; Newman (2010a).
80 Newman (2000).
81 Bakunin (1964) 156.
82 Bakunin (1964) 239.

root in "man's very animality".[83] Yet these natural laws, like the concept of 'domination', have their root in Euro-modernity and epistemic paradigms of coloniality. Anarchist natural laws re-create European thought and values. But on this point Agamben raises a criticism: anarchy lacks an origin or ground, but both Bakunin and Proudhon do not think of a 'true anarchy'. By emphasising the natural laws of man, both thinkers merely "displaced the origin", substituting a rational principle of man's essential goodness for the principle of State authority.[84] Agamben wants to think of a 'true anarchy', which is "what becomes thinkable only at the point where we grasp and render destitute the anarchy of power",[85] meaning an acceptance that political power more broadly has no objective basis.[86]

Unfreedom and neoliberalism

Adam Kotsko contends that neoliberalism starts from the conviction that the only true source of political legitimacy is the economic realm. Neoliberal theorists know that markets and market competition do not happen naturally. They are human constructs.[87] Walter Benjamin saw capitalism as a cultic religion, the most extreme that has ever existed. It is a permanent cult, and one which creates guilt.[88] For Agamben, capitalism is a religion entirely founded on faith.[89] The neoliberal system states that the individual is in control of their destiny, meaning any failures are the fault of the individual, not the system.[90] The market is a creation designed to resemble unfettered human choice, but every part of human life becomes subsumed under the logic of market competition.[91] Capitalism controls our labour and our life activities. Capitalist reproduction requires the production and reproduction of labour power.[92] Most goods and services necessary for this task are commodified, but domestic labour and the processes of social reproduction itself is largely confined to the private sphere, unpaid and primarily performed by women *on top* of their participation in the labour market.[93] Capitalism even imposes the imperatives of market relations ever deeper into our lives, a central dynamic

83 Bakunin (1964) 121.
84 Agamben (2016) 276.
85 Agamben (2016) 275.
86 Agamben (2019) 76.
87 Kotsko (2015) 185.
88 Benjamin (2004) 288–9.
89 Agamben (2019) 69.
90 Kotsko (2018) 96.
91 Kotsko (2015) 185.
92 Gordon (2019) 930.
93 Gordon (2019) 930; Bezanson and Luxton (2006).

of the neoliberal drive to privatise and commodify public services and nature itself.[94]

This is why living in the CMP can be connected to living in the Anthropocene, a new geological epoch brought about by human consumption, production and habitation.[95] This is a destructive period caused by the social and environmental impacts of liberal industrial regimes.[96] Capitalism has always depended on racial subsidies to exploit the planet's resources, and it is today recolonising its own centre.[97] Neoliberal capitalism has heightened the prevalence of unfree labour.[98] Today, the despoiling and pollution of the earth, along with the creation of human detritus poisoned by that technological despoilment, precisely mirrors the way enslaved people were used by the means of production throughout the history of the West.[99]

At the same time, capitalism has no object. It believes in the pure fact of believing, in pure credit.[100] Everyone lives on credit, or debt.[101] Debt is at the heart of the contemporary economy. This is a machine that extracts surplus value from behaviour by excluding unprofitable individuals.[102] Debt is the assertion of power of one party over another. The opposition between workers and the owners of the means of production has been transformed into an opposition between debtors and creditors.[103] Mbembé argues that neoliberalism gives all events and situations a market value. There are no longer workers, only labouring monads, who are subject to the market and to 'debt', a 'superfluous humanity'.[104] Financial markets will decide which lifestyles and forms of life are viable and which do not deserve credit (and therefore deserve to be indebted).[105] Debt relies on individual virtue, with the economy based on the existence of virtuous individuals who will pay what they owe.[106] This means control over the future of the individual and the individual's behaviour, a future in which they promise to honour their debt.[107] The psychic life of neoliberalism is shot through with anxiety and shame.[108]

94 Gordon (2019) 929–30.
95 Birrell and Matthews (2020) 233.
96 Wakefield (2023) 121.
97 Mbembé (2017) 179.
98 Rioux, LeBaron & Verovšek (2020) 710.
99 Blackburn (1988).
100 Agamben (2019) 69–70.
101 Agamben (2019) 71.
102 Lazzarato (2014) 162–8.
103 Lazzarato (2012) 7.
104 Mbembé (2017) 3.
105 Christiaens (2018) 257.
106 Lazzarato (2012) 11.
107 Lazzarato (2012) 45–6.
108 Kotsko (2018) 95.

The debtor is excluded from the profits of surplus value, reduced to a mere bodily existence, a form of bare life.

Neoliberal governance has historically been accompanied by increasingly repressive state violence. For Lazzarato, contemporary neoliberalism selects some forms of life to the detriment of others, and this selection is always non-democratic:

> Popular sovereignty is conditional, since the only vote that matters is that of the market and financial institution of international governance, which express their 'political' will every day and in real time via the stock market and the spread.[109]

The deregulatory state and the national security state nearly always go hand in hand.[110] Market competition, which entails inequality and winners and losers, is emphasised.[111] Capitalism is corrosive of traditional institutions. The institutions of race, family and nation are reasserted to try and ensure wealth and income is unequally distributed.[112]

Agamben observes that after the Last Judgment, there is one place where the economy persists – hell, where demons eternally punish the damned. Meaning that in Christian theology the notion of eternal government (the basis of modern politics and the modern nation state) is infernal.[113] Agamben equates contemporary politics with the Christian hell, meaning that for him there is no legitimate authority left on earth.[114]

Unfree labour exists on a continuum. Today's unfree labour forms part of the broader history of unfree labour within capitalism.[115] The creation of unfree labour was always a racialised process, where extreme forms of subjection like forced labour were reserved for Black and Indigenous labour.[116] Mbembé explains that the experience of enslavement by Black slaves during early capitalism is now the norm for most of subaltern humanity. Today's practices of capital borrow as much from the slaving logic of capture and predation as from the colonial logics of occupation and extraction.[117] The

109 Lazzarato (2013) 103.
110 Kotsko (2015) 187–8.
111 Kotsko (2018) 89.
112 Cooper (2017) 18.
113 Agamben (2011) 164.
114 Agamben (2012) 40–1.
115 Gordon (2019) 925; Banaji (1977) 1–44; LeBaron and Ayers (2013) 878–9.
116 Gordon (2019) 926; Allen (1997); Allen (1994).
117 Mbembé (2017) 4.

colonial desire to produce difference and hierarchies created a fault line that we still live with.[118] Today race has become a technology of governance.[119]

Today's world is populated by 'outsiders', including hyper-exploited populations of colour who prop up capitalism from the margins but are treated as expendable.[120] Erased bodies are still useful to capital, either as direct cheap labour, or through motherhood – a source of reproduction of more cheap labour.[121] Temporary migrants who migrate from the Global South to the Global North are a product of neoliberal economics. Gordon explains that the background to their 'voluntary' movement is hunger and poverty caused by externally enforced structurally adjustment programmes, global capital and CMP and the ongoing impact of coloniality.[122] Populations across Africa have been abandoned through the creation of 'private indirect government'.[123] There has been a proliferation of export-processing zones with exceptional legal frameworks.[124]

In today's neoliberal world, space is also 'raced'. Particular spaces are designated as being dominated by persons of specific 'races'.[125] The *dispositif* of race controls which groups can circulate and which places they can occupy, and also ensures they do not threaten state control.[126] Racialised presence in particular is made illegal in a number of ways, from confinement to plantation, to strict immigration laws, to the creation of White spaces.[127] The restricted body is held perpetually in space, without power beyond this confinement, to use space for its own and communal possibilities.[128] Silvia Federici summarises:

> [C]apitalism must justify and mystify the contradictions built into its social relations ... by denigrating the 'nature' of those it exploits: women, colonial subjects, the descendants of African slaves, the immigrants displaced by globalisation.[129]

'Free' wage workers have a very shallow form of freedom. In reality, they are compelled to dispose of their labour power by the law and capitalist

118 Mbembé (2017) 6.
119 Mbembé (2017) 35.
120 Phipps (2020) 123.
121 Adébísí (2023) 73.
122 Gordon (2019) 932.
123 Mbembé (2001) 78–9.
124 Sassen (1988) ch 4.
125 Mills (1999) 41–53.
126 Mbembé (2019) 35–6.
127 Mbembé (2019) 79.
128 Adébísí (2023) 102.
129 Federici (2014) 17.

economics.[130] Even the most secure 'free' wage workers cannot escape this precarity. Even if employment is found there is no control for the worker over the conditions of work (apart from those gained by struggle and campaigns).[131] Selling one's labour power is a way of mediating the 'economic bondage' at the centre of the capitalist labour market,[132] but there is no certainty that there will be a buyer for this sale.[133] The worker's subjectivity is constituted around the loss of his humanity, as they could be thrown onto the street if they fail to pay rent.[134] Private property, supported by the deregulation of markets, working in conjunction with the bureaucrats of hollowed-out nation states have created a new biopolitical economy based on bare life.[135] Capitalist freedom in this light becomes its opposite – unfreedom.[136]

Slavery and technology

Many problems have had technology thrown at them as a way of 'fixing' the issue.[137] But technology will not save us. The machine, like the figure of the slave, intends to liberate human beings from necessity. For the ancient Greeks, the liberation promised by slavery was political life. For us moderns, technology promises the possibility of mastering the forces of nature:

> [T]he symmetry between the slave and the machine … concerns the ultimate achievement of anthropogenesis, the becoming fully human of the living human being. … In this sense, slavery is to ancient humanity what technology is to modern humanity: both as bare life, watch over the threshold that allows access to the truly human condition.[138]

Agamben contends that the slave is an ancient category of technology. How Western philosophy has always thought of technology is connected to the figure of the 'slave'.[139] Agamben's charge is not original (although he makes no claims for it being so). This evokes Marx's critique of Aristotle, where Marx claimed that to say technology would help us escape from slavery was equivalent to claiming that slavery was natural and would endure forever.[140]

130 Gordon (2019) 932.
131 Gordon (2019) 930.
132 Marx (1990) 723.
133 Gordon (2019) 930.
134 Timofeeva (2017) 439; Marx (2007) 135.
135 Barkan (2009) 244.
136 Gordon (2019) 930.
137 DeCook (2021) 1160.
138 Agamben (2016) 78.
139 Agamben (2016) 11.
140 Marx (1990) 532–3.

I have explored how artificial intelligence has always had a close relationship with the figure of the slave. Robots were created to produce the same jobs as slaves.[141] Robots in classical Greek literature functioned as a utopian substitute for slavery and forced labour.[142] Aristotle conceived of a system where enslaved people come together with artificial servants to do useful work, both acting as different types of instruments.[143] Technology would still require slavery, and such an economy would never be revolutionary.[144]

Agamben's comments on technology must be read in light of Heidegger's essay, 'The Question Concerning Technology'. Heidegger considers the 'essence' of modern technology as a mode of being, or revealing, not something that we make. To consider the 'essence' of technology involves the ordering of everything around us, and ourselves.[145] Modern technology looks to manipulate nature, impose on it, and extract from it, stockpiling resources, and is distinct from earlier technologies.[146] In a manner evocative of Heidegger's framing, Agamben argues that by today's dependence on technology, we have estranged ourselves from the animal and organic and drawn close to the machine and the inorganic to the point of nearly identifying with them, as a human-machine. This master-slave relationship tracks historical change simply by how it is captured in law and then formally abolished and superseded by the alienation of technology.[147]

Heidegger stated that technology comes to presence in the realm where revealing and unconcealment take place, and where *alētheia*, truth, happens.[148] This revealing is the 'open',[149] and it is because human beings occur in this openness that something like a *polis* and politics are possible.[150] The essence of technology is a 'challenging', *Gestell*, Enframing.[151] But we are challenged to impose order everywhere as if it were already there before we imposed it. This is the 'standing-reserve', where everything is 'challenged' to be an orderly resource for technical application, which in turn we take as a resource for further use.[152] Humanity is also made to be on call as a standing-reserve, made to wait for a series of revelations whose only real consequence is to place man in the position of those who are ordered.[153]

141 LaGrandeur (2020) 232.
142 Devecka (2013) 52.
143 Devecka (2013) 60–1; Aristotle (1984b) 1253b28–34.
144 Devecka (2013) 66.
145 Heidegger (1977) 12.
146 Heidegger (1977) 14–15.
147 Agamben (2016) 79.
148 Heidegger (1977) 13.
149 Agamben (2004) 57–8.
150 Agamben (2004) 73.
151 Heidegger (1977) 19.
152 Heidegger (1977) 13.
153 Campbell (2011) 55.

Technology replaces the familiar connection from parts to wholes; everything is an exchangeable piece. Machines and human beings become exchangeable pieces. Isolated machine pieces are uniform and exchangeable.[154] In a sense, Heidegger is warning against the way technology makes the human being into a kind of animated instrument. Technology mediates the relationship between the living being and the world, but also estranges this relationship. Technology has *become* the world. Its domination makes us forget our understanding of ourselves as the beings who can stand within this realm. We no longer realise the world that we have lost.[155]

Agamben reads technology as an apparatus dividing the living being. This Enframing is a hegemonic force at the heart of the essence of modern technology.[156] The Foucauldian apparatus or *dispositif* is etymologically related to Heidegger's *Gestell*, being similar to *dis-positio*, just as the German *Stellen* corresponds to the Latin *ponere*, the root from which the *dispositio* can trace its origins.[157] The Enframing of modern technology is a practice or form of knowledge that seeks to manage, govern, control and orient the behaviours, gestures and thoughts of human beings.[158] To add to Heidegger: technology or machines that could liberate if put to common use, fell into the hands of a few and became tools for subjection.[159] Technology and artificial intelligence are today facets of the domain (coloniality of knowledge) that is taken over, including the actors and institutions generating them.[160]

This is why Agamben sees technology as watching over the threshold of the truly human condition. But this focus has led to Agamben reaching some deeply problematic conclusions regarding modern technology. In writing about the coronavirus pandemic, and the measures taken around the world to promote social distancing, vaccinations and restrictions on individual mobility to prevent the spread of the virus, Agamben viewed this as allowing national governments to turn our politics into a permanent state of exception.[161] Preventative measures were read as a 'health religion',[162] modern medicine was a 'cultic practice' no longer free or voluntary but was mandatory.[163] Instead, Agamben advocated a "humbler, simpler form of life", which was previously lived and which we were said to have memories of.[164] For

154 Heidegger (1977) 20–1.
155 Heidegger (1977) 19.
156 Heidegger (1977) 21.
157 Agamben (2009b) 12; Campbell (2011) 54.
158 Agamben (2009b) 12.
159 Devecka (2013) 65.
160 Mignolo and Walsh (2018) 197.
161 Agamben (2021) 28.
162 Agamben (2021) 115.
163 Agamben (2021) 51.
164 Agamben (2021) 115.

Benjamin Bratton, Agamben learned the wrong lessons about the pandemic. The pandemic revealed pre-existing conditions, including the consequences of poor government planning and broken social systems.[165] Countries used the pandemic to remove populations of people to their countries of passport with little notice.[166]

Agamben's view of technology does not focus on its misuse, or on how the modern technology industry is rooted in the exploitation of people of colour across the globe.[167] His arguments about technology appear to reflect a broader critique of modernity. On this reading, technology in all its forms has eventually led to the concentration camp and the production of dominated subjects. When Agamben has written of human potentiality, he does not mention technology. Instead, he states that potentiality has a lapidary formula, mentioned in relation to Aristotle's *Metaphysics*,[168] and Melville's Bartleby.[169] Agamben's position means he does not engage with the literature exploring how technology is shaped by race and the CMP.

To accept technology as an apparatus also does not mean an implicit rejection of all technology, especially considering the slave-as-technology is identified as a use of the body. But there is no discussion in Agamben of how racial capitalism has shaped the development of today's digitally based society,[170] and how racial capital uses digital resources as a way to accumulate and expropriate,[171] and to shape the creative industries.[172] Digital technologies are presented as neutral and progressive but have a racialising potential.[173] Corporations have used surveillance capitalism to create digital communication technologies that govern and structure how we understand the world. This has been tied to 'White world-making', with digital bias reified on racial lines.[174] Technology is created by humans, so it carries with it the same limitations as humanity in terms of its ability to transcend our categorisations of race, class, gender and ability.[175] The 'source code' already holds the assumptions of all of these categories of difference, as it is written from the epistemological standpoint and values of those who create it.[176]

165 Bratton (2021) 5.
166 Bratton (2021) 15.
167 Hampton (2023).
168 Agamben (1998) 32; Aristotle (1984a) 1046a.
169 Agamben (1999) 262.
170 McMillan Cottom (2020).
171 Melamed (2015) 78.
172 Turner and Hui (2023).
173 Franklin (2021); Beller (2021).
174 Jooste (2021).
175 Benjamin (2019).
176 Umoja Noble (2018).

Even optimistic predictions of technology reaffirm racialised and gendered paradigms. The surrogate human performs degraded work meant to be invisible.[177] This hybrid of machine (technology) and organism is what Haraway called a cyborg.[178] It is "a cybernetic organism, a hybrid of machine and organism, a creature of social reality as well as a creature of fiction".[179] The cyborg appears in myth at the point where the human/animal boundary is transgressed. This is also where the figure of the slave is situated.[180] Haraway uses the cyborg to investigate how and why boundaries and dichotomies between the human and non-human are created. These artificial divisions shape our understanding of bodily capacities, desire and power in certain ways, and the construction of bodies is caused by the effects of capitalism.[181] Today's technology makes ambiguous the difference between natural and artificial.[182] The cyborg has potent fusions, as well as dangerous possibilities. A hopeful interpretation of the cyborg points towards "lived social and bodily realities in which people are not afraid of their joint kinship with animals and machines, not afraid of permanently partial and contradictory standpoints".[183] It is not clear who is made and who is doing the making in the human-machine relationship.[184]

But the cyborg also represents the universality of Euro-modern gender formations and a hegemony of Western biologism.[185] As a result, the boundary between the human and non-human are subject to the judgments and prejudices of Euro-modernity. The idea of the cyborg is borne out of a Western philosophy of selfhood and technology. Epistemic sites of thought in theorising the relationship between technology and the living being exist within the same epistemic paradigms upon which science and technology are built – colonial, Euro-modern, White – and therefore are limited in conceptualising any figure beyond the Euro-modern subject.[186]

Technology also forms what Lazzarato termed 'machinic enslavement'. For Lazzarato, the relationship between subjectivity and the mode of production has become dysfunctional to the extent that "today the weakness of capitalism lies in the production of subjectivity".[187] Lazzarato's work, like Agamben's, is Eurocentric, and does not engage with the logics of racial

177 Atanasoski and Vora (2015).
178 Haraway (1985) 5.
179 Haraway (1985) 149.
180 Haraway (1985) 11.
181 Haraway (2016).
182 Haraway (1985) 11.
183 Haraway (1985) 154.
184 Haraway (1985) 60.
185 Oyěwùmí (1997).
186 DeCook (2021) 1164.
187 Lazzarato (2014) 8.

capitalism.[188] But he offers insights into the way capitalism and technology interact to produce new structures of domination and enslavement. Again evocative of Heidegger's view that technology makes machines and human beings into interchangeable pieces, machinic enslavement describes the way sub-individual and supra-individual human elements are put to work as cogs in complex machines that are not just technical machines.[189] Lazzarato explains:

> Intelligence, affects, sensations, cognition, memory, and physical force are now components whose synthesis no longer lies in the person but in the assemblage or process.[190]

Just like with Aristotle, and the Atlantic slave trade, machinic enslavement repeats the principle that some people are to be enslaved naturally, whilst the 'owners' control the means of production and the production of credit. This can be connected to the CMP and the racialised nature of the neoliberal economy. More than this, those enslaved by the neoliberal regime and racial capitalism, and stuck in an unending cycle of debt, underpaid work or unemployment, 'deserve' such an outcome and it is their fault they do not amount to more. Just like the Black African deserved to be enslaved and was only good enough to till the cotton fields in the American South, or cut down sugar cane in Jamaica, today's indebted worker is no good for anything else. The commodity comes to know herself only through being subject to exchange and being embedded in a society that itself is shaped by exchange.[191]

Machinic enslavement arises out of the growing reliance of capitalism on processes of production that function increasingly independently of human awareness or intention.[192] These vast machinic assemblages are akin to Marx's critique of how technology created large-scale machines of production to which the worker was an appendage.[193] Today, the machinic is everywhere. Financial capitalism is run by unaccountable financial traders and computer algorithms. These assemblages have human and non-human components, like stock markets, currency exchanges and mathematical equations, that are indifferent to our sense of ourselves as individuals. They can intervene in material flows, capturing, evaluating and transferring to harness and extract value from a range of divergent activities.[194] This is, to me, a direct analogy

188 Rose (2016) 103.
189 O'Shaughnessy (2019) 197.
190 Lazzarato (2014) 17.
191 Moten (2003) 9.
192 Deleuze and Guattari (1985) 451.
193 Lazzarato (2014) 81.
194 Lazzarato (2014) 41.

with Agamben's own definition of technology as a modern dominating apparatus that brings the human being into relation with the machine. Just as in Marx's time, the new slave is invisible, which involves being recognised as the unrecognisable, and as a metaphor which has a distinct meaning apart from the living being who is enslaved.[195]

How can we resist and transform such a situation?[196] It is necessary to hide from human beings the fact that they have no set purpose.[197] Human inoperativity is something that emerges only when the economy, neoliberalism, is stopped. In this sense, the outcome of capitalism is not communism, but the dead end of neoliberalism.[198] Lazzarato terms this form of inoperativity 'laziness'. Tim Christiaens sees the practice of laziness as separating life from the capitalist demands of productivity and therefore releasing blocked potentialities.[199] Laziness, as the refusal to work, opens the possibility for new ways of life outside racial capitalism. This is a kind of escape, a human mobility which the State must prevent.[200]

Lazzarato's laziness is analogous to the way I contend hyper-hermeneutic gestures expose humanity's creative semi-indifference to any task.[201] This laziness is akin to an experience of creativity during moments of rest.[202] Likewise, *kairotic* gestures, fulfilled in the moment of the now, are creative in the way they change time.[203] These are moments that must be seized.[204] Such 'now-time' means that the present is inseparably linked to the past as well as the future. Time is created by events within a community, events which must be experienced to be real.[205] 'Now' gives a crucial symbolic value to an event. These events are enacted by remnants, who resist prevailing apparatuses.[206] Life's various moments (the past and the present especially) are "infinitely connected",[207] liberating forms of life from continuous linear time.[208]

The issue with a focus on laziness is that such behaviour could be accommodated within neoliberal capitalism. Christiaens gives the example of Joseph Schumpeter's theory of entrepreneurship. For Schumpeter, entrepreneurs are not economic agents conforming to market conditions, looking for

195 Moten (2003) 68.
196 Kotsko (2015) 184.
197 Kotsko (2015) 191.
198 Kotsko (2015) 198.
199 Christiaens (2018) 259.
200 Agamben (2007c) 86.
201 Agamben (2000) 141–2.
202 Christiaens (2018) 259.
203 Agamben (2007a) 99, 110–111.
204 Aarons (2020) 51.
205 Mbiti (1969) 17.
206 Agamben (2005) 57.
207 Agamben (2023b) 309–10.
208 Agamben (2007a) 115.

the highest possible profits. Instead, they make risky investments in promising ventures.[209] Laziness involves a potential to exceed the bounds of immediate capital accumulation. But this is precisely what Schumpeter is advocating too.[210] This laziness is therefore part of the imaginary of neoliberalism. The creative space opened by laziness is part of the entrepreneurial framework in terms of innovation and seeking future profits.[211]

But this is too harsh. What we see with Agamben's own conception of potentiality and inoperative resistance is a deeper questioning of the economic system. Agamben's form-of-life suggests that we can maintain a positive relationship with this inappropriable or impersonal part of life, the empty centre which the economic sphere continues to try and grasp and control. Christiaens states that instead of panic, shame, or disgust, we should learn to love this part of ourselves and others.[212] Human unity is not found in the body or the cultural or legal construct of the individual, but in form-of-life.[213] We overcome the *whatness* of our constructed identities, the socio-institutional categories designed to reinforce our separation, by becoming a *how* together, as we interact by means of shared gestures.[214]

Constituting a form-of-life means destituting the social and biological conditions into which it finds itself thrown.[215] These conditions are the CMP, the coloniality which has constructed our world and the existence and operation of racial capitalism. In Kieran Aarons words:

> To destitute an order of relations is first of all to deprive it of any relevance, to strip it of any significance. However, far from a strictly negative project, destitution is inseparable from the positive elaboration of a new evaluation of the important and the interesting, the alluring and the repugnant, the tolerable and the intolerable.[216]

Inoperativity coincides with destitution, and the fact of a life, the basis of the coming politics, and a politics based in paradigmatic gestures.[217] Destituent power is no longer simply the immediate recuperation of alienated human beings but rather an always latent possibility of non-alienated living perpetually deferred and rendered increasingly impossible.

209 Schumpeter (2008) 81–6.
210 Christiaens (2018) 264.
211 Christiaens (2018) 265.
212 Christiaens (2018) 269; Zartaloudis (2010) 286–7.
213 Tiqqun (2010).
214 Aarons (2016).
215 Agamben (2014) 74.
216 Aarons (2016).
217 Agamben (2014) 65.

Hope in the present

Today, the *Zong* is recreated in the Mediterranean every day. Men, women and children who are not recognised as rights-bearing figures belonging to European legal orders still risk their lives trying to reach Europe. Indigenous peoples around the world are marginalised, racially ordered and subjected to brutal state violence and control. Exploitation is necessary for the lucky few to enjoy a political system founded on claims of justice, equality and fairness. Yet this is no surprise. The Enlightenment was creating modern ideas of democracy and liberty whilst the sugar cane fields of the Caribbean were full of kidnapped men, women and children. Just as Aristotle could write of 'natural slavery' and divide humanity, all the while ignoring the lived experience and actions of enslaved persons in Athens, today legal and political theory and philosophy grapples with questions of right, anti-discrimination and sustainability whilst ignoring the lives and actions of liminal figures.

So where do we find hope today? The success of neoliberalism has led to a new form of enslavement. Racial capitalism has created liminal figures. We need to be attentive to shared sites of resistance and refusal, beyond the focus of constituent and constituted power to the formal political process in a democratic state. The point is not to change the machine, but to deactivate it, destitute it, and create possibilities which the CMP and racial capitalism deny exist. Form-of-life destitutes existing social conditions by using them.[218]

As Agamben states, the coming politics will not be a struggle to control the State. It will be a struggle between the State and the non-State, humanity.[219] But the State cannot tolerate singularities that form a community without affirming an identity recognised by the State.[220] I have traced ways in which enslaved people in both the ancient world, and throughout the CMP, have done just this. These are singular beings who have sought to live lives outside of the nation state or empire. But whenever singularities demonstrate their being in common, the State reacts.[221] For example, Papadopoulos, Stephenson and Tsianos understand the formation of power other than the nation state from the perspective of escaping people. People's escape, flight, subversion, refusal, desertion, sabotage or acting independently of existing political structures forces state sovereignty to manifest itself in response.[222]

Forms of life seek to maintain their singularity and mobility to live as a form-of-life. In response, modern states in the CMP claim authority and power over all forms of human mobility and political belonging. It is in these actions and gestures, these slight glimmers of hope, that we can see the image

218 Agamben (2016) 274.
219 Agamben (2007c) 85.
220 Agamben (2007c) 86.
221 Agamben (2007c) 87.
222 Papadopoulos, Stephenson and Tsianos (2008) 43.

of a life that is not divided, that does not depend on division and remainders, and which threatens the very structures of politics that we exist under. These past events, *kairological* in nature, have shaped today's world. These actions and forms also presented past gestures which could be, and were, of influence on other (later) forms-of-life, providing inspiration and influence on other forms of resistance to coloniality. These are (in Jesi's terms), revolts which crystallise a shared horizon of experience, generating a distinct 'common'.[223] In a revolt a human being determines their self-realisation as part of a collective.[224]

What is at stake in these lives (viewed as liminal from the perspective of racial capitalism) is living itself.[225] Inactivity is not non-activity. Seeking inactivity outside of the confines of racial capitalism does not become devoid of value because the apparatuses of capitalism seek to reappropriate this zone of being. Human life is idle and aimless in the sense that it has no inherent purpose. Racial capitalism seeks to appropriate this and transform it into an endless busyness. Inactivity is reduced to appearances in dreams and political utopias.[226] But just like a work of art, such action can acquire political significance. It is an operation that contemplates and renders non-operational man's senses and usual actions, thus opening them to new possible uses. What art achieves by the senses; politics has to achieve by the power of action.[227] Both politics and art name the dimension in which works are deactivated in order to liberate the inoperativity that remained imprisoned within them.[228]

Agamben's writings have needed development to combat their Eurocentricity. An example: for Agamben the face is an opening, a threshold, to another person.[229] It is also the way through which the human being exposes himself and communicates, in a gesture.[230] All living beings manifest themselves in their appearance, and politics causes appearance to appear.[231] The face is a fundamental opening and the only location of community.[232] For Agamben, if a face is encountered by the subject, the subject experiences an exteriority, another person. This is characterised as having "an *outside* happen to me".[233]

223 Aarons (2019) 1024.
224 Jesi (2014) 53.
225 Agamben (2014) 73.
226 Agamben (2008) 138.
227 Agamben (2008) 140–1.
228 Agamben (2016) 278.
229 Agamben (2000) 91.
230 Agamben, (2022) 14.
231 Agamben (2007c) 39.
232 Agamben (2000) 91.
233 Agamben (2000) 100.

But what of the human being who covers their face (or, for that matter, their body)? There appears to be a presumption here that an exposure of the face is what is the source of politics. French republicanism states that it exercises a colour-blind universalism,[234] in its radical indifference to difference.[235] Connecting the commentary on the cyborg, technology, neoliberalism and the *dispositif* of race: in recent years the French Republic has criminalised face coverings in public spaces (*racing* space), remaking particular spaces for certain 'races'. This legislation has specifically targeted Islamic dress, which is constituted through difference. The desire for others to recognise us is what makes us human. This recognition is essential, so much so that people even risk their lives to obtain it.[236] Under Agamben's schema, a covering of the face could restrict or remove the encounter between humans, removing the relation of recognition that underscores all politics and ethics. As he stated, a country that 'renounces' its face, and which masks the faces of its citizens, is a country that has "purged itself of any political dimension".[237]

This illustrates a category-error in Agamben's thought (which Mbembé identifies), namely a colour-blindness with respect to race which actually reinforces a colonialist logic. As Kimberley Brayson explains, the policy of assimilation toward minority migrant Muslim communities has been the colonial method of the French state since the nineteenth century to the present.[238] In Algeria the French colonial authorities systematically unveiled women, using the language of liberation to describe their actions.[239] The veil came to represent Algerian resistance against colonialism, and in criminalising Islamic dress in the present, the French state evidences the attachment of the colonial past to the present and future.[240] This produces the Whiteness of public space, making it inhospitable to Muslim women, their families and their communities.[241] The term 'Muslim women' is also inherently problematic for the universalism that it propagates, denying cultural variations and specificities.[242] To follow a logic which equates the naked face with politics is to reconstruct a Eurocentric logic whereby face coverings are born elsewhere.

Agamben's philosophy reflects a form of anarchism, but again an anarchism that is understood as a destituent, rather than a constituent power. Anarchy deactivates apparatuses.[243] What would it mean to translate into

234 Mbembé (2021) 60.
235 Mbembé (2021) 123.
236 Agamben (2010) 46.
237 Agamben (2021) 87.
238 Brayson (2019) 62.
239 Fanon (1965) 62–3.
240 Brayson (2019) 62.
241 Brayson (2019) 79–80.
242 Brayson (2021) 238.
243 Agamben (2016) 277.

action a destituent potential in a constituted political system? For Agamben, it would mean thinking of an element that, while remaining heterogeneous to the system, was able to render decisions destitute, suspending them and rendering them inoperative.[244] Agamben gives the example of Plato's Nocturnal Council at the end of the *Laws* as an example of such a destituent element.[245] The status of the Nocturnal Council is unclear amongst scholars.[246] One view reads the role of the Council as attempting to improve the laws of Magnesia through the application of philosophic knowledge.[247] Alexander Verlinsky has argued that the Council was intended to have law-making and law-enforcing powers.[248] George Klosko was of the view that the Council, endowed with supreme political authority, was close to the dictatorial rule of the philosophers Plato outlined in the *Republic*.[249] 30 years later, Klosko wrote of the contradictory position of the Council and its powers in Plato's thought, with the *Laws* being an incomplete major theoretical shift on his part.[250]

Agamben's reading of the Council is one which does not subsume it into either constituted or constituent power.[251] Agamben presents the Council as a protector of the city, which is not an institution in "a technical sense" because it is impossible to lay down the Council's activities until it has been established.[252] Sergei Prozorov reads Agamben as claiming the Council does not give philosophers constituent sovereign power (as was the case in the *Republic*), but only giving them the destituent power of contemplating changes to the laws of the city.[253] But Prozorov critiques Agamben's reading by turning to another passage of the *Laws*, the Council's function of punishing atheists.[254] Atheists who are honest about their atheism are to spend five years in a reformatory and can only speak with Council members who are responsible for saving their souls. Prozorov asks how the philosophy of the Council would save those stuck in a deficit of existence, and how this is not a form of repressive apparatus of re-education targeting the youth of the city.[255]

244 Agamben (2016) 278–9.
245 Agamben (2016) 279.
246 Prozorov (2017) 159.
247 Morrow (1993) 501–11; Lewis (2018) 1–20.
248 Verlinsky (2016).
249 Klosko (1988) 74–88.
250 Klosko (2008) 466–71.
251 Prozorov (2017) 159; Plato (2005) 968c.
252 Agamben (2016) 279; Plato (2005) 968c.
253 Prozorov (2017) 159–60.
254 Prozorov (2017) 160; Plato (2005) 908a–909a.
255 Prozorov (2017) 160.

Agamben's aim is to display the radical heterogeneity of destituent potential.[256] I propose, following my arguments throughout this study, that enslaved people have provided examples of destituent potential throughout history and especially in the world of the CMP. The enslaved person (and for that matter, the person living under colonialism) could not have a juridical *persona* and was considered inhuman. But some humanity always remains, and these actions and gestures of persons abandoned beneath the abyssal line actually show us a form of life that is not dependent upon a remnant or residual remainder in order for it to constitute itself.[257] Enslaved people have been carving out forms of life in the face of statist and imperial oppression, showing the potential for non-statist and non-capitalist politics today. Such gestures perforate and deform the modern state, showing how statist recognition is not needed for form-of-life. We must build our political future starting with liminal figures. Writing in 1995, in relation to the figure of the refugee, Agamben predicted that:

> Only in a world in which the spaces of states have been thus perforated and topologically deformed ... only in such a world is the political survival of humankind today unthinkable.[258]

What is our task? We must be contemporary, to focus on our own time and perceive not its light, but its darkness.[259] We must not be blinded by the lights of modernity, and the CMP, which obscures the glimpse of the shadows of those lights.[260] What is unlived in the present is what is contemporary, a present where we have never been, given modernity's fascination with capitalism, the nation state, and charters of human rights.[261] To be contemporary is to encounter other times and generations, transforming time and putting it in relation to other times.[262] We must read history in unforeseen ways. Darkness today is an invisible light that casts a shadow on the past. The past is touched by this shadow and acquires an ability to respond to the darkness.[263]

Throughout Western political and legal philosophy, the *figure* of the slave has acted as a light, obscuring the myriad lives and ways of being that enslaved people have lived. In focusing on the way the figure of the slave helped apparatuses of power construct ideas of freedom and belonging, we lost the light in the shadows. I have used Agamben's thought to focus back

256 Agamben (2016) 279.
257 Agamben (2010) 52–3.
258 Agamben (2000) 26.
259 Agamben (2009b) 44.
260 Agamben (2009b) 45.
261 Agamben (2009b) 51.
262 Agamben (2009b) 53.
263 Agamben (2009b) 53.

on this darkness, on the records of forms of life striving to exist just as they are, without remainder. From the unruly slaves chastised in Aristotle's writings, to the rebels of the Roman Empire, to the men, women and children in Maroon communities, living in the face of the CMP, enslaved people have been attempting to live lives through their gestures and actions. The state and power relations have, brutally and without mercy, consistently sought to crush those shoots of potential. And yet they still stand as an exemplum from which we can be influenced today.

Around the modern capitalistic world, we must search for similar acts of potential, and live our lives as a form. This would involve forging new relationships outside of the power of the State, or of modern capital. It would involve accepting that a philosophy of hyper-hermeneutics can mean that even seemingly small and insignificant acts can lead to apparatuses of control being rendered inoperative. It would involve understanding that any future revolt does not require large-scale planning or a manifesto for radical change, and that living our lives as a form is a decision that we can all make ourselves. It would involve destituting apparatuses (of the state, of the social order, of dominant power relations) and turning them to a new use. It would involve a rejection of the CMP and any definition of life or politics which requires a remainder of humanity for it to be built on. It would involve a lack of prescription in our politics, an acceptance that the landscape of the world in which we live is being exploited in the name of racial capital, and an acceptance of the fact that justice demands our futures on this planet are sustainable for all. Finally, it would involve an acknowledgment that any destituent politics would face determined opposition, and whether or not we would be successful in this task is a question I, and you, cannot answer. But this is a task that is demanded of us, and one that, if we are serious about justice and the ability of philosophy and politics to make the world better, we cannot ignore.[264]

Reference List

Aarons, K (2016) 'No Selves To Abolish: Afropessimism, Anti-Politics and the End of the World', *MetaMute* (29 February 2016) http://www.metamute.org/editorial/articles/no-selves-to-abolish-afropessimism-anti-politics-and-end-world.

264 It is not possible to complete a project of any length without support and guidance. I am deeply grateful for the conversations I had and advice I received from Carin Tunåker, Suhraiya Jivraj. Vidya Kumar, Maria Drakopoulou, Alex Damianos, Kim Brayson, Philipp Kender, Gian-Giacomo Fusco, Connal Parsley, Thanos Zartaloudis, and many others as well. Thanks also go to Sally Kyd and Rosemary Hunter who provided help and support as Heads of School. Lastly, my thanks go to Tanya Palmer, who proof read much of the text and provided very valuable comments and feedback, without which this project would not have been completed.

Aarons, K (2019) 'Cruel Festivals: Furio Jesi and the Critique of Political Autonomy', *Theory & Event*, 22, 1018–46.

Aarons, K (2020) 'Destitution and Creation: Agamben's Messianic Gesture', *Journal of Italian Philosophy*, 3, 51–89.

Achinte, A A (2012) 'Epistemes "otras" ¿Epistemes Disruptivas?', *KULA. Antropólogos del Atlántico Sur*, 6, 22–34.

Adébísí, F (2023) *Decolonisation and Legal Knowledge: Reflections on Power and Possibility*, Bristol: Bristol University Press.

Agamben, G (1998) *Homo Sacer: Sovereign Power and Bare Life,* Heller-Roazen, D (trans.), Stanford: Stanford University Press.

Agamben, G (1999) 'Bartleby, or On Contingency' in *Potentialities: Collected Essays in Philosophy*, Heller-Roazen, D (trans.), Stanford: Stanford University Press, 243–71.

Agamben, G (2000) *Means Without End: Notes on Politics*, Binetti, V and Casarino, C (trans.), Minneapolis: University of Minnesota Press.

Agamben, G (2004) *The Open: Man and Animal*, Attell, K (trans.), Stanford: Stanford University Press.

Agamben, G (2005) *The Time That Remains: A Commentary on the Letter to the Romans*, Dailey, P (trans.), Stanford: Stanford University Press.

Agamben, G (2007a) *Infancy and History: On the Destruction of Experience*, Heron, L (trans.), London: Verso Books.

Agamben, G (2007b) *Profanations*, Fort, J (trans.), Princeton: Princeton University Press.

Agamben, G (2007c) *The Coming Community*, Hardt, M (trans.), Minneapolis: University of Minnesota Press.

Agamben, G (2008), 'Art, Inactivity, Politics' in Backstein, J, Birnbaum, D, and Wallenstein, S-O (eds.), *Thinking Worlds: The Moscow Conference on Philosophy, Politics, and Art*, Berlin: Sternberg Press, 131–41.

Agamben, G (2009a) *The Signature of All Things: On Method*, D'Isanto, L and Attell, K (trans.), New York: Zone Books.

Agamben, G (2009b) *What Is an Apparatus? and Other Essays*, Kishik, D and Pedatella, S (trans.), Stanford: Stanford University Press.

Agamben, G (2010) *Nudities*, Kishik, D and Pedatella, S (trans.), Stanford: Stanford University Press.

Agamben, G (2011) *The Kingdom and the Glory: For a Theological Genealogy of Economy and Government*, Chiesa, L and Mandarini, M (trans.), Stanford: Stanford University Press.

Agamben, G (2012) *The Church and the Kingdom*, de la Durantaye, L (trans.), London: Seagull Books.

Agamben, G (2014) 'What Is a Destituent Power?', *Environment and Planning D: Society and Space*, 32, 65–74.

Agamben, G (2016) *The Use of Bodies*, Kotsko, A (trans.), Stanford: Stanford University Press.

Agamben, G (2019) *Creation and Anarchy: The Work of Art and the Religion of Capitalism*, Kotsko, A (trans.), Stanford: Stanford University Press.

Agamben, G (2021) *Where Are We Now? The Epidemic As Politics*, Dani, V (trans), London: Eris Books.

Agamben, G (2022) *When the House Burns Down: From the Dialect of Thought*, Attell, K (trans.), Calcutta, Seagull Books.
Agamben, G (2023a) *Destituent Potentiality and the Critique of Realization*, The South Atlantic Quarterly, 112, 9-17.
Agamben, G (2023b) *Hölderlin's Madness: Chronicle of a Dwelling Life, 1806–1843*, Price, A L (trans.), Chicago, University of Chicago Press.
Allen, T (1994) *The Invention of the White Race, Volume 1: Racial Oppression and Social Control*, London: Verso.
Allen, T (1997) *The Invention of the White Race, Volume 2: The Origin of Racial Oppression in Anglo-America*, London: Verso.
Aristotle (1984a) 'Metaphysics' in *The Complete Works of Aristotle, Volume Two*, Barnes, J (ed.), Princeton: Princeton University Press.
Aristotle (1984b) 'Politics' in *The Complete Works of Aristotle, Volume Two*, Barnes, J (ed.), Princeton: Princeton University Press.
Atanasoki, N and Vora, N (2015) 'Surrogate Humanity: Posthuman Networks and the (Racialized) Obsolescence of Labor', *Catalyst: Feminism, Theory, Technoscience*, 1, 7. https://catalystjournal.org/index.php/catalyst/article/view/ata_vora.
Bakunin, M (1964) *The Political Philosophy of Bakunin: Scientific Anarchism*, Maximoff, E (ed.), London: Free Press of Glencoe.
Banaji, J (1977) 'Modes of Production in a Materialist Conception of History', *Capitalist and Class*, 1, 1–44.
Banaji, J (2010) *Theory as History: Essays on Modes of Production and Exploitation*, Leiden: Brill.
Barkan, J (2009) 'Use Beyond Value: Giorgio Agamben and a Critique of Capitalism', *Rethinking Marxism*, 21, 243–59.
Beller, J (2021) *The World Computer: Conditions of Racial Capitalism*, Durham: Duke University Press.
Benjamin, R (2019) *Race After Technology: Abolitionist Tools for the New Jim Code*, Medford: Polity Press.
Benjamin, W (1999) 'Theses on the Philosophy of History' in *Illuminations*, Zorn, H (trans.), London: Pimlico, 245–55.
Benjamin, W (2004) 'Capitalism as Religion' in *Walter Benjamin, Selected Writings, Volume 1: 1913–1926*, Bullock, M & Jennings, M (eds.), Cambridge: Harvard University Press, 288–91.
Bezanson, K and Luxton, M (eds.) (2006) *Social Reproduction: Feminist Political Economy Challenges Neoliberalism*, Montreal and Kingston: McGill-Queen's University Press.
Birrell, K and Matthews, D (2020) 'Laws for the Anthropocene: Orientations, Encounters, Imaginaries', *Law & Critique*, 31, 233–38.
Blackburn, R (1988) *The Overthrow of Colonial Slavery, 1776–1848*, London: Verso.
Blackburn, R (1997) *The Making of New World Slavery*, London: Verso.
Bratton, B (2021) *The Revenge of the Real: Politics for a Post-Pandemic World*, London and New York: Verso.
Brayson, K (2019) 'Of Bodies and Burkinis: Institutional Islamophobia, Islamic Dress, and the Colonial Condition', *Journal of Law and Society*, 46, 55–82.

Brayson, K (2021) 'Swimming Pools, Islamic Dress and Colonial Differentiation: The Cleansing Role of the Law in 'the Republic [That] Lives through an Uncovered Face', *Journal of Gender Studies*, 30, 237–52.

Campbell, T (2011) *Improper Life: Technology and Biopolitics from Heidegger to Agamben*, Minneapolis: University of Minnesota Press.

Césaire, A (1973) *Discourse on Colonialism*, New York: Monthly Review Press.

Christiaens, T (2018) 'Neoliberalism and the Right to Be Lazy: Inactivity as Resistance in Lazzarato and Agamben', *Rethinking Marxism*, 30, 256–74.

Cooper, M (2017) *Family Values: Between Neoliberalism and the New Social Conservatism*, New York: Zone Books.

Critchley, S (2007) *Infinitely Demanding: Ethics of Commitment, Politics of Resistance*, London: Verso.

DeCook, J (2021) 'A [White] Cyborg's Manifesto: The Overwhelmingly Western Ideology Driving Technofeminist Theory', *Media, Culture & Society*, 43, 1158–67.

Deleuze, G and Guattari, F (1985) *A Thousand Plateaus: Capitalism and Schizophrenia*, Massumi, B (trans.), Minneapolis: University of Minnesota Press.

Devecka, M (2013) 'Did the Greeks Believe in Their Robots?', *The Cambridge Classical Journal*, 59, 52–69.

Douglass, F (2018) *Lessons of the Hour*, New Haven: Yale University Press.

Fanon, F (1965) *A Dying Colonialism*, Chevalier, H (trans.), New York: Grove Press.

Federici, S (2014) *Caliban and the Witch: Women, the Body, and Primitive Accumulation*, 2nd edn, New York: Autonomedia.

Foster, J B, Holleman, H and Clark, B (2020) 'Marx and Slavery', *Monthly Review*, 72, 96–117.

Franklin, S (2021) *The Digitally Disposed: Racial Capitalism and the Informatics of Value*, Minneapolis: University of Minnesota Press.

Gordon, T (2019) 'Capitalism, Neoliberalism, and Unfree Labour', *Critical Sociology*, 45, 921–39.

Hampton, L M (2023) 'Techno-Racial Capitalism: A Decolonial Black Feminist Marxist Perspective' in Browne, J, Cave, S, Drage, E and McInerney, K (eds.), *Feminist AI: Critical Perspectives on Algorithms, Data, and Intelligent Machines*, Oxford: Oxford University Press, 119–36.

Haraway, D (1985) *A Cyborg Manifesto: Science, Technology and Socialist-Feminism in the Late Twentieth Century*, Minneapolis: University of Minnesota Press.

Haraway, D (2016) *Staying with the Trouble: Making kin in the Chthulucene*, Durham: Duke University Press.

Hartman, S (1997) *Scenes of Subjection: Terror, Slavery, and Self-Making in Nineteenth-Century America*, Oxford: Oxford University Press.

Hartman, S (2008) 'Venus in Two Acts', *Small Axe*, 12, 1–14.

Heidegger, M (1977) *The Question Concerning Technology And Other Essays*, Lovitt, W (trans.), New York and London: Garland Publishing, Inc.

Jesi, F (2014) *Spartakus. The Symbology of Revolt*, Toscano, A (trans.), Chicago: Chicago University Press.

Johnson, W (2004) 'The Pedestal and the Veil', *Journal of the Early Republic*, 24, 299–308.

Jooste, Y (2021) 'Surveillance Capitalism as White World-Making', *Acta Academica*, 53, 44–67.

Kinna, R and Prichard, A (2019) 'Anarchism and Non-Domination', *Journal of Political Ideologies*, 24, 221–40.
Klosko, G (1988) 'The Nocturnal Council in Plato's *Laws*', *Political Studies*, 26, 74–88.
Klosko, G (2008) 'Knowledge and Law in Plato's *Laws*', *Political Studies*, 56, 456–74.
Kotsko, A (2015) 'The Theology of Neoliberalism' in Dickinson, C and Kotsko, A (eds.), *Agamben's Coming Philosophy: Finding a New Use for Theology*, New York: Rowman and Littlefield International, 183–200.
Kotsko, A (2018) *Neoliberalism's Demons: On the Late Political Theology of Late Capital*, Stanford: Stanford University Press.
LaGrandeur, K (2020) 'Artificial Slaves in the Renaissance and the Dangers of Independent Innovation' in Cave, S, Dihal, K and Dillon, K (eds.), *AI Narratives: A History of Imaginative Thinking about Intelligent Machines*, Oxford: Oxford University Press, 95–118.
Lazzarato, M (2012) *The Making of the Indebted Man*, Amsterdam: Semiotext(e).
Lazzarato, M (2013) *Governing by Debt*, Jordan, J D (trans.), Los Angeles: Semiotext(e).
Lazzarato, M (2014) *Signs and Machines: Capitalism and the Production of Subjectivity*, Los Angeles: Semiotext(e).
LeBaron, G and Ayers, A (2013) 'The Rise of a 'New Slavery'? Understanding African Unfree Labour through Neoliberalism', *Third World Quarterly*, 34, 873–92.
Lewis, D (2018) *Greek Slave Systems in their Eastern Mediterranean Context, c. 800–146 BC*, Oxford: Oxford University Press.
Marx, K (1968) *Theories of Surplus Value, Part II*, Moscow: Progress Publishers.
Marx, K (1971) *The Poverty of Philosophy*, Quelch, H (trans.), New York: International Publishers.
Marx, K (1973) *Grundrisse: Foundations of the Critique of Political Economy*, Nicolaus, M (trans.), Harmondsworth: Penguin.
Marx, K (1990) *Capital: A Critique of Political Economy, Vol. 1*, Moore, S and Aveling, E (trans.), Harmondsworth: Penguin.
Marx, K (2007) *Economic and Philosophical Manuscripts of 1844*, Milligan, M (trans.), Mineola: Dover.
Marx, K and Engels, F (1975) *Collected Works, Volume 30*, New York: International Publishers.
Mason, E (2020) 'Thing: A Fugitive in( )operation'', *Journal of Italian Philosophy*, 3, 163–89.
Mbembé, A (2001) *On the Postcolony*, Chicago: University of Chicago Press.
Mbembé, A (2017) *Critique of Black Reason*, Dubois, L (trans.), Durham: Duke University Press.
Mbembé, A (2019) *Necropolitics*, Durham: Duke University Press.
Mbembé, A (2021) *Out of the Dark Night: Essays on Decolonization*, Daniela Ginsburg (trans.), New York: Columbia University Press.
Mbiti, J (1969) *African Religions and Philosophy*, London: Heinemann.
McMillan Cottom, T (2020) 'Where Platform Capitalism and Racial Capitalism Meet: The Sociology of Race and Racism in the Digital Society', *Sociology of Race and Ethnicity*, 6, 441–49.
Melamed, J (2015) 'Racial Capitalism', *Critical Ethnic Studies*, 1, 76–85.

Mignolo, W and Walsh, C (2018) *On Decoloniality: Concepts, Analytics, Praxis*, Durham: Duke University Press.
Mills, C (1999) *The Racial Contract*, Ithaca and London: Cornell University Press.
Morrow, G (1993) *Plato's Cretan City: A Historical Interpretation of the* Laws, Princeton: Princeton University Press.
Moten, F (2003) *In the Break: The Aesthetics of the Black Radical Tradition*, Minneapolis: University of Minnesota Press.
Moten, F (2018) *Stolen Lives*, Durham: Duke University Press.
Newman, S (2000) 'Anarchism and the Politics of Ressentiment', *Theory & Event*, 4.
Newman, S (2010a) 'The Horizon of Anarchy: Anarchism and Contemporary Radical Thought', *Theory & Event*, 13.
Newman, S (2010b) *The Politics of Postanarchism*, Edinburgh: Edinburgh University Press.
O'Shaughnessy, M (2019) 'Beyond Language and the Subject: Machinic Enslavement in Contemporary European Cinema', *Studies in European Cinema*, 16, 197–217.
O'Connell Davison, J (2015) *Modern Slavery: The Margins of Freedom*, Basingstoke: Palgrave Macmillan.
Oyěwùmí, O (1997) *The Invention of Women: Making an African Sense of Western Gender Discourses*, Minneapolis: University of Minnesota Press.
Papadopoulos, D, Stephenson, N and Tsianos, V (2008) *Escape Routes: Control and Subversion in the Twenty-First Century*, London: Pluto.
Patterson, O (1982) *Slavery and Social Death: A Comparative Study*, Cambridge: Harvard University Press.
Phipps, A (2020) *Me, Not You: The Trouble with Mainstream Feminism*, Manchester: Manchester University Press.
Plato (2005) 'Laws' in *The Collected Dialogues, Including the Letters*, Hamilton, E and Cairns, H (eds.), Princeton: Princeton University Press.
Proudhon, P-J (1994) *What Is Property? Or, an Inquiry into the Principle of Right and of Government*, Kelley, D R and Smith, B G (trans.), Cambridge: Cambridge University Press.
Proudhon, P-J (2011) 'Letter to Bastiat' in Tucker, B and McKay, I (eds.), *Property Is Theft!: A Pierre-Joseph Proudhon Anthology*, Edinburgh: AK Press.
Prozorov, S (2017) 'Living *à la mode*: Form-of-Life and Democratic Biopolitics in Giorgio Agamben's *The Use of Bodies*', *Philosophy and Social Criticism*, 43, 144–63.
Rioux, S, LeBaron, G & Verovšek, P (2020) 'Capitalism and Unfree Labor: A Review of Marxist Perspectives on Modern Slavery, Review of International', *Political Economy*, 27, 709–31.
Robinson, C (2021) *Black Marxism: The Making of the Black Radical Tradition*, London: Penguin Books.
Rose, M (2016) "It's Not the Money But the Love of Money That Is the Root of All Evil': Social Subjection, Machinic Enslavement and the Limits of Anglican Social Theology', *Religions*, 7, 103.
Sassen, S (1988) *The Mobility of Capital and Labor*, Cambridge: Cambridge University Press.
Schumpeter, J (2008) *Capitalism, Socialism, and Democracy*, New York: Harper.

Shilliam, R (2012) 'Forget English Freedom, Remember Atlantic Slavery: Common Law, Commercial Law and the Significance of Slavery for Classical Political Economy', *New Political Economy*, 17, 591–609.
Sorentino, S-M (2019a) 'Natural Slavery, Real Abstraction, and the Virtuality of Anti-Blackness', *Theory & Event*, 22, 630–73.
Sorentino, S-M (2019b) 'The Abstract Slave: Anti-Blackness and Marx's Method', *International Labor and Working-Class History*, 96, 17–37.
Timofeeva, O (2017) 'Freedom Is Slavery', *Crisis & Critique*, 4, 425–45.
Tiqqun (2010) *Introduction to Civil War*, Los Angeles: Semiotext(e).
Turner, J R and Hui, J (2023) 'Racial Capitalism Online: Navigating Race Among Creative Professionals of Color', *Proceedings of the ACM on Human-Computer Interaction*, 7, Article No. 85. 1–23.
Umoja Noble, S (2018) *Algorithms of Oppression: How Search Engines Reinforce Racism,* New York: New York University Press.
Verges, F (2021) *A Decolonial Feminism*, Bohrer, A (trans.), London: Pluto Press.
Verlinsky, A (2016) 'The Nocturnal Council in Plato's *Laws*', *Philologia Classica*, 11, 180–222.
Wakefield, S (2023) 'Anthropocene Destitution', *South Atlantic Quarterly*, 122, 121–36.
Wilderson III, F (2003) 'Gramsci's Black Marx: Whither the Slave in Civil Society?', *Social Identities*, 9, 225–40.
Zartaloudis, T (2010) *Giorgio Agamben: Power, Law and the Uses of Criticism*, Abingdon: Routledge.

Index

Kolibri 360 GmbH
Ferdinand-Jühlke-Straße 7
99095 Erfurt, Deutschland
produktsicherheit@kolibri360.de